FORKED TONGUES?
Comparing Twentieth-Century British and American Literature

FORKED TONGUES?
Comparing Twentieth-Century British and American Literature

Edited by Ann Massa and Alistair Stead

Longman
London and New York

Longman Group UK Limited,
Longman House, Burnt Mill,
Harlow, Essex CM20 2JE, England
and Associated Companies throughout the world.

Published in the United States of America
by Longman Publishing, New York

First published 1994

ISBN 0 582 07554 8 CSD
ISBN 0 582 07555 6 PPR

British Library Cataloguing-in-Publication Data

A catalogue record for this book is
available from the British Library

Library of Congress Cataloging-in-Publication Data

Forked tongues : comparing twentieth-century British and American literature / edited by
    Ann Massa and Alistair Stead.
    p. cm.
    Includes bibliographical references and index.
    ISBN 0-582-07554-8 (CSD). — ISBN 0-582-07555-6 (PPR)
    1. English literature—20th century—History and criticism.
2. American literature—20th century—History and criticism.
3. Literature, Comparative—English and American. 4. Literature, Comparative—American
and English. I. Massa, Ann. II. Stead, Alistair.
PR129.U5F67 1994
820.9'0091—dc20   93-39018
                                            CIP

Set by 14B in 10 / 12 pt Bembo Roman

Produced by Longman Singapore Publishers (Pte) Ltd.
Printed in Singapore

Table of Contents

Table of Contents

Foreword

The title, *Forked Tongues?*, is allusive, a little playful, and intended to glance at least at the commonplace paradox of the two nations divided by the barrier of a common language (an observation, we suspect, dubiously attributed to the likes of Oscar Wilde, G.B. Shaw, Winston Churchill, Dylan Thomas, on the grounds that they were gifted phrasemongers and significantly were all borderers or marginals themselves). The phrase suggests simultaneously the potential for deception and the potential for empowerment. Deception, not in the manner of the accused white man of the old Cowboys-and-Indians movies (it was always a white *man*), but in the manner of the 'false friends' of translation from one language to another, where we may be accidentally deceived by the near-likeness of the word in the alien tongue to one in our own. Expanded to cultural terms, that means we may easily misread each other, Britain and America, from overconfidence in what we appear to share. But historically, we *do* share a great deal, and the positive charge of the forked tongue may be realised if we recognise that *bilinguis* is the Latin for split- or double-tongued. The vigorous hybrid of Anglo-American is today a modern *lingua franca* that may differ in certain respects in its spoken form but is virtually identical in its written form. The truth may be that, as Homi K. Bhabha says, 'All forms of culture are continually in a process of hybridity', that bilingualism is not simply the condition and opportunity of Anglo-American culture (British English and American English) but that of the minority culture within these communities (for example, African American, Hispanic, and Asian American in the United States; Scottish, Welsh, Northern Irish within the United Kingdom). Hence the appropriateness, from one point of view, of the plural *Tongues*. From another, it argues for the sheer number of differences and divergences, grounded in language and the literary culture which language articulates, that the essays in the book propose and expose, both within the British and American texts under discussion and among the readers of those texts. If tongues fork, this collection neither assumes nor argues for a consistent and predictable forking. Rather, it suggests a variety of multilingual transactions, polyphonic conjunctions and disjunctions, interactions and reactions, recognitions of dependence and declarations of independence.

Forked Tongues? was conceived as a response to students in Europe and America who have expressed their need to see addressed, in fresh ways and through fresh texts, what seem to them to be the curious and compelling differences between British and American writing in the twentieth century. The transatlantic scholarly community responded zestfully to such student curiosity and itself generated ideas and topics for exploration and comparative analysis that went beyond the fairly basic set of questions that we had considered appropriate for study. An enlightened and non-prescriptive publisher provided a mandate which did not restrict *Forked Tongues?* to canonical and best-selling authors. The result is a volume of eighteen essays which individually and collectively raise a substantial number of comparative issues and demonstrate a variety of methodological practices. The contributors approach the volume's central concern from diverse backgrounds and disciplines: they are drawn from both major cultures; some are Americanists, others teachers and students of twentieth-century literature in English; and the perspectives and emphases within their work are correspondingly and stimulatingly various. Their essays attend to transnational and cross-cultural themes as well as establishing some of the significant elements that correlate and differentiate the shaping and the shapes of British and American writings of the period.

Our contributors have here exemplified many of the ways in which our writers or texts may be compared to throw light on national identities and cultural difference. Writers or texts may be juxtaposed against a background of subtly differentiated preoccupations with a common theme (as Edward Bond and Sam Shepard are in Ruby Cohn's examination of their images of the artist) or made to confront each other (as in Brian Harding's interpretation of the difference in political purpose in the historical fictions of E.L. Doctorow and John Fowles). Writers may be in dialogue with each other (as Olga Kenyon shows that Alice Walker and Buchi Emecheta are aware of each other as leading women writers of African descent in their respective countries) or may owe each other significant debts (as Eric Mottram indicates in his account of the inspiration that British performance-poets have taken from their American precursors); or the nature of the dependency may be more broadly intertextual (as in the case of Alison Lurie's practice of the Anglo-American International Novel in *Foreign Affairs*, as Judie Newman maintains). Studies may be focused on a single author or text yet still support the comparative project by furnishing an illuminating case study (as in Peter Egri's close reading of Edward Albee's Absurdist refashioning of Giles Cooper's more traditionally realistic satire in *Everything in the Garden*, or Brian Scobie's exploration of how the textual terrain of 'Carver Country' – the world of Raymond Carver's short stories – may be obliquely inscribed with quite specific cultural meanings). On the other hand, enquiries may range across many authors and periods to exhibit moments of conjunction and disjunction in matters of the deployment and reception of a style or mode (as in Keith Tuma's exposition of the neglect, dismissal and acknowledgement of a British modernism in poetry, or Alistair Stead's selective history of the differently timed and accented derivations of modern and postmodern pastoral from a common store of myth and convention).

These are the kinds of explicit groupings that our contributors have usefully proposed. We would expect, and seek to encourage, our readers to recognise and formulate other potential interrelations among the heterogeneous materials provided, to take our enquiry further and enter into a lively comparative activity within the volume itself. We are anxious to open up the argument and to suggest rather than to delimit pertinent reading strategies. It would clearly be instructive, for instance, to read across the period, genre, topic, text and author-centred interests of the individual essays and to regroup them accordingly. Several essays direct attention to a single decade or well defined phase in cultural development but draw on differing genres and writers. Thus the reader might construct contrasted images of the American and British literary cultures of the thirties from essays by Ann Massa (on theatre) and David Peck (on reportage and novel) where American drama appears more engaged, inventive and passionate than the British, American prose more radicalised than the British. But qualifications suggest themselves from within these pieces, in Mark Jarman's (on Eliot and Pound) and Tuma's (on Modernism), for in the thirties the expatriate American poets produced works seriously damaged by anti-Semitism, yet while Eliot enjoyed New Critical adulation and bicultural prestige in his efforts to revive poetic drama – and enliven the British scene – the other American Modernists (Pound, Williams, H.D., Oppen and Zukofsky), who were to mean so much to American poets emerging in the fifties and sixties, were not well received in this decade. Or the reader might track the fortunes of women's writings and feminist issues which, on the evidence of the essayists, differ markedly in the two cultures during the earlier part of the century, with the successes of Willa Cather in the novel, Hilda Doolittle and Marianne Moore in poetry, Susan Glaspell and Lillian Hellman in drama, reflecting a vigorous cultural and political movement in the United States and overshadowing such British counterparts in the same period as Naomi Mitchison, Sylvia Townsend Warner, and Mina Loy, even if these are receiving some tardy and merited recognition late in the century. In the climate of the last quarter of the century, when feminisms are renascent and politically diversified on both sides of the Atlantic, a significant number of British women have produced work to match the Americans. Paulina Palmer attests to this in her citation of novelists, both heterosexual and lesbian, who tackle urban experience (for example, Zoë Fairbairns, Angela Carter, Jeanette Winterson and Rebecca O'Rourke).

Another interesting extrapolation would be to divide the material into the major literary and artistic movements of the century: the premodern, the Modern and the Postmodern. Taking as a starting point Egri's assignment of one mid-century British dramatist (Cooper) to the premodern and his American near-contemporary (Albee) to the Postmodern, the reader might consider whether, regardless of history, the tradition-bound conservative British writer might feel more at home in the premodern modes while the American, ever more experimental and up-to-the-moment, would be relentlessly heading for the outpost beyond the Modern. The reader might note the Georgian cultural context which semi-circumscribes the work of Forster and Lawrence, the premodern attachments of Hartley and Waugh and the anti-modern reactions of Orwell and Larkin, even the decent traditionalisms of Margaret Drabble and Buchi Emecheta. But this reading might be contested by reference to the British versions of both the Modern (Tuma's alignment of Ford Madox Ford, Hugh MacDiarmid, David Jones, Mina Loy, Edith Sitwell, Basil Bunting, and D.H. Lawrence as poet; David Seed's claims for Wyndham Lewis as satirical novelist) and the Postmodern (Richard Brown's anatomy of the attitudes and styles of Angela Carter, Martin Amis and Ian McEwan; Bryan Cheyette's sensitivity to the considerable talents of the Jewish novelists, Clive Sinclair and Elaine Feinstein). It is arguable that both movements in British literature are belated in comparison with American developments, and that in many instances (Mottram offers many poetic specimens, from Bunting to Ken Smith) the former owes a self-conscious debt to the latter. Yet this high-relief cross-cultural map would still probably need to be redrawn, not merely to cope with very individual writing talents and the idiosyncratic contours inscribed by the critic, but to note how the United States continues to hold to *its* premodern (in the work of Marge Piercy, for example, as Palmer presents her) as well as to its Modern and Postmodern. Adventurous American writers, whatever the period or genre, have repeatedly identified or renewed themselves in direct contact with British culture (whether it is Frost, as Jarman sees him, or Cather, according to Lee; Shepard, in Cohn's account, or Lurie in Newman's).

Some writers, as may by now have become apparent, are dealt with in more than one context in this volume (Eliot, Cather, Lawrence, Bunting, Orwell, Fowles, and Carter, among others). This affords the opportunity to see how the writer may figure differently at different times in the transnational debate: Ezra Pound, for instance, is present in our first essay very much as the companion-at-arms of T.S. Eliot in an energetically pursued modernist campaign, an outstandingly American poet in both his strengths (aesthetic ambition, dedication, reintegrative projections) and weaknesses (virulent anti-Semitism); in Mottram's survey of the British poetic scene in the sixties and seventies he makes a more ambiguous appearance, as a possibly now anachronistic modernist saint and as part of a generally approved American inspiration to esteemed British poets like Bunting; in Tuma's essay, more evidence accumulates for a fluctuating status: first, modernist classic on both sides of the Atlantic, then an internationalist neglected in the anti-modernist reactions of the thirties and forties, but a surviving force in British Modernism that has seemingly little to contribute to the Language poetry of the recent American Postmodernists.

In spite of our incitement to such pattern-making on the part of the individual reader, we have elected to divide our initial Table of Contents into four broad topic areas (*Cultural Identities, Literary Relations, Generic Perspectives, Gender and Race*) to reflect what we take to be the dominant interests of our contributors and the important issues that are being explored in comparative studies in this field. Each of our divisions has a Prefatory Note glossing the categories we have constructed, but such categories, it should be understood, cannot be hermetically-sealed compartments. We are especially conscious as producers of no single-author, single-thesis book, that our initial division may seem to imply only one set of directions for handling the data. To obviate any misunderstanding on this point, and to be as serviceable as possible to the student, we have provided an Alternative Table of Contents (on which, more later) and a Contents Arranged Historically which appears at the back of the book. We had considered giving more prominence to both a generic and historical arrangement. The possibility of reading through genre is substantially addressed in the Prefatory Note to the third division of our initial Table of Contents, but it may be worth dwelling for a moment on an example not cited there to bring out the way different periods generate different answers to the quest for distinguishing factors: Hermione Lee's study of Cather's encounters with British culture in the early years of the century graphically exposes this ex-drama critic's typical sense of national inferiority when confronted with an ebullient Edwardian theatre (powerfully reinforced by the Irish); by the time we reach Massa's comparison of theatres between the wars, there seems no room to doubt, that if we except Noel Coward, T.S. Eliot, and the Irish (again), the American theatre is more earnest, professional, and innovative; Cohn's collection of Bond and Shepard reminds us that Bond is only part of a whole generation of British playwrights emergent and triumphant in the later fifties and in the sixties (most of whom are still productive today) that have shifted the hegemony away from mid-century

America; Shepard is seen as equally talented, strikingly indigenous, but he is less closely bound up with the ethos and collective endeavour of a diversely gifted, prolific generation. Egri's analysis of Albee's adaptation of Giles Cooper is wonderfully specific but its emphasis on the dynamic American reshaping of British material ought not to hide from view Cooper's place in the British theatre renaissance, the degree to which his work is only one kind of writing being practised there, and, conversely, the relation of Albee to the less stable contemporary American theatre. Egri pertinently points out, however, that Albee's drama tends to decline when he has not the kind of external support that Cooper's stronger control of narrative structure (among other things) supplies on this occasion.

The point we make is inevitably a historical one. A reading through history is also addressed in, more than one site, elsewhere in this volume, but an example or two might suffice to underline the importance of taking into consideration the historical factors conditioning style and theme in both literatures. In the essays on poetry and its reception by Mottram and Tuma, for instance, it becomes apparent that a more centralised literary culture in Britain, cherishing its own rather insular mannerly image, has done a great deal to smother more modernist and innovatory voices, such as those of Bunting and the more performance-orientated poets. Tensions and possibilities are also the products of changes in the historical role of the nations: an expansionist America, coupled with the energy of its indigenous feminist movement, tends to create those more optimistic visions of city life and its exciting opportunities that Palmer's conspectus of women's fiction affords. In Stead's study of aspects of the pastoral impulse in both literatures, there is a British tendency to dwell nostalgically on the vanished past that might be seen as more than by-product and symptom of national, more precisely, imperial decline: it may be good part of the cause. American writers, traditionally feeling themselves part of a still developing, though deeply flawed, democratic society might more readily seize on the oppositional power of the critical and liberating countercultural visions which pastoral forms may be adapted to carry. But it is arguable that the early twentieth-century British pastoralists also found the relatively lightweight forms a convenient mode of resistance, a retort to imperialist monumental ideals of conformity, duty, industry, progress, war and all gross displays of power. Increasingly aware in the latter half of the century of economic and political decline, Britain had tended to impose more conservative pressures on culture and to create a self-consciously conservative wing to British literature, the kind of work that poets like Harrison and Silkin, dramatists like Bond and Barker, novelists like Carter and Amis, have sought to subvert; for it would be wrong to overlook the evolving range of contemporary British writing (particularly as it evolves from the margins, or what was formerly considered such), or fail to recognise that similar processes are at work in the United States, for both cultures inhabit the postmodern condition of blurred differences. With a steady growth in the sense of a transatlantic identity (certainly on this side of the ocean), Britain adapts to a more pluralist, multicultural society and some certain loss of autonomy in the European Community.

We conclude with a brief commentary on our Alternative Table of Contents to demonstrate how another reading of our materials might work. The essays in 'Textual Reconstructions' are all concerned at some point with re-presentations, treating individual works and the cultures in which they are embedded as texts, texts to be reworked and reconstituted, whether consciously or not: in Jarman's essay, Pound and Eliot's rejected America returns in ideal form, in the ambitious reconstructive gesture, making a new order out of the old disintegrations. Lee makes plain how Cather's mythopoetic versions of English culture contribute to her efforts to define the 'marginal' American self in her mature fictions; Albee's wholesale reworking of Cooper's more traditionally British, understated realism in *Everything in the Garden* is, Egri argues, a radical Americanisation, foregrounding absurdity and disordering the naturalist text. Newman shows how Alison Lurie's *Foreign Affairs* replays with wit the strategies of Anglo-American international fiction, throwing into relief thereby the intertextual nature of all culture; the displaced American heroine's sense of personal and national identity is transfigured, her stereotypes radically revised, and she passes from one intertextual scene to another. In Brown's essay, three contemporary British writers (Angela Carter, Martin Amis and Ian McEwan) project images of America with postmodern self-consciousness and flamboyance to reflect on the ambiguous and complex construction of cultural identity in a time when traditionally perceived boundaries and distinctions have become strikingly transgressable. In these works, more notably in Carter's and Amis's, America seems to have less and less to do with observable geopolitical differentia and more to do with the confusing pantextualism of Baudrillard's hyper-reality: 'America' is reconstituted as style and symptom in British and European settings. This concluding essay of the group highlights the mediating role that representations increasingly play in our investigations into quests for some sense of national or cultural identity.

In the second group, 'Myths of History / History of Myths', the approach is through history or myth, or rather the interface between them. Peck's revised literary history of the thirties, a 'mythical' decade for both countries, speculates about how the post-McCarthy Cold War retrospects of the surviving apostates from left-wing and liberal persuasions have misrepresented the nature of American literary culture. Harding, working on a genre that epitomises formally and problematises radically the theme of this section, i.e. historiographical metafiction, proposes that Doctorow and Fowles achieve unequal results in their postmodern manipulations of historical fiction for the demythologisation of familiar perceptions of our respective pasts. Kenyon's title foregrounds the shared project of two women from differing black cultures to demystify the role of the mother-worker; although both Alice Walker and Buchi Emecheta draw on acute personal experience and some historical awareness of misconstructions about gender and race, the rethinking of personal and social roles tends to be more radical and mystical in Walker's highly coloured images than in Emecheta's more documentary realism. Stead sets up a history of the two cultures' self-identifications through variants of pastoral myth within which specific transformations of pastoral 'heroes' (indicative of sexual attitudes) trace patterns of parallel and divergent response; the interface here, as in the examples above, is not simply between the new historical situations and the functions of old representations but the negotiations between individual perception and collective assumption in any given period.

The third grouping of essays, 'Parallel Traditions' offers the chance to focus on a frequent duality in the interface between British and American literatures. The relationship is formed by a parallel identification of issues generated by period and genre; it is also characterised by separate development, by divergence of conception and execution. Thus Seed on Jazz Age novels exhibits dialogic elements as well as a resonance of theme and structure; yet the British novelists ridicule postures of postwar nihilism while the American project a cynicism that thinly covers a lament for what was a hope for what might be. Massa's essay on theatre between the First and Second World Wars detects a dissonance that outweighs resonances of period and genre. It argues a British tendency to see theatre as a locus for entertainment in familiar terms, and American commitment to confrontation and experimentation. Mottram's 'Poetic Interface' is a study in intimate intertextuality; British poets reflect exposure to American theory and practice from Pound through Olson to the Beat poets. But while there is assonance here – the cultures 'rhyme', on page and in performance – the voice print remains idiosyncratic and, in Pound's word, 'uncounterfeitable'. The correspondence between Edward Bond and Sam Shepard is greater. Each functions as a critic of contemporary society, each utilises a comparable stagecraft. Nevertheless, Shepard's plays, like David Mamet's, are as much hymns as dirges; to a degree they look to the future, they posit change, while Bond's plays like many of John Arden's refer to the past to explain the continuum of the unsatisfactory present. Johnsen's essay suggests that a species of consonance is evident in the poetry of Bly, Silkin, Hill and Heaney. While the Vietnam War engendered in Bly a differentiating involved response to violence, there is still a parallel harmony of anguished witness before it, which may prefigure collective responsibilities and collective solutions.

In the final group *Revisionary Practices* our essayists adopt, or explicitly reflect upon, a pronounced scepticism toward standard accounts of various aspects of literary production in the two cultures: the critics' and their subjects' revisionary practices tend to betray suspicion of any totalising myths of distinctive cultural character or achievement. Tuma, for instance, seeks to rescue from the misconstructions and mystifications of commentators and practitioners on both sides of the Atlantic a British form of poetic modernism. Scobie's tight focus on Raymond Carver's short fiction revises an overhasty formulation of the writer, not just as peculiarly American but as readily categorisable as a postmodern minimalist or regional realist; by attending scrupulously to the level of textuality in his analysis of selected stories, Scobie teases out the cultural specifics of an elusive case. In the last two essays, the critics approach the revisionary process through representations of and by women and Jews respectively. Palmer's wide-ranging survey of urban fiction from a feminist perspective revises masculinist readings of the institutions and practices of the city, exploring the manifold divergences within women's responses to an ambiguous site as well as the distinctions between American and British women's orientations toward it. Cheyette analyses the common effort of distinguished British-Jewish and American-Jewish writers to revise stereotypes of the Jewish novel and its protagonist by displacing their subjects from the suffocating interdictions and decorums of the parochial community to the perilous but liberating cosmopolitan settings: through relocation of character and action to 'imaginary homelands' they paradoxically, if precariously, reconnect them with their authentic Holocaust-haunted history. Within this revisionary practice lies another, for Jewish women novelists like Cynthia Ozick and Elaine Feinstein may be seen to correct the gender-distortion which Philip Roth's and Clive Sinclair's emphatically male representations of Jewishness are liable to.

Ann Massa and Alistair Stead
University of Leeds, 1993

Alternative Table of Contents

Notes on Contributors

Richard Brown is a lecturer in the University of Leeds. He is the author of *James Joyce and Sexuality* (Cambridge, 1985) and *James Joyce: A Postculturalist Perspective* (London and Basingstoke, 1992) as well as numerous articles on modern and contemporary literature. He is currently at work on a study of Postcultural fiction of which the current essay is a part.

Bryan Cheyette was a British Academy postdoctoral research fellow in the School of English, University of Leeds (1989–1992) and is now a lecturer in English, Queen Mary and Westfield College, University of London. He is the author of *Construction of the Jew in English Literature and Society: Racial Representations, 1875–1945* (Cambridge, 1993), and is editing a book of essays on English and American literary antiSemitism. He is currently working on a critical history of British-Jewish Literature in the twentieth century.

Ruby Cohn is Emeritus Professor of Comparative Drama at the University of California (Davis). For some forty years, she has been shuttling between American and European theatre. An editor of several theatre journals, she has published three books on the work of Samuel Beckett, and a variety of others on both American and British drama, most recently *New American Dramatists 1960–1990* (London and Basingstoke, 1991) and *Retreats from Realism in Recent English Drama* (Cambridge, 1991).

Peter Egri, Professor of English, American and Comparative Literature at L. Eötvös University, Budapest, Hungary, has published widely on modern literature, including studies of Hemingway, Joyce, Proust, Mann and Kafka. He has a particular interest in European and American drama in a comparative context. Among his recent publications are *Chekhov and O'Neill* (Budapest, 1986), *The Birth of American Tragedy* (Budapest, 1988) and *Literature, Painting and Music: An Interdisciplinary Approach to Comparative Literature* (Budapest, 1988).

Brian Harding is Senior Lecturer in American Literature at the University of Birmingham. He is the author of *American Literature in Context II, 1830–1865* (London and New York, 1982). He has edited two volumes of Nathaniel Hawthorne in the Oxford University Press World Classics Series: *Young Goodman Brown and Other Tales* (Oxford and New York, 1987) and *The Scarlet Letter* (Oxford and New York, 1990).

Mark Jarman is an American poet. His most recent books of poetry include a collection, *The Black Riviera*, (Middletown, Connecticut, 1990) and a book-length narrative poem, *Iris* (Brownsville, Oregon, 1992). He lives in Nashville, Tennesee where he teaches at Vanderbilt University.

William A. Johnsen is Professor of English, Michigan State University, and has completed several tours teaching and studying in England, Ireland and Italy. Associate Chair for Graduate Studies in the English Department at MSU, his appointments include serving on the University's Committee on Overseas Study and The University's Committee on Graduate Education. His principal topics of interest and publication are James Joyce, W.B. Yeats, Virginia Woolf, and Henry James. His book on Modernism is forthcoming.

Olga Kenyon, formerly Head of Humanities, Morley College (London), now lectures at the University of Bradford. Her publications include *Women Novelists Today: A Survey of English Writing in the Seventies and Eighties* (Brighton, 1988), *Women Writers Talk: Interviews with Ten Women Writers* (Oxford, 1989), and, recently, *800 Years of Women's Letters* (Stroud and Wolfeboro Falls, N.H., 1992) and *The Writer's Imagination: Interviews with Major International Women Writers* (London, 1992).

Hermione Lee grew up in London and read English at Oxford. She has lectured at the College of William and Mary in Virginia, at Liverpool University, and at York University, where she is a Reader in English Literature. She is well known as a critic and broadcaster and reviews for *The Independent on Sunday* and for the *New Republic*. Her books include *The Novels of Virginia Woolf*

(London, 1977); *Elizabeth Bowen: An Estimation* (London, 1981); *Philip Roth* (London and New York, 1982); *Stevie Smith: A Selection* (London 1983); *The Mulberry Tree: Writings of Elizabeth Bowen* (London, 1986); *Willa Cather. A Life Saved Up* (London, 1989) and an edition of Willa Cather's stories. She is now working on a new life of Virginia Woolf.

Ann Massa has studied, researched and taught at a number of American Universities (Brown, Chicago, The College of William and Mary, Brooklyn College of CUNY, CSULB). In England she has taught at Nottingham and Essex and is currently Senior Lecturer in American Literature at Leeds. Among her books are *Vachel Lindsay* (Bloomington and London, 1970); *American Literature in Context, 1990–1930* (London and New York, 1982); *American Declarations of Love* (London and Basingstoke, 1989).

Eric Mottram is Professor Emeritus of American Literature at London University. He is one of the disseminating pioneers of American Studies in Britain. A distinguished poet, he has published his *Selected Poems* (Twickenham, 1989) and coedited *The New British Poetry* (London, 1989). His many publications on nineteenth-century and twentieth-century American writers include *William Burroughs* (London, 1977) and, most recently, his fourth essay on Pound, in *Ezra Pound and America* (ed. Jacqueline Kaye, London and Basingstoke, 1992). He has recently cofounded *Democratic Vistas*, an American Studies journal.

Judie Newman was educated at the Universities of Edinburgh and Cambridge, and is the author of *Saul Bellow and History* (London and Basingstoke 1984), *John Updike* (London and Basingstoke, 1988) and *Nadine Gordimer* (London and New York, 1988), the editor of Harriet Beecher Stowe, *Dred: A Tale of the Great Dismal Swamp* (Halifax, 1992), Associate editor of the British Association for American Studies Pamphlets Series, she has written a variety of essays on American and post-colonial writers in scholarly journals and collections. She is Reader in American and post-colonial Literature at the University of Newcastle upon Tyne.

David Peck is Professor of English and Director of the American Studies Program at California State University, Long Beach. He is the author most recently of *Novels of Initiation: A Guidebook for Teaching Literature to Adolescents* (New York, 1989), and *American and Ethnic Literature: An Annotated Bibliography of Native American, African American, Hispanic American, and Asian American Writers and Their Backgrounds* (Pasadena, California, 1992).

Paulina Palmer teaches an undergraduate course in "Feminist Perspectives on Literature" in the English Department at the University of Warwick and contributes to the teaching of the Women's Studies MA. Her publications include *Contemporary Women's Fiction: Narrative Practice and Feminist Theory* (Hemel Hempstead, 1989); an essay on Angela Carter in Sue Roe (ed.), *Women Reading Women's Writing* (Brighton, 1987); and a discussion of "Contemporary Lesbian Fiction" in Linda Anderson (ed.), *Plotting Change: Contemporary Women's Fiction* (London, 1990). She has a lesbian reading of Antonia White's *Frost in May* in Susan Sellers (ed.), *Feminist Criticism: Theory and Practice* (Hemel Hempstead, 1991) and an essay on lesbian crime fiction in Elaine Hobby and Chris White (eds), *What Lesbians Do in Books* (London, 1991). She is currently working on a book on *Contemporary Lesbian Writing* for the Open University Press.

Brian Scobie has recently spent two years as Visiting Professor of Comparative Literature at the College of Wooster, Ohio and is currently teaching at Leeds University. His specialities are Modernism, literary theory (especially narration). He has strong interests in short fiction, which he regularly teaches at graduate level, and in Samuel Beckett.

David Seed is Senior Lecturer in the Department of English at Liverpool University. He took his first degree at Cambridge, subsequently taught in a London secondary school, and pursued research for a Ph.D. on Henry James at Hull University. He has published *The Fictional Labyrinths of Thomas Pynchon* (London and Basingstoke, 1988), *The Fiction of Joseph Heller* (London and Basingstoke, 1989), *James Joyce's 'A Portrait of the Artist as a Young Man'* (Brighton, 1992) and *Rudolph Wurlitzer* (Lampeter 1992). In addition he has published numerous articles mainly on the Gothic novel and modern American fiction.

Alistair Stead is Senior Lecturer in English at the University of Leeds. He has taught both English and American literature in Leeds and at Michigan State University. He coedits the *James Joyce Broadsheet*. He was coeditor (with W.J. McCormack) of *James Joyce and Modern Literature* (London, Boston, Melbourne and Henley, London, 1982). He has contributed entries on British and American authors to Webster's *New World Companion to English Literature* (London, 1973) and *The Fontana Biographical Companion to Modern Thought* (London, 1983).

Keith Tuma is an Assistant Professor of English at Miami University in Oxford, Ohio. His essays on modern and contemporary poetry have appeared in *American Literary History, Chicago Review, Contemporary Literature, Paideuma,*

Sagetrieb, ELH, Sulfur, The Dictionary of Literary Biography, and other publications. He is currently completing a manuscript on the intersection of English and American poetry and co-editing a volume of essays on Mina Loy.

Introduction

As the British historian Howard Temperley pointed out in his charming and instructive essay on 'Anglo-American Images' (in *Contrast and Connection*, ed. H.C. Allen and Roger Thompson, London, 1976) the accumulating oft-repeated perceptions that the Americans and the British have had of each other constitute a kind of 'international folklore', a dialogue, one might add, of the almost-deaf at times, that engages in myth-making rather than the strenuous pursuit of something more objectively verifiable. Comparative studies of this kind undertaken in the present volume, though shifting the focus to the products of the individual imagination, inevitably deal in something like the same coin. The works are composed of and circumscribed by such perceptions, mythologisings, misconceptions, improvised hypotheses, acts of translation. Sometimes the works will define each other against the national Other quite self-consciously; more often, they emerge from an only faintly apprehended background of cultural stereotyping and patriotic prejudice. The images of difference and identity that traverse or preoccupy them have their shifting historical dimension, of course; Temperley reminds us, for instance, that for Europeans America was once, from the Renaissance to the end of the eighteenth century, the Past, potential location of the Golden Age, the Noble Savage, recapturable prelapsarian simplicities; for some time now, America has been the Land of the Future, variously interpreted in terms of political, economic, cultural power and technological ingenuity.

Such symbolic constructions of a national identity reflected, projected, or rejected have traditionally been considered matter for more self-conscious shaping by the American writer. In American studies in general, exceptionalism has until comparatively recently been the dominant. Such exceptionalism means 'the notion that the United States was created differently, developed differently, and thus has to be *understood* differently – essentially on its own

1

terms and within its own context.' So writes Byron E. Shafer, the editor of the recent re-examination of the topic, *Is America Different?* (Oxford, 1991), in his preface (p.v.). The essays in the collection respond to the challenge made to the old cliché, providing some basis for holding on, for the time being, to a renewed sense of their American difference in the political and cultural spheres. Seymour Martin Lipset, in 'American Exceptionalism Reaffirmed' argues that a surprisingly resilient ideological consensus, a myth of America unites wildly varying sects and antagonistic factions within the country. Shafer's 'What is the American Way? Four Themes in Search of Their Next Incarnation' sees populism and individualism at the personal level, and democratisation and market-making at the institutional level constituting, until now, the identifiable, continuing, interacting components of the national mode. In literary studies the attachment of distinguished mid-century American critics – F.O. Matthiessen, Henry Nash Smith, Leo Marx, Richard Chase – to idealist and essentialist conceptions of the American character has been seriously challenged by those who see the American tradition as one of *dissensus* rather than *consensus* (by Sacvan Bercovitch, for example, in 'Ideology in American Literary History', *Critical Inquiry*, 12 (Summer 1986), and in *Ideology and Classic American Literature* coedited with Myra Jehlen, Cambridge, 1986). Nevertheless, writers of fiction, from Henry James in *The American* (1877) to Bret Easton Ellis in *American Psycho* (1991), have themselves persisted in self-conscious exploration of national types, culturally specific experience, the defining traits of Americanness, betraying that very common sense among Americans of *being different* as grounds more sufficient than topography for the sentiment of national identity. Such nationalist insistence on efforts at self-understanding in works of literature may lead to ideologically suspect conclusions and effects, particularly when found in a society that appears to become increasingly fractured and plural in its composition. But such efforts seem to correspond to the needs of a still insecure self-questioning, ever-mobile country, and, beyond the specifics of the American case, to depend on 'notions of identity, tradition and provisional closure without which no society can survive' (to adapt Terry Eagleton on Irish culture, *TLS*, 10–16 February 1989: 134).

Bernard Bergonzi very valuably draws attention to the important fact that there is also an ideology of Englishness (in 'The Ideology of Being English', Chapter 3 of *The Situation of the Novel* (London, 1970, revised 1979), one that clings to tradition and liberalism, privileges continuity and accommodation over radical transformations and modernist innovation, an Orwellian vision (Bergonzi acknowledges the precariousness) of unpretentious decency. More significantly Bergonzi, professing some anthropological as well as literary-critical comparison with America, was scenting in the seventies that fiction was beginning to participate in a new sense of cultural crisis in the period of postwar economic uncertainty and post-imperial political decline; that it was beginning to throw up novels like Nigel Dennis's *Cards of Identity* (1955) and Andrew Sinclair's *Gog* (1967) which reflect on the problematics of personal and cultural identity and, in the latter case (under the influence of Pynchon's *V.*, 1963), project a vision of national character in the mythic and fabulated terms more conventionally associated with the Americans. It might be thought that self-consciousness of this kind is the concomitant and symptom of a broader political and social crisis, as in the thirties (Orwell's *England Their England*, Priestley's *English Journey*, Auden's *The Orators: An English Study*, to draw examples from beyond the novel too); and the crisis in the stabler forms of the old society has deepened, as Thatcher's England, uglier, greedier, more violent and dispirited, soon dated Bergonzi's vision.

Since Bergonzi's book appeared, social and literary historians have been probing the myths of essential Englishness, exposing the origins in the early twentieth century of a still influential construction of a coherent national culture (see Robert Colls and Philip Dodds (eds), *Englishness: Politics and Culture 1880–1920*, London, 1986) and arguing that the pastoral version of the national myth continues to flourish in conservationist, tourist-friendly Heritage England (see Raphael Samuel (ed.), *Patriotism: the making and unmaking of British national identity*, London, 1989; in particular Vol. III, 'National Fictions'). Correspondingly, there has not only been a revival of The Condition of England fiction (in the novels of Margaret Drabble and the plays of left-wing dramatists like Howard Brenton and David Hare), but renewed preoccupation with defining national character in very explicit terms, from John Fowles's ambitious but flawed study of the Englishman in a crisis of identity, *Daniel Martin* (1978), to the conservative pastoral dreaming of Peter Ackroyd's *English Music* (1992). In *Daniel Martin*, Fowles's hero, a Jamesian transatlantic figure caught between producing filmscripts in Hollywood and writing a novel about England in transition, meditates on English – American difference as matter of personal urgency: 'Nothing distinguishes us more clearly from the Americans, nothing characterises better the very different ways we use our shared language – the way they use it as a tool, even when they are being poetic, and the way we treat it as a poem, even when we are using it as a tool; and it is the same with the enormous semantic subtleties of middle-class English intonation and the poverty of nuance in even the most intellectually sophisticated American equivalent' (pp. 78–9).

Bergonzi's sense of the distinctiveness of the American contribution to fiction in the twentieth century took its cue from Richard Poirier's powerful, seminal study *A World Elsewhere* (New York, 1966), subtitled 'The Place of Style in American Literature'. It is the attention to language and the foregrounding of style that are so frequently perceived as characteristically American. Fowles may seem to slight what William Faulkner, back in 1922, had seen as the great boon to a new American drama, a native language which was 'action rather than communication between minds' (*The Mississippian*, 24 March, 1922 p. 5.). Fowles is particularly negligent of the poetry in the outrageous and devious idioms of American humour, not just as it is evinced in literature – in Ring Lardner's low laconicism, in James Thurber's whimsy, in T.S. Eliot's sly self-mockery, in Faulkner's Southern tall tales, in Donald Barthelme's surreal collages, in Stanley Elkin's bursting inventories, in Garrison Keillor's low-relief drollery, or Roth's vaudeville of angst – but as it is disseminated massively through American popular culture worldwide in the performances of Mae West, Groucho Marx, Lenny Bruce or Woody Allen. (Britain's most remarkable return gift for all this has been Charlie Chaplin, the great silent screen star!) But Fowles does unerringly focus on linguistic difference as important. Similarly, Philip Roth, in response to the question 'What does America mean to you?' (posed in 1981), acknowledges the importance of the fact that 'my consciousness and my language were shaped by America' (*Reading Myself and Others*, London, 1985, p. 128).

For the American, more than for the Englishman, language and the construction of national identity have been inter-involved. Language and style were caught up in the political struggle to make and assert 'America', 'a linguistic construct and a legal fiction' as Tony Tanner points out, in the title essay of *Scenes of Nature, Signs of Men* (Cambridge, 1987, p. 5.). In 1789, the year in which Britain's former American colonies ratified the Constitution, drafted the Bill of Rights and had their first Presidential Election, Noah Webster, who in 1828 was to publish the first American dictionary argued with some passion that an independent American language and its corollary, an independent literature, was both desirable and inevitable:

> As an independent nation, our honour requires us to have a system of our own, in language as well as government. Great Britain, whose children we are, and whose language we speak, should no longer be our standard; for the taste of her writers is already corrupted, and her language on the decline. But if it were not so, she is at too great a distance to be our model, and to instruct us in the principles of our own tongue. . . . Several circumstances render a future separation of the American tongue from the English necessary and unavoidable. . . . Numerous local causes, such as a new country, new associations of people, new combinations of ideas in arts and sciences, and some intercourse with tribes wholly unknown in Europe, will introduce new words in the American tongue. These causes will produce, in a course of time, a language in North America as different from the future language of England as the modern Dutch, Danish and Swedish are from German, or from one another: like the remote branches of a tree springing from the same stock, or rays of light shot from the same centre, and diverging from each other in proportion to their distance from the point of separation. . . . We have therefore the fairest opportunity of establishing a national language and of giving it uniformity and perspicuity, in North America, that ever presented itself to mankind. Now is the time to begin the plan. (Quoted in H.L. Mencken, *The American Language*, New York, 1937, p. 10).

As examples of British 'corruption' Webster offered Dr Johnson's 'intolerable . . . affected smoothness, scholastic accuracy, and roundness and periods' and Gibbon's tendency to make 'the mind of the reader constantly dazzled by a glare of ornament, or charmed from the subject by the music of the language'. This attack on corrupt style was deeply complicit with a political concern, and Webster's was only an early instance of those 'fore-doomed gestures', as Tanner puts it, 'towards a wholly new American language, purged of the imperialism inherent in the hegemonic English which had ruled the colony, autonomous and independent as befitted the Adamic American in his liberated paradise' (p. 4). Over one hundred years later, H.L. Mencken quoted Webster's words approvingly and cited twentieth-century examples to demonstrate American linguistic difference and primacy:

> Let the American confront a novel problem alongside English, and immediately its superior imaginativeness and resourcefulness become obvious. *Movie* is better than cinema; and the English begin to admit the fact by adopting the word. Bill-board is better than hoarding. . . . The English, seeking a figure to demonstrate the wedge-shaped fender in front of a locomotive, call it a plough; the American, characteristically, give it the far more pungent name of cow-catcher.
>
> (pp. 95–6)

The implication for literary difference was clear: 'Standard English now has the brakes on, but American continues to leap into the dark, and the prodigality of its movement is all the indication that is needed of its intrinsic health, its capacity to meet the ever-changing needs of a restless and emotional people, inordinately mongrel, and disdainful of tradition' (p. 97).

Mencken's argument is as potent as it is tendentious, and has been made on the British side of the Atlantic, too. Mencken himself quoted Basil de Selincourt's provocative generalisations, made in 1929:

> The English are uncommunicative, the Americans are not. In its coolness and quiet withdrawal, in its prevailing sobriety, our language reflects the cautious economies and leisurely assurance of the average speaker. We say so little that we do not need to enliven our vocabulary and underline our sentences, or cry 'Wolf!' when we wish to be heard. The more stimulating climate of the United States has produced a more eager, a more expansive, a more decisive people. The Americans apprehend their world in sharper outlines and aspire after a more salient rendering of it.
>
> (p. 95)

Daniel Martin's reflections echo de Selincourt's, but his British contemporaries, or at least Fowles's, are more likely to pass from any reserve or pretence to even-handedness to outright envy (and indeed emulation) of the linguistic verve and versatility of the American author; so, Gordon Burn in the recent *Alma Cogan* (1991) essays some of the exuberance of Michael Herr and Don DeLillo and celebrates American English as 'a language that climbed on the table and danced its energy' (pp. 130–1), while Martin Amis with his 'bicultural credentials', as Richard Brown says in this volume, has produced in his novel *Money* (1984) at least the signal instance of the successful reinvention of British English along American lines, jetting an idiom to confound the de Selincourt complacencies about English caution and leisureliness and aligning himself with the heteroglossic high of Rushdie's migrant fantasies from *Midnight Children* (1981) to *The Satanic Verses* (1988).

To mention Rushdie, the defiant migrant and internationalist who disavows and repudiates a limiting 'national identity' in *Imaginary Homelands* (London, 1991) and finds his imaginary homelands in India and Bombay, 'Indias of the Mind', raises the pertinent question of the nature and extent of the cultural determination of the writer. Stephen Spender's insightful study of Anglo-American sensibilities, *Love–Hate Relations* (London, 1974), had thrown some light on the issue in proposing in his Introduction the term *patria* (Latin or Italian for 'fatherland') for the poetic construction of 'the true nation' to set in opposition to the extant state to which the writer as citizen theoretically owed allegiance. (Here the *patria* or country of the mind, functioning as a strategic ideal, anticipates Seamus Heaney's similar poetic concern, in his essays in *Preoccupations* (London, 1980) and *The Government of the Tongue* (London, 1988) to locate a space between cultural imperatives and elegant linguistic refuges. Heaney's analysis of the forms that attachment to a a place take in the works of three English poets, Larkin, Hughes and Hill, is called 'Englands of the Mind'.) Bryan Cheyette develops Rushdie's concept suggestively in his study in this volume of the strategies of Philip Roth and British-Jewish and American-Jewish writers; and we would propose the general truth of the dialectic between nation and imagination, between formative social texts and nonconformist aesthetic constructions, that conditions our interpretations of national characteristics and cultural predispositions.

Theories of national literatures, predicated on cultural homogeneity or consensus, may nowadays have to yield not only to the imaginative counterpull of the *patria* but to the sense that all writing tends to fall into transnational, transcultural categories, be they Modernist, Postmodernist, magic realist, dirty realist. This internationalist context for the reading of British and American texts may be reinforced by the tendency of postmodernisation to eliminate or play down cultural identity. More specifically, both societies have to live with the multicultural facts of life. The British, compounding substantial traditions, racial fantasies and besetting nostalgias, have resisted them more stubbornly with a fetishisation of national identity that may betoken the paranoia of a country obsessed with decline in its status. American society was always a multiculture but only comparatively recently has its literature appeared to recognise the case and its criticism, particularly in its preoccupation with revising the canon that has privileged white, middle-class, Christian, male, heterosexual constructions of culture, begun to operate on this crucial premiss.

This currently dominant view has its sceptics. For example, the American literary critic Louis Menand, reviewing the recent *Faber Book of America* (ed. Christopher Ricks and William L. Vance, London, 1992) for the *Times Literary Supplement* (30 October, 1992), challenges the statistical basis for the claim that the United States is becoming more racially and culturally diversified: 'A smaller percentage of the population is foreign-born than was the case sixty or seventy years ago; the rate of interracial marriage has increased dramatically; the Census Bureau projects that the country will maintain roughly its present racial proportions . . . well into the next century; 93 per cent of Americans who say that they are religious are Christian . . .'

Furthermore, Menand argues forcefully that multiculturalism should not be equated with genuine cultural diversity. America may have enjoyed this in the past when groups distinguished by their ethnicity, religion, gender and sexual preference, were able to lead 'culturally, largely segregated lives', but when self-conscious 'diversity' afflicts the whole culture, promoted as it is by America's 'fantastically aggressive popular culture', the consequence is flavourless homogenisation. Most identity groups, according to Menand, aspire to be 'different flavours in the same dish', a view that harmonises closely with that of the novelist Willa Cather as Hermione Lee presents her in this volume.

It is nevertheless true, that if our focus is on literature the very term America may no longer have unitary force here; American literature may have to be situated transhemispherically, in the Americas – North America, the United States of America, Central and South America, and the linguistic hegemony of American English may be passing to Spanish. The emphasis on hyphenated or hybrid American literatures in academic studies (for example, African-American, Hispanic) appears to be hastening the collapse of an homogenous American literature; nor should one underestimate the contribution of gay and feminist studies to this fission. It has also been claimed that American literary experience is the model for all later post-colonial writing. It may be that all comparative literature studies will in future be pursued under the headings pre-colonial, colonial and post-colonial. This does, however, raise the tricky question of when a country and a literature cease to be colonial. Does a country like Mexico, politically autonomous but economically dependent on the United States now produce post-colonial texts? Has America itself, a colonising power exploiting not only its economy but its culture, passed beyond the colonial stage of literature? Or is it already, as some would allege, into the post-imperial? Is Britain, with its colonial days in the remote past and its colonising now vestigial, writing out of a phase and experience which America has yet to achieve?

In these postmodern times, Britain, an ethnically diverse and nationally pluralistic society begins to look less distinct from the United States, perhaps. But it should also be recalled that only recently, as Keith Robbins informs us in *Nineteenth-Century Britain: England, Scotland and Wales: The Making of a Nation* (Oxford, 1988) was the notion of a cohesive Britishness established with its suppression or muting of the vigorous peripheries. In the later twentieth century, literary and cultural resistance to the dominance of the metropolitan centre has been intensifying, paralleling the nationalist and devolutionary movements in Wales and Scotland, the unresolved tensions in the relationship of Northern Ireland to the United Kingdom. Literature from the regions or the peripheries, from Tony Harrison's Yorkshire, Alasdair Gray's Scotland or Tom Paulin's Northern Ireland, refuse the 'tone of the centre', Matthew Arnold's neutralising middle ground, in their attitude, subject matter, and, above all, their aggressively local pronunciation of lexicon. In matters of British dialect, it is worth noting that, as Richard N. Coe has observed in his 'Introduction to a Comparative Mythology of Childhood', *Proceedings of the Leeds Philosophical and Literary Society*, 19 (1984),the dialects of the 'peripheral' communities (such as Wales and Scotland) have been regarded as exotic, even glamorous, whereas the 'internal' dialects (such as those of Birmingham or Liverpool) have been despised or ridiculed, and even rejected by the speaker. This situation has been changing, and the success of Harrison's sonnet sequence *The School of Eloquence* (from 1978) testifies to the crack in the centralist monolingualism of the dominant culture. Processes of restitution or recovery, declarations of independence and assertions of identity, are the socio–political realities that are becoming culturally vocal, from the immediately popular 1980 comedy, *Gregory's Girl*, directed by Scottish film-maker Bill Forsyth, to the poorly received but well-intentioned historical fiction, *People of the Black Mountain* (1989), by Raymond Williams from the Welsh–English border country. In 1976, in the already cited essay 'Englands of the Mind', Heaney the North-ern-Irishman slyly suggested: 'The poets of the mother culture, I feel, are now possessed of that defensive love of their territory which was once shared only by those poets whom we might call colonial' (pp. 150–1). Olga Kenyon's essay on Alice Walker and Buchi Emecheta bears witness that immigrant subcultures are making inroads into 'the mother culture' too, with transforming energies. Emecheta is only one of the British-based writers one would cite in order to contest Kathryn Hughes's claim (in *New Statesman and Society*, 12, July 1991) that the success of Chinese-American Amy Tan's second novel, *The Kitchen God's Wife*, draws attention to our own lack of stories by women from immigrant cultures: 'in Britain we have as yet no female equivalent of Mo and Rushdie'. As in America, there is much assimilation and accommodation, but also defiant ethnicity and bilingual interplay, from the likes of Emecheta, Rushdie, Timothy Mo, Mustafa Matura, Grace Nichols and Joan Riley.

Issues of language and ethnicity within the convergent multiculturalism of Britain and America cannot be divorced from the question of class, and no discussion of the differences between their respective literatures fails to animadvert the imaginative profits and deficits accruing to a strongly or a weakly demarcated class system. For the most part, the 'international folklore' prevails. British writers work within an overtly class-conscious society, where the Thing (what Cobbett called British class deference) and the prestige of the patricians have surprising long life, and fictions are consequently informed either by the high drama of mutual antagonisms of the common assumption that middle-class values and mores are the natural matrix of artistic production. American writers operate in a more fluid medium, where social mobility has blurred class boundaries and egalitarian ideology and rhetoric have inhibited recognition of both subtle and gross discriminations. (Matthew Arnold's middle-class nation has been collapsing, in later years into two cultures: the cultures of contentment and of poverty). They can proceed as if class were as readily excised from the text as the notorious stanza of 'All Things Bright and Beautiful' from so many American hymnals (as Alex Cockburn observes in *Corruptions of Empire* (London and New York, 1987), p. 16):

> The rich man in his castle,
> The poor man at his gate,
> God made them high and lowly,
> He ordered their estate.

Yet there is also an honourable tradition of American social fiction, extending from Dreiser to Doctorow, that addresses the collisions, exclusions and depredations, that have fractured the bland surface of the liberal democratic dream, while practitioners of the novel of manners, from Edith Wharton to Alison Lurie, have elaborated the analysis of the hidden complexities of the resilient structure. From Henry James on, there have been American writers who have envied the fictional resources of the already famed and certified social identity: you know where you are. But, more and more, the American's contact with British and European life and letters has resulted in the archetypal moment of the writer's self-recognition as an *American* (consider Shepard, or Roth, or Ed Dorn). After all, the typical American question: 'Where y' from?' is not primarily concerned with eliciting *social* position. On the other hand, Tony Harrison as an English working-class poet with class as one of his major muses has admitted in interview with John

Haffenden (1983) that the United States relaxes his guard: 'I don't read America with the same spiky class instincts as I read England', and the verse born of his American experience (living and working in New York and Florida) invokes a different muse. America has been even more of a role model for recent British writers of fiction: Russell Celyn Jones, the Welsh author of *Small Things* (1992) and graduate of the Iowa Writers' Workshop has sought to appropriate the subject matter of American, mostly populist writers dealing with 'a less class-orientated society' and re-root it in British circumstances, as Kevin Jackson reports in *The Independent,* 7 February, 1992. Martin Amis is probably the best-known example of the British creative attention to the American precedent, but his transference of Saul Bellow's concern with 'the moronic inferno' to *London Fields* (1989) has not displaced traditionally English sensitivities to social nuance or cross-class incomprehension: rather, he has attempted to refocus the bilious comedy-of-manners concerns of so many British novelists from Evelyn Waugh to Kingsley Amis within a postmodern (and post-nuclear) world of less localised, more mobile and devious, seductive and reductive determining forces.

A comparison of multicultures and transnational phenomena proves ever more hazardous. But reading through filters of literary and cultural types and stereotypes, however limiting it may be, is inevitable, and, if practised self-consciously and with attention to detail, may demonstrate how rewarding it is to work from context to text as well as from text to context (and from text to text, for that matter). Exemplarily, Stephen Spender, in *Love–Hate Relations* (pp. 224–31) offers a bravura analysis of a tendency that he found equally in life and literature in America. In life, it was in the Beatnik and Hippy movements at Berkeley in the sixties; in literature, it was not just in Beat writing but in productions from Charles Olson's manifestos for projective verse to Norman Mailer's *Armies of the Night* (1967): 'The personal forces of being and behaving are set up in opposition to the impersonal ones of society. The individual becomes a bundle of physical and psychic – sometimes psychotic – reactions to the forces of depersonalised power acting upon him' (p. 229). Spender christens such writing 'orgasmic', in its American manifestation taking to extremes the evasion of the constriction of an all-powerful modern society through an irreducible individuality 'opening up to forces beyond self-awareness', 'forces of darkness instinct, dream and passion stronger than the "I" and, ultimately, subversive to society' (p. 224). This trend which reaches back to Emerson is only marginally present in English writing (D.H. Lawrence and Aldous Huxley are cited). The British tend to opt for irony over radical protest, self-satire over self-assertion. Although one might argue, particularly after the sixties, that maverick passion, savage indignation and subversive dreams, have continued to break out of old cultural habits in Britain (consider the theatrical explosions of Heathcote

Williams's *AC / DC* (1970) and Steven Berkoff's many self-scripted high-octane performances, or the Blakean tigers of Angela Carter's imagination), Spender's perception enjoys the support of Tony Tanner's *City of Words: American Fiction 1950–70* (London, 1970) which pays considerable attention to the 'American writer's dread of all conditioning forces to the point of paranoia' (Introduction, p. 16), and Tanner's review of Stephen Fender's *Plotting the Golden West* (Cambridge, 1981), where he claims 'that the two dominant, or most recurrent, styles in American writing have been the rhapsodic and the paranoid'. (*London Review of Books*, 18 February–3 March, 1982).

Spender and Tanner boldly and eloquently speculate on the salient national characteristics of the literatures they survey, and Tanner, as one might have expected, has gently rebuked the American novelist Richard Ford for not risking in his Introduction to the *Granta Book of American Short Stories* (London, 1992) any exploration of the reasons for the American writer's peculiar concentration on and exploitation of the short story form. But doubts about the possibility of locating any transhistorical national features remain. George Orwell's famous and highly influential account of the English genius in 'England Your England' (first published in *The Lion and the Unicorn* in 1941), though generous and wonderfully particularised – laying stress on English anti-intellectualism and suspicion of philosophical systems, hypocrisy, privateness and devotion to home, gentleness, antimilitarism, respect for the law, and lack of artistic ability, except for literature) – is brilliant impressionism, and more particularly the child of its historical moment. (The emphasis on patriotism and the capacity of the heterogenous nation to pull together under external threat relates it emotionally to Olivier's 1944 film version of *Henry V*, which more crudely and explicitly serves the war effort). In reflecting on and deploying such profiles of a nation or culture, the comparative critic's eye will have to be on the calendar: something amusingly illustrated by John Carey's review (*The Sunday Times*, 18 February, 1990) of John Lucas's recent *England and Englishness: Ideas of Nationhood in English Poetry 1699–1900* (London, 1990). He plays a little game with his readers by supplying what seems to be a contemporary list of English characteristics: 'The English are temperamentally easygoing. They live in an atmosphere of comedy, and resist a tragic view of life. They are attached to safety and comfort. They hate science, abstract ideas and dramatic behaviour, and can see no reason for exactness or intensity. They dislike proceeding to extremes, and fight, if at all, good temperedly.' He then admits that they need some slight revision for they are (in paraphrase) H.G. Wells's, or his *alter ego*'s, drawn from his First World War novel, *Mr Britling Sees It Through* (1916). The resemblances to Orwell's inventory may be linked to an identity crisis at the outbreak of another war, and any resemblances to the British reader's current impressions are at least in part attributable to their enthralment by what Carey calls 'self-flattering national superstitions'; in part though, they might testify to plausible continuities of experience, like finding 'essential Englishness' in Mr Britling a 'little Briton' who is Essex man. Alternatively, he is Graham Coster, an English novelist, author of *Train, Train* (1989), who too readily accepts an inevitable Englishness and its concomitant constraints on English writing. For him, Englishness means, in literature, E.M. Forster, Philip Larkin, John Betjeman, and Anita Brookner, redolent of the English tone, 'pensive, wistful, given to reticence and understatement' . . . 'humorous melancholy', 'self-deprecating gaucheness', 'insularity' ('In my View', *The Sunday Times*, 30 July, 1989). The experimentalist Fowles puts the point more bracingly in *William Golding: The Man and His Books* (ed. John Carey, London, 1986), where he pays homage to the brilliantly unpredictable William Golding on his seventy-fifth birthday: 'expectability' is the English novel's great defect and virtue: 'Defect in its sometimes too eager and complacent willingness to obey the conventions of the genre (as in life, so those of society) . . . virtue in the richness it can derive from an outwardly narrow range and restricted palette' ('Golding and "Golding" ', p. 151).

Forked Tongues? will go some way to reviewing and testing both the daringly speculative and the regularly handed-on definitions and identifications of the British and American dialogues, conducted both inside and outside literary texts. (To what extent are certain materials, certain manners, culturally specific? Perennial? Bound up with particular genres? Translated by nationally shaped attitudes to gender, class, and race? Products and producers of a certain historical moment?) Take as exemplary Graham Coster's resignation to a non-migrant English condition that cannot 'speak out of painful personal displacement' and 'radical homelessness'. For all its honest, humble self-appraisal, this stays too close to the clichéd perspective on the nature of English fiction (and creativity) propounded by both Britons and Americans. See, for instance, the interviews that the American journalist Richard Critchfield has drawn on in his *Among the British: An Outsider's View* (London, 1990). Should one resist the castigations and self-castigations, since, according to Martin Amis, 'American writers take on more and try harder' (*The Observer*, 16 February 1986), while Gore Vidal alleges that they are 'much blacker and stronger' than the cosy British? Vidal's remark appeared in 1984, what one might reasonably call an *annus mirabilis* for contemporary British fiction, flourishing Angela Carter's *Nights at the Circus*, Martin Amis's *Money*, Julian Barnes's *Flaubert's Parrot*, Peter Ackroyd's *Hawksmoor*, Alasdair Gray's *1982 Janine*, Iain Banks's *The Wasp Factory*, Muriel Spark's *The Only Problem*, J.G. Ballard's *Empire of the Sun*, Elaine Feinstein's *The Border* . . . If we widen the net, what's cosy about Pinter and Orton, Bond and Barker? About the poetry of Hughes and Hill? But let us return, finally, to the year of Coster's piece (1989), for a strong example of the attempt to revise and reverse the stereotypes. In 'The Flavours of the Decade' (*The Observer*, 31 December, 1989) Lorna Sage stands the customary epithets on their head: fiction in English (produced in Britain) in the eighties was not 'insular, provincial, timid, inward-looking, and disappointing', but 'bold, various, satiric, serious, funny and subtle'. Even if the outstanding achievements of Rushdie, Mo, and Kazuo Ishiguro may seem unconventionally British, their preoccupations are 'historically' such. Once more 1984 provides a test: the works by Carter, Barnes and Ballard could hardly be called provincial; and it is not only these 'mental travellers' but others, like Jonathan Raban and Bruce Chatwin who have experimented with a new kind of travel writing, who have been concerned with mobility rather than roots. In a postmodern era of fragmentation, when the discrete parts fail to fit into any preconceived tradition, the crisis of identity in English fiction should be embraced.

Following William Carlos Williams (*In the American Grain*, New York, 1925) the American writer has sometimes been seen as never in crisis because always in reactive flux. Mid-century, though, Lionel Trilling (*A Gathering of Fugitives*, London, 1957, p. 65) projected the American writer as limited by the consciousness of international status. S/he must 'respond to the growing isolation of his / [her] country amid the hostility which is directed against it.' Currently, what are seen as classic American literary stances receive critical validation (Richard Poirier is quoted in Bantam-Windstone's publicity as praising Thomas Pynchon's *Vineland* (1991) for inhabiting 'a wilderness . . . a randomness where you might hope to find your true self.') Even more recently Toni Morrison, writing in and of *Jazz* (1992) seeks to advance the abandonment of authenticating voice and of any hierarchy of voices: a theory which owes as much to historical indignation as to narratology. To whatever degree she is heeded, Morrison succeeds in problematising the direction of American writing.

Angela Carter, who died in New York in 1992, was a British writer who poured scorn on the stock notion of the British novel, 'the kind of novel where people drink tea and commit adultery', as she put it, in a BBC Radio 3 interview in the year of her death. She knew her America and her American literature well. Her choice of favourite novel for *The Observer Magazine* series in 1980 (24 February) was, at first blush, a surprise: *The Great Gatsby*. Scott Fitzgerald's book was 'the most perfect romance of high capitalism' *and* 'one of the great middlebrow classics'. In *Nights at the Circus* (1984), her most popular novel, there is among so much else an allegory of international relations, and, at the heart of this, an emblematic affair between twentieth-century artists from the United States and Britain. The American appears as a male reporter, a Jack London figure from California. Jack Walser is the handsome 'innocent' who has travelled and seen much but whose professional

stance of scepticism is combined 'with a characteristically American generosity towards the brazen lie' (p. 10). His British counterpart is Fevvers,
aerialiste (and winged creature) from the metropolis of the confidence trick
(the *other* London). He is boldly committed to direct engagement (exposing
humbugs), to art for society's sake. She practises an insouciant art, taking to
the high wire with self-pleasuring panache. Their liaison, taken as symbolic
of the state of play between American and British literatures, would revise
the Spender model of *Love–Hate Relations* (as it exorcises, too, the
sado-masochistic tenor of sexual relations in Carter's earlier fictions). Now
we have the attraction of opposites within an unpredictable, mutually
illuminating, momentarily consummated affair. It is true there is parody in
the air, a feminist revision of romance with the woman on top and having
the last (carnivalesque) laugh. It might then seem to privilege one party, the
British, to excess. But apart from the iconographic contradictions in imagining Fevvers as both Mae West and Continental New Woman *à la* Apollinaire,
we may remark that Carter has furnished her unusually sympathetic hero with
a proper 'sentimental education', so repaying the compliment she once paid
to Fitzgerald's portrayal of the narrator of *his* great romance: 'the only
authentic American account of a sentimental education that I know of'. In
the complex interchanges here, we may find an appropriate closing (and
opening) image for the tensions and *rapprochements,* the indifference and
responsiveness, the similarity and incompatibility, the occasional influence
and frequent misconstruction, even ignorance, that typifies the negotiations
between British and American writing in the twentieth century.

I Cultural Identities:
T.S. Eliot to Martin Amis

Cultural Identities

> Since Donne, since Blake, America can be a shifting, ambiguous and contradictory
> sign ineradicable from all our cultural discourses. As such it expresses the shifting,
> ambiguous and contradictory nature of many of the desires and anxieties we might
> experience both as individual selves and as a culture. America may be an 'other' to
> our senses of identity and yet also an 'other self' that may either be represented as a
> younger and more callow partner or else as that future on whose threshold with
> increasing eagerness and terror we suspend ourselves.

The words are Richard Brown's in the last essay in this section, addressing
contemporary British fiction. In her essay on the early work of Willa Cather,
Hermione Lee notes that 'no American writer of the nineteenth and early
twentieth century could mark out an imaginative territory without looking
back at England and Europe . . . For many of these writers the transatlantic
bridge had either to be crossed, or blown up.' This attempt to define cultural
identity in transnational terms has been a consistent and mutual preoccupation
of British and American writing in the twentieth century. And if American
writing has trafficked increasingly with Europe, not simply with Britain, the
familial relations between American and Britain have been considerably more
marked.

But the balance of cultural interest has shifted. As the essays in this section
demonstrate, an American fascination with Britain has given way to a British
obsession with America. The American writer no longer feels the automatic
need, expressed from James Fenimore Cooper onwards, to look over the
shoulder to British culture with chastening deference or patronising referral.
The process is now reversed; American passion for British rituals and
traditions has been replaced by an envious British preoccupation with the
inventive life of American culture, high and low. A sense of American
inferiority – Cather romanticised Britain, celebrating a vigorous barbarism –
has given way to a British sense of the superior energy and vitality of American
literature. Yet, in the fictions of Angela Carter, Martin Amis and Ian
McEwan, for instance, images of America as a site of liberation and experiment are juxtaposed with counter-images of America as a nightmare of excess
and desolation (a paradox postulated influentially by D.H. Lawrence, in
Studies in Classic American Literature, London, 1923). In their writings, the
issues of relative cultural identity are further complicated by the projection
of cross-cultural myths and by the transgression of established / assumed
cultural borders. All three are conscious of the role of representation in
defining national and cultural identities.

Projections of transcultural possibility, in the sense of one tongue, one
voice, one subject, one experience, one art, are still relatively rare (and the
simultaneous phenomenon of multiculturalism may prove more potent).

Cultural stereotyping dies hard on both sides of the Atlantic. The English elements in Philip Roth's *The Counterlife* (1987), the missionaries and capitalists of *The Color Purple* (1983), the campus fiction of Malcolm Bradbury and David Lodge testify to this. Novelists and cultural commentators such as Paul Theroux and Jonathan Raban derive from, thrive on and utilise, albeit with sophistication, a range of sarcastic observations and self-consciously naive responses to 'alien' sights, sounds, attitudes and phenomena. But if there is an element of exaggeration and invention here, there is also a persistent sentiment of difference which can often be empirically grounded. For example, Britain bans risqué telephone chat lines at the same time that America produces Nicholson Baker's neo-documentary *Vox* (1992), subtitled 'a novel about telephone sex'. American writers (Mailer, Pynchon, for example) treat the idea of God in broad ethical and metaphysical contexts; the nature of their engagement with issues of good and evil is such that Manichean possibilities are advanced. British literature offers a range of Catholic and Anglican writers (Anthony Burgess, Barbara Pym and A.N. Wilson, for instance) who are more narrowly concerned with doctrinal and institutional Christianity. Arguably, such differences can be grounded in cultural identity. In Britain an established church and the counter churches have reduced God to a rule-maker, as powerful and as suspect as a politician, while in America the dissociation of church and state has worked to the deity's benefit.

Calvinism's continuing legacy to American literature has been effectively invoked by William H. Shurr in *Rappaccini's Children* (1981), one of a number of by now traditional essentialist studies of cultural identity which retain their significance. The theses of these books are multifaceted, but we draw attention to some of the symptomatic distinctions they have foregrounded. D.H. Lawrence's *Studies in Classic American Literature* (1923), argues a characteristic duplicity in the American text. Richard Chase, in *The American Novel and its Tradition* (New York 1957), posits a British practice of concretion and reconciliation, an American predilection for abstraction and alienation. Leslie Fiedler's *Love and Death in the American Novel* (New York, 1960; see too the revisionist *American Declarations of Love*, ed. Ann Massa, London and Basingstoke, 1989) finds ubiquitous homo-eroticism in American writing. In *The Reign of Wonder* (Cambridge, 1965), Tony Tanner finds in American writings on the child an unencumbered simplicity less emphatically present in British prose; British texts privilege an analytic perspective, American a stance of wonder. In *City of Words* (1971) Tanner distinguishes the British assumption that form enables from the American fear that form restricts. There is a continuing need to attend to such mythopoetic concepts which are both imaginative constructs and cumulatively part of the past with which the present negotiates (the essays on Cather and Lurie particularly illustrate this point). There is also a need to recognise, in spite of Poststructuralist scepticisms about humanist notions of agency, totality and presence that may be thought to underpin traditional projections of national or cultural identity, the force of social and historical and ideological construction. Lawrence Buell, the most penetrating of recent commentators on America's persistent self-identification in pastoral terms (in 'American Pastoral Ideology Re-Appraised', *American Literary History*, Spring 1989, I: 1–29), deftly negotiates between the old ideological criticism of Henry Nash Smith (*Virgin Land*, New York, 1950) and Leo Marx (*The Machine in the Garden*, New York, 1964) and the newer kind of Bernard Rosenthal (*City of Nature*, Newark, N.J., 1980) and Myra Jehlen (*American Incarnation*, Cambridge, Mass., 1986), as well as between respect for the experiential and representational basis of American pastoral and awareness of its complex status as cultural construct. He sees the value in placing American pastoral in a post-colonial context that tends to confirm its ideological multivalence. Current post-colonial theory still works with the concept of the nation (as Benedict Arnold's 'imagined community'), however ambiguous, fissured and contested it may be now, as Homi K. Bhabha's collection *Nation and Narration* (London and New York, 1990) testifies; and such theory may license the politically strategic deployment of non-reactionary forms of essentialism that would enable the dispossessed to disrupt oppressive hegemonic formations (see Diana Fuss's analysis of Gayatri Spivak's critique of Subaltern Studies in *Essentially Speaking: Feminism, Nature and Difference*, London, 1989). Self-conscious alternatives, strategic occupation of subject positions and reformulated essentialisms may well be entailed (see, for example, *Comparative American Identities: Race, Sex and Nationality in the Modern Text*, ed. Hortense J. Spiller, London and New York, 1991). Johnsen's essay, 'The Treacherous Years of Postmodern Poetry in English' recognises 'the endlessly corroborated truths of cultural differences'; Bryan Cheyette's essay on 'Philip Roth and Clive Sinclair' valorises an inevitably historicised Jewishness.

As Mark Jarman indicates in his essay on Pound and Eliot, Americanism is often a matter of attitude and subject: iconoclasm, pragmatism, puritanism. He argues that Pound and Eliot continued a nineteenth-century tradition of reaction against American vulgarity and pluralism'. But even as they fled diversity they sought to recreate it in their poetry; to arrange fragments of the old order in new combinations. From this perspective *The Waste Land*, 'like the American constitution, is a thoroughly American project'. Whether expatriation is ever intended as a constructive act of affirming American identity is questionable, but Jarman suggests that Americanism will out, not least in terms of speech. 'The indulgence in incorrect grammar for its own sake . . . the facetious disapproval . . . and the adverb . . . employed for its relative mystery are all characteristic of an American mixture of the down-to-earth and the fanciful.' Richard Brown also notes that Martin Amis 'uses a fast-paced and slangy "Americanised" narrative idiom as a means of defamiliarising West London public house life'.

Willa Cather's *oeuvre*, as Hermione Lee demonstrates, invokes large questions about the relations of culture to ethnicity, about the creation of nationality and the life available to an individual at a crossing point between possible identities. (The issues are very much the multicultural ones of today.) Cather, who preferred peculiarity to sameness, and who was unwilling to throw herself into the melting pot, chose to look outside America for her personal and literary sense of self. Rightly or wrongly, she identified Englishness as 'a melancholy lyricism . . . a wildness or energy, something rough and passionate' and England as a place where marginality and nonconformity is readily possible; where a tradition of romantic escapism offers a desirable alternative to a harsher, materialistic American reality.

But, as the essays on theatre between the wars and on Bly and Silkin demonstrate, cultural identity doesn't have to be defined by reference to the other or experience of the other. William Johnsen sees Robert Bly's work as developing, not untypically for American poets of his generation, through opposition to the Vietnam war, resulting in a public poetry that took him outside his internal pattern of development. ' "The Teeth Mother Naked at Last", as a poem, but also a public event, broke out into a horizon of cultural politics that has not been attainable by English poets since the Thirties . . . The poetry of Silkin and Geoffrey Hill, on the other hand, reflects a steady internal logic of development.' Unlike Bly, Hill can project 'the poor "victimised self" now contaminated by those awful images, whose pleasure is relief'. He has the luxury of being able to register war and violence ironically, elegiacally.

Johnsen cites Henry James as a complex register of varieties of Britishness and Americanness. James had a strong and prescient sense of the tendency of each culture to export and import artefacts and customs with the inevitable result of 'duplication, circulation, and devaluation'. Hermione Lee cites James's examination of the 'latent preparedness of the American mind' for English life, and by implication James figures in the other essays in this section. Richard Brown deals with writers who have reversed James's international theme; now the British find art and life in America. James could well have figured as a presence in the essay on theatre between the wars, which explores the continuation of what James identified: a largely isolationist, apolitical British theatre with an affection for tradition and unwilling to be visually, formally or thematically extended, a more outward-looking, experimental and politically engaged American theatre. The twenties and thirties were decades in which the two countries shared much experientially. But the British looked to theatre as a way of escaping the issues of the day; the Americans embraced it as a way of confronting and even solving those issues.

Forked Tongues?

A forking of intention, a forking of tongues, evident too in a British musical theatre of continuing eclecticism (*The Boy Friend, Evita, Blood Brothers*) and an American musical theatre (*Oklahoma, The Music Man, Assassins*) which, by contrast, regularly concerns itself with the geographical, historical and political dimensions of cultural identity.

CHAPTER ONE

Brer Rabbit and Brer Possum: the Americanness of Ezra Pound and T.S. Eliot

Mark Jarman

LOCATING THE AMERICAN

How much easier it would be to talk about the Americanness of Robert Frost or Wallace Stevens, of Marianne Moore or William Carlos Williams. Though Frost lived in England for three years, from 1912 to 1915, he wrote there some of his most unmistakably American poems – poems which include the landscape of New England and the flat accents of its speech. That speech with its dry inherent understatement is audible in these lines from 'Birches', a poem composed in England when, Frost says, he was 'a little homesick'.

> I'd like to get away from earth awhile
> And then come back to it and begin over.
> May no fate willfully misunderstand me
> And half grant what I wish and snatch me away
> Not to return: Earth's the right place for love:
> I don't know where it's likely to go better.

William Carlos Williams, the other master of American speech in poetry, is also immediately recognisable as an American, from this poem of 1917 (the year *Prufrock and Other Observations* was published in England). Addressing his mother at the end of the poem 'January Morning', he writes:

> All this –
>   was for you, old woman.
> I wanted to write a poem
> that you would understand.
> For what good is it to me
> if you can't understand it?
>   But you got to try hard –
> But –
>   Well, you know how
> the young girls run giggling

on Park Avenue after dark
when they ought to be home in bed?
Well,
that's the way it is with me somehow.

The indulgence in incorrect grammar for its own sake ('you got to try hard'),
the facetious disapproval ('when they ought to be home in bed?'), and the
adverb 'somehow' employed for its relative mystery are all characteristic of
an American mixture of the down-to-earth and the fanciful.

Moore and Stevens are rather more exotic than Frost or Williams and
rarely affect an earthy tone in their poems, but their very individuality
bespeaks an Americanness. We do see this in Pound and Eliot, as well, a
characteristic that often puzzles their British biographers. But Moore sounds
especially American, if it is American to say directly, about her own art, in
her famous poem, 'Poetry':

I, too, dislike it: there are things that are
important beyond all this fiddle.

To employ a vernacular figure of speech ('all this fiddle') without attributing
it to a character's dialect but letting it characterise the poet herself is clearly
an American mannerism. As for Stevens, to an American he seems
thoroughly American, walking to work with the rhythm of his stretched
iambic pentameter line and imagery of the tropics crystallising in his head.
Though isolated from his society on the enchanted, coral lagoon of his
imagination, still he located himself in his own country, in the state of Florida,
finding there:

A few things for themselves,
Convolvulus and coral,
Buzzards and live-moss.
. . .

The dreadful sundry of this world,
The Cuban, Polodowsky,
The Mexican women,
The negro undertaker
Killing the time between corpses
Fishing for crayfish . . .

('O Florida, Venereal Soil')

Like Whitman, that most American of poets, Stevens in these lines includes
the 'sundry of this world'. It is with something of an aesthete's distaste that
he calls them 'dreadful', but he's willing to employ a pretty dreadful American
pun in the line about the negro undertaker who is '[k]illing the time between
corpses'.

Frost, the Californian, adopting New England as his home, Williams with

22

his general practice in Paterson, New Jersey, Moore living with her mother in Brooklyn, and Stevens, the insurance executive, vacationing yearly in Florida – all were contemporaries of Pound and Eliot. All, especially Stevens and Frost, were exposed to the same *fin de siècle* ideas, including the aestheticism that drove Pound and Eliot abroad in revulsion from America's vulgarity and from the literal increase in this vulgarity – humanity itself – during the great influx of immigrants from Europe. Yet Frost and Williams, Moore and Stevens, remained (or came home to stay), and their poetry as an American product is, to an American reader, much less problematic than the subject before us.

Why is it harder to locate the American in the poetry of Pound and Eliot? It can and has been done. Probably I am confining the issue too narrowly to the language and the sound of the language, but these are distinguishing factors of poetry. For all their critical pronouncements and the size of their historical presence, Ezra Pound and T.S. Eliot are poets first. To identify their Americanness based solely on their poetry is not easy and critics tend not to make a completely successful job of it, as if listening for that inconsistency of speech whereby the non-native speaker betrays his foreignness. I am going to broaden the issue and describe ideas and conditions that formed them as individuals as well as American poets of their time.

In 1938, when he was in his early thirties, Louis MacNeice commented upon the poets Pound and Eliot in this way, in his book, *Modern Poetry, a Personal Essay*:

> Eliot and his early model, Pound, are both first and foremost American tourists. They wish to shake off the vulgarity of America – of Sweeney, Miss Nancy Ellicott, Mr Hecatomb Styrax, to become European, cosmopolitan. They take long trips through history and the history of art and literature, eagerly 'aware that the mind of Europe . . . is a mind that changes, and that this change is a development which abandons nothing *en route*, which does not superannuate either Shakespeare, or Homer, or the rock drawing of the Magdalenian draughtsmen'.

This opinion of Pound and Eliot seems to have changed very little, at least in the minds of their most recent biographers, both of whom – Peter Ackroyd, author of *T.S. Eliot, a Life*, and Humphrey Carpenter, author of *A Serious Character: the Life of Ezra Pound* – are English. The opinion is just, though perhaps more trenchant coming from the young poet MacNeice whose intention is to clear ground for himself and others of his generation, particularly his friends, W.H. Auden, C. Day Lewis and Stephen Spender. Ackroyd and Carpenter include with this belief a reflex response to anything non-English or non-European about their respective subjects. They conclude that it must be an aspect of Pound's or Eliot's Americanness. Thus, for Ackroyd, all signs of self-denial in Eliot are facets of his American puritanism. For

Carpenter, Pound's energy and entrepreneurial spirit mark him, at worst, as a P.T. Barnum, an American huckster.

Actually, this contrast might be useful to establish an important difference between Pound and Eliot, especially to examine generalisations about their Americanness. For it is just as possible that their differences identify them just as well as Americans and perhaps more so. Their strongest similarity was that as young men they came to Europe before the First World War, from America, and there began their careers as writers. They brought with them two similar traits that served their modernism and their poetry. One was an iconoclasm, bred in the bone, as Monroe K. Spears has said in his book *American Ambitions*, and formed by the habit of revolution in American society. The other was a desire for unity or syncretism, another American paradox founded on the intellectual conundrum of *E Pluribus Unum* ('From the Many, One'). The very diversity that Pound and Eliot seem to have fled, they sought in their own ways to recreate and unify.

Their biographers justly take them to task for another aspect of their Americanness – their anti-Semitism, which flourished in England. Its roots were in the growth of the immigrant population in America at the turn of the century. This anti-Semitism was met and nurtured by the English sort, which regarded any attempt to assimilate, to become English, with raised eyebrows, and the more virulent European variety, which sent many Jews in flight from Europe and led eventually to the Holocaust. Eliot managed diplomatically to suppress his. Pound, as we all know, gave his free rein and it stampeded through his poetry, marring much of his *magnum opus*, *The Cantos*.

Finally, an essential feature of both men is that they were American natives and grew up in the United States. To use Monroe Spears's useful phrase again, they had bred in the bone not only indigenous American qualities, like Eliot's puritanism and Pound's pragmatism, but individually each possessed a set of experiences that marked him from childhood. These experiences are much clearer in the poetry of Eliot, whose late work returns to the scene of his boyhood. His story of reading *Huckleberry Finn*, a book forbidden to him as a boy in St Louis, the city on the great river of the novel, is poignant; implicit in the opening lines of 'The Dry Salvages' is his own feeling for Huck's Mississippi River. Pound's childhood is harder to tease out of his poetry, though one significant biographical event – his visit to his boyhood home after his release from St Elizabeth's in 1958 – is told romantically by Hugh Kenner at the end of *The Pound Era* and also by Carpenter, with equally characteristic matter-of-factness, in his biography. Pound is really best at recalling his American apprenticeship and journeyman status in England. His less-than-minor poem, 'L'Homme Moyen Sensuel' and his famous farewell to England, 'Hugh Selwyn Mauberley' tell us much about Pound, the young

American, in England. Eliot's Americanness can be traced through poems in his first two books, and also in part of *Four Quartets* and in the childhood scenes recaptured in two of his so-called minor poems, 'New Hampshire' and 'Cape Ann', from the group entitled 'Landscapes'. Eric Sigg in his book, *The American T.S. Eliot*, has also identified a self-portrait of Eliot as a child in his poem 'Animula' from *The Ariel Poems*.

Iconoclasm, the desire for unity, anti-Semitism, and the influence of childhood – these are the ideas and conditions I will examine in order to describe the Americanness of Pound and Eliot and its effect on their poetry.

AMERICAN ICONOCLAST

An iconoclast needs an icon to destroy and for Pound and Eliot these were actually different images. Though a convincing argument has been made for their reaction against American vulgarity and pluralism, their early poetry shows something else for each man as a motive for revolt.

Pound's first good poem, 'Cino', portrays his antagonist and target in the form of two fat burghers of the Italian Middle Ages, conversing about an itinerant poet:

> Once, twice, a year –
> Vaguely thus word they:
>   'Cino?' 'Oh, eh, Cino Polnesi
>   The singer is't you mean?'
>   'Ah yes, passed once our way,
>   A saucy fellow, but . . .
>   (Oh they are all one these vagabonds) . . .

This bourgeois attitude might be found anywhere, yet it appears to be one Pound associated especially with America, that 'mass of dolts' to which he refers in 'To Whistler, American'. In this belief, he was to remonstrate with Eliot's father when his compatriot first came to England to make his fortune. Living as a poet and not, as Eliot had to do, as a banker and then as a publisher, was something Pound succeeded at, finally with the aid of his wife Dorothy Shakespear's fortune. Self-justification against a perceived animosity in society permeates Pound's early work. 'I', he writes in 'And Thus in Nineveh',

> Am here a Poet, that doth drink of life
> As lesser men drink wine.

He sees that poetry itself can bait the bourgeois and '[r]uffle the skirts of prudes', and he commissions his poems to confront 'practical people':

go! jangle their door-bells!
Say that you do no work
and that you will live forever.

As he aims at the sensibilities of a society that would dismiss him as a poet
and dismiss poetry as a marginal activity, he sounds a note echoing the attitude
of the French symbolists. But as he finds that the language of poetry itself
must change from the late Victorian diction he favors in his early work, he
begins to sound like his nearest American relative, Walt Whitman. As if to
cast a spell to hide this proximity, he writes 'A Pact':

I come to you as a grown child
Who has had a pig-headed father;
I am old enough now to make friends.
It was you that broke the new wood,
Now is the time for carving.　　　*
We have one sap and one root –
Let there be commerce between us.

Pound's own father, Omar, an employee of the US Mint, approved of his
son, and in his old age was a disciple of his son's craziest theories. If Pound
was to revolt successfully he had to choose another father. When later he was
to write, 'to break the pentameter, that was the first heave', he acknowledged
implicitly that it was Whitman who heaved and broke it. Whitman's
apparently artless excesses repelled Pound, but it was especially Whitman's
inclusiveness, his democratic vision, that Pound recoiled from, as did Eliot.
Pound would not model himself on Whitman. His model would be another
American expatriate, the aesthete of the previous generation of Americans in
England – James MacNeil Whistler. Pound saw him as the ancestor of those

Who bear the brunt of our America
And try to wrench her impulse into art.

You were not always sure, not always set
To hiding night and tuning 'symphonies',
Had not one style from birth, but tried and pried
And stretched and tampered with the media.

'To Whistler, American'

Nowhere else in his early poetry does Pound himself sound quite so American
as here, with his directness, his colloquial invective, and his casual use of the
iambic pentameter line.

In 'L'Homme Moyen Sensuel', Pound writes of his character Radway that
he learned of Poe, Whitman, Whistler and Henry James. He also asserts that
their recognition they 'got abroad'. But America's poor taste in literature he
ascribes to one of its greatest literary documents:

The constitution of our land, O Socrates,
Was made to incubate such mediocrities . . .

Compounded in his iconoclasm is an élitism that would also repel the likes of Louis MacNeice. America as it was founded, so Pound believes, is incapable of recognising genius – the sort of genius, anyway, that must regard itself as special.

Eliot's iconoclasm is more subversive and really more devastating than Pound's, for it appears in *Prufrock and Other Observations* that he wishes to break with the very society that might acknowledge his special artistic gift. In poem after poem of the first book he depicts and demolishes an American society that aspires to gentility despite hopeless provincialism. Yet it is not to assert his role as poet that he does this, but simply to overturn and with much less discretion even than Pound shows. Women are clearly the pillars of the society that Eliot would undermine – caryatids as icons, if you will. In 'The Love Song of J. Alfred Prufrock' they utter inanities and dismiss his own attempts at communication. In 'Portrait of a Lady', the woman is seen as pressing her advantage, even if she were to die. In the figures of Cousin Harriet, Aunt Helen, Cousin Nancy, and the laughing woman in 'Hysteria', woman is variously boring, irrelevant, mannish and dangerous. But she is always or almost always in the company of the poet, making him feel ineffectual. When she is exposed to other, stronger forces, like Mr Apollinax and the man who leaves the weeping girl in 'La Figlia Che Piange', she wilts. In every case, even the exotic one of 'La Figlia Che Piange', she looks American. Against her society, the poet can only pose the resources of his private imagination and his ability to sympathise. Thus, the tenderness of 'Preludes' and the brief moment of empathy in 'Morning at the Window' for 'the damp souls of housemaids' and the surreal floating image of a passing woman's 'aimless smile' are all the more shocking. The woman in 'Rhapsody on a Windy Night' and the figure in 'Preludes' with her yellow-soled feet clasped in her hands appear on the margins of society, where Eliot himself, in these early poems, has chosen to loiter and frame the world he assaults.

Eliot's background in America was clearly different from Pound's, not on the other side of the tracks but certainly higher up on the social scale. Yet Eric Sigg has pointed out that growing up in St Louis the son of a successful industrialist in a prominent family, still Eliot had to endure life in an area of increasing dilapidation, because of the family's attachment to the ancestral home. The meliorist attitudes of his Unitarian background have also been pointed to as motives for his revolt. Sigg indicates that the sensibilities of Henry James and Henry Adams, disaffected Americans who returned to Europe and a traditional and coherent culture, appealed enormously to Eliot. Unfortunately, the antidote of William James did not affect him. The author

27

of *Varieties of Religious Experience* expresses more of the American ideal of inclusiveness and the relative virtues of diversity than does his brother. But Eliot had had a bellyful of that thinking by the time he was grown. His first poems not only clear ground but appear to burn the very ground beneath his feet.

THE DESIRE FOR UNITY

To revolt is to reject. To smash an icon is rarely to put a new image in its place. Both poets rejected what America offered them and at the same time acted as if to some degree it had offered them nothing. By blaming America's mediocre literature on the Constitution itself, Pound showed his incipient political concerns and his belief that the poet had a role to play in the government of nations. By satirising genteel American society, Eliot sought to put another sort in his frame of urban degradation. But as Americans, as the products of an eighteenth-century revolution and its intellectual legacy, and as a new generation living in the memory of a civil war fought for the principles of the founding fathers, Pound and Eliot would have acted uncharacteristically if they had resorted merely to nihilism. Along with *E Pluribus Unum*, another motto of the nation was, and is, *Novus Ordo Saeculorum* ('A New Cycle of the Ages'). Eliot and Pound set about to make new unities and to bring to life a new confederation of ideas. Their ends were quite different, but the impulse towards those ends was distinctly American.

Eliot's new world is depicted in *The Waste Land*, where the fragments of the old order offer, in new combinations, another way to regard the world. It is clear from recent scholarship that the poem could almost be considered a collaborative effort between Pound and Eliot, for it was Pound's editing that gave the poem its distinct character. Still, it was Eliot's intention from the start to set his lands in order, lands that he had himself laid waste. He comes to the old world as an explorer, in a reverse of the pilgrim migration. For every act of Eliot in these early years, though a negation, is actually a mirror image of the making of America. Eliot makes up a new world out of the old, but the materials and images with which he does so have analogues in America.

In Part I of *The Waste Land*, the unreal city is surrounded by or approached through desert, the land of red rock. The island city surrounded by hostile terrain is, indeed, a feature of the American landscape. The land of red rock is in the southwestern part of the United States, however, not in Eliot's Missouri. Still, as in previous poems, Eliot invests desert margins of the city with more reality than the city itself. In Part II, he depicts a woman at the heart of the unreality, a figure who seems to a reader today to represent Eliot's own unhappy relationship with his first wife. Demotic and vulgar as they are, Lil's friends in the pub have much more reality about them in their frankness and their appetites. Once again, there on the margins, Eliot feels free. He cannot connect with the world from which he derives; he cannot connect with it intellectually or physically. Part III is about connection, sexual connections in particular. Most of them appear to be distasteful, whether they be the one suggested by Mr Eugenides or the one effected by the young man carbuncular. Yet the song of the Thames' maidens, though it resolves itself in the anguish of Augustine's flight from his own sensuality, suggests pleasure, swelling with the Thames' tide. The enigmatic fourth part of *The Waste Land* depicts the drowning of Phlebas. It is his role to drown, just as Prufrock drowns. Here Eliot leaves behind the old body and, in fact, all that is represented by body and mind in the previous sections. In the fifth and final part, and in the footnotes attached (which must be seen as a sixth part to the poem, as the Bill of Rights must be seen as a part of the US Constitution), he makes the new world.

St Louis, on the Mississippi River, is the gateway to the American West and what was once called the great American desert. The vastness of empty space around the American city must be considered in the milieu of *The Waste Land*: it is part of the American imagination. So much space must mean so much potential. It takes that sort of mind to work as Eliot does, implying that ruins can be propped up, shored up by fragments. It is interesting, as well, that at the end of the poem Eliot offers a spiritual resolution derived from India. This would seem to be further repudiation of his intellectual heritage, his family's Unitarian faith in works. Yet the wisdom of the East enters American thinking with Transcendentalists like Emerson, who also were engaged in the ongoing American project of, in Pound's phrase, making it new. (The scale of meaning in this phrase of Pound's, by the way, ranges from the sublime to the ridiculous in American life.)

The Waste Land, then, like the US Constitution, is a thoroughly American project, an attempt at making something new. Though the language is Europeanised and literary, and the best dialect bits are take-offs on British speech, its place as Eliot's most American achievement profoundly affected American poets on the other side of the water. Young poets like Hart Crane and Eliot's own contemporaries like William Carlos Williams felt obliged to respond. Older American poets like Frost and Stevens seem to have been unaffected. And yet we can find in their work poems like Frost's 'Directive' and Stevens's 'The Man on the Dump', poems about ruins and fragmentation, that read differently because of the existence of *The Waste Land*. In a century of American innovations, *The Waste Land* is that thing on which Americans pride themselves – it is a first.

Or is it a second? Pound had already written 'Hugh Selwyn Mauberley', his attempt to write a Jamesian novel in verse. Perhaps this claim has obscured his own significant syncretic achievement. I think so. Humphrey Carpenter argues that much of what Pound wrote and much of the way Pound lived displays a love of the mask, the persona. So, we see Pound moving from the role of Provençal troubadour to Chinese poet, in his *Cathay* series, to Roman wit, in 'Homage to Sextus Propertius'. In 'Hugh Selwyn Mauberley' he dons the mask of the French neo-classicist, Théophile Gautier. All of these masks form the shifting personae of *The Cantos*, as well, and, in truth, that work bears more of an analogous relationship to *The Waste Land*, in terms of its syncretic structure and its status as a new vision of world history. But much occurs in 'Mauberley' that anticipates *The Waste Land*. It may be possible that having made his own attempt at a major work that would hold a series of pieces together, Pound as Eliot's editor was all the more ready to recognise the direction in which Eliot ought to go in 'He Do the Police in Different Voices', the original draft of what became the most important poem of the modern era.

'Mauberley' is just as ambitious as *The Waste Land*, and in one regard, more formally original. After the twelve sections plus the 'Envoi' of the poem, 'Hugh Selwyn Mauberley, Life and Contacts', the poem begins again, with a section entitled simply, 'Mauberley', which Pound considered both an extension of the poem and a commentary on it, like Eliot's notes to *The Waste Land*. 'Mauberley', the second part, in five sections, contains no narrative material, and the writing is both more compressed in places and windier, too. The epigrammatic wit of the last stanza of Part IV,

> 'I was
> And I no more exist;
> Here drifted
> An hedonist.'

exists nearby the mushy-mouthed attempt at onomatopoeia and self-criticism of the previous section:

> Nothing, in brief, but maudlin confession,
> Irresponse to human aggression,
> Amid the precipitation, down-float
> Of insubstantial manna,
> Lifting the faint susurrus
> Of his subjective hosannah.

Throughout the poem there are macaronic combinations of Latin and Greek, French, allusions to the ancient world and to the First World War, portraits of friends, such as Ford Madox Ford, and suspect characters like the venal Mr Nixon, modelled on Arnold Bennett. In other words, it tries out much of the same staging as *The Waste Land*. But Pound's poem is also an album of English memories and as such a farewell to England. In a way the memories are those of an American tourist, the sort Louis MacNeice accused both Eliot and Pound of being; they are the keepsakes of an American gone abroad and bent on looking for the best art of the day, like Henry James's Newman in *The American*. Pound's saving grace might be that he hopes also to remember who made the art and who condemned it. He manipulates Gautier's trim quatrains to create his own attic grace with a practical American sense of workability, stretching and contracting the form as he sees fit. The stanzas are meant to last, to be, as Donald Davie has observed, carved in time, as an antidote to what the times demanded.

> The 'age demanded' chiefly a mould in plaster,
> Made with no loss of time,
> A prose kinema, not, not assuredly, alabaster
> Or the 'sculpture' of rhyme.

The poem represents what is for Pound the one integral good, his proposed replacement for a world turned upside down. That good is beauty, chiefly the beauty of art. His aim is 'to convey the relation / of eye-lid and cheek-bone / by verbal manifestation'. When he imagines himself drowning, like Phlebas and Prufrock, it is for him 'to designate / His new found orchid'. When he pictures himself and his beloved as nothing more than 'siftings on siftings in oblivion', still he insists that change will break down '[a]ll things save Beauty alone'.

Beauty alone continues to be Pound's obsession throughout his poetry. How beauty is made and preserved leads him, I believe, to his disastrous economic theories and these in turn provide the growth hormone for his anti-Semitism. Pound wished, as he says in the final Canto, 'to write Paradise', to create the heavenly city on earth. 'Mauberley' gives us our first look at his values. The tragedy of Ezra Pound was his belief that beauty could be an accomplishment of the correct economic policies; thus, he projected the aims of art along vectors like Social Credit. His suburban anti-Semitism, as he was later to call it, developed monstrously because he perceived an enemy to his project. His foolishness stems from his mistaken belief that he could have a larger role in the world than the role of poet.

Though *The Cantos*, as I have said, are by rights the work that should be placed beside *The Waste Land*, I do not believe they add much to Pound's vision that is not already expressed in 'Mauberley'. Pound's sense of how things ought to be and of what ought to be preserved in the world is determined almost completely by his aesthetic judgements. These were often first rate, and his expression of beauty by 'verbal manifestation' few have ever contested. Both his ear for language and his eye for the image are unparalleled.

But it is Eliot whose vision holds together and continues to cohere, because Eliot has more than the good of art on his mind. I am not, however, particularly interested in creating a contest between them as poets, assigning place to each for various reasons. It is an American quality that made each wish to make a new unity out of the pieces he perceived and in some ways created. I think the success and failure in each case is related to how they dealt with another American trait they brought with them to England – their anti-Semitism.

ANTI-SEMITISM AND THE LOST CHILDHOOD

American anti-Semitism (of the sort bred in Pound and Eliot) and English anti-Semitism are rather different strains of the same disease. Their biographers correctly locate Pound's and Eliot's in the American xenophobia resulting from the great increase in the country's immigrant population around the turn of the century. Americans extended their prejudices to the Irish as well as the Jews, but the hatred of Jews was all the more pernicious because it could be fed by notorious and ancient conspiracy theories. Books like *The Protocols of the Elders of Zion*, a proven fraud, did their damage. The English brand of anti-Semitism is fed by the general English disdain for the non-English, but mingled with it is the fascination with and distaste for Mediterranean culture, a repulsion – attraction syndrome for the South, which includes the Levant. There is also the anomaly of non-Christians living in a country where Protestant Christianity is the state religion. And there is the larger European issue of Jewish residence there since the Diaspora. English anti-Semitism is older than the American type on which Pound and Eliot were weaned. But the ingrained prejudice that could lead Henry James to refer to all bank loan officers as 'the Jews', as he does in *Roderick Hudson*, could be found on both sides of the Atlantic.

Eliot's anti-Semitism mars a number of his poems in *Poems, 1920*. In 'Gerontion', 'the jew squats on the window sill, the owner'; in 'Burbank with a Baedeker; Bleistein with a Cigar', Bleistein is described gratuitously as 'Chicago Semite Viennese', and once again 'The Jew' is caricatured. This time the rats below the Rialto of Venice are given a higher place, for 'The jew is underneath the lot.' Princess Volupine entertains 'Sir Ferdinand / Klein' who, caught astride an enjambment, is deflated by the pun on his German name. In this case, Eliot indulges in a typically English *bêtise* about the aspirations of such people, for whom a knighthood is no disguise. In 'Sweeney Among the Nightingales', 'Rachel *née* Rabinovitch', who tears at the grapes with her 'murderous paws', is the last of the anti-Semitic cartoons to appear in Eliot's poetry during his lifetime. It is sad stuff to catalogue these weaknesses, but sadder still I think to excuse them, as critics have done.

Pound's anti-Semitism is worse; it is the tragic flaw running through and undermining his great work, *The Cantos*. Though his letters were often laden with references to 'kikery', and all his life he entertained a belief that during his days as a railroad magnate his father had to endure the conspiracies of Jewish bankers, Pound's own first poetic expression of his prejudice appears in 'Mauberley', in the section called 'Brennbaum':

> The sky-like limpid eyes,
> The circular infant's face,
> The stiffness from spats to collar
> Never relaxing into grace
>
> The heavy memories of Horeb, Sinai and the forty years,
> Showed only when the daylight fell
> Level across the face
> Of Brennbaum 'The Impeccable'.

Compared with Eliot's caricatures, this one is mild, a curious sketch speculating on what forms the mind and manner of someone perceived to be Jewish. For Pound is depicting here the author and artist Max Beerbohm, whom he mistakenly took to be a Jew. This mistake is related to the much larger disorder that Pound enjoyed. His theories about Jews ranged widely and outlandishly and ran the gamut from believing the dulling effect of circumcision led to a desire to make money as a compensation, to issues of racial purity touching on his own background. (He was anxious to make it clear that he had no Jewish ancestors.) But Pound always had to have a theory or theories to knit together. His anti-Semitism enters forcefully into *The Cantos* in the thirties, when he discovers Douglas's theory of Social Credit, and thus he begins to elaborate a petty prejudice into a social vision. Fascism helps him, too. Many who came into his sphere caught the anti-Semitic bug, like his American publisher James Laughlin, but were able later to shake it off. Only the nasty bunch of sycophants surrounding him at St Elizabeth's, described devastatingly by his daughter, persisted in their prejudice. Humphrey Carpenter reports in his biography of Pound that Ernest Hemingway wrote to Allen Tate: '[Pound] ought to go to the loony bin, which he rates and you can pick out the parts in his cantos at which he starts to rate it.' He starts to rate it, I would argue, in Canto XXXV, which begins, 'So this is (may we take it) Mitteleuropa.' He proceeds in that poem to describe the Jewish family in absurd terms (its warmth is 'intravaginal', for example) and to depict European Jews as the pivot of artistic commerce, involving the production of art in the production of money. From there on, he is in the grip of his obsession, and it works a vein of rot through the poem which, from the 1930s until his death, was his primary literary endeavor.

Prejudice begins in childhood. Few would look back nostalgically to the roots of their prejudice, yet Pound's reported remark to Allen Ginsberg about his 'suburban anti-Semitism' does look back. 'Suburban' does actually describe Pound's American experience. Though born in the state of Idaho, where his father was constructing railroads, he was bred in Pennsylvania and his family lived on the edge of Philadelphia. As his biographer mentions, there was little 'immigrant blood' in the neighbourhood around him. He and his family were members of a Presbyterian church and he made his confession of faith there when he was about twelve. His father's work in the US Mint in Philadelphia seems to have excited Pound most when he reflected on his childhood. This association with the making of money had an ominous relationship with his later obsession. But his association with the West, the influence of his father's telegraphic style of writing letters, his exposure to the Uncle Remus stories as a boy and his grab-bag Americanism (which he could reach into at will for the rest of his life) all colour the character who wrote his own letters in phonetically Americanised English and gave himself the name Brer Rabbit after dubbing his friend T.S. Eliot even more memorably, Brer Possum. (For both men these nicknames were like calling cards from their American past.) One looks in vain, however, for a nostalgic or searching reminiscence of childhood in Pound's poetry. That sort of self-knowledge is absent in most of his writing and his life and may account for the moral lapse of his unrepentant prejudice.

There is one interesting story about Pound's relationship to his childhood. Humphrey Carpenter mentions that while Pound was incarcerated in St Elizabeth's, the mental asylum where he lived after the Second World War (following the decision that his psychological state made a trial for treason impossible), he had contacted the family that occupied his old family house in Wyncote, Pennsylvania. In 1958, when he was released, they invited him to visit, and Pound amazed them at how much he remembered of his childhood. He excitedly inspected the house, and during the night he went down the road to the Presbyterian church where he had made his first confession as a boy, to see if a tree he and a friend had planted still stood. Hugh Kenner, at the end of *The Pound Era* tells the story like this:

> At Wyncote, last, a summer night, in 1958, St Elizabeth's freshly behind him, in bed in his old house for the last time (and aged 72), he had somehow wakened – always a brief sleeper; genius enjoys long days – and tiptoed downstairs in his pajamas, out into the dark street, and down to the Presbyterian Church, to sit on its steps looking over the moonlit lawns of great estates: sitting where a boy had sat 60 years before, his eye on trees before dawn, his mind on a poet's destiny, which should be that of dreaming old men's silences; the old man's memory now in turn accessible

to the still older man in Venice, to be guessed at but never experienced by any comer. 'Shall two know the same by their knowing?' Thought is a labyrinth.

Pound himself never wrote any such poetry about his childhood in America. But Kenner's assumption, lavishly as it is expressed, closes on a kernel of truth. The boy who made his confession of faith in that church, who grew up in that suburb of Philadelphia, became the poet Ezra Pound, a figure of such dimensions that his most unquestioning followers, like Kenner, are able to create myths out of his life without contradiction from the man himself.

Eliot as he grew older showed more of the actual roots of his imagination. Perhaps, because his childhood was the beginning of a lifelong unhappiness, not really assuaged until his marriage to his second wife, he could return to parts of it when he knew he was happy and he could recall its painful loneliness as well. Eric Sigg quotes these lines from 'Animula' to give an oblique but sharp portrait of the boy, Tom Eliot:

> The pain of living and the drug of dreams
> Curl up the small soul in the window seat
> Behind the *Encyclopedia Britannica*.

Eliot also offers, in contrast, portraits from landscapes associated with his childhood and adolescence, not in St Louis but in New England. Thus, 'New Hampshire', in 'Landscapes',

> Children's voices in the orchard
> Between the blossom- and the fruit-time:
> Golden head, crimson head,
> Between the green tip and the root . . .

and the beginning of 'Cape Ann',

> O quick quick quick, quick hear the song-sparrow,
> Swamp-sparrow, fox-sparrow, vesper-sparrow
> At dawn and dusk. Follow the dance . . .

modulate into the children's voices woven through *Four Quartets*:

> Go, said the bird, for the leaves were full of children,
> Hidden excitedly, containing laughter.
> Go, go, go, said the bird: human kind
> Cannot bear very much reality.

And these voices from his childhood echo as well in the line of Verlaine quoted in Part II of *The Waste Land*– 'Et O ces voix d'enfants, chantant dans la coupole!' The human voices that wake and drown Prufrock become, as Eliot strains to hear them again, voices of the past and of another place. And behind these voices, like the river Wordsworth heard in his nursemaid's song, are, for Eliot, both a river and a sea. Both these natural features figured in his

35

growing up: the Mississippi River, the 'strong brown god' of 'The Dry Salvages', and the Atlantic off the north-east coast of Cape Ann where he enjoyed sailing as a teenager and young man. 'The river is within us, the sea is all about us', he writes, convincingly, locating his understanding of this metaphysical condition in his original experience. Eliot's poetry seems to quest after something which he discovers; in practical American terms, he finishes what he starts. Pound's failure – his life ended in silence and his work in pieces – is just as American as Eliot's success. That I choose these terms at all to describe the work and life of the two poets betrays an American affliction: the desire to divide the world between winners and losers.

Eliot found his end, in his poetry at least, in his beginning. Pound in his touching last Canto acknowledges his original plan, too, way back at the beginning, which was to write Paradise. He asks to be forgiven, invoking the language of his Presbyterian background, by the gods and those he loves. Eliot, too, ends his final great poetic work with a vision of paradise.

> And all shall be well and
> All manner of thing shall be well
> When the tongues of flame are in-folded
> Into the crowned knot of fire
> And the fire and the rose are one.

Both endings come from a need to create a unitary vision. In Pound's case, it was of this world, where art would be made in the perfect society it needed, to be unblemished by financial practicalities. In Eliot's, it was of a transcendent religious reality. In the case of both poets, the pursuit began with an American belief that the attempt was possible and that its accomplishment could be measured in terms of success or failure.

POSTSCRIPT

When I began drafting this essay in the first weeks of December 1990, I opened with the following paragraph:

> It feels unreal to be looking back across the century at two men who had so much to do with how we experience the daily fragmentation of our lives, if we are readers of poetry, and yet who believed, in their poetry, that they were trying to put the pieces back together in a new way. As the century's third global conflict begins, it feels strange to try to apprehend a quality – Americanness – in two Americans who left their country to escape characteristics they carried in their genes and social make-up. It is, in part, something in Americanness that has brought the world to war this time. So, it feels unreal, strange, and yet as the century looks back at us,

through the eyes of Ezra Pound and T.S. Eliot, it seems all too familiar, all too real, all too in keeping with this era of catastrophes.

The actual outcome of the Gulf War, the end of the Cold War, and the state of the globe wracked by the AIDS epidemic, all persuade me that the world described prophetically by Pound and Eliot has come and gone. Modernism is over and has been over for a long time. Even the term Postmodernism is anachronistic. We read Pound and Eliot for their artistry – what music is like Pound's? What voice like Eliot's – and for their historical importance. Would either of them recognise the world as a global village that is also torn by conflicting cultural desires? As Americans they might suffer the same bewilderment Americans are now suffering, even as their system of government innately encourages diversity. But as poets, I think they would offer the same redemption as they did before – art and faith.

FURTHER READING

Primary

T.S. Eliot, *The Complete Poems and Plays, 1909–50* (New York, 1971).
Ezra Pound, *Collected Shorter Poems* (New York, 1970).
——*The Cantos* (New York, 1981).

Secondary

Peter Ackroyd, *T.S. Eliot, a Life*, (New York, 1984).
Humphrey Carpenter, *A Serious Character: The Life of Ezra Pound* (New York, 1988).
Donald Davie, *Ezra Pound: Poet as Sculptor* (New York, 1964).
Jacqueline Kaye, (ed.), *Ezra Pound and America* (London and Basingstoke, 1992).
Hugh Kenner, *The Pound Era* (Berkeley, 1971).
Louis MacNeice, *Modern Poetry, a Personal Essay* (London, 1938).
Eric Sigg, *The American T.S. Eliot: A Study of the Early Writing* (Cambridge, 1989).
Monroe K. Spears, *American Ambitions* (Baltimore, 1987).
Wendy Stallard Flory, *The American Ezra Pound* (New Haven and London, 1989).

Cather's Bridge: Anglo-American crossings in Willa Cather

Hermione Lee

CATHER AND THE 'MARGINAL MAN'

I begin with three locations in the fiction of Willa Cather. The first is the Cuzak farm at the end of *My Ántonia* (1918), protected from American space inside its 'triple enclosure' of wire fence, locust hedge and tall mulberry hedge, with the Czech family inside it, boasting of their mother's *kolaches*, playing Bohemian airs on the grandfather's fiddle, speaking to each other in their 'rich old language', and reading items from the Bohemian illustrated papers about a singer from Prague. The second is the night-time scene in *Death Comes for the Archbishop* (1927) where Bishop Latour, sitting outside the pueblo at Laguna, talks to his Indian guide Jacinto in Spanish and English about the names of the stars, and they agree to differ:

> 'The wise men tell us they are worlds, like ours, Jacinto'.
> The end of the Indian's cigarette grew bright and then dull again before he spoke.
> 'I think not', he said in the tone of one who has considered a proposition fairly and rejected it. 'I think they are leaders – great spirits.'
> 'Perhaps they are', said the Bishop with a sigh. 'Whatever they are, they are great.'[1]

The third is the house where Cécile Auclair, the seventeenth-century French apothecary's daughter in Quebec (*Shadows on the Rock*, 1931), brings her mother's parsley inside, in the depths of the icy winter weather. Auclair listens to her 'softly stirring about, moving something, covering something: "Papa, j'ai peur pour le persil." ' It had never frozen in her mother's time, and it should not freeze in hers.'[2] These three examples depict local New World cultures which are perceived to be in transition. By means of a (characteristic) apparent simplicity and with a secure use of specifics – family life, food, naming, domestic habits – Cather invokes large questions on the relation of culture to ethnicity, on the creation of nationality, and on the best life for an individual at a crossing-point between possible identities.

Cather occupies an interestingly ambivalent position in her country's historical debate between cultural pluralism, or 'ethnic diversity',[3] and nationalism. It is too easy to describe her as a simplifying nostalgic, as Henry Steele Commager did, under the heading 'The Traditionalists'. Cather has frequently been characterised in this way: a writer who located what Commager called a 'peculiarly American' tradition in the idealism of the first pioneers, and who retreated, after she perceived that idealism to have been defeated, into earlier heroic phases of New World history and in the direction of Catholicism.[4] The three examples I began with do not quite bear out that version of Cather. Jim Burden goes back out of the enclosed Czech farmhouse into modern American spaces, where the old roads are ploughed under, and the story of Ántonia, however 'incommunicable', must find its audience. Cécile grows up to marry a Canadian backwoodsman and become one of the new Québécois bourgeoisie – attractive to Cather because they have success-fully adapted to the territory but have *also* remained distinctively French. Latour's job is supposed to be to convert the New Mexican Native American Jacinto to French Catholicism, but he holds off. Bridges between pluralisms are only half-crossed; distinguishing factors between cultures are celebrated, while at the same time the necessity for assimilation, and the threats to distinctiveness, are clearly perceived. Cather's characters are 'peculiar Americans' rather than 'peculiarly American'.

Always writing about cultural confrontations and crossovers, she preferred peculiarities to sameness. Though she was emotionally sympathetic to the historian Frederick Jackson Turner's pessimistic and influential account of the closing of the Westward frontier, she did not subscribe to its cultural premise that the frontier had created an amalgamated, homogenous American char-acter. And at the point when the exciting theory of the 'melting pot' was proving useful to American sociologists and political commentators, Cather stood apart.

> There she lies, the great melting pot – listen! can't you hear the roaring and the bubbling? There gapes her mouth – harbour where a thousand mammoth feeders come from the ends of the world to pour in their human freight. Ah, what a stirring and a seething – Celt and Latin, Slave and Teuton, Greek and Syrian, black and yellow . . .[5]

That theory of 'Anglo-conformity', optimistically embracing the idea that a new culture would bubble up from the amalgamation of minority groups, preceded a more threatened and xenophobic movement of assimilation, a more sinister boiling-up, out of a mixture of related events: the huge wave of Eastern European immigrants, the rise of Klan membership, the war with Germany and post-Darwinian theories of biological inequality. Cather began to write at this point of transition. There are strong attacks on American racism in her books, like the small-town xenophobia in *My Ántonia*, or, in *One of Ours*, the vendetta against the German farmer in wartime Nebraska. *My Ántonia* was written at the time of Madison Grant's *The Passing of the Great Race* (1916), which drew on the nineteenth-century social theorist Gobineau's racist conviction of the innate superiority of the Anglo-Saxon race. Madison Grant described the man of the old stock – Nordic, Protestant – being swamped by Jews, Slavs and Negroes. Grant's theory (the sort of thing that Tom Buchanan quotes enthusiastically in *The Great Gatsby*) bolstered wartime and postwar 'nativist' movements to restrict immigration, introduce literacy tests and pressurise immigrants to adopt 'American ways'.[6] It may be that Cather's writing, at least in the 1910s, came partly out of her resistance to this nativist ideology of assimilation. But her version of American cultural or ethnic pluralism is never simply nostalgic or celebratory. Nostalgia and celebration coexist with feelings about American identity which are ambiguous, unresolved and troubled.

Cather's work coincided with the formulation by the pioneering Chicago sociologist Robert Park (and, later, by Everett Stonequist) of the concept of the 'marginal man'.[7] The marginal man is *'par excellence* the stranger'. He is the man of mixed blood, 'the man who lives in two worlds but is not quite at home in either'.[8] He is the immigrant, the cosmopolite, the wanderer. Park gives as his leading examples Heine, the Jew in Germany, and Santayana, the Spaniard in Boston. His 'marginal man' is a 'cultural hybrid', 'a man living and sharing intimately in the cultural life and traditions of two distinct peoples; never quite willing to break, even if he were permitted to do so, with his past and his traditions, and not quite accepted, because of racial prejudice, in the new society in which he now sought to find a place'.

> The marginal man is a personality type that arises at a time and a place where, out of the conflict of races and cultures, new societies, new peoples and cultures are coming into existence. The fate which condemns him to live, at the same time, in two worlds is the same which compels him to assume, in relation to the worlds in which he lives, the role of a cosmopolitan and a stranger. Inevitably he becomes, relatively to his cultural milieu, the individual with the wider horizon, the keener intelligence, the more detached and rational viewpoint. The marginal man is always relatively the more civilised human being.[9]

Like the convert, as described by William James in *Varieties of Religious Experience* (a book which was very important to Robert Park), the marginal man's characteristics are 'spiritual instability, intensified self-consciousness, restlessness, and malaise.'[10] It is a telling historical coincidence that the term 'marginal man' was felt to be an attractive and useful one at the same time as the idea of the 'melting pot'. The two notions jostle uncomfortably against each other, yet are related. In Cather's fiction, the processes of immigration and assimilation are heroically rendered but presented in a tone of elegiac mournfulness: in *O Pioneers!*, for instance, the triumph of endurance coexists with the sense of something lost.

Robert Park's account of the psychic effects of marginality has an odd appositeness, not so much for Cather's immigrants – the Auclairs or the Shimerdas or the Bergsons, studies in survival and adaptation – as for her troubled, self-divided American heroes, Jim Burden or Bartley Alexander or Godfrey St Peter. The parallel is imperfect because they are not men of mixed blood or mixed faith, nor are they essentially 'cosmopolite'. But they feel alienated and separate from their 'cultural milieu', and that alienation has a great deal to do with an internalised conflict between different, opposing kinds of Americanness. No doubt Cather's sense of herself as sexually isolated and unconventional intensified her interest in 'marginal men' of this sort. But her absorption in the psychic effects of *cultural* conflicts is as much a factor as her sexual orientation. In her study of American identity (which might be one way of describing her life's work) it is the unassimilated, the peculiar, the maladjusted, the person who has the 'more civilised' 'self-consciousness', who arouses her imagination.

CATHER AND THE 'PASSIONATE PILGRIM'

No American writer of the nineteenth and early twentieth century could mark out an imaginative territory without looking back at England and Europe. The malaise and self-consciousness of the marginal figure, identified by Park as a significant twentieth-century construct, was paralleled by the self-consciousness and need for self-identification of the American writer, who frequently felt him or herself to be an alien to the community, the 'parish', yet a stranger in any other world. For many of these writers the transatlantic bridge had either to be crossed, or to be blown up.

Cather's interest in the tensions between acculturation and alienation came from childhood observations and from powerful private emotions, but it derived, also, from a lifelong literary debate, embarked on in her early journalism and expressed throughout her writing. Of course she was not unique in this negotiation between the claims of American materials and European literary models. But she belongs, interestingly, neither to the 'passionate pilgrims' (in Henry James's phrase) who gladly claimed their inheritance in England or Europe, nor to the 'lost generation' – Stein, Anderson, Hemingway – who couldn't go home again. European and English culture – literature, art, music – lifted Cather out of Red Cloud, Nebraska, and sent her to London and Paris and Avignon and Italy. She chose to stay in America and write about it, but her American writing never disengages from her 'passionate pilgrimage'.

The phrase is the title of James's 1871 story about a romantic American's first visit to England:

> The latent preparedness of the American mind for even the most delectable features of English life is a fact which I never fairly probed to its depths. The roots of it are so deeply buried in the virgin soil of our primary culture, that, without some great upheaval of experience, it would be hard to say exactly when and where and how it begins. It makes an American's enjoyment of England an emotion more fatal and sacred than his enjoyment, say, of Italy or Spain.[11]

This idealised, neo-colonial – and comical – account of the sacred and inevitable homecoming of the American mind to its 'primary culture' is more benign and assured than anything in Cather. But 'latent preparedness' brilliantly describes the preconceptions and desires which Cather shared with many American writers setting out for Europe. 'Latent preparedness' meant openness to the European experience; but it also meant (as James wittily illustrated in his story) a romantic prejudice in favour of a culture which had been prejudged in terms of the literary and the pictorial. If for Cather, as for James and for many others, the European experience felt as much like a homecoming as a discovery, it was because the landscape and the architecture and the society were a confirmation of well-known, long-loved books and paintings. The literary American's response to these wonders could be extremely equivocal: the old political hostility towards England, a resentment of Europe's cultural dominance, a distaste for the vestiges of medieval feudalism and a failing of the spirits before the ruins of ancient empires affected writers as different as Hawthorne, Twain and Henry Adams. The European experience frequently induced a feeling of marginality and inferiority, rather than of homecoming. For Cather, the difficulty of these cultural crossings was most acutely felt in England.

Cather's literary negotiation between what her mentor Sarah Orne Jewett called 'the parish and world' has been much discussed: her 'Russianising' of Nebraska, her lifelong attraction to French culture both in its native and in its exiled forms, her passion for German and Italian opera, her appropriation of a Virgilian tone for American landscapes. But Cather's 'latent preparedness' for England has not been thought of so much account, perhaps because her friend Edith Lewis said that though Cather felt 'a deep blood kinship with England', French culture spoke 'more directly to her imagination'.[12] Yet the influence of certain English writers on her work – Shakespeare, Bunyan, Carlyle, Kipling, Lewis Carroll, Keats, George Eliot – is well known, and so is her youthful preference for the dark, unwieldy Anglo-Saxon language over the 'fatal' perfection of French:

> The Anglo-Saxon . . . came without an inherited classical sense of fitness and proportion, into a language as dark and unexplored as his own forests, unwieldy as his own giant battle-axe matched with the French rapier. It has never been perfected. Every English author has known the continual torment and stimulus of writing an inexact tongue . . . He [The Anglo-Saxon] made the most spiritually suggestive language ever written. He made it the tongue of prophecy, he gave it reverence, that element of which French is as barren as a desert of dew . . . it is in the pages of Carlyle, when those great, chaotic sentences reach out and out and never attain, and through them and above them rings something that they never say, like an inarticulate cry.[13]

In this early manifesto for the value of suggestiveness, of 'the thing not named', Anglo-Saxonness – wild, deep, dark, prophetic, ancient – is thoroughly romanticised. When she came to match the language and the literature to the place, she would have to work hard, as a tourist, to sustain that prejudice in favour of the sacred and the meaningful. All of Cather's writing about England, whether in journalism, fiction, or poetry, shows her making it up to meet her imaginative needs. Of course this is a commonplace of cross-cultural literature, as a British writer on transatlantic crossings observes: 'Mythopoesis came into play as soon as the nations and national characters were described, [since] the subject matter of a people was one that destabilised scientific discourse at the same time that it provoked imaginative expression.'[14] But Cather's mythopoesis of England is particularly revealing, and tells us a great deal about her construction of a 'peculiar', marginal, complex American identity.

She went to England first in 1902 as a wide-eyed tourist, and then, in 1909, while working for McClure, as an experienced editor, meeting literary people and going to the theatre. If she revisited England later in her life, she made no record or mention of it. Later journeys abroad were to France in 1920, researching *One of Ours*, to Europe for seven months in 1923, while writing *A Lost Lady*, to Europe for six months in 1930, for background to *Shadows on the Rock* (when she had her 'chance encounter' with Madame Grout, Flaubert's niece, and came to know the Menuhin family) and a last journey to Italy and France in 1935, to look after her dying friend Isabelle Hambourg. She also made two English connections in America, one in the mid twenties with D.H. Lawrence, whom she met in New York and New Mexico (an encounter which may have influenced the pantheism of *The Professor's House*), and one with her eccentric, flamboyant admirer, the Hon. Stephen Tennant,[15] who came to visit her in 1935 after an impassioned correspondence. No two Englishmen could have been more grotesquely unlike, but Cather's interest in both does suggest, again, the appeal of the marginal man, whether this took the form of a self-exiled, nomadic genius, or of a reclusive, elaborately camp homosexual. But with these two peculiar exceptions, Cather's perception of England remained largely framed in a pre-war past, and this is reflected in her infrequent but significant uses of it: first, in her 1902 travel journalism, in her poems of 1903, and in a 1905 story called 'The Marriage of Phaedra'; then, in her first novel, *Alexander's Bridge*, (1912); and lastly, in her late, posthumously published story, 'The Old Beauty', of 1936.

Cather's 1902 letters to the *Nebraska State Journal* about the beauty of Chester, the Shropshire countryside, the London poor and the British theatre express the 'succession of emotions' which Henry Adams said (in 1919) 'millions of Americans have felt' and 'possibly very young and ingenuous tourists feel them still'.[16] Cather may have been ingenuous, but she was aware of how the passionate pilgrim's mind is constantly adjudicating between prejudice and actuality. As she says in her letters home: 'Constant comparisons are the stamp of the foreigners; one continually translates manners and customs of a new country into the terms of his own before he can fully comprehend them.'[17] But she cannot avoid looking at the country through the lens of the English culture she had already imbibed: painting, poetry, theatre, fiction. So she makes pictorial and literary readings of England: the Norman tower at Hawarden outside Chester explains Maurice Hewlitt's historical novels; her shocked view of the London poor makes Kipling seem to her 'a greater man than I ever thought him before', and proves to her that Hogarth 'was the only realist and the only man who knew his London': 'Every day faces from "The Idle Apprentice", "Cruelty", and "The Harlot's Progress" pass one in the streets like the hideous distortions of a nightmare.'[18]

If her metropolitan views were derived from Kipling and Hogarth, her sense of English pastoral was at this time overwhelmingly coloured by Housman, whose elegiac classicism, muted homosexuality and bitter scepticism spoke very powerfully to her. Shropshire was inevitably perceived as real Housman country; she was even lucky enough to spot 'a company of lads with their pigskin ball' racing over the Green, a living illustration of Housman's schooldays. So scenic is her response that she describes Shropshire *as painted* by the American painter Abbey, because the trees look like painted trees in a child's Noah's Ark set. Cather looked, in the landscape she identified with Housman, for what she already wanted to find: a melancholy lyricism, a twilit arcadia. (It was those preconceptions which made her visit to the recessive poet so embarrassing on both sides.)[19] Characteristically, though, since she was always equally attracted to the aesthetic and the robust, she identified 'Englishness' also as wildness or energy, something rough and passionate, to match those dark inchoate prophetic notes she had heard in

Carlyle. She found this aspect of 'Englishness' in the gypsy-style boatwomen on the canals, or in the rough flower-selling Hogarthian London street-girls. In art, she found it in Burne-Jones, whom she admired for his unsentimental and erotic medievalism, and in the 'elasticity' and 'wildfire wit' of Ellen Terry's performance of Mistress Page. Cather saw Terry in Beerbohm Tree's unfunny, prim and over-elaborate ('real' cobblestones, and so on) 1909 production of *The Merry Wives of Windsor*. She picked out Terry's performance as the only thing which gave 'the spirit of things Elizabethan', the 'faintest aroma of all that jumble of fisticuffing and jocular horse-play'.[20]

Cather's scenic view of Edwardian England is expressed throughout the pieces she wrote for her Midwestern readership in a language of spectatorship: London is a 'procession', a 'pageant', an artist's studio, a stage-show. She concluded her letters to Nebraska, after a meditation at Arles on the decadence of the subtle, 'beauty-making' Latin races, with a description of Kitchener's return to London with his troops from the Boer War. She notes with enthusiasm the spectacle of 'the trains of rajahs from the east . . . moving this way and that, glittering in gold and crimson, the nobles of a conquered race'. But what strikes her most are the hundreds of children proudly and earnestly patting the horses:

> There they were: 'Cook's son, Duke's son, son of a hundred kings', each whispering a vow to the horses of the cavalry. One felt in a flash of conviction from what blood the world's masters were to come. The poet of the line said that 'On the bones of the English, the English Flag is stayed.' From the time the Englishman's bones harden into bones at all, he makes his skeleton a flagstaff, and he early plants his feet like one who is to walk the world and the decks of all the seas.[21]

Cather's passion for a fine show, her love of Kipling and of Anglo-Saxon brutality and her belief in the inevitable conquest of the lesser breeds by the Nordic races entirely gets the better of her here. This envious imperialism (not unusual for its time, of course) makes a startling contrast to her cultural sympathies and flexibility in an American context. But it is bound up with her desire to locate and experience true Englishness, powerful, spiritual, democratic, robust, with no bad blood. The fear that 'bad blood' might lurk within this Anglo-Saxon pageant haunted her; it is an odd and unattractive feature of her English writings that they bring out her areas of racism. Interested though she was in marginal or deracinated figures, remote though she is from the rampant xenophobia of Madison Grant or Gobineau, she nevertheless had a horror of 'degeneracy'. And where she most cherished romantic illusions about a nation, this fear was most pronounced.

The derivative Edwardian poems which Cather wrote out of her first English visit are superficial and imitative. 'Poppies on Ludlow Castle', for example, makes an inert frieze of romantic 'English' associations.

Of love and song and warring
Of adventure and play
Of art and comely building
Of faith and form and fray.[22]

The only story in her early collection, *The Troll Garden*, directly derived from her English travels, is an artificial piece of work, too, inspired by her visit to Burne-Jones's studio. But it is extremely revealing about what she wanted from England. 'The Marriage of Phaedra' is told by a 'gallicised,' American painter, MacMaster, a passionate pilgrim ('I'm a man with a mission') who is let into the secrets of the late 'Treffinger's' life and work through the painter's faithful Cockney valet. This character, though taken 'from life' (Cather had been delighted by her meeting with James, the faithful guardian of Burne-Jones's studio,)[23] reads like an awkward amalgam of Dickens and a Punch cartoon: 'He bore himself in a manner strikingly capable, and there was a sort of trimness and alertness about him, despite the too-generous shoulders of his coat. In one hand he held a bulldog pipe, and in the other a copy of *Sporting Life*'.[24]

Though his valet is a typical Brit, Treffinger is revealed, through his servant's narrative, as an exception to 'the fold of national British art'. Like Carlyle, he is the misfit who appeals to her imagination because his qualities are at once representative of a certain kind of Englishness, and exceptional. Cather, explaining to herself in her story the appeal of Burne-Jones's art, at once 'naive and remote', dresses up the painter's democratic origins. The real Burne-Jones grew up in genteel poverty in Birmingham and went to St Edward's School and Oxford. Cather's Treffinger, like the boat-women and flower-girls she had admired, is 'raw clay out of the London streets'. It is that 'fisticuffing' background which gives her the true Anglo-Saxon roughness. But this is mixed with a European education from and Italian political exile, (Cather's version of Rossetti) who moulded 'the blank soul of the London boy' into an imagination impassioned by 'medieval romances'. So Nordic roughness is mixed with Latin aestheticism. Hence the frank brutality and religious mysticism of the fifteenth century in the artist's work, especially in his most famous painting, 'The Passing of Venus'. And one can see why the original for this, Burne-Jones's 'Passing of Venus', would have appealed so strongly to Cather. In its strange landscape, statuesque women out of Puvis de Chavannes crouch in fear as the naked form of Venus zooms in from the left on a monumental winged chariot. Mystery, paganism and an ethereal eroticism are fused.

At the end of the story, bad blood creeps in. The dead man's greatest painting is sold, in spite of the efforts of the valet, to an obnoxious Jewish dealer: the native treasure is traded into culturally predatory, racially inferior hands. The 'true' English spirit is overpowered by corrupt extortionism and by the sort of smug, unimaginative philistinism which always infuriated Cather, whether it came out of England or Nebraska. It is the cold, prim, jealous wife of the painter who is responsible for the sale. (There are similarities here with 'The Sculptor's Funeral' and with *The Professor's House*.) 'The Marriage of Phaedra' is a story about how an inheritance can fall into the wrong hands, and it suggests how anxious Cather was to lay claim, herself, to a certain kind of English inheritance. But that emotion could only be mediated through an imitatively Jamesian narrative (the story resembles his 'The Author of "Beltraffio" ' (1884), with its unsympathetic, fatally censorious writer's wife) and through a tourist's view of the English artist's studio.

Cather's second visit to England, in 1909, was not so naive, but it confirmed her theatrical, scenic approach to the country. She had the good luck to encounter the Edwardian theatre at its most ebullient, with Marie Lloyd, Vesta Tillie, Gertie Millar in full swing, the Follies at the Apollo, Florence Smithson, 'The Nightingale of Wales', in *The Arcadians* at the Shaftesbury, J.M. Barrie's *What Every Woman Knows* at the Empire, and the first London Abbey Theatre season.[25] Cather went with Lady Gregory to the first night of *The Playboy of the Western World*, in which the late Synge's fiancée, the enchanting Maire O'Neill, played Pegeen. Of course this was not a new interest for Cather. Since her early years of reviewing in Lincoln and Pittsburgh, Cather had been interested in and knowledgeable about British actors, plays and theatre (she had reviewed Pinero, Shaw, Barrie and Wilde). In many of these reviews of the 1890s and 1900s she had lamented the lack of an indigenous American theatrical tradition of any distinction, and the dependency of the American stage on imports from England and Europe for the best plays and players. Her enthusiastic 'latent preparedness' for the English theatre was mixed with an acute sense of national inferiority. No wonder, then, that the dazzle and power of London took shape in her mind in theatrical terms.

That 'latent preparedness' made for a friendship with William Archer, the leading theatre critic of his day, whose championing of Ibsen had had a powerful effect on Henry James in the 1890s. Archer's responsiveness to Ibsen and to other foreign drama did not preclude his campaign – not unlike Cather's in her reviewing years – for a native theatre: 'plays which mirror our own life, utter our own thoughts, deal with our own problems, satirise our own foibles, interpret the character, the ideals, the genius of our race.'[26] Archer's expressive verbs make a rubric for a realist British theatre. In her conversations with him, Cather would have found points of comparison with the personal manifesto which she was beginning to evolve, for an American fiction which would be true to experience and would fuse the realistic and the romantic. In her writings on English subjects, she never found a way of applying the rubric satisfactorily. She did not know enough to 'mirror', 'satirise' or 'interpret' the character of the race, and she was too preoccupied in imposing her romantic, preconceived idea of English types – melancholy lyricists or rugged barbarians – to escape from caricature or simplification. The chivalric, the traditional, the picturesque, the impressionistic are foregrounded; political or economic complexities are ignored. She must, for instance, have been well aware of the raging controversy over the Abbey's production of *The Playboy*, and of the politics of that whole season, which included the banning of Shaw's *The Showing Up of Blanco Posnet* and protests at Lady Gregory's Irish republican one-acter, 'The Rising of the Moon'. When she came to make use of the Irish theatre in her first novel, *Alexander's Bridge*, however, all that is expurgated and submerged in favour of a charming, silly Celtic pastiche, complete with real donkey, fairy rings, potheen smugglers and fairy wreaths, as a backdrop for her heroine's light, expressive Irish charm. Yet her struggle in this first novel, however awkward, to make use of her English experiences is extremely revealing of her anxieties about herself as an American writer.

MASQUERADING: *ALEXANDER'S BRIDGE*

Alexander's Bridge is a transatlantic novel which reflects in its crossings of the ocean and in its contrasts of cultures, the divided and 'marginal' psyche of its hero. Its first title was 'Alexander's Masquerade', and, like so much of Cather's work, it is a novel about performance. Bartley Alexander is an elevated figure on a heroic stage, and he is also a dissimulator, a bad actor trapped in conflicting roles. (He owes a good deal to Ibsen's Master Builder, for whom youth and troll-like power are embodied in 'Hilda' Wangel.) Bartley's Hilda is, like her Irish play, a fairy-tale illusion to satisfy Bartley's romantic escapism. The theatrical conception of the whole novel allows Cather to project Bartley's split self into the dramatic breaking of his bridge.

When Cather referred to *Alexander's Bridge*, which she always did dismissively, she used terms of artifice for it, calling it 'a studio picture', 'mechanical', 'like riding in a park, with someone not altogether congenial, to whom you had to be talking all the time'.[27] It was made, she said in her 1922 Preface to the reissue, of 'external material', reflecting 'the glitter of the passing show'. This is partly camouflage, to prevent readers from looking too closely at a self-revealing fiction. Alexander, the heroic bridge-builder divided between two women and two kinds of selves, acts out Cather's own sense of distress from her conflict between writing and journalism, and projects her own sexual doubleness. He reflects her fears of what is happening to her own country. And he stands in for the novelist who must decide where to choose her materials for her buildings. Cather is attracted by Bartley Alexander's 'natural force', the pioneering energy he has applied to his bridge-building. The male world of technology and construction always held a romance for her: she loved the big transcontinental trains and the old railroad pioneers, and she makes heroes out of businessmen, tycoons, explorers and scientists. Those great modern emblems of the American machine age, John Roebling's bridges in Brooklyn and over the Allegheny River at Pittsburgh, were familiar sights to her. But in the American celebration of the machine there was also, great dread and anxiety, feelings Cather shared with Henry Adams and Henry James. New York, particularly, seemed a catastrophic enclosing prison. In a story of 1912 called 'Behind the Singer Tower', she represented the city as a barbaric monster, devouring its human slaves. These American fears dominate *Alexander's Bridge*.

Bartley Alexander is also enslaved. He feels that his younger self – the outdoor self from the Midwest – is being crushed out of him under the pressure of public success and official commitments. He is becoming simply a machine, carrying out the 'functions of a mechanism useful to society'. This self-alienation is compounded by his sexual 'masquerade'. He is torn between his marriage to the gracious, supportive Winifred and his return to the love of his youth, the seductive Irish actress Hilda. Winifred embodies the civilising constrictions of Boston; she nourishes his finer feelings, but not his energy. Hilda is supposed to represent freedom, youth and a world elsewhere. But the clash between the two relationships is not really as interesting as the tension within Bartley between his public self and his 'second man', who is 'fighting for his life at the cost of mine'. Alexander's split self, his sense of his own marginality, is dramatised by placing him for half the novel in an England where he feels, like the young Cather, at once estranged and beglamourised. This world, which is not his, is presented as a stage-play, or as a painted scene. He is in it, but he cannot enter it. It is the perfect location for the 'spiritual instability, intensified self-consciousness, restlessness and malaise' of the marginal man.

Alexander is introduced to England by 'Maurice Mainhall', a fossilised Edwardian, 'the nephew of one of the standard Victorian novelists' and author of books like a 'Key To Shakespeare's Sonnets' and a study of 'The Poetry of Ernest Dowson'. He looks 'astonishingly like the conventional stage-Englishman of American drama,'[28] and it is he who sweeps back the curtain for Alexander on to London, and Hilda. It is a neat touch: if Mainhall is an American's idea of a stage-Englishman, then perhaps Bartley Alexander is his idea of a stage-American. The possibilities of mutual caricaturing and mysti-fication (of the sort that preoccupy Henry James in many of his stories and

novels) are just suggested here. But *Alexander's Bridge* is a romance, not a
social satire.

Because she is setting a romance of escape against a harder, materialistic
American realism, Cather feels free to stir in a vaguely evocative mixture of
seductive transatlantic references. So Hilda's Irishness, and the younger
Alexander's lost idyllic days in Paris, blur gently together. Bartley sits on the
Embankment gazing at a scene by Monet: 'He . . . sat down to watch the
trails of smoke behind the Houses of Parliament catch fire with the sunset.
The slender towers were washed by a rain of golden light and licked by little
flickering flames; Somerset House and the bleached gray pinnacles
about Whitehall were floated in a luminous haze.'[29] Thinking his way back
into the past (uncannily like Gatsby at his station on West Egg), he goes home
as 'the red and green lights [are] blinking along the docks on the farther
shore, and the soft white stars shining in the wide sky above the river'.[30] And
returning from their jaunt to Richmond, Alexander and Hilda drive
through

> one of those rare afternoons when all the thickness and shadow of London are
> changed to a kind of shining, pulsing, special atmosphere; when the smoky vapours
> become fluttering golden clouds, nacreous veils of pink and amber; when all that
> bleakness of gray stone and dullness of dirty brick trembles in aureate light, and all
> the roofs and spires, and one great dome, are floated in a golden haze.[31]

Inside this magically Monet-like city they find the summer crowds out on
the streets, standing in 'long black lines' before the pit entrances of the
theatre,[32] and hear a noise everywhere from street pianos, cab horses, street
calls, like the 'deep vibration of some vast underground machinery, and like
the muffled pulsations of millions of human hearts'. It is Monet crossed with
Bleak House, or *The Princess Cassamassima*, or even *The Secret Agent*: a
half-delighted, half-horrified rendering of the spectacle, in which the human
lives of the city have been 'hazily' generalised and pictorialised. Like Cather,
Bartley Alexander is a tourist here: a marginal man, a passionate pilgrim, who
cannot make a bridge into this scene to inhabit it as a home.

Alexander's sense of estrangement reflects Cather's struggle to come to
her own imaginative terrain, to inhabit a writing where she would feel at
home. It is interesting, then, that although England is supposed to figure in
the novel as the alluring alternative to mechanised America, it has its ominous
aspects too. For Bartley and Hilda, the sinister side of England is located in
the British Museum, which has appropriated and fossilised artefacts of world
culture. To Bartley, the British Museum is the place 'where all the dead things
of the world were assembled', and the mummy in the Museum is referred to
several times in threatening opposition to Hilda's energy, power and life force.
Evidently there is a cultural difficulty for Cather in locating a free alternative

to contemporary America in the Old World. She is terrified of being buried alive in either place. That fear of being stifled and ossified never leaves her (a mummy is discovered at the heart of the pioneering idyll in *The Professor's House*), but she will find landscapes and figures which release her more fully than the England of *Alexander's Bridge*.

BEHIND THE SCREEN: 'THE OLD BEAUTY'

> They sat talking about people who were no longer in this world. She knew much more about them than he. Knew so much that her talk brought back not only the men, but their period; its security, the solid exterior, the exotic contradictions behind the screen; the deep, claret-coloured closing years of Victoria's reign. Nobody ever recognises a period until it has gone by, he reflected: until it lies behind one it is merely everyday life.[33]

In the last years of her life, by which time Cather's tendencies towards ossified nostalgia had hardened, she made use of England once more as a cultural reference (mixed, as in *Alexander's Bridge*, with her stronger sympathies for France). In 'The Old Beauty', England, from which the narrator has been absent about as long as Cather, is the focus for a romantic regret for what 'lies behind one'. The story is full of reactionary lachrymose elegies for vanished courtesies and traditions. But, surprisingly, in a narrative where England seems more than ever to be fixed as a painted scene, deepened and claret-coloured in the memory of two displaced and marginalised old people, some unsettling details are allowed to peer through, 'exotic contradictions' from 'behind the screen'.

The first disconcerting thing about the story is the insecure status of what is remembered. The narrator, a middle-aged Jamesian American bachelor, Mr Seabury, returning to Europe from a lifetime of business in China, is in search of 'some spot that was more or less as it used to be'. His old age is dominated by his desire to find a way to go back. But when he has a 'chance meeting' at Aix-les-Bains with an old lady called Mme de Couçy, he does not immediately recognise that she was once Gabrielle Longstreet, a famous Edwardian beauty. Only gradually does the story admit to the extent of his memories, as if the narrator, though longing to live in the past, cannot bring himself to acknowledge all of its contents. Not for nothing is 'bury' in his name. Gabrielle's romantic past is duly unfolded (picked up from Martinique by an English lord, queen of Edwardian society, divorced, moved to New York and Paris, remarried, widowed by the war). In the company of his re-found 'lost lady', Seabury is returned, as he desires, to an English 'society

51

whose manners, dress, conventions, loyalties, codes of honour, were different from anything existing in the world today'.

Between them, Seabury and Gabrielle repulse modernity, as Cather so notoriously did in her late years. Madame de Couçy, a 'grim', 'mirthless' 'personage', travels with her photograph albums of dead heroes and believes 'one should go out with one's time'. She confirms Seabury's prejudice that the beauties of the past (as opposed to the 'cinema stars' of the present) had benefited by 'a romantic tradition . . . an attitude in men which no longer existed'. Their high moment together is a ghostly dance in the hotel ballroom, where they put the enervated young couples to shame by a stylish performance of the 'Blue Danube'. The two old waltzers are left alone on the floor, amid comments from the spectators: 'It's so quaint and theatrical.' Gabrielle's last performance is a trip with Seabury to the monastery of the Grande-Chartreuse. On the way back their chauffeur swerves to avoid two young American women driving on the wrong side of the road. (On the wrong side of the road in more senses than one: they are dressed in 'knickers' and call each other 'Marge' and 'Jim', and Gabrielle refers to them as 'those creatures'.) The old lady is not hurt, but the rude shock of this brush with the contemporary actually kills her. She dies in the night, and is buried in Père Lachaise, where 'ladies who once held a place in the world' used to buy burial lots.

Like Madame Grout in 'A Chance Meeting', the old beauty is a forbidding, restrictive, matriarchal figure. But her companion, once the English music hall star Cherry Beamish, disrupts the story's fixed glare of nostalgia. She herself doesn't mind 'young things': 'the present . . . is really very interesting', she tells her friend, 'if only you will let yourself think so'. Cherry brings a democratic, popular note into the proceedings. Seabury makes friends at the hotel with a touching English family from Devonshire, who have been visiting their son's war grave. The English father remembers Cherry as a principal boy in a popular coster song: 'Remember her in that coster song, Mother? It went round the world, that did. We were all crazy about her, the boys called her Cherish Beamy. No monkeyshines for her, never got herself mixed up in anything shady.'[34] Times have changed, as Mother points out, for Cherish Beamy now to be the companion of Lady Longstreet. The grave which the English family has come to France to grieve over is the symbol of everything that has brought to an end the music hall, the innocent cross-dressing, the empire, the class hierarchies. But Cherry and the English family alleviate the snobbish nostalgia of Seabury and Gabrielle. They stand for the rough, jolly, democratic street-life which had always been part of Cather's fantasy of England, derived from Dickens and Kipling and the music hall.

Gabrielle herself comes out of another branch of English theatre, the 'claret-coloured' late Victorian melodrama. It takes a long time, in this short story, for Seabury to arrive at his earliest memory of her, in a sinister episode which is recalled like an account of a play. But nothing like this was ever featured in 'The Second Mrs Tanqueray' or 'A Woman of No Importance'. It is as if Pinero has been crossed with Zola:

> As he approached the wide doorway leading into the drawing-room, he was conscious of something unusual; a sound, or perhaps an unnatural stillness. From the doorway he beheld something quite terrible. At the far end of the room Gabrielle Longstreet was seated on a little French sofa – not seated, but silently struggling. Behind the sofa stood a stout, dark man leaning over her. His left arm, about her waist, pinioned her against the flowered silk upholstery. His right hand was thrust deep into the low-cut bodice of her dinner gown. In her struggle she had turned a little on her side; her right arm was in the grip of his left hand, and she was trying to free the other, which was held down by the pressure of his elbow. Neither of those two made a sound. Her face was averted, half hidden against the blue silk back of the sofa.[35]

This is an unusually explicit sexual scene for Cather, buried in the centre of what is supposed to be her nostalgic memory of romantic, courtly English life. Gabrielle – unlike Cherry Beamish – has certainly been mixed up in something 'shady'. It is made clear that Gabrielle's brutal assailant is Jewish – 'an immigrant who has made a lot of money', not 'English speaking', like the Jewish dealer who raped the sanctuary of the dead painter in 'The Marriage of Phaedra'. As in that story, the old world has its villains, intruders of bad blood, portrayed as sexual and cultural predators. This coarse, perfunctory bout of anti-Semitism complicates Cather's picturesque romance of England. There are 'exotic' – and erotic – complications behind the screen. What has been repressed in Cather's expurgated, picturesque version of England – jolly music hall, decent ordinary folk, chivalric love, spiritual art, passionate language – sneaks back as something fearful, like the mummy in *Alexander's Bridge*. Lurking inside the enviably traditional old world is the presence of the alien.

This is unpleasant, but it shows that Cather understood what a fragile masquerade she had made out of her English illusions. Even in this sentimental late story, the attempt to find a safe home by a process of idealisation is not allowed to succeed. (The same is true for the narrators of *My Ántonia* or *A Lost Lady*.) Cather is famously authoritative at identifying the tensions between cultures – between Catholic France and pre-Christian New Mexico, or between Bohemia and Nebraska. What is profound and powerful in her work is that she uses these cultural struggles as ways of writing about personal fears, repressions and confusions. Her American pilgrim's investment in England as the locus of certain fantasies about romance and tradition is undermined by the intrusion of sexual cruelty, racism and voyeurism. Elsewhere, attempts to romanticise 'innocent' territories – France in *One of Ours*, the Mesa in *The Professor's House*, the Forresters' house in *A Lost Lady*

– also come undone. The construction of any identity – sexual, cultural, authorial – requires the forging and sustaining of numerous illusions. Cather makes us perceive how perilous and fragile this process is, for those who do not feel they have a cultural identity ready-made, or are not at home with the one on offer. That her first novel ends with the cracking in half of a bridge mades a fine theatrical metaphor for the difficult crossing-points that lie ahead in her work.

NOTES

1. *Death Comes for the Archbishop* (London, 1981), p. 93.

2. *Shadows on the Rock* (London, 1984), p. 27.

3. James Stewart Olson, *The Ethnic Dimension in American History* (New York, 1979), p. xvii.

4. Henry Steele Commager, *The American Mind* (New Haven, 1950), p. 155.

5. Olson, op. cit., p. xvii (quoting Israel Zangwill, 1909).

6. Ibid., p. 213.

7. Robert Ezra Park, *Race and Culture* (New York, 1964), Part IV, 'The Marginal Man'; Everett V. Stonequist, *The Marginal Man: A Study in Personality and Culture Conflict* (New York, 1961). The concept was first formulated by Park in 1928: see Peter Rose, *They and We: Racial and Ethnic Relations in the United States* (New York, 1964), 'Marginal Men and Marginal Cultures', pp. 124–9.

8. Park, op. cit., p. 51.

9. Ibid., pp. 375–6.

10. Ibid., p. 355.

11. Henry James, 'A Passionate Pilgrim' (1871), in *The Complete Tales of Henry James*, ed. Leon Edel, Vol. 2 (London, 1962), p. 227. The wording is much altered in the New York Edition of 1908.

12. Edith Lewis, *Willa Cather Living* (Athens, Ohio, 1989), p. 56.

13. Willa Cather, 'On Language: French and English' (March 1898) in *The World and the Parish: Willa Cather's Articles and Reviews, 1893–1902* (ed.) W.M. Curtin (Lincoln and London, 1973), II, pp. 583–4. Quoted in Robert J. Nelson, *Willa Cather and France: In Search of the Lost Language* (Urbana and Chicago, 1988), p. 14, who argues for the dominant influence of France and the French language on her work.

14. Christopher Mulvey, *Transatlantic Manners* (Cambridge, 1990), p. 7.

15. See my *Willa Cather: A Life Saved Up* (London, 1989), pp. 332–3, for an account of their relationship.

16. Henry Adams, *The Education of Henry Adams*, (1918), quoted by Walter Allen, *Transatlantic Crossing* (New York, 1971), p. 114.

17. 13 July 1902, *The World and the Parish*, p. 892.

18. 10 Aug. 1902, Ibid., p. 911.

19. See *Willa Cather: A Life Saved Up*, p. 60, for an account of Cather's unsatisfactory visit to Housman.

20. 24 April 1902, *The World and the Parish*, p. 920.

21. 19 Oct. 1902, Ibid., p. 952.

22. Willa Cather, *April Twilights* (1903), Rev. edn (ed.) Bernice Slote (Lincoln and London, 1962), p. 42.

23. 'London: Burne-Jones's Studio' in *Willa Cather in Europe: Her Own Story of the First Journey*, intr. George N. Kates (New York, 1956), reprinted with emendations in *The World and the Parish*, describes 'James . . . sitting the day long with his pipe and a copy of *Sporting Life*, watcher and warden still'.

24. Willa Cather, *Collected Short Fiction 1892–1912* (Lincoln and London, 1965, 1970), p. 220.

25. For the London theatre in 1909, see J.C. Trewin, *The Edwardian Theatre* (London, 1976); W. MacQueen Pope, *Carriages at Eleven* (London, 1947) and J.P. Wearing, *The London Stage 1900– 1909*, Vol. II (New Jersey, 1981). For the Abbey Theatre see W.B. Yeats, 'The Controversy over The Playboy of the Western World' and 'On Taking the Playboy to London' in 'The Irish Dramatic Movement', *Plays and Controversies* (London, 1927), pp. 192–8.

26. William Archer, *Study and Stage* (London, 1899), p. 40.

27. *Willa Cather on Writing* (New York, 1949), pp. 91, 93.

28. *Alexander's Bridge* (London, 1990), pp. 27–8.

29. Ibid., p. 46.

30. Ibid., p. 52.

31. Ibid., p. 118.

32. The sight of the 'pittites' waiting for two or three hours a night, three nights a week, to get into the shows, was a familiar one in Edwardian London. See Trewin op. cit., p. 19.

33. 'The Old Beauty' in *The Short Stories of Willa Cather*, selected by Hermione Lee (London, 1989), p. 425.

34. Ibid., pp. 426–7.

35. Ibid., p. 433.

An earlier version of this article was given as a paper at the 1990 Fourth National Seminar on *Willa Cather: Multiple Traditions of American Culture* at Santa Fe, New Mexico, in June 1990, and I would like to express my thanks to Susan Rosowski, the Seminar Director.

FURTHER READING

Willa Cather, *Alexander's Bridge* (London, 1990).

——*Collected Short Fiction 1892–1912* (Lincoln and London, 1965, revised edition, 1970).

——*The Professor's House* (London, 1981).

——*Selected Stories* (London, 1989).

——*The World and the Parish: Willa Cather's Articles and Reviews 1893–1902* (Lincoln and London, 1973).

George Kates (ed.), *Willa Cather in Europe: Her Own Story of the First Journey* (New York, 1956).

Hermione Lee, *Willa Cather: A Life Saved Up* (London, 1989).

Sharon O'Brien, *Willa Cather: The Emerging Voice* (New York and Oxford, 1987).

James Woodress, *Willa Cather: A Literary Life* (Lincoln and London, 1987).

CHAPTER THREE

Theatre of Manners, Theatre of Matters: British and American Theatre between the Wars

Ann Massa

In a platform performance at London's National Theatre in August 1990, David Mamet argued that the simultaneous presence in the National's repertoire of Harley Granville Barker's *The Voysey Inheritance* (1905) and Mamet's own *Speed-the-Plow* (1989) neatly represented classic distinctions between British and American theatre. British theatre, Mamet maintained, is for the most part trivially domestic and technically unexperimental. Its plays move inexorably toward tidy resolutions and formulaically allow an audience to leave the theatre in a comfortable and unchallenged frame of mind. American theatre, by contrast, is innovative, deliberately uneven, provocatively open-ended and sends its audience away disturbed and questioning. While to a degree Mamet's theory attempts to justify his own linguistic freedom and dramatic unpredictability, and is tendentious (can a Barker revival and a recent Mamet play be appropriately compared) it pinpoints a significant difference between British and American theatre which was perhaps never more evident that in the twenties and thirties. It is the purpose of this essay to chart, to explore and to account for such difference in terms of cultural identity.

The radical differences between the two theatres at this time is all the more striking because the twenties and thirties were decades in which the two countries apparently shared so much, experientially. Both had come out of the war with cruel losses (America lost more troops in her year's involvement in the First World War than in the four years of the American Civil War); both had a 'Jazz Age'; a time of what George E. Mowry calls, in his book of that title 'Fords, Flappers and Fanatics'; both had stock-market crashes, Depressions and the accompanying phenomenon of mass unemployment; both were confronted with the facts of the Spanish Civil War, the growth of Fascism and the rise of Nazi Germany. But Britain's entertaining theatre of manners (with its drawing-room sets, familial structures, domesticated social relationships) and America's theatre of matters (Was Freud right? Was Nietzsche? How to achieve as women; how to exist without God and with machines) seemed the products of opposed realities and the reflections of contradictory and incompatible histories and experiences. Why *did* so many British playwrights seem casually to ignore the world? Why *did* most American playwrights so passionately engage with it?

Three reasons are conventionally advanced for the British non-response.[1] First, that audiences, actors and writers were deliberately disengaged. They perceived the function of their theatre as escapism and entertainment. The British, this argument runs, decided to equate peace with fun. The tough realism of Granville Barker and John Galsworthy was consciously supplanted by the fanciful plays of J.M. Barrie, James Bridie, J.B. Priestley (also a solid regionalist) and the clever superficiality of Noel Coward. Second, the number of potential dramatists was decimated by war casualties. Third, in a symptomatic display of philistinism and poverty, no new theatre was established in London between 1914 and 1959, when the Mermaid Theatre opened. All three factors can be seen as indicative of theatre as a known quantity and a social event rather than a social force. Prewar interest in Ibsen was, typically, diluted into vestigially problem plays. Henry Popkin indicts British playwrights from the nineteenth century onwards as unambitious artists who wrote primarily for a living and who often wrote down to their audiences. Such playwrights were

> so intent on making their pieces capture the interest of their audiences that, in the true spirit of their day, they 'domesticated their "poetic" drama, emphasising the sentimental and the pathetic, bringing out the "sanctity" of such relationships as husband–wife, parent–child. That they succeeded in this domestication' is undeniable and the audiences did respond, but this success often came at the expense of meaningful drama and vital poetry.[2]

Eric Salmon, in his chastening study *Is The Theatre Still Dying?* (1985) diagnoses a naively sentimental British theatrical world rather than an escapist one, though it was characterised by recidivist writing which lacked the 'genuine' seriousness of Galsworthy and Granville Barker. What seriousness there was was spurious, what comedy there was lacked the wit and pace of pieces by George S. Kaufman and Moss Hart (*You Can't Take It With You* (1939), for example). Moreover, Salmon contends, images of family life in plays of this period were not original, but derived from earlier texts. Orwell notwithstanding, this was less a class-conscious society than one which sought to deny any kinds of division. The watchword was reconciliation. And fiction. The purveyors and the consumers of the British theatrical product conspired to deny reality. Salmon ascribes this to an issue of cultural identity. The British need their privacy protected and the unchanging unreality of British theatre (which thriftily throve on the few characters and single sets needed for drawing-room plays) permitted that.

> The degree of flattering reassurance that this kind of play communicated to its audiences was even greater in the provinces than in London, since the setting of the play in London – as was most usually the case – added an even greater distance between the easy, comfortable and desirable world of the play and their own often rather monotonous existences. Given this audience, the play could the more readily function as fairyland. London was to these provincial audiences what Moscow was to Chekhov's three sisters. Unlike Congreve and Sheridan, too, this new Town play has left no considerable examples of work which, while arising from the immediate circumstances of their own narrow, urban circle, yet by the accident of genius so transcend those origins as to become plays of universal application and permanent worth.[3]

Henry Popkin is a little less harsh on the British theatre of this time. He sees some diminution but some continuation (in Priestley and Bridie) of 'the major concern of the serious Edwardian playwrights . . . the conflict of man and his society with certain themes predominating, especially those involving economic, religious, social and political questions'. Such major Victorian realists as Shaw, Pinero, Jones and Barrie defected from realism though their influence remained. But in the second decade of the twentieth century 'most of the talented writers, notably Somerset Maugham, Noel Coward and Frederick Lonsdale, were, after 1920, going into boulevard comedy' (though Maugham, *For Services Rendered* (1932), and Coward, *Post Mortem* (1931), produced occasional angry plays).

COWARD AND COMPANY

Popkin praises Coward for his cynicism, 'congenial both to him and to us . . . a highly successful antidote to sentiment',[4] and Salmon concedes that of their kind Coward's plays are perfect, though conceptually and theatrically too modest to be more than minor texts.[5] But J.C. Trewin writes insightfully of Coward's considerable talent. He was 'a technician who knew just how to time and present his clipped dialogue; he could write as laconically as another, and entirely different dramatist of a succeeding period, Harold Pinter'[6] (and, one might add, Mamet). It is appropriate here to suggest parallels with Evelyn Waugh's dialogue, with Hemingway's and Gertrude Stein's, for Coward makes comparable use of silence, pause, minimal, repetitive, and non-adjectival syntax. Like Salmon, Trewin concludes that Coward's aim and talent was primarily to amuse. This is to judge and misjudge

Coward simply through his surfaces and as a painter of surfaces. If his plays are read and presented as period pieces they can seem mannered and dated. But once we question cripplingly received readings and performances and treat the plays with a fresh seriousness, we find texts and spectacles that insist on the inference of something frightening and substantial underneath that superficial febrility of speech and action (a febrility that is in itself disturbing). An exchange between Richard and Jackie in *Hay Fever* (1925) makes the point.

Richard	Spain is very beautiful.
Jackie	Yes, I've always heard Spain was awfully nice.

[Pause]

Richard	Except for the bull-fights. No one who ever really loved horses could enjoy a bull-fight.
Jackie	Nor anyone who loved bulls either.
Richard	Exactly.
Jackie	Italy's awfully nice, isn't it.

[Pause]

Richard	Rome is a beautiful city.
Jackie	Yes, I've always heard Rome was lovely.
Richard	And Naples and Capri – Capri's enchanting.
Jackie	It must be.

[Pause]

Richard	Have you ever been abroad at all?
Jackie	Oh, yes; I went to Dieppe once – we had a house there for the summer.
Richard	*[kindly]* Dear little place, Dieppe.
Jackie	Yes, it was lovely.[7]

On the one hand there is nothing to say; the language (nice, beautiful, charming, lovely) is possessed of distressingly undifferentiated meanings and is as seemingly vacuous as the 'exchange'. What has happened to language, Coward surely asks. Perhaps, like Hemingway, he is identifying and utilising a defensively and strategically devalued use of language; perhaps, as in Stein, there is a refreshing, minimalist revaluation of language. On the other hand, Coward's text suggests the urgent need of Jackie and Richard to talk to each other, to deny the differences that exist between them (their attitude to bullfighting). But in spite of the linguistic similarities and the forced social harmony, there is no common ground. Richard has to pretend interest to sustain the conversation because Jackie hasn't travelled, and he is uncurious about the 'we' she refers to.

The exceptionalism of Coward is also apparent in his collection of short plays, *Tonight at 8.30* (1936). Rarely for an English playwright of the period there is evidence of the impact of Freud (*The Astonished Heart, Shadow Play,*

We were Dancing) and effective use of middle-class and lower-class materials and characters (*Red Peppers, Hushed Autumn*). *Still Life* utilises everyday artefacts and referents (Boots' Library Books, Huntley and Palmer's biscuits, Three Star Brandy, Nestlé's Nut Milk Chocolate, Marie biscuits, Banbury cakes) in a manner which anticipates Sam Shepard's use of toasters in *True West*. The inanimate consumer icons achieve a primacy of status; their animate dependants are diminished.

Coward's *Design for Living* (1933) also deserves attention, not least in the context of this essay because it parallels O'Neill's important play *Strange Interlude* (1928). In both texts one woman and a trio (Coward) and a sextet (O'Neill) of men desperately use each other in sexually and socially perverse manipulations. The permutations and combinations of relationships astound and appall. In Coward's play a series of impersonal rented dwellings provides a sequence of settings in which the characters try to manage their profound disenchantment at the human condition by snatching at pleasure or giving way to weariness. 'We can only sit here flicking words about' says Gilda. In O'Neill's play a cosy library and a pleasant sitting room become progressively destabilised, as do the figures who try and fail to inhabit them with ease. 'How we poor monkeys hide from ourselves behind the sounds called words', says Nina Leeds in *Strange Interlude*. 'Our lives are merely strange dark interludes in the electric display of God the Father',[9] she concludes. Coward's 'comedy' is in some ways darker than Neill's tragedy; he doesn't have God to blame, and forcibly expresses a period ambience of unmitigated impotence and frustration; Gilda speaks:

> The human race is a let-down, Ernest; a bad, bad let-down! I'm disgusted with it. It thinks it's progressed, but it hasn't – it's still wallowing in it! It's still clinging to us, clinging to our hair and our eyes and our souls. We've invented a few small things to make noises, but we haven't invented one big thing that creates quiet, endless peaceful quiet – something to pull over us like a gigantic eiderdown; something to deaden the sound of our emotional yellings and screechings and suffocate our psychological confusions.[10]

What made Coward buck the system? Why should he, uniquely, react against the sentimental, repetitive and nostalgic British theatrical norms? Perhaps he was a product – or triumph? – of the British class system. His relatively lower-middle-class origins (and his early experience as a minor actor) inclined him to mock, query, subvert; his ambition to be top of the upper class heap led him to push his mockery only so far. He was also (homo)sexually marginalised. Perhaps he should be explained away, as Emily Brontë has been, as an American *manqué*, a dissenting exception that proves the rule. But Coward is only in part such a figure. There are crucial differences of cultural identity between him and O'Neill. If both are diagnostic and cynical, O'Neill has a purpose and a passion that Coward eschews. Coward is a disturbing commentator but comically contemporary too; analytically penetrative, but not reformist. He allows for saving illusions rather than the strategic cultivation of pipe dreams. He doesn't develop his thesis in the obsessive, prophetic manner of O'Neill. Indeed, he offers texts of such subtlety that their savagery can be overlooked. He is arguably British in that when he does do more than entertain an audience, he doesn't contemplate changing it. His view of human nature and of the power of the theatre isn't tinged with that kind of American social and cultural idealism. Mamet, for instance, argues that 'through [theatre] the artistic community elects and forms our national dreams'. He adds: 'in the theatre we must strive to recognise and to ratify the universality of our desires and fears as human beings'.[11] Typically, the American dramatist sees theatre as a necessary tool and weapon in the construction of individual and national health (themselves inseparable). Before Mamet, O'Neill sought to preach and improve.

> The playwright today must dig at the roots of the sickness of today as he feels it – the death of the Old God for the failure of science and materialism to give any satisfying new One for the surviving primitive religious instinct to find a meaning for life in, and to comfort its fears of death with. It seems to be that anyone trying to do big work nowadays must have this big subject behind all the little subjects of his plays or novels, or he is simply scribbling around on the surface of things and has no more real status than a parlor entertainer.[12]

Coward doesn't deny the implications of his texts; but, like the ironic Jason Compson Sr in William Faulkner's *The Sound and the Fury* (1929) would surely say 'no battle is ever won. . . . They are not even fought. The field only reveals to man his own folly and despair, and victory is an illusion of philosophers and fools.'[13] While Coward identifies dilemmas he sees no point in moving beyond identification to polemical and urgent engagement.

Unlikely stablemates though they may be, T.S. Eliot stands alongside Coward as a 'British' playwright of rare seriousness and stature. His work was in part generated and made accessible by the Religious Drama movement, a response to a war which had called the comforts, creed and cause of Christianity into question. John Masefield's *The Coming of Christ* (1929; music by Gustav Holst) inaugurated a series of plays which included Eliot's *Murder in the Cathedral* (1935). Gareth Lloyd Evans[14] describes the play as 'a noble failure', in which language had to do too many jobs; but Eliot's interest in the theory and practice of dramatic language (what he called dramatic poetry) is of lasting worth. MacNeice, Spender, Auden and Isherwood also tried their hands at 'Poetic Dramas' and showed some skill in utilising Brechtian techniques, cabaret elements and music hall elements. If these plays function best as literature rather than theatre they were nevertheless commendably imaginative and, by British standards, innovative.

Coward and Eliot notwithstanding, British theatre of this period would have been thin and impoverished without its Irish dimension. The brilliance of the Anglo-Irish contribution of the 1890s and 1900s – Yeats, Wilde, Shaw and Synge – was sustained between the wars by Shaw and O'Casey. In addition to their verbal bravura – Shaw's witty urbane and conversational transformation of ideas into drama (his plays are otherwise fairly static) and O'Casey's creation of a language 'as capable of communicating a fierce naturalism as it is able to take flight into the world of the imagination',[15] both writers were, unusually for British dramatists, consistently raising topical, spiritual and metaphysical questions. O'Casey's trilogy *The Shadow of a Gunman* (1923), *Juno and the Paycock* (1924), *The Plough and the Stars* (1926), deals with events of the Irish war of independence and embraces the contemporary facts of poverty, war, nationalism and colonialism. But if, as Emil Roy notes, everything in these plays is emblematic of 'the terrible political and religious divisions'[16] everything is also to do with immemorial and universal issues of despair and joy, survival and resilience, hopelessness and hope. Shaw embraced the lessons of the First World War, together with the possibilities of a second, and issues raised by socialism, Marxism and Fascism. His *Back to Methuselah* (1923), often described as a Shavian *Ring*, looked historically, politically, and metaphysically at human experience from Eden to a world 'as far as thought could reach'. For A.R. Jones, the eccentric, ambitious play was not Irish, 'As a metaphysician, Shaw is an embodiment of the English spirit of amateurism. He was willing to pronounce on any subject and took all knowledge as his province.'[17] In a number of plays he attempted to ask and answer the what-is-England, why-is-England, whither-England questions. *Pygmalion* (1913), for instance, addressed issues of class and language, and offered the bleak images of Alfred Doolittle trapped by his inheritance of £3,000 into a loss of freedom and a 'gain' of middle-class morality and Eliza unreformed, uncomprehended, unregarded by the comfortable middle class. *Heartbreak House* (1921), as Benedict Nightingale notes, argues that 'the cultured people in England, as in the Russia of *The Cherry Orchard*, are politically and socially futile. They shrink from contact with the public world thus ceding to the barbarians.'[18]

Shaw was a gigantic yet ultimately isolated figure, with somewhat superficial influence on his contemporaries or subsequently, perhaps because he was relatively cautious in terms of technique and inimitable in terms of ideas. Perhaps he too was an American *manqué* who put entertainment second and who believed in art for truth's sake (or perhaps O'Neill was an Irishman once removed). Neither he nor O'Neill would sacrifice ideas. *Back to Methuselah* had to be staged on four consecutive nights; audiences had to arrange for a sustaining dinner between the acts of O'Neill's *The Iceman Cometh* (1946).

In making a St Joan or a Napoleon accessible, conversational, normal and not simply a historically unique mover and shaker, Shaw arguably reflected the tradition of British dramatic domestication. Whatever the material, his point of view is so consistent that his work as a whole reassures and homogenises, though in individual texts, whatever he addresses – power, gender, class, history – he addresses disturbingly. The reverse is true of O'Neill, many of whose plays, individually, can seem cranky or crude, and in some ways dismissable, but whose work as a whole shows mastery of existing dramatic forms, a formidable range of bravura technical experimentation and a dark vision of art as a Frostian 'momentary stay against confusion'.

AMERICAN VARIETY

It is sometimes assumed that as Shaw was an intimidating and inimitable force for British dramatists to reckon with, so the figure of O'Neill overshadowed American drama. But although his contemporaries, both critics and playwrights, bore testimony to the excitement of reading and seeing O'Neill, he was only one of an immensely talented group of playwrights who burst upon the American scene between the wars. As an expressionist he was no more distinguished than Elmer Rice; as part of the influential Provincetown Players he was probably no more important than its co-founder, Susan Glaspell. Glaspell in turn was by no means the sole or dominant force among American women dramatists. Judith Olausen demonstrates in *American Women Playwrights*,[19] the existence of an amazing sequence and range of plays, in the 1930s, for instance. Glaspell's *Alison House* (1930) set a fictionalised Emily Dickinson against a presumably more liberated niece who discovers her aunt to have been more boldly capable of illicit love, more subversive, more gender assertive than herself. Rose Franken's *Another Language* (1931) has a boy falling in love with his aunt and examines the aunt's dilemma as her family ostracises her for what they perceive as *her* unacceptable conduct. Rachel Crothers' *When Ladies Meet* (1923) – her 1924 satire *Expressing Willie* wittily targeted high society's cult of Freud – was a powerful text, in which as Lois Gottlieb comments, 'Crothers locates the greatest and most comic obstacles of modern woman's freedom and progress as her need for men.'[20] The year 1934 saw Lillian Hellman's *The Children's Hour*, which addressed the issues of lesbianism, and Zoë Akins's *The Old Maid*, which examined the figure of the spinster and the double standard which condones male sexual exploits and condemns women who are not monogamous. Hellman's sensitivity to the issues of lesbianism and Akins's dramatic sophistication are arguable; but in terms of women playwrights addressing women's issues there is nothing contemporaneously comparable in Britain. The reasons currently advanced for the low profile of the women's movement in Britain may be relevant here: British women either consider themselves liberated or are happy to be doormats and therefore tend to be relatively non-vocal about gender issues.

Olausen argues that women dramatists placed their own sex 'in the conventional female attitudes, the predictable ones, passive, intuitive, materialistic, possessive, being the most characteristic'.[21] But if the plays are to a degree products of the patriarchy they also question and challenge that structure. Clare Boothe's *The Women* (1936), for instance with its cast of thirty-five women – the men are offstage or at the end of a telephone – has a privileged sharpness of observation.[22] The 'existence' of men in her text through implication and inferral has something of the effect, albeit more light-hearted, more bitter-sweet, of Lorca's *The House of Bernarda Alba*. Olausen's theory does not hold good for Susan Glaspell's *The Verge*, whose 'botanist–visionary–feminist hero is obsessed with the dream of creating a new form of life', and is frustrated by the inability of species (human, botanic) to stop 'running back to what it broke out of'.[23] She destroys her creation, the Edge Vine, and her lover, because they both threaten her with the familiar, the known, and can't continue to 'Make It New'. With its contorted plants, jagged towers, bulging windows and distorted staircases, *The Verge* is also remarkable for a set whose surrealism is as radical as the play's content.

If we accept Richard Chase's argument that the American literary imagination shapes characters who tend toward the 'abstract and ideal', who seem to be 'merely a function of plot' and texts in which 'astonishing events may occur' and 'mythic, allegorical and symbolistic forms'[24] will prevail, then expressionism, with its emphasis on 'type characters' and 'symbolic abstractions', with its diminishment of plot in favour of an 'intense subjectivism'[25] is likely to commend itself to American writers, and such strikingly effective expressionist plays as Elmer Rice's *The Adding Machine* (1923) are, to a degree, predictable. *The Adding Machine* is remarkable in a number of ways. As Thomas Greenfield points out, it anticipates by thirty years C. Wright Mills' supposedly seminal analysis of 'the impact that widespread use of office machines would have upon the devaluation of white-collar clerical skills'.[26] It also anticipates that present-day technology which so intrusively and crucially shapes modern sensibilities, relationships and patterns of life.[27]

Rice's rigorous expressionism conveys a surreal world not confined to the human automata who are altogether shaped by the workplace (Mr Zero's home is papered with sheets of foolscap covered with accounting calculations), but which extends to the dehumanised adherence of society in general to the petty and the material. Friendship is parodied in the scene where Mr and Mrs One, Two, Three, Four, Five and Six visit Mr and Mrs Zero. Verbal vacuity and social savagery characterise the gathering. The attractions of marriage are mocked in encounters between the Zeros. 'He is thin, sallow, undersized, and partially bald. . . . She is shapeless in her long-sleeved cotton nightgown. She is wearing her shoes, over which sag her ungartered stockings.'[28] Emotions and states of being are as indifferent and undifferentiated as day and night-time clothes. The encounters between Zero and Daisy show the sexual urge as just that: an urge, and ephemeral. A thousand (plus)-word monologue by Mrs Zero, which opens the play, suggests shallowness and lack of self-knowledge.

It is difficult not to see Rice's three most influential plays, *The Adding Machine* (1923), *Street Scene* (1929) and *We The People* (1932) as the accumulating antecedents of Thornton Wilder's work in *Pullman Car Hiawatha* (1931), *The Happy Journey from Trenton to Camden* (1931) and *Our Town* (1938). Though the Rice texts are voluminous and complexly staged, and the Wilder plays are short, economical, laconic and minimally staged, both playwrights seek to suggest a cross-section of American society; both represent issues of class and type in America; both call into question the ability of individuals to control their destiny, to live intelligently, to work usefully. What testimony to the vibrancy, experimentation and innovation of American drama at this time that such a variety of approach to the whither-America, whither-humanity questions was so successfully employed. Wilder recalls his commitment to change in a 1958 preface to his plays in which he projects a theatre which questions, which is not 'soothing', which disturbs, which is universal. He doesn't want theatre to make 'childish attempts to be "real" '; he wants 'new ways to express how men and women think and feel in our time'.[29] *Our Town* uses the device of the 'character' of the stage manager who is narrator, stagehand, props man and the verbal and physical scene-setter to point to the absolute theatricality of his piece. It is fiction, though it relates to and derives from fact. It is meant to provoke, profoundly, not to mirror or divert, comfortably. The graveyard scene in *Our Town* when Emily Gibbs, recently dead, is initiated into 'terrible regret', the knowledge that life is invariably wasted; in *The Adding Machine*, when Mr Zero and the other corpses rise and reflect; in Irwin Shaw's *Bury the Dead* (1936) where recently killed soldiers, outraged at being cannon-fodder, at being cut off in their prime for other men's reasons and mistakes, reflect the often grim nature of American drama during this period.

DOUBLE BILL

Why the existence of this dark, passionate, experimental, engaged, rich theatre of matters in America and what Steven Berkoff[30] has characterised as the stultifying, constipated, superficial British tradition? Partly because Britain had a dramatic tradition to rest in; America had no hampering precedents, no reason for complacency, and it was probably inevitable that, when it gave birth to a theatre, both the birth and the theatre would be exaggeratedly energetic, self-conscious, ambitious, as if to compensate for what had not gone before. The reasons for the failure of America to produce plays of any distinction before the early years of the twentieth century are obscure. Was the Puritan hostility to entertaining spectacle slow to die? Did a naive American earnestness make it difficult to see theatre, generically, as anything except a secondary or tertiary art form? Were plays encoded in novels and stories, especially those by Poe and Melville? What is certain is that when the dam broke, and it began to do so with Little Theater experiments and original stagings in Chicago and elsewhere from the early 1900s (Chicago itself, with its urge to be first city, culturally superior, culturally different, gave an impetus to American theatre), writers would be liberated by the lack of any tradition other than that of competent imitation. It was open season, open space. And given the qualities of the American literary tradition and imagination that did exist, that recognised the 'aesthetic possibilities of radical forms of alienation contradiction and disorder',[31] then the theatre of O'Neill, was, like the theatre of Elmer Rice, to a degree predictable. (The superior attractions of New York and New England for new writers at this time was culturally predictable; two generations later, though, Mamet was content to write and work in Chicago for much of his career.)

European stimuli were also crucial for American theatre. There were cultural influences – Freud, Nietzsche, Schopenauer and Munch, for instance, were important for O'Neill. There was the impact of European theatre and theory: Susan Glaspell responded enthusiastically to Sorge and Toller, Rice and Kaiser and Sternheim. (These stimuli were, of course, equally available to British dramatists, but they, for the most part, were culturally imperme-able.) The political isolation, the introversion, intolerance and self-regarding hedonism of America immediately after the war not only led novelists and poets into expatriation, it led American dramatists to seek to counter national narrowness. Harold Clurman has written powerfully of how the visits to New York of the Moscow Art Theatre and the importation of the Stanislavsky system revolutionised not only his sense of technique but a sense of

> The theatre and society. There was no question that we were concentrated on the theatre, pondering over all the outstanding productions, searching foreign and domestic periodicals for special articles and new illustrations, going to see all the European productions that the favorable foreign exchange made it possible to import.[32]

67

Interest in theatre was not confined to New York. In *American Theatre Companies, 1888–1930*, Weldon B. Durham outlines a diverse and dynamic regional theatre. During 1928 there were 160 companies in flourishing existence. In the mid twenties, typically, the Lyceum Players in Rochester might have on the bill O'Neill's *Strange Interlude, Recessional*, William Hurlbut's African–American play and Molnar's *The Guardsman*. The Lyceum's visiting star might be Gregory Matoff of the Moscow Art Theatre.[33] By contrast, in the same period, England's Birmingham Repertory Theatre had some success with modern dress Shakespeare and premiered *Back to Methusalah*; it made such theatre available by regularly touring to Manchester, Malvern and London. But it found that financial survival depended on a conservative repertoire.[34] In America there was an epidemic of experimental theatrical activity between the wars, in part engendered by George Pierce Baker, who taught first Workshop 47, a play-writing course at Harvard (O'Neill was a student, with Philip Barry and Sidney Howard) and then a course in play-directing at Yale (Elia Kazan was a student). The Washington Square Players (1915), the Provincetown Players (1917), were succeeded in the twenties by the Theatre Guild, which built its own theatre on West 52nd Street, performed the best European and American texts of the period, had its own magazine, the *Theatre Guild Quarterly* and its Guild School of Theatre. And fifty-cent tickets.

In the thirties impetus passed to the Group Theater, influenced equally by Stanislavsky and Marx. Clifford Odets' work typified this new wave of topical, political, agit-prop theatre. *Awake and Sing* (1935) raised issues of poverty, ethnicity and ethics in the context of the Depression. Christopher Bigsby usefully classifies such plays as works which 'emerged out of the press of events, out of the individual's struggle to relate to public myths and private vision'. Bigsby charts an abundance of little-known radical theatre groups of the twenties and thirties: the Workers' Laboratory Theatre, the Theatre of Action, the Theatre Collective, the Workers' Drama League, and the New Playwrights, whose manifestos cast the theatre artist on as the historian, toastmaster and clown for such mentors of the age as Einstein and Edison.[35] Such theatre was as crude as it was innovative, the polemics as obstrusive as integrated, and nowhere more so than in Odet's *Waiting for Lefty* (1935) in which the taxi-drivers' union struggles against corrupt employers. At the end of the play Odets had the audience standing to join in the play's last words: 'STRIKE! STRIKE! STRIKE!'

No account of American theatre between the wars would be complete without description of the Federal Theatre Project (FTP:1936–39) and no better example exists of the complex causality of American theatrical activity at this time. The professed aim of the FTP was to be

'National, Regional, and American', and its scope included every phase of the performing arts. During its short life it presented classical, modern, dance, religious, radio, and children's drama, including puppet shows; it staged pageants and spectacles, musicals, Americana, vaudeville, and circus; it presented plays in several languages, including French, German, Spanish, Italian, Chinese and Yiddish; it encouraged community theaters and sent touring troupes into small towns and rural areas; it staged plays by unknown as well as famous playwrights; and, quite predictably, it experimented with tremendous enthusiasm.[36]

The FTP staged over 1,200 classic and experimental plays in its short lifetime: the avant-garde *One Third of a Nation*, a critique of American housing and housing policy, is estimated to have been seen by 200,000 people.

Perhaps there had to be some such one-off event as the Depression to generate government subsidies for the FTP (the Works Progress Administration, a government Agency, financed a range of artistic activities) and the patently inspirational subject matter. But there also had to be an established – endemic – belief among both the producers and consumers of plays that at any given time that theatre properly expressed the specific aspirations and ailments of society and that the artistic presentation of issues was at once diagnostic, therapeutic, reformist; at once social, political and artistic. As Hallie Flanagan wrote in 1936: 'Drama, through rhythms, speech, dynamic movement and contagious listening, can influence human thought and lead to human action.'[37] There was no sense of theatrical form running a poor second to content, but a determination to use pressing social issues to develop appropriate theatrical forms. Hence 'The Living Newspaper'; a 'committed documentary that informed the audience of the size, nature and origin of a social problem, and then called for specific action to solve it'. The call was made in dramatically innovative terms:

> Projections, masks, spotlights, loudspeakers, ramps, and characters in the audience were some of the devices used to force the facts upon the audience in an unforgettable fashion. The projections, still a new theatrical concept in maps, and headlines, or they could be more visual: photographs, animated cartoons, and short film sequences. The projections could provide a startling counterpoint to the action occurring downstage. They dramatically extended the stage space and forced the spectator to sit up in his seat in order to catch all that was happening about him. Another assault on the traditionally passive spectator's senses was an offstage loudspeaker, occasionally called the 'Voice of the Living Newspaper'. Essentially an American creation, this was a transitional figure who introduced new characters, established time and place, and linked the episodes. On occasion the loudspeaker became the voice of the public, posing questions and pressuring officials.[38]

Triple-A Plowed Under, which dramatised the ways in which the Agricultural Adjustment Act affected farmers, typically utilised such devices.

In his thesis *The Development of the Unity Theatre Between 1936 and 1939*,

Stephen J. Nicholson[39] has charted the genesis of the British equivalent of FTP. After 1918 political and social drama festivals proliferated in Britain. For the most part the message prevailed at the expense of form. But unlike its most significant predecessor, the Workers' Theatre Movement, Unity sought not only 'to produce and present, among as wide an audience as possible, stage plays dealing with social problems and issues of interest to the working class', but also to 'devise, import and experiment with new forms of dramatic art . . . to work for the regeneration of the Commercial Theatre along the above lines'.[40] Few indigenous plays of quality were forthcoming, however; one-act plays with a mass recitation in between were the favoured format. British political dramatists showed little interest in European theatre (and a poor understanding of Stanislavsky), and were apparently ignorant of the American Living Newspaper, though two comparable texts were devised and presented in England between the wars. Perhaps the most effective and original Unity production was the 1938 Political Pantomime, *Babes in the Wood*, 'featuring Austria and Czechslovakia as the innocent Babes, Hitler and Mussolini as the wicked uncle who is secretly in league with the robber'.[41] It is an index of the rigorous and dogmatic focus of Unity Theatre that Elmer Rice was not staged; he was declared too committed 'to a humanism which demands only humanitarianism as a remedy'.[42] *Waiting for Lefty* proved acceptable, and was one of Unity's more successful productions. The other was *Where's That Bomb?* (1936), written by two London taxi-drivers, Roger Gullan and Buckley Roberts (aka Herbert Hodge and Buckland Roberts), which effectively utilised farcical and cinematic techniques and audience participation in a powerful attack on capitalism.

The contrast between British and American theatre between the wars is well illustrated in a comparison between two publications. Victor Gollancz's *Famous Plays Of . . .* series, first published in 1931, usually included the text of five or six plays, date and place of first performance and the original cast list. Its American equivalent was Burns Mantle's *Best Plays Of . . .*, subtitled 'the year book of the drama in America'. Typically the 1936–37 edition of Mantle included, in addition to 288 pages of play text (nine plays), 256 pages of comment and information. A descriptive and evaluative introduction commented on what shaped the season in question: motion picture capital had been withdrawn from Broadway and as a result productions were relatively unspectacular, more minimal; the FTP, which Mantle hoped might lead to the founding of a national theatre, throve; John Gielgud's Hamlet had led to a revival of interest in Shakespeare. The table of contents included the seasons in New York, Chicago, San Francisco and Southern California; biographical data; an annotated list of all plays produced in New York that season, including off-Broadway productions and such categories of theatre as monodrama, puppet, children's college, foreign language plays (French,

Argentinian / Spanish, Italian, German, Ukrainian), statistical summaries, a review of earlier years, obituaries, indexes of authors, plays and casts. The volume demonstrates how professionally and seriously drama was taken in America. By comparison the Gollancz looks amateur and perfunctory.

Two productions in 1991 of Thornton Wilder's *Our Town* nicely represent the continuing strands of difference between British and American theatre. The British production starred Alan Alda as the Stage Manager, and reflected a sweetness and a wryness in Alda which made the play into a light comedy with serious touches. The importation of Alda suggested the exclusive Americanness of the text. It was an entertaining, unadventurous production which avoided or diminished the tragic and universal elements of the play. Arena Stage's production in Washington DC imaginatively cast ethnic minority actors in key roles normally reserved for Wasps (Dr and Mrs Gibbs, Wally Webb, for example). What in theory was a technically risky and politically insensitive multicultural tokenism proved no such thing in practice. The effect was to make the play undated, widely not narrowly American, and to direct attention, in fresh ways, to the theatrical process and to the ways in which an audience is manipulated by casting, production and staging strategies. Once again the American urge to experiment was symptomatically contrasted with the British affection for tradition.

NOTES

1. See J.C. Trewin, *The Theatre Since 1900* (London, 1964): Frank N. Magill (ed.) *Critical Survey of Twentieth Century British Drama*, 6, (Englewood Cliffs, N.J., 1985).

2. Michael Timko, 'Nineteenth-Century and Edwardian Drama' in *Encyclopaedia of World Theatre*, ed. John Gassner and Edward Quinn (London, 1970), p. 232.

3. Eric Salmon, *Is the Theatre Still Dying?* (Westport, London, 1985), pp. 62–3.

4. Henry Popkin, 'Post-Edwardian Drama' in Gassner, op. cit., pp. 237, 242, 243.

5. Popkin, 'Noel Coward', in Gassner, op. cit., p. 156.

6. Allardyce Nicoll, *British Drama*, 6th ed, rev. J.C. Trewin (London, 1978), p. 234.

7. Noel Coward, *Hay Fever* (London, 1979), pp. 34–5. I am indebted to Trewin's (differently focused) discussion of this exchange in Nicoll, op. cit., p. 235, for drawing my attention to this passage.

8. Noel Coward, 'Design for Living' in *Plays: Three* (London, 1979), p. 21.

9. Eugene O'Neill, 'Strange Interlude' in *Three Plays* (New York, 1952), pp. 91, 221.

10. Noel Coward, *Design for Living*, p. 58.

11. David Mamet, *Writing in Restaurants* (London, 1986), p. 9.

12. Quoted in Oscar Cargill, N. Fagin, W.J. Fisher, *Eugene O'Neill and his Plays* (London, 1964), p. 115.

13. William Faulkner, *The Sound and the Fury* (Harmondsworth, 1970), p. 73.

14. Gareth Lloyd Evans, *The Language of Modern Drama* (London, Melbourne, Toronto, 1977), p. 28.

15. Ibid., p. 25.

16. Emil Roy, *British Drama Since Shaw* (Carbondale, 1972), p. 73.

17. A.R. Jones, 'George Bernard Shaw' in John Russell and Bernard Harris (eds)., *Contemporary Theatre* (New York, 1962), p. 71.

18. Benedict Nightingale, *An Introduction to Fifty Modern British Plays* (London, 1982), p. 71. See too Shaw's own preface to *Heartbreak House.*

19. Judith Olausen, *The American Woman Playwright: A view of Criticism and Characterisation* (Troy, NY, 1981).

20. Lois C. Gottlieb, *Rachel Crothers* (Boston, 1979), p. 151.

21. Olausen, p. 145.

22. See James Agate, *The Amazing Theatre* (New York, London, 1939; reissued 1969), p. 255, for Boothe on her text's targets.

23. Sherrill E. Grace, *Regression and Apocalypse: Studies in North American Literary Expressionism* (Toronto, Buffalo, London, 1989), p. 73.

24. Richard Chase, *The American Novel and its Tradition* (London, 1959), p. 13 and *passim.*

25. Gerald Weales, 'Expressionism', in Gassner, op. cit., p. 251.

26. Thomas Allen Greenfield, *Work and the Work Ethic in American Drama 1920–70* (Columbia, Missouri, 1982), p. 13.

27. Elmer Rice, 'The Adding Machine' in *Seven Plays* (New York, 1950), pp. 106–7.

28. Ibid., p. 62.

29. Thornton Wilder, 'Preface' in *Our Town . . .* (Harmondsworth, 1984), pp. 8, 11, 14.

30. Chase, op. cit., p. 2.

31. Steven Berkoff, 'Desert Island Discs', BBC Radio 4, 11 January, 1992.

32. Harold Clurman, *The Fervent Years: The Story of the Group Theatre and the Thirties* (New York, 1957), p. 16.

33. Weldon B. Durham, *American Theatre Companies 1888–1940* (Westport, 1987), p. 271.

34. J.C. Trewin, *The Birmingham Repertory Theatre 1913–63* (London, 1963). See too Wendy and J.C. Trewin, *The Arts Theatre, London, 1927–81* (London, 1988), which cites no play policy at this supposedly Fringe theatre at this time.

35. C.W.E. Bigsby, *A Critical Introduction to Twentieth Century American Drama*, Vol. I, 1900–40 (Cambridge, 1982), pp. 185, 197, and the excellent Chapter 5, 'Left-wing theatre'.

36. James V. Hatch, 'Introduction', in E. Quita Craig, *Black Drama of the Federal Theatre Era* (Amherst, 1980), p. 3.

37. John O'Connor and Lorraine Brown, *The Federal Theatre Project* (London, 1980), p. 25.

38. Ibid., p. 10.

39. I am indebted for this section on Unity Theatre to Dr Stephen J. Nicolson's fine MA thesis cited in the text (University of Lancaster, 1986). Nicolson is shortly to publish a much-needed book on British Political Theatre, 1918–39.

40. Quoted in Nicolson, p. 27.

41. Nicolson, p. 75.

42. Quoted in Nicolson, p. 51.

FURTHER READING

Christopher Bigsby, *A Critical Introduction to Twentieth-Century American Drama*, 1900–40 (Cambridge, 1982). Useful bibliography.

Enoch Brater (ed.), *Feminine Focus: The New Playwrights* (New York, 1989).

Elizabeth Brown-Guillory, *Their Place on the Stage: Black Women Playwrights in America* (Westport, 1988).

Robert Brustein, *The Theatre of Revolt* (Boston, 1964).

Denis Donoghue, *The Third Voice: Modern British and American Verse Drama* (Princeton, 1959).

Alan Downer, *American Drama and its Critics* (Chicago and London, 1965).

Eleanor Flexner, *American Playwrights, 1918–38* (Freeport, 1938).

Malcolm Goldstein, *The Political Stage: American Drama and the Theatre of the Great Depression* (New York, 1974). (Useful bibliography.)

Nilouber Harben, *Twentieth-century English History Plays from Shaw to Bond* (Totowa, N.J., 1988).

Ian McDonald, *The 'New Drama', 1900–14* (New York, 1986).

Edward Mendelson (ed.), *The English Auden: Poems, Essays and Dramatic Writings 1937–39* (New York, 1977).

Norman Page, *The Thirties in Britain* (London, 1990).

Jack Poggi, *Theatre in America: the impact of economic forces, 1870–1967* (Ithaca, 1968).

Gerald Rabkin, *Drama and Commitment: Politics in the American Theatre of the Thirties* (Bloomington, 1964).

Leslie Catherine Sands, *The Development of Black Theatre in America: From Shadows to Selves* (Baton Rouge, 1987).

Jane Schlueter, *Feminist Rereadings of Modern American Drama* (London and Toronto, 1989).

Gerald Weales, *Religion in Modern English Drama* (Philadelphia, 1961).

CHAPTER FOUR

The Treacherous Years Of Postmodern Poetry In English

William A. Johnsen

CULTURAL BEHAVIOURS

The question of cultural differences in England and America is a difficulty for the postmodern period, because it touches on the rift between what Anglophone literary intellectuals, especially academic intellectuals can see for themselves of each other's differences, as they circulate through Chicago and London, New York and Leeds, Dublin and Los Angeles, but what current theoretical taboos against the referential value of language won't allow them to write about. We are, in effect, living a kind of double life. We treat each other, with such evident pleasure, to stories about the behaviour of Brits and colonials, yet the postmodern turn to theory in the universities makes any writing on American, British, or Irish native character susceptible to being an example of a pitifully out-of-date belief that recurring features of collective behaviour can be verified.

So what? There are many contradictions in late twentieth-century culture, not all of them are interesting. It would be very easy, of course, to mock literary intellectuals as either insufficiently or shallowly theoretical, in favour of greater rigour. We could as well mock theory, before the endlessly corroborated truths of cultural differences, acknowledged everywhere except in the academies.

I *do* think we have gone about as far as we can in ridding the intellectual workplace of an uncritical belief in referentiality, to such an extent that we risk losing the properly reductive potential of theory, without which any real knowledge is impossible. In fact, I think that risking embarrassment by writing about cultural differences carries the opportunity for recovering the progressive power of theory.

How? First of all, by asking ourselves, 'what follows from the fact that these contradictory attitudes towards cultural differences in Anglo–America coexist, often in the same person?' I confess to being such a person – committed to theory, but in love with the stories we tell on each other. I will summon up my courage to tell one, but I do not intend to settle for mere differences.

I believe most of us who circulate ourselves by choice in England, Ireland and America demonstrate our belief in cultural differences in two related ways – we tell stories on each other, and we put on, for the pleasure of our friends, exaggerated but recognisable versions of our national character.

Any cultural behaviour is, properly understood, a form of collective research. (And research, even story-telling is part of that collective behaviour as well.) The stories we hear about typical 'native' behaviour, which, in turn, cap some of our own intuitions about cultural differences give a pleasure beyond mere corroboration, because their ease of circulation and reception intimates as well a common research 'team', perhaps even a family practice among English speakers, and holds out the possibility of real knowledge about our own collective human behaviour.

I want to acknowledge my own addiction to stories of cultural difference by an anecdote (now ten years old). Sequestered at Leeds University for the Joyce Centenary in 1982, we heard with astonishment an announcement about the Falklands crisis break into our scholarly seclusion: 'We've just been invaded by the Argies.' I still remember, even before the image of the Argentine infantry marching up the Otley Road had passed, my (American) pleasure in this (essentially Brit) wry understated acknowledgement of the end of empire, the colloquial, casual, even familial relation to history, the unfussed confidence that this postcolonial adventure could nevertheless be 'sorted out'. (Of course the popular response in England to the Argentine threat was anything but unfussed.)

The connection between literary study and a growing comprehension of collective human behaviour, especially violent human behaviour, is more than anecdotal. I have written elsewhere about the pertinence of René Girard's victimage hypothesis for an understanding of modern literature. [1] I always have my eye on Girard these days, but here I mean to stay close to poetry, to put together the work of certain Anglophone poets (American, English and Irish) of the postwar period to suggest an understanding of collective violence from what might be called a post-essentialist theory. Theorising collective behaviour must not fall victim to a fetishing nativism on the one hand, blaming particular races for violence, or a scapegoating process within the culture on the other, blaming particular interests or individuals for that which everyone is in some way responsible. Such a theory is necessarily a non-violent theory, in so far as it disbelieves each culture's vindication of its own violence. Such a theory is partially implied in each national poetry, but only available through a frankly comparative and cumulative approach to American, British and Irish postwar writing.

The deceptively similar careers of Robert Bly and Jon Silkin may initiate a more extended opportunity to essay the distinguishing factors of cultural difference for Anglo-America, and, more importantly I believe, articulate the common theoretical ground that makes distinction possible. Both Bly and Silkin have kept their distance from academic positions, and put greater distance between themselves and the dominating cultural centres; both have run their own magazines, since the fifties; each has believed that translation is important cultural work; and each has written a poetry that is at once pastoral and political.

THE VIOLENT OTHERS

Yet there is a profound difference in the way Bly's work develops, not untypical for American poets of his generation who opposed the Vietnam War. That is, the opportunity for oppositional practice depends upon a Vietnam kind of war, a war against which a large-scale, popular opposition could be organised. 'The Teeth Mother Naked At Last', as a poem, but also as a public event, broke out into a horizon of cultural politics that has not been attainable by English poets since the thirties. Opposition to the Vietnam War amassed an audience not readily available to an English poet, but the felt presence of a large audience took poets like Bly outside their own internal pattern of development (often in very subtle ways), which they can only return to (if at all) much later. *This Tree Will Live Here For A Thousand Years* (1979) tried to find its way back to the kind of poetry Bly was writing before the anti-war poems, in the late fifties.[2] But Bly's early poetry, profoundly isolated and private, does not easily address itself to the kind of popular audience he has gathered now.

The poetry of Silkin and Geoffrey Hill, on the other hand, reflects a steady internal logic of development, roughly matched by a gradual widening of their audience over time.[3] For the opposition of American and British poets, the work of Irish poets like Seamus Heaney (and I would add Tom Paulin and Hugh Maxton) gives us a useful middle term: disrupted by a history which hurts, but restrained by the existence of recognisably compelling alternative Provisional and Loyalist sympathies which cannot be reduced to an all-against-one popular oppositional practice, they develop as they oppose, steadily.

There is no better authority for marking distinguishing national factors on the common ground of an Anglophone community than Henry James, whose avuncular relation to Anglo-America, even his Irishness grants him strategic location on all his nephews and nieces. What guided James's own sense of cultural production was the way representations of local and insular virtues in the modern world, driven by a motive one could name by shorthand 'Americanisation', were circulated across national boundaries: in *The American* Christopher Newman's preference for the *copies* of masterworks he can purchase over the originals in the Louvre; the alacrity with which the Touchetts Americanise an English tea-time, with bigger cups, longer hours, etc., at the beginning of *The Portrait of a Lady*; Waymarsh's 'sacred rage' to make a grand purchase, along The Rows at Chester in *The Ambassadors*. These humorous characterisations of national behaviour show James's prescience in establishing the transatlantic continuity of the modern rage to acquire unique art objects, as well as their inevitable postmodern duplication, circulation and devaluation.

James's strange gambolling sense of humour is also transatlantic, English and American traits exaggerated for the pleasure of a common postnational Anglophone audience. More ominously, James also anticipates the way violence can be surrendered to as an ontological entity, separate from the will and work of men.

> The plunge of civilisation into this abyss of blood and darkness by the wanton feat of those two infamous autocrats is a thing that so gives away the whole long age during which we have supposed the world to be, with whatever abatement, gradually bettering, that to have to take it all now for what the treacherous years were all the while really making for and *meaning* is too tragic for any words.[4]

James realises, belatedly, the way that even the idiosyncratic syntax of his fictions has been forced to take its meaning in the abyss of blood and darkness. This remarkable letter to Howard Sturgis in one sense comes round to face the beast at last, but it gives no hope of influencing or talking back to events. Two infamous autocrats determine meaning for everyone. James's phrase 'the treacherous years' gives authority to some anonymous force which has tricked and betrayed all.

Postmodern Anglophone writing, at different locations, within different histories that are nevertheless recognisably common, is now struggling with this debilitating hypothesis of 'the treacherous years'. 'Counting Small-Boned Bodies' fairly caught the Johnson administration on its quantification of the advances of daily struggle, but the mass anti-war demonstrations of thirty years ago are gone. Bly's male affinity groups, perhaps not as silly as they look, were not positioned to say much about the Gulf War, caught as they must have been trying to distinguish their language of the warrior in *Iron John* (1990) from the briefings offered to the American news network, CNN. Grenada, Panama and the Gulf War more nearly resemble the Falklands War as it was represented in the British media: the exercising of a popular and righteous violence that could organise the whole nation into pure opposition against a common enemy.

If James's fictions are guarantors that Anglo-America yields distinguishing factors on a common ground, George Orwell calls Oceania's (Anglophonia's) future, accurately forecasting what I am calling here the treacherous years, and what I have called elsewhere an age of hypocriticism,[5] the uniquely contemporary situation (post-1984) of knowing everything and doing nothing. The post-1984 narrator of *Nineteen Eighty-Four* knows, as we his readers are assumed to know, exactly how the Two-Minute Hate deploys racism, anti-Semitism and sexism, but never breathes a word of it, and certainly never uses our common critical terminology to describe its operation. 'Whatever you say, say nothing.'[6]

In the Gulf War, the poets and oppositional intellectuals from the sixties who even bothered to resist were outmatched. Postwar Anglophone writing has entered 'the treacherous years', where poetic failure surrenders meaning to anonymous forces: lobbies, interests, national leaders, the state, the media. Modern Irish poets have shown remarkable prescience in holding their ground as politics grows in sophistication, in answer to poetic resistance. Heaney's 'The Unacknowledged Legislator's Dream' (with a shrewd and unservile deference to Yeats) shows us a poet who can grow to estimate the media's capacity to represent violence as spectacle and commodity.

In the title essay of *The Government of the Tongue*, Heaney argues two conflicting estimates of poetry's power to effect social change. 'In one sense, the efficacy of poetry is nil – no lyric has ever stopped a tank. In another sense, it is unlimited. It is like the writing in the sand in the face of which accusers and accused are left speechless and renewed.'[7] Heaney takes up the most compelling analysis of collective violence our culture has, in his allusion to the story of the woman taken in adultery (John 8: 1–11), but mistakenly, I believe, identifies Jesus's writing with his finger in the sand as the force which delivers accusers and accused from mob action. It is not the writing, but what Jesus says to the adulteress and her accusers which returns to them their individual consciences surrendered to the imperfect solidarity (all minus the victim) of the scapegoat mechanism. They can no longer convince themselves that their violence to the woman proves her singular guilt and their righteousness innocence. They are offered, in effect, a perfect solidarity which excludes no one, a solidarity of sinners who will sin and accuse no more.

Seamus Heaney, but also Bly, Silkin and Geoffrey Hill, when read comparatively, say something not already known about collective violence misread as anonymous and omniscient, the work of all these violent others.[8] What we will see is a position, repeated in poem after poem, of a refusal to accuse or sin anymore. With the notable exception of Hill, these poets have placed their poems in political contexts, yet each poet dramatises a position away from politics, the point of pause, limit, or inertia. This can be the testing of limits, like a broadjumper coming up to the line before a leap, but the poem can also represent a self-blinded man stopping before a wall he knows is there. In the worst cases, it is a matter of showing how easy it is to wash one's hands of all these violent others, in despair or righteousness.

THE PUBLIC AND THE PRIVATE BLY

Bly has become the most considerable *popular* poet in America since Frost and Sandburg. (Bly often jokes in performance that, when he reads at places where he is mistaken for Frost, he reads 'Stopping by Woods On A Snowy Evening' without giving himself away.) But popularity has come to mean something different for Bly now, than it did in the sixties and early seventies; the coordinates of Gramsci's famous distinction between political and civil society have fundamentally changed, so that *Silence in the Snowy Fields* (1962), an intensely private collection of poems, cannot serve as a guide for *This Tree Will Be Here For A Thousand Years* (1979) and *The Man in the Black Coat Turns* (1981). Nor is it easy for the popular audience these poems imply in their very mode of address (in contrast to the earlier private voice of *Silence*) to detect Bly's longstanding interests.

It is probably impossible to write a nature poem in English, that is not also pastoral. (Perhaps one of my readers will be challenged to write a slash-and-burn advocacy poem.) Against the intensely local and particular visionary poems of *Silence in the Snowy Fields* there is concern for human relationship:

> You raise your face into the rain
> That drives over the valley –
> Forgive me, your husband,
> On the streets of a distant city, laughing,
> With many appointments,
> Though at night going also
> To a bare room, a room of poverty,
> To sleep among a bare pitcher and basin
> In a room with no heat –
>
> Which of us two then is the worse off?
> And how did this separation come about?

The title 'A Man Writes To A Part Of Himself' assures us that both urban and rural contexts represent neighbouring regions in Bly's consciousness as well. (The intensely pastoral writing of Bly, Silkin and Heaney should not be taken to mean that they would ever get lost in New York or London.) The title also reflects the aloneness typical of most of the poems, yet anticipates as well Bly's interest in personal growth, and the character of gender. The first question of the concluding lines confirms that both contexts are diminished by real poverty, not ennobled by an aestheticised spareness and simplicity.[9]

The uneven and shifting recognition of contiguousness and separation between country and city maps the developments of any single pastoral poem *and* its tradition. 'A Man Writes To Part of Himself' is an unusually self-reflective pastoral in that its sense of separation worries the very possibility of signification, by which rural and urban values comment on each other. Bly's answer to the gap between two separate worlds has always been to make long soaring leaps back and forth between them, whether in the idiom of the seventeenth-century German mystic Jacob Boehme, the American neurologist Paul McClean, or the modern Peruvian poet César Vallejo.[10] What changes across time is the ratio of civil to political tincture of the areas he inserts himself into, or the discourse permits, of which his audience is the living representative, and the kinds of use to which the energy of these leaps can be put. 'It's because the milk trains coming into New Jersey hit the right switches every day that the best Vietnamese men are cut in two by American bullets that follow each other like freight cars.'[11] The shock of plugging the infrastructure of the home-front into the battle-front propels the leaps of 'The Teeth Mother Naked At Last', and the shorter poems of the sixties, like 'Asian Peace Offers Rejected Without Publication'. Such leaps reconnect civil and political society, which may be taken as the historical moment's variants for the pastoral's codes of country and city.

The prose section of *Sleepers Joining Hands* (1973), 'I Came Out of the Mother Naked' yokes martial and colonialist values with ecological despoilation: barges full of buffalo tongues floating down the Mississippi.[12] Further, 'The Teeth Mother Naked At Last' puts itself at odds with the appropriation of the self-sacrificial ethos of the pastoral elegy, which would reconcile us to death by the cycle of renewal to which it purports to belong.

> The Marines think that unless they die the rivers will not move.
> They are dying so that the mountain shadows will continue to fall east in the afternoon,
> so that the beetle can move along the ground near the fallen twigs.

The poem accuses the Marine Corps ethos of perverting the pastoral: the traditional connection between the genius of the shore and the land has become an abomination. At the same time, the poem reveals the suppressed essential link between the 'country' of origin and of deployment, and the most sophisticated and technologically developed commitments of the Capitol.

Bly's polemical accusation that this is what 'the Marines think' still offends.

Wilfred Owen identified the sentiment of *dulce et decorum est pro patria mori* with bloodthirsty civilian elders, never with his own fellow soldiers. Curiously enough for a work that was a rallying point for mass demonstrations, the poem does not close in full and unanimous opposition to the war. The last section of 'The Teeth Mother Naked at Last' withdraws itself from further observation:

> I want to sleep awhile in the rays of the sun slanting over the snow.
> Don't wake me.
> Don't tell me how much grief there is in the leaf with its natural oils.
> Don't tell me how many children have been born with stumpy hands all those years
> we lived in St Augustine's shadow.

Bly (like Geoffrey Hill in 'September Song') marks the limits of his resistance, and the edges of his complicity, by indicating what he cannot bear to see. (He can turn away from what soldiers were forced to see.) This is the note which allows him to admit his responsibility, but it also runs the risk of conceding everything to the treacherous years.

Bly has written of the Chilean poet Pablo Neruda's political commitments on several occasions, and has chosen his most famous political poems for translation and anthologising. Neruda's name cannot be disassociated from resistance, yet 'Mourning Pablo Neruda' in *The Man in the Black Coat Turns* (1981) stays away from politics, and does what all moderns do – resists the conventions of the pastoral elegy as it reconnects itself to the pastoral's deeper motives of remembering. The poem begins by a sober valuing of water's practicality, [13] but solaces itself on water's indifference as an emblem of death's irreversible flow away from us.

> For the dead remain inside
> us, as water
> remains
> inside granite –
> hardly at all –
> for their job is to
> go
> away,
> and not come back,
> even when we ask them

Bly does not mention the inevitable association of Neruda's last illness with the fall of Allende. The poem is reticent, even grateful for its ability to keep to water. 'This is plenty.'

The poem stays away from the pastoral's reigning idea, that the mourned one is a heroically perfect victim, whose sacrifice returns blessed springtime to the country (and the audience of the poem). Bly's poem lives by the recognition that the dead, like water, are not here – they are gone. By not celebrating the fruits of sacrifice Bly contributes to the possibility of a victimage hypothesis whose only future is to regard all sacrifice as abomination. Like the many poems in Bly's anthology for the Sierra Club, *News of the Universe* (1980), 'Mourning Pablo Neruda' leaps back and forth between ecology, politics and a nature poetry which cannot but be pastoral. We might say that this poem, like most of the poems in *The Man in the Black Coat Turns*, emphasises the leap away from politics, for the sake of better relations among men: fathers, sons, fifty males at a time.[14]

SILKIN, HILL, AND POLITICAL POETRY

Silkin's *Out of Battle*, a study of the First World War poets, gives a fine example of a practising poet reading another's verse. The subtle and detailed readings sustain Silkin's argument that the best and the most politically alive poetry comes from recognising the necessary intimacy between the home and the battlefront. Silkin's own generation of poets comes after the Second World War, without the credit of active duty. How do the most gifted and productive poets of that generation, such as Silkin and Geoffrey Hill, write out the consequences of the war closest to them?

'Astringencies', from *The Re-ordering of the Stones* (1961) splits into two parts, 'The Coldness' and 'Asleep', to propose two cleansing agents produced from, and perhaps for, the way a British / European postwar intellectual's anguish over the Nazi atrocities dredges up England's own ancient pedigree in anti-Semitism. As Silkin asks himself why the citizens of York seem to him so cold, he brings to mind the historical absence of Jews since the massacre of the Jews of York in 1190.

> Why have they been so punished;
> In what do their sins consist now?
> An assertion persistent
> As a gross tumour, and the sense
> Of such growth haunting
> The flesh of York
> Is that there has been
> No synagogue since eleven ninety
> When eight hundred Jews
> Took each other's lives
> To escape christian death
> By christian hand; and the last
> Took his own.

The question Silkin poses cannot be answered, except to admit that no guilt deserves such punishment, whether it is the York or Nazi atrocities. Silkin wishes to take away any easy British sense that anti-Semitism is *echt deutsch*. Silkin is Jewish, and would probably admit to having sussed out prejudice once in a way, somewhere in his travels in Anglophonia. And he served on active duty in the early fifties, so he knows something about martial force. Silkin has praised those soldier poets who, 'once out of battle', recognise that the customs on the home-front sustain the blood-rites of the battlefront. But Silkin does not, and cannot represent himself as out of battle on the strength of his military service, as could the First World War poets, and cannot count on whatever he knows personally of anti-Semitism to speak as an internee from the concentration camps. He cannot speak directly, in his own voice, about the victimisation of the Jews. To show postwar Europe '. . . touched / With some of frigid York, / As York is now by Europe', 'Astringencies' represents the Jews of York through their absence.

How can such coldness serve as an astringent? '. . . the cold / Blood of victims is colder, / More staining, more corrosive / On the soul, than the blood of martyrs.' Silkin's insistence on the difference between a victim and a martyr will take us far in understanding the service of poetry in comprehending all forms of collective violence, especially its most spectacular mobilisations into sacrifice and war.

Martyrs, of course, are normally understood to suffer or even solicit their persecution as marks of their faith. Persecution benefits the faithful, and curses the persecutors. Martyrdom marks both persecuted and persecutors within the single ethical system of the persecuted: persecutors stand for all those others who love violence and sacrifice.

How does victimisation mark both more deeply? The victimised serve no horrific belief of their own. They are innocent of any charge of 'masochism', and critical reflection is thrown on (1) the beliefs of the persecutors, not the persecuted as responsible for this action; (2) the desire behind the (violent) beliefs of the persecutors: what form of recognisably human misunderstanding made them believe that persecution of the Jews would bring them peace; and most importantly (3) the possibility of a victimisation hypothesis itself, arising out of the recognised capacity to distinguish victims from martyrs, which is capable of comprehending both persecutors and victims, 'christians' as well as 'Jews' (in Silkins's spellings).

'Resting Place', from *The Psalms With Their Spoils* (1980), returns to this same instance of victimisation. It begins by demonstrating how poetry can serve a theory of victimisation in a way that prose cannot – in other words, the specific theoretical potential of poetic representation. Drama and prose characteristically confer a superior reality on the ordinary reader. Stage directions and narrative situate dialogue and voice within a sanity judged superior to the characters, shared between author and reader. Poetry leaves the speaking voice on the field, necessarily imbricated in the situation. Silkin prefaces 'Resting Place' by quoting from R.B. Dobson, *The Jews of Medieval York and the Massacre of March 1190*, who marks the site of a plot of land sold by John le Romeyn, the subdean of York Minster for an ancient Jewish cemetery now under a carpark tarmac, where '. . . archaeologists will no doubt one day disturb the posthumous tranquillity of Jews who can have rarely been completely tranquil while alive'. By such nicely balanced 'English' prose irony Dobson assures us that he and we are no anti-Semites.

If 'Astringencies' offered two separate solutions to sweal away York's tumorous growth, 'Resting Place' offers two voices, victim and 'christian' victimiser, who can only be understood from a victimisation hypothesis. The poem first embodies the voice of a medieval Jewish corpse nearly gagged by the motor oil dripping from the car park above: 'Judah'd with oil / their iron drips into our mouths.' Dobson's ironic prose makes all readers honorary Englishmen to regret the 'disturbing' of 'the Jews' by these 'turbulent' others. Silkin represents a more comprehensive position than 'Astringencies' by invoking this Jewish voice from the dead, and identifying their Christian benefactor as their persecutor.

> Of that Church, John; by whose furled lamp I sold
> our loam for dormitory to the Jews.
> Earth hold them gently, and be gentler to
> this woman than her child is, nursing her
> each part of death's submissions. To mind so
> the flesh is nurse to death. If more life is,
> then they must each become a door of selves
> each enters by in suppliant need: their own.

John prays for their peace, although 'hold them gently' will take on a more sombre tone as what he can and cannot say takes hold on the reader. John, in effect, disagrees with this woman's mothering. To care for such flesh is to nurse death; rather, mother and child must enter the afterworld unmindful of their family bonds.

> They never heard of this. Angel of death
> made of desire and mercy raise your wings.

The terrible combination of John's peremptory 'they never heard of this' to seal his own faith, with his prayer for their death, reveals his own complicity to her persecution. Silkin still cannot speak directly 'out of battle', but now he arranges a 'strange meeting' of John le Romeyn with the Jewish mother and child. I do not think we would say that Silkin indicates himself as complicitous in anti-Semitism because he shares a common Christian name with le Romeyn.

Geoffrey Hill will allow himself no unmediated mark of authorship on what postwar European intellectuals must say about the atrocities in their own name. 'September Song' carefully plays the measures of victimisation.

> Undesirable you may have been; untouchable
> you were not. Neither forgotten
> nor passed over at the proper time.
> As estimated, you died. Things marched
> sufficient to that end.
> Just so much zyklon and leather, patented
> terror, so many routine cries.

The chilling difference established between *undesirable* and *untouchable*, casual synonyms for outcasts, the ironic resonances of 'passed over', and the deadpan poetic measures for precisely calibrated exterminations, do what a posing of guiltless outrage at the violence of others cannot in representing atrocity.

But that is not all. The poem was first published in Silkin's journal *Stand* (vol. 8, No. 4, 1967: 41), with the usual *Stand* page format of heading poems with a biographical blurb on the contributing poet. Below the notation of Hill's birth year and career credits, 'September Song' begins with its own headnote: '*born 19.6.32; deported 24.9.42*'. That the subject of deportation shares birth year (and month) with the author can only point up this peremptory modification of the usual headstone formula of birth and death, read against the regular successes of Hill's life. It is as fine and close an example as I know, of how Hill exploits the circumstances in which his poems are likely to be received.

After the lines quoted above, the poem turns on itself.

> (I have made
> an elegy for myself it
> is true)
>
> September fattens on vines. Roses
> flake from the wall. The smoke
> of harmless fires drifts to my eyes.
>
> This is plenty. This is more than enough.

The rhetorical position of the first lines of 'September Song' is not unlike Dobson's, which Silkin quotes in 'Resting Place': one voice speaking ironically for all who (of course) abhor violence. But the first part of the poem is not allowed to stand as a collective rejection of Nazi discipline. These last lines go beyond the admission that all are (regrettably) touched or barbarised by the concentration camps, to note that the secret motive of the earlier observations is elegiac, for oneself: the poor 'victimised' self now contaminated by these awful images, whose pleasure is relief. The smoke of (thank

God) harmless fires is more than enough, the floating reference of 'this' to potentially nightmarish images is 'plenty'.[15] Thus Hill dramatises a special way to forfeit the revelation of kinship between accusers and accused. The speaker has scandalously appropriated victimisation for his own comfort – he too knows what it is to be punished, to be a 'Jew'.

HEANEY'S GROUND

It is startling to see the ungainly trace of political violence intrude itself into the pastoral tradition in the first lines of the first poem, 'Digging', in *Death of a Naturalist* (1966), Seamus Heaney's first book of poems: 'Between my finger and my thumb / The squat pen rests; snug as a gun.' The poem rehearses the ease of Heaney's father and grandfather with a shovel, and his feeling of being apart from that grace.

> The cold smell of potato mould, the squelch and slap
> Of soggy peat, the curt cuts of an edge
> Through living roots awaken in my head.
> But I've no spade to follow men like them.
>
> Between my finger and my thumb
> The squat pen rests.
> I'll dig with it.

The lines which describe the fathers honour their physical dexterity with dexterous verse, but no rhythm supplied by the reader can grace the dogged final line of the poem, which characterises the violence done by putting a gun into Heaney's penhand: bang / bang / bang / bang.

In general, for those poems in *Death of A Naturalist* not expressly political, politics 'provides' metaphors for personal observations. This reversion of the more usual priority of pastorals (where 'the wolf is in the fold' points out from the pasture towards politics) stands for the inversion of collective life in Northern Ireland: a poem about farm-life discipline which requires drowning unwanted kittens ('wee scraggy shits') is dubbed 'The Early Purges'.

'Act of Union', from *North* (1975) recovers the possibility of exchange between sexual, political and geographical contexts,[16] although the title invariably would first get a political read, at least if one knew it was a poem by an Irishman. The poem conjures up the two islands as bedpartners, whose positions begs those frank Anglo-Saxon terms for unequal congress:

> Your back is a firm line of eastern coast
> And arms and legs are thrown
> Beyond your gradual hills. I caress
> The heaving province where our past has grown.
> I am the tall kingdom over your shoulder
> That you would neither cajole nor ignore.

Heaney tags the language of politics omnipresent in Ireland with Anglophone oral culture's resisting practice of converting sober realities into 'country matters'. Any subsequent look at a map of the two islands or use of the phrase 'act of union' must bear Heaney's poem.

'Whatever You Say Say Nothing', from *North* (1975) begins speaking after having talked with an English journalist searching for 'views / On the Irish thing' / 'Polarisation' / and / 'longstanding hate' / are evidently washed up as pseudo-analytical media-terms to serve as substitutions for a proper response to the troubles. Yet the poem moves on to catch the same dodge in local voices:

> 'Oh, it's disgraceful, surely, I agree',
> 'Where's it going to end?' 'It's getting worse.'
> 'They're murderers.' 'Internment, understandably . . .'
> The 'voice of sanity' is getting hoarse.

An English journalist representing Northern Ireland for his country's readers necessarily has already in place a 'view', especially if he thinks he lacks one. (Haines told Stephen that history was to blame.) But the commentary of the locals is no better, each washing their own hands of the other's violence.

'Exposure', the sixth poem in the 'Singing School' sequence which ends *North*, wonders for whom it speaks: 'For the people? / For what is said behind-backs?' / This necessary interrogation of motive frees the poet from sides / neither internee nor informer, 'an inner emigré'. The poet will be neither helpless victim nor victimiser. Yet this position deprives him of 'The once-in-a-lifetime portent, / The comet's pulsing rose.' In other words, merely avoiding the twin pressures of the treacherous years, to victimise others or himself, is to say nothing.

How then can the poet do more than avoid the mirror-popularities of resistance and consent, a stage-Irish or a stage-English voice? In the twelfth poem of the title sequence of *Station Island*, which echoes 'Little Gidding', Joyce's spirit warns the poet away from surrendering his vocation to resistance, conformity, or the times. When the poet dutifully mentions the 13 April 'tundish' entry in Stephen's diary in *Portrait*, Joyce jeers back:

> The English language
> belongs to us. You are raking at dead fires,

a waste of time for somebody your age.
That subject people stuff is a cod's game,
infantile, like your peasant pilgrimage.[17]

Closer to Joyce's point than the tundish diary entry would be Stephen's refusal to subjugate himself or others,[18] and Joyce's lifelong refusal of sacrificial solidarity in favour of political systems that do not exclude anyone.

Against the reigning orthodoxies that insist that everything is always and only political, *The Government of the Tongue* (1988) argues that the poetic voice can find a way to speak for itself. Heaney, as much as Hill, Silkin and Bly, situates poetry in a place where contact, if not complicity, with sectarian positions must be recognised, but the recognition itself is a critical reflection which opens up the distance necessary for theoretical advances. Because these are poems which mark out their own limits, which will not pretend to maintain a position superior in nature to collective violence, the last word is never spoken, as the reading mind plays the stops as temporary rests. The reader is empowered to ask what theoretical advance made the recognition of limit possible.

Postwar Anglophone poetry, read comparatively, does reflect certain nativist assumptions about American massification and megalomania, British scrupulousness and Irish loquacity, but it would be wasteful to stop at what are now media stereotypes and commodities, or transnational comic routines. Properly read, these cultural differences serve a common understanding which can theorise collective violent behaviour. The more comprehensive that reflection is, the more comprehensive the theory will be. Each increase in comprehensiveness is necessarily an increase in the non-violent potential of the theory. Each comparison that each member of the community of accusers and accused makes (let he who is without sin among you cast the first stone), increases the likelihood of arriving at a common non-violent society.

NOTES

1. See 'Myth, Ritual and Literature After Girard', *Literary Theory's Future* (ed.) Joseph Natoli (Urbana, 1989) pp. 118–45.

2. See Bly's prose beginning, 'The Two Presences', in *This Tree Will Be Here For A Thousand Years* (New York, 1979), pp. 9–11.

3. By steady development, I do not mean to say that anyone, even Hill himself, could have predicted *Mercian Hymns* from *King Log*, *Tenebrae* from *Mercian Hymns*, and *The Mystery of the Charity of Charles Péguy* from any of these books. No poet

whose primary interest was increasing and consolidating his audience would ever have dared to follow the success of each of these books with such radically different work.

4. *The Portable Henry James*, (ed.) Morton Dauwen Zabel(New York, 1968), p. 672.

5. 'Myth and Ritual After Girard', op. cit.

6. Heaney's caught phrase for 'the famous / Northern reticence, the tight gag of place / And times': see *North* (London 1975).

7. *The Government of the Tongue* (New York, 1988), p. 107.

8. In Girard's terms, violence as sacred. See *Violence and the Sacred* (Baltimore, 1978).

9. If this poem looks as if it might support some dreary Jungian reading, that would make gender and location an extension of the self, see *Iron John*: 'Another mistake Jungians make is to adopt that hideous word *anima*, and to regard every goodlooking woman you meet as your *anima*. / When a man says to a woman, "You are my anima", she should quickly scream and run out of the room' (Reading, Mass., 1990, p. 137).

10. See No. 1 of *The Seventies* (Spring 1972), on 'Leaping Poetry'.

11. From 'The Teeth Mother Naked At Last', in *Sleepers Joining Hands* (New York, 1973), p. 23.

12. See also *News of the Universe*, an anthology which presses opposition to war and exploitation through nature poems.

13. In fact, the poem obliquely downplays the opening of Pindar's First Olympian Ode: 'Best of all things is water; but gold, like a gleaming fire by night, outshines all pride of wealth beside.' *The Odes of Pindar* trans. Richmond Lattimore (Chicago, 1947, Second edn 1976), p. 1.

14. See 'Fifty Males Sitting Together' in *The Man in the Black Coat Turns* (New York, 1981), pp. 55–57.

15. *The Lords of Limit* (London, 1984) as well as *The Enemy's Country* (Oxford, 1991) assay the trouble for poets who must work against the small unbreakable phrases in the language like 'this is plenty', by which the speaker of this poem slides by his trouble.

16. Thus *The Government of the Tongue* (London), where Heaney argues for poetry as fighting for its own right to govern itself.

17. *Station Island* (New York, 1985), p. 93. An earlier version, where Heaney identified the tundish entry date as his birthday, was read at the James Joyce Centenary at Leeds University in 1982. See *James Joyce and Modern Literature*, Boston, Melbourne and Henley (ed.) W.J. McCormack and A.J. Stead (London, 1982), pp. 74–6.

18. Joyce argued against subjugation as early as the second school essay collected in *The Critical Writings* (New York, 1959), misleadingly titled 'Force' by the editors, Ellsworth Mason and Richard Ellmann.

FURTHER READING

Robert Bly, *Leaping Poetry* (Boston, 1973).

René Girard, *Violence and the Sacred* (Baltimore, 1978).

Seamus Heaney, *Preoccupations: Selected Prose 1968–78* (London and Boston, 1980).

——*The Government of the Tongue: The 1986 T.S. Eliot Memorial Lectures and Other Critical Writings* (London and Boston, 1988).

Geoffrey Hill, *The Lords of Limit: Essays on Literature and Ideas* (London, 1980).

——*The Enemy's Country* (Oxford, 1991).

Jon Silkin, *Out of Battle: The Poetry of the Great War* (London, 1972).

CHAPTER FIVE

Postmodern Americas
in the fiction of Angela Carter, Martin
Amis and Ian McEwan

Richard Brown

'I think I'll call it America'
(Bob Dylan's 115th Dream)

That summer she was fifteen, Melanie discovered she was made of flesh and blood.
O my America, my new found land. She embarked on a tranced voyage, exploring
the whole of herself, clambering her own mountain ranges, penetrating the moist
richness of her secret valleys . . .[1]

ANGELA CARTER'S NEW FOUND LAND

The opening of Angela Carter's sixties' classic, *The Magic Toyshop*, immediately sets up a spectrum of semantic possibilities. Here is the Renaissance
America of Donne's Elegy XIX: 'Going to Bed', that continent of
discovery and enjoyment serving once again as a metaphor for the
erogenous body. But the image has been taken from the world of poetry
and put into prose and the implied male colonial explorer of Donne's
poetry has been translated into the image of female self-possession characteristic of much new women's writing.[2] Here America is the erotic body
and, since Melanie's partly thwarted creative self-discovery is the substance of Angela Carter's novel, America may also stand in some way for a
place of writing and, indeed, in all its post-Enlightenment ambiguities, for
the 'Self'.

The language of the passage neatly encapsulates the way in which, since
Donne, since Blake, America can be a shifting, ambiguous and contradictory
sign, ineradicable from all our cultural discourses. As such it expresses the
shifting, ambiguous and contradictory nature of many of the desires and

anxieties we might experience both as individual selves and as a culture. America may be an 'other' to our senses of cultural identity and yet also an 'other self' that may either be represented as a younger and more callow partner or else as that future on whose threshold with increasing eagerness and terror we suspend ourselves.

In tandem with its increasingly explicit use of 'South American' methods of subverting the real, Carter's fiction (as her work became prominent among that of a 'younger' postwar generation of British novelists through the seventies, eighties and up until her untimely death at the start of the nineties) offers an exemplary case in which some of these issues of representing North America (the United States) can be explored. In this essay I proposed a reading of her work along with that of Martin Amis and Ian McEwan, two other prominent figures from this discernible 'new generation' of British novelists, in these terms. In their work – as in that of many other distinguished contemporaries which I am not able to treat here – the terms of critical discourse surrounding our fiction and its supposed postwar provinciality and smugness have been decisively shifted and new possibilities for the relationship between place and linguistic sign are explored. The America of Carter, Amis and McEwan is describable as a postmodern or postcultural space where writing, selfhood and cultural identity can be defined. Each of them create a sense of their British selfhood in relation to an 'American' elsewhere but also communicate that such an 'elsewhere' is also present and can be observed within the originating 'self'.

The Magic Toyshop (1967), Carter's second novel, tells the fantastic or magically tinged narrative of the fifteen-year-old Melanie, who is forced to live with her evil or oppressive Uncle Philip amongst the images he creates, and who tries to liberate herself from his authority. Carter uses a narrative perspective which is coloured by Melanie's consciousness and which blurs the borders between fantasy and reality and at the same time gives simple details much meaningful and disturbing potential. Melanie's discovery of herself, with which the novel opens, is quickly interrupted by the loss of her parents. It is they, not she, who, on the more literal level, have 'gone to America' – perhaps representing the world of adult sexuality that she has yet to enter – though they, as we gradually learn, have died on a 'routine internal flight' in Nevada (p. 31).

These things are marked as 'American' in the novel, whereas the housekeeper Mrs Rundle, with whom she is left, is described as having 'an old-world, never-never land stateliness' (p. 3). The toyshop of the book's title, where Melanie is sent to live with her uncle, is a place that is repeatedly labelled as being both 'traditional' and 'British', and Uncle Philip's intimidating theatre, in whose Yeatsian pageant of sexual violence Melanie is forced to perform, stands for traditional patriarchal British culture.

93

The loss of Melanie's parents (as Kleinian or Lacanian theory of the psychology of bereavement might suggest)[3] and the restrictions placed on the awakening of her sexuality compete as psychological determinants of her mental disturbances. As one of Melanie's two new younger Irish uncles, Francie, hints: 'The distress of your loss might make you see things. It is only natural' (p. 121). Melanie's loss of a sense of security and of her hopes for self-development to 'America', her growing alliance with her other young Irish uncle, Finn, and the final conflagration of the Toyshop may all have their cultural as well as psychosexual subtexts, particularly in the context of the emerging feministic political consciousness of the time. Perhaps the book's imagined bodily America may be identified with what the theorist Julia Kristeva has called the realm of the 'semiotic' and Uncle Philip's intimidating theatre with the realm of the 'symbolic'. If so then both Melanie and Carter's writing may be thought to occupy what Kristeva calls the characteristic space for women's writing and, perhaps for all writing, 'between'.[4]

In *The Passion of New Eve*, Carter's sixth novel published in 1977,[5] her play with the semantics of place darkens and she provides another fantasy of America that is now recognisably postmodern. Its epigraph – 'In the beginning all the world was *America*' – sets up a conundrum of pasts and futures, implying that the book may be read either as a creation myth or as a dystopia. The phrase comes from Locke's *Second Treatise of Government* which described late seventeenth-century colonial America as a 'state of nature', as yet uncomplicated by the written laws and contracts that, in Locke's view, founded civil government.[6]

This un-written and un-Europeanised America may be one goal of the hero / heroine Evelyn's quest for his Hollywood screen idol Tristessa, but it is set against the nightmarish city of New York which he / she must pass through in order to find it: 'the country where Mouth is King, the land of comestibles' (p. 10); a place of beggars and disordered streets where 'a kamikaze squad of syphilitic whores' is rumoured to be prosecuting a sex war (p. 17). This America is, in the old examination question remembered by Evelyn, 'the bastard child of the French Enlightenment' (p. 16), at a time when the Age of Reason that postdated Locke has already clearly run down. 'It was chaos, dissolution, nigredo, night' says Evelyn. Slave to his sexual desires, he follows the exotic black prostitute Leilah into a relationship that ends with a visit to a Voodoo abortionist. He then sets off for the 'desert', 'the waste heart of the vast country', the desert that (in Jean Baudrillard, Sam Shepard, or the cinema of Wim Wenders)[7] has recently become one of the most potent European postmodernist images of America. Here it is offered as the place where Evelyn might find: 'that most elusive of all chimeras, myself' (p. 38).

In the fantastical city of Beulah that, like one of the instant mirage-cities described by Baudrillard, Evelyn discovers in the desert, he is seized by the leather-clad women guards of a Cybelean female deity called Mother, raped and castrated before being given a new female identity. In this place where 'myth is a made thing, not a found thing' (p. 56), where feminist propaganda is the only law and where Mother 'has made symbolism a concrete fact' (p. 58) Evelyn becomes the Tiresias of Southern California, the new Eve.

To make the polemical point that gender is a constructed rather than a natural thing is the primary stated intention of this mythic mutilation[8] (as, no doubt, of Carter's erotically male narrative perspective), though here again Baudrillard's sense of postmodern America as a new sexual culture based on the problematics of gender provides a useful clue to a place where 'liberation is over; it is not sex one is looking for but one's "gender" '.[9]

Evelyn / Eve learns his / her lessons so well that he / she is soon subjected to the 'female' experiences of rape and enslavement at the hands of the violently autocratic poet Zero. He / she also is obsessed by the film goddess Tristessa who he / she believes has robbed him / her of his / her fertility. In the background American thanatopic dissolution continues – the Siege of Harlem rages and California secedes from the Union – as Evelyn / Eve and Zero at last discover the glass palace hideaway and transsexual secret of Tristessa. In the unmasking of the screen goddess's true sexual identity Evelyn declares: 'I saw all the desolation of America, or of more than that – of all estrangement, our loneliness, our abandonment' (pp. 121–2).

Los Angeles and California are Sodom and Gomorrah in this apocalyptic chaos, and there is some poignancy in Evelyn's bemused 'I am a British citizen. I do not understand the political situation' (p. 175), as civilisation collapses and he / she, him / herself, sets out on a curious psycho-mythical return journey to Mother who 'having borne her, now abandons her daughter forever' (p. 186). Eve is set adrift to some other continent (back to Europe? away to China?) than the America that is ruled and destroyed by this irrationalist female god.

From the mythically feminist thanatopia that Carter reveals beneath both Lockean and Enlightenment myths of America in this extraordinary and fantastic book, it may seem no small step to the historical pastiche of *Nights at the Circus*, published in 1984,[10] but here too images of America serve to represent aspects of postmodern culture.

The heroine is Fevvers, a Cockney winged circus trapeze performer or *aerialiste*, whose wings are presented not as costume but as symbolically real. She tours with the circus from turn-of-the-century London to Imperial St Petersburg and Siberia. The semantics of place and nation are not lost on Walser, the journalist who is transcribing details of Fevver's extraordinary life at the start and who eventually joins the circus as a clown. '*Russia is a sphinx*' he begins his article on arriving in St Petersburg, '*a city built of hubris, imagination and desire*' (pp. 96–7).

Carter herself acknowledged some specific allegorical intentions in the work: that Mignon (the Ape-Man's abandoned wife adopted by Walser) 'is supposed to be Europe, the unfortunate bedraggled orphan – Europe after the war'.[11] America figures in a double guise since Walser is presented as one kind of American stereotype and the circus owner, Colonel Kearney, as another. Walser is rational, inquisitive and eager, but has to undergo a series of humiliations, first in his assumed role as circus clown and then in falling in love with Fevvers who, as circus star, and as a type of the New Woman of the century takes a dominant role in their relationship. Colonel Kearney, who enters in the second section, is an exaggerated version of the parodic colonel who appeared in *New Eve* 'all for the stars and stripes' with his buckle 'in the shape of a dollar sign' (p. 99) and his flag-waving, performing Patriotic Pig. The Colonel's crusade is both for profit and for the particular brand of circus entrepreneurialism which he calls the 'Ludic Game' and which he gleefully spreads across all of Russia. In fact, 'He is the living image of the entrepreneur' (p. 147).

Each of the characters meets his or her apotheosis in Siberia in Part Three where the narrative economy itself seems to become expanded or dissolved. The circus, seized by outlaws, leaves the Colonel's enterpreneurial ambitions in tatters, though he vows to return. Walser's separation from the party and lapse into semi-madness is another version of the collapse of Enlightenment rationality and forces him to learn from the forest dwellers who harbour him a new Shamanistic form of reason where fact and fiction merge. This new language is named, like Carter's own fiction and that of the South American postmodernists Donoso, Marquez and others, 'magic realism', and it is a language into which the North American 'Stars and Stripes' cannot, apparently, be translated (p. 262), though both stars and stripes are included on the new embroidered gown that Walser wears as a symbol of his power, on which the prime symbol is a winged woman.[12] His new wisdom outside of history is compared to that of the American Indians in 1492, except that it is 'able to incorporate the future into itself and so prevent its believers from disappearing into the past' (p. 265) and is, at least, an advance on the rationality which has allowed him to be 'fooled' by Fevvers all along.

Carter's movement from 'demystificatory' to 'celebratory' modes, as it has been charted by Paulina Palmer, continues into her infectiously celebratory *Wise Children* (1991), second of the twin peaks of her literary achievement.[13] This is the garrulous, affirmatively female and multilayered reminiscence of the seventy-five-year-old Dora Chance who, with her sister Nora, has lived a riotous life on the borders between high and popular culture along with the famous theatrical Hazard family of which she is the bastard child. Illegitimacy is a primary metaphor throughout a text which is packed with playfully popular allusions to Shakespeare as well as to Joyce, Marquez and the magic of popular theatre. Such bastardised forms occur as the carnivalised postcultural chaos of the *Twelfth Night* costume ball thrown by Dora's biological father, Melchior Hazard, the 'To butter or not to butter' advertisement that shows how Melchior's third wife has 'planned for the twentieth century' (p. 37), and the extravagant Hollywood thirties' filming of *A Midsummer Night's Dream*, to which Dora brings along a jar of 'real' Stratford-upon-Avon earth.

Further postmodern confusions or, to use Lyotard's phrase, 'crises of legitimation'[14] include the mixtures of place signalled by the opening account of the cultural connotations of south as opposed to north London and the inevitable transgressions of the cultural borders between Britain and the 'bastard child' of *New Eve*, America. In *Wise Children* Anglo-American difference seems defined in terms of differences between high and low styles of culture, yet at the same time no absolute difference can be said to exist along these lines since cross-cultural transgressions are shown to be part of the history of both cultures, at least since the appearance of Dora's grandmother as a female Hamlet in New York. Many aspects of the text will remind readers of the wild Shakespearean discussion in James Joyce's *Ulysses* and the climax of the action at Melchior Hazard's 100th birthday party, which all but brings the chandelier to the ground, is more Joycean still (pp. 220–1).[15] There, after Dora's identity as Melchior's natural daughter has been revealed, she offers Peregrine, her previously supposed father, a wild moment of drunken sex: an act whose apparent incest is legitimated by her actual illegitimacy.

The America of *Wise Children* is still less a place in the social or geographic sense than it is in the adolescent fantasies of Melanie, the surreal future of *New Eve*, or the magically transfigured strains of rationalism and entrepreneurialism seen in *Nights at the Circus*. The world of the novel implies a cross-cultural mixture in which the borders between the written and the spoken, the male and the female, high and low culture, Britain and America, are all inextricably transgressed and, indeed, the traditions of both cultures based on such transgressions.

MARTIN AMIS'S MORONIC INFERNO

The importance of America to Martin Amis has long been recognised, not least in the collection of cogent and stylish interviews, essays, articles and reviews that he wrote in the seventies and eighties and republished under the title *The Moronic Inferno* (1986), which also imagines America as a chaos of collapsed rational ideals.[16] In the Introduction to that volume Amis is keen to point to his bicultural credentials (his year at an American school, his American wife), the fact that 'like Thatcher', he sees the closeness of the Anglo-American relationship.[17] He is never a more British writer than when he is writing satirically about America, even though his writing often works to erode that distance on which satire depends. This may be evident in his choice of the more exotically foreign, or least English of American writers to treat (Mailer, Capote, Vidal) as well as in his placing of them among the symptoms of American excess (the Atlanta serial child-murders, Claus von Bulow, Reagan and new Evangelism) that he treats with equally ironic curiosity. His museuming of Hugh Heffner and Gay Talese, as well as his sympathetic commentary on the AIDS-stricken gay community, imply that we are here again in the post-liberationist territory defined by Baudrillard as the territory of American sex. His tone, somewhere between amazement and bemusement (and not always synthetically redeemed as amusement) marks a distance from the things he describes, though it is a distance that is never far from being broken down.

Saul Bellow, with whom he begins and ends the collection, is the writer he most reveres (performing the questing 'reader' Charlie Citrine to Bellow's 'author' Humboldt, perhaps?). There is, no doubt, something Oedipal in his deference to both Bellow and America. There is something discernibly English about the way he admires Bellow's characters who are down-to-earth but still intellectual heroes, his form of 'High Style', which 'attempts to speak for the whole of mankind' (without the characteristically English complications of social class) and Bellow's good luck in having Chicago ('a great city, vast, bloody, hugely mercantile, and not trodden flat by writers') in which to locate his fictional world.

Amis's curiosity betrays (to recall Stephen Spender's term for such ambivalence) both love and hate for the American societies he can anatomise and for those American writers whose symptomatic statuses he can both envy and evade. It would make much sense to say that in his first three instantly acclaimed novels *The Rachel Papers* (1973), *Dead Babies* (1975) and *Success* (1978), he was attempting to provide a British version of the American fictions of the sixties (seen by many British critics both as excitingly liberated and yet as somehow superficial or self-indulgent).[18] Such fictions could transcend the class divisions over which the British critics of the time were agonising (Murdoch's crystalline / journalistic, Lodge's 'crossroads' between fictional and empirical, and then later between metaphoric and metonymic modes) because, as Philip Roth put it: 'The American writer in the middle of the twentieth century has his hands full in trying to understand, describe and then make *credible* much of American reality. It stupefies, it sickens, it infuriates, and finally it is even a kind of embarrassment to one's own meagre imagination.'[19] To show that this 'American' reality could be seen to be present in Britain too is the very substantial achievement of these books.

American stereotypes appear in the first two novels. Charles Highway, who fast-talks, writes and womanises his way through cramming college into Rachel and Oxford in *The Rachel Papers*, is a Londoner. The smooth, wealthy De Forest Hoeniger, principal rival for Rachel's affection is an American: a stereotypical one (Charles's imagination is full of satirical grotesques) before whom he is at first embarrassed and over whom he eventually triumphs, only to sicken with disgust at the achievements of his predatory sexual acquisition. When Charles's shadowy natural father appears with Vanessa 'just flown in from New York', he can give full vent to a construction of American identity that justifies his hatred: 'Because they're violent. Because they only like extremes. Even the rural people, the old reactionaries in the farms, go out blowing nigger's heads off, roast a Jew or two, disembowel a Puerto Rican. Even the hippies are all eating and mass-murdering each other' (p. 107). Much of Highway's sex-life and mind-life are a reflection of Anglo-American semiotics. Being clever about the English literary tradition of Milton and Blake is a potential means of advancement for Charles but the 'most violent and tuneless of all his American LPs, *Heroin* by the Velvet Underground' is his best strategic tool for casual seduction. The copulation and disgusted sex-fantasy that emerges in the souring of his relationship with Rachel in the tenth chapter is justified in the context that he 'has been reading a lot of American fiction' (p. 184, evidently a reference to the scene from *An American Dream* that Amis describes in *The Moronic Inferno*)[20].

It might be said of Charles Highway that he becomes or nearly becomes the symbolic America that he hates. Indeed the narrative of his personal development may be another version of the flawed Eden-cum-Utopia which he describes in one of his own more inspired passages of student literary criticism (p. 112). Ironically what may save Charles is the academic canon of English Literature, the safe classics his adolescent brilliance can engage, evade or subvert but which can still (as is shown in the put-down / acceptance he receives from the Oxford don who examines him for University entrance at the close) show him to himself for what he is.

Amis is a postmodern satirist whose narrative tricks work to prevent us from escaping complicity with the objects we are made to despise. In *Dead Babies* this ambiguous genre is set in a useful context by the epigraph from Menippus, whose satires made him a favourite for ancient writers like Petronius and for modern and postmodern critics from Bakhtin, to Kristeva or McHale.[21] Here again we have stereotypes. One group of the party of sick hedonists whose wild debauch at the Appleseed Rectory leads them to well-deserved destruction is classified, in the cast list that prefaces the novel, as 'The Americans'. During the stylised introductions to the suave, cynical and / or grotesque sex-and-drug crazed Brits, what we first hear of the trio of Americans is that they are involved in a sexual grouping described as a 'Troy'. They enter as an absurd version of Rabelaisianh erotic dystopia from the country of the unrestrained self. Roxeanne (at least from Keith's point of view) is: 'one of those terrifying, genetics-experiment, gate-fold American girls – well over six foot in her platforms, a bonfire of lambent red hair, breasts like zeppelins, large firm high backside, endless legs' (p. 54). And the leading figure in the American group Marvell Buzhardt (counterpart to the British host Quentin Villiers) offers up the philosophy that justifies their deeds: '*Fuck* all this dead babies about love, understanding, compassion – use drugs to kind of . . . cushion the consciousness, guide it, protect it, stimulate it' (p. 56).

American literature comes in for its usual roasting in the book. To 'Mailer' is part of the group's porno-taxonomy (p. 40), and there is some clever comedy where the English and American languages clash in dialogue. Andy Adorno's memorable definition of the British team as 'ecstatic materialists' who 'grab whatever the fuck's going' (p. 155) suggests that they are as bad, if not worse, themselves. It may or may not be significant that it is when the English and American characters are fully merged in their transatlantic meeting of competitive self-destruction that their own death wish drives them to destruction, just as their worst nightmare, the mysterious Johnny, had turned out to be none other than an 'other self' of Quentin Villiers.

A key term that recurs throughout *The Moronic Inferno*, producing and defining the Dickensian grotesques of America whom Amis seeks out, is 'money'. *Money*, Amis's fifth novel published inevitably in the year of dystopias 1984, might be read in and through these essays.[22] He wrote of the popular American TV evangelists in 1980: 'Money is the two-way traffic of the religious TV industry: money is taken from the viewers in the form of sacramental contributions; money is returned to them in the form of celestial jackpots . . . Money is its own vindication; money is its own just cause.'[23] The circularity of such money / religion figures largely in the novel, whose anti-hero John Self survives as 'commercial director' in the financial hinterland of the movie industry, linking actors; writers and directors to the all-important 'money genius' Fielding Goodney in order to make a film called *Good Money* that turns out to be little more than a financial trick played on Self in which he is duped into bankrupting himself.

The novel begins with a pointedly American scene: a New York in which Self seeks Goodney to set up the first deal through a minefield of junk food and pornography. Even the cab driver has views which make him an extension of Charles Highway's nightmare exaggeration of American violence and racism. The reader is thrown into America immediately not only by settings but also by the personality and the language of the first-person narrator John Self whose very body is the city; his toothache its 'upper west side'. Amis creates for him a brilliantly fast-paced new idiom packed with brand names (his car is a Fiasco; he takes a sleeping pill called Serafim), and terms like 'rug rethink', 'handjob', 'sack talent' and the word 'pornography' used as a positive term (which are types of usage that the British reader will probably register as 'Americanisms'). As Self says on the comic names of characters in the book: 'lots of Americans are called things like that. They've all got names like Orifice and Handjob. They don't notice. They think its cool' (p. 233). So it is something of a shock to the English reader (no doubt a relief to the American) to find that stereotypically Mailerish and American John Self has, in fact, an English background and even refers to himself as an Englishman (p. 24), though he also admits to being 'half American and half asleep' (p. 14). 'I pitched my voice somewhere in the mid-Atlantic' (p. 196), says Self in his own defence, implying that Amis, like Carter, may find aspects of his writing emerging from that space between.

The narrative alternates between an American film industry, with its vain and self-seeking 'stars' Lorne Guyland and Butch Beausoleil, seen through vestigially English eyes, and a west London publand (the pub that Self frequents in London, since he was 'born upstairs' and where he meets the English writer 'Martin Amis' is called the Shakespeare) defamiliarised as through the eyes of an American. But Anglo–American cultural mixedness prevents the polarities from stabilising. Self's 'American but English-raised' girlfriend Martina Twain 'a real boss chick . . . with a terrific education on her' (p. 41), who teaches him to read George Orwell and *Othello*, helps both to identify England as a place of culture in the novel's Anglo-American dichotomies and also to subvert such identifications. Selina street, his London girlfriend, whose 'brothelly knowhow and top-dollar underwear' call up American currency, similarly serves to destabilise stereotypes.

Self's eventual undoing at the hands of American Fielding Goodney may be prefigured in the story of his Uncle Norman who had believed America to be 'the land of opportunity' but ended up coming home none the richer and living in a 'home' (a 'home' is significantly defined as a place 'where money isn't worth anything', p. 198). Self too ends up back 'home' and almost inadvertently begging in the London Underground with his dubious new girlfriend, Georgina. But this opposition too is undercut, perhaps, by Fielding's Enlightenment English writer's name, and by the fact that it is Martina's English husband, Ossie Twain, who works 'in pure money . . . nothing to do with anything except money, the stuff itself' (p. 117), who is both Selina's secret lover and the true instigator of Self's supposedly clandestine relationship with his wife, as well as sharing his name with America's comic genius Mark Twain.

In *London Fields* (1989) Amis continues the process of exploring his narratorial selfhood and complicity through images of America in a novel which plays still further with the possibilities of a fast-paced and slangy 'Americanised' narrative idiom as a means of defamiliarising west London pub life.[24] The narrator has just flown in 'on a red-eye from New York' (p. 1) and his mid-Atlantic perspective allows Amis to play games with his English as against Keith Talent's cockney and to make a distanced commentary the English disease of social class. Though it doesn't alternate locations between London and America like *Money*, the narrative does switch between the supposedly objective third-person story of Talent and Nicola Six and the first-person, diary-like account of the narrator's 'self' and increasing self-involvement in the plot. As in *Other People* and *Money* the Heisenbergian 'surprise' trick played on the reader by the ending of the novel is that the narrator is no detached observer but a participant who is guiltily involved in the action.

The narrator is called Samson Young, or sometimes just Sam (Uncle Sam?), whose house swap with English writer Mark Asprey (another MA as we are reminded in Amisian, Oxford? code, pp. 160, 240 etc.) may just be an echo of the seventies' Anglo-American identity-swapping *Changing Places*.[25] In a contorted piece of rhyming slang he is spotted as being a 'four-wheel Sherman'. ('Four wheel = four wheel skid = yid; Sherman = Sherman tank = Yank', p. 81.) Asked 'How's America?', he responds, 'Crazy, like an x-ray laser' (p. 78). Glimpses of a soured 'American Dream' (pp. 262–3) and of American 'insanity' (pp. 366–7) punctuate the narrative, but its cleverest metaphor may be a postmodern version of the familiar Enlightenment concept of the *tabula rasa*, continuing the identification of America and writing noted in Angela Carter. Samson returns to America for a brief six-day visit in the middle of Chapter 12, during which time he is unable to write. Between the end of one section, 'Let's go to America', and the start of the next one, 'Well I'm back', what we have represented of America is p. 237 – a blank page.

If *Money* complicated and inverted Amis's play with Anglo-American stereotyping in line with the newly aggressive economic stance of the British Government and commercial community in the 1980s, then *London Fields* further extends that play in certain areas. The gradual undercutting of Young's supposed reasonableness and sanity and the subtle humanising of Talent's grotesque appetites, petty criminality and naive enthusiasms make a complex contribution to Anglo-American dialectic but also to the psychopathology of narration and nationhood. To allow the exporting of narrative, and perhaps also of national *self*-hood to America may be to create a kind of schizophrenic doubling of freedom and constraint, to build the Gothic monster that Samson Young has become at the close in the 'dead-end street' of the 'I', a powerless creation of the fiction of others: 'As if someone made me up, for money' (p. 470).

That there is no way back from such dead-end 'streets' to the mysteriously undefined 'Fields' of the title is one of Young's closing realisations (p. 463). Along with these associations, Young's dark intimations of the 'script' of history, his own piece of writing 'on the way America has started to fulfil –', and Talent's worrying darts-lore reminder that 'Those Pilgrim Fathers are said to have thrown darts while sailing to America in 1620 on the so-called Mayflower' (p. 313) add up to the powerfully serious geopolitical theme of global extinction said to be 'coterminous with' the sex-death-wishing 'Necropolitan Nicola' Six (p. 467).

Either a nightmarish confirmation of that global death wish or else a euphoric unravelling of the century's most crippling social guilt – or even both alternative readings – may be drawn from Amis's sensationally serious *Time's Arrow* (1991).[26] In this book the still more guilty and complicit figure of the narrator passes in a reversible narrative mode from his death in the American suburbs as the cheerful Tod Friendly backwards through his earlier assumed identity, John Young, under which he had emigrated to escape the consequences of his involvement in the Nazi holocaust. The technique of reversible narration may owe something to the *Counter-Clock World* of Philip Dick[27] or to the celebrated final episode of David Lynch's postmodern television series *Twin Peaks*, or even to controversies about the hidden reversed messages in contemporary popular music lyrics. Most importantly though it makes a potent historical metaphor for transvaluation out of the reversal of Semitic script, and erodes the reader's learned habits of distance from such a traumatic theme.

It is, of course, the nightmare of European history in the post-holocaust, post-cultural era that is unpacked in the book but some of its most haunting images are again images of America, such as the uncannily familiar space that Odilo has come to inhabit at the end of his life which is the start of the book: 'I live, out here, in washing-line and mailbox America, innocuous America, in affable, melting-pot, primary colour, You're-okay-I'm-okay, *America*,' (p. 14). Innocuous America, in-nocuous America, the ambivalence suggested by Amis's phrasing and syntax calls up all the suburban gothic Grant Wood terror of an innocent country peopled by a chaos bred from a mass-murderous European past. In this image the creation and subversion of stereotypes is again at work and the 'coterminous' worlds of personal life and history once again confirmed.

IAN MCEWAN'S POSTMODERN GEOGRAPHIES

The apparently fantastical world of Ian McEwan's first two collections of short stories also gives way to something more like geopolitical allegory in his work as it develops through the increasingly politically charged eighties, and some of the allegorical implications may be teased out by attempting to read the ways in which America is imagined in the works as a complex cultural or post-cultural sign. America, absent from the stories of *First Love, Last Rites* (1975), except in the reference to Americans as people 'who often indulge in fantastic tales' in 'Solid Geometry' (pp. 35–6), becomes important in *In Between the Sheets* (1978).[28] The final story in the collection begins: 'Mary worked in a part-owned feminist bookstore in Venice' (p. 103), that Venice being part of Greater Los Angeles, the 'Psychopolis' of the story's title. Mary, with her paradoxical fetish for insisting that the narrator of the story chain her to the bed, is a symbol of one kind of feminism (her feminism recurs later in the story when she attempts a feminist critique of Christianity, pp. 122–3) but also represents the indescribable postmodern insanity of the city.

According to Edward Soja's *Postmodern Geographies* (1989), massively expansive, once gold-rushed Los Angeles enjoys a number of features which make it 'a *prototopos*, a paradigmatic place' or '*mesocosm*' (a place which is in some sense everywhere at the same time) for the postmodern, urban capitalist world.[29] For Soja to describe such a place empirically is literally impossible. Its wild accumulations of multinational capital are incommensurate with its acute housing crises which leave more people than anywhere else in America living in cardboard boxes. Its 'polynucleated decentralisation' which has made it 'a hundred suburbs in search of a city' sort ill with the centripetal economic forces that cause both recentralisation and a sense of the re-creation of the centre as another kind of periphery. The extreme multicultural diversity and drive towards personal individuation seem only to lead to new totalities and the accelerating erosion of difference.

McEwan's story uses strikingly similar figures. Mary's paradoxical sex game, in which the English narrator bemusedly participates, is followed by a scene in which he dwells on the absurdity or paradox of a hire shop dealing in both 'items for party givers' and 'equipment for sick rooms' (p. 106). The hugeness, uncentredness, absurdity and representativeness of this 'heterotopia' all feature as both background and foreground in the story. 'It's a city at the end of cities', says Mary, and 'It's sixty miles across', the narrator is said to have 'agreed' (p. 105). His friend Terence Latterly says: 'It's OK for the British. You see everything here as a bizarre comedy of extremes, but that's because you're out of it. The truth is it's psychotic, totally psychotic' (p. 109). The narrator thinks mesocosmically: 'Everywhere on earth is the same. Los Angeles, California, the whole of the United States seemed to me then a very fine and frail crust on the limitless, subterranean world of my own boredom. I could be anywhere . . .' (p. 112).

The climax of the story occurs in a final scene in which the characters meet together in an increasingly wild discussion of the corporal punishment of children, Christianity, the America of 'God, Guts and Guns' and so on. George's sceptical but pragmatic Christianity and his loud patriotism and Mary's attractive but ultimately limited and futile version of socialist feminism are both silenced by Terence's mad practical joke with George's gun. Throughout the story the nameless English first-person narrator has described in minute detail his flute-playing and, in particular, his practising of a Bach sonata, 'No. 1 in A Minor'. He plays without perfection or even ambition towards perfection, repeating the same familiar errors on his instrument and achieving only an imagined coherence 'remembered from gramophone records and superimposed over the present' (p. 113). At the close the coherence implied by such 'Classical' rationalistic music as a Bach sonata has itself come to seem misplaced. In the light of his experience of the 'vast, fragmented city without a centre, without citizens, a city that existed only in the mind' he begins to see Bach as 'inane in its rationality, paltry in its over-determination' (pp. 126–7). If Bach represents culture then this America is 'postcultural': an incommensurable; absurd and grown beyond the powers of imagination. Cultural Bach is set up in opposition to those postcultural representatives of Dionysian licence and irrationality, English representatives, of course, The Rolling Stones, from whose song 'Live With Me' the title of McEwan's story 'In Between the Sheets' and his collection are taken.[30] The fact that McEwan subsequently chose to write his second novel, *The Comfort of Strangers*, with another poignantly futile feminist heroine called Mary, but this time set in the thanatopic, capitalistic nightmare city of Venice, Italy, confirms the presence of this 'America' in the centre of Europe too.[31]

The cultural politics of McEwan's fiction are far less explicit than those of the television and other dramas whose excursion into a more public genre McEwan describes in the metaphorical title of his *A Move Abroad* (1989) in which the libretto of the pacifist–feminist oratoria *Or Shall We Die?* and screenplay of the 1983 television film *The Ploughman's Lunch* were published.[32] In shifting from fiction McEwan describes himself as having been concerned to engage more directly with the new authoritarianism of Britain in the eighties, and also, like James Penfield in *The Ploughman's Lunch*, to be contributing to the redefinition of Britain's place in 'World History since 1945'.[33] *The Imitation Game* (1981) portrayed a frustratingly secret, hierarchical and impotent British society at the time of the Second World War.[34] *The Ploughman's Lunch* dissects the no less anxious but sharply thrusting world of yuppy journalists and ad-men at a time when Britain was forced back into place as a world power through the Falklands War. This Britain is once again defined in relation to America both as a newly successful competitor ('We're the best, it's as simple as that. Even the Americans will admit it now', says Matthew Fox in the pivotal scene 82) and as a place whose supposedly authentic traditions can no longer be held up against American artificiality, since even the archetypally 'traditional' Ploughman's Lunch was the product of an early sixties' advertising campaign, suggesting that British culture may be best understood in 'American' terms as a Baudrillardian culture of simulacra too.[35]

The expansion of McEwan's creative range through the performance works of the eighties fed into his two most recent novels *The Child in Time* (1987) and *The Innocent* (1990).[36] In the *The Child in Time* the setting is once again a political insider's London from a slightly marginalised or semi-outsider's point of view and (though apparently set slightly in the future) the British political restructurings of the past decade, are obviously powerful undercurrents of the novel's appeal. America appears as a monstrous super-power stereotype in the incident of Cold War tension that has marred the year's Olympic games (pp. 34–5). But the most obviously relevant figure to the semiotic encoding of America in the novel is Thelma Darke: the wife of Charles Darke, ambitious British political careerist on whose friendship Stephen depends for his commissions. Far from the Californian bondage fetishist Mary in 'Psychopolis', Thelma is a serious-minded thoughtful and relaxed counterpart to Charles's frenzied and ultimately self-destructive political ambitions. Academically trained, she has relinquished her post in order to assist Charles but also in order to write a book on the New Physics that McEwan uses as a vehicle for, or at least as a partial attempt to articulate, the positive values he wishes to promote in the novel. More substantial than the dangerously naive 'womanly times' of McEwan's oratorio, Thelma may be described as a kind of 'Good America' or positive imagined future akin to the stars and stripes transformed by magical realism at the end of Carter's *Nights of the Circus* or the cultured figure of Martina Twain and the near-humanised final Self of Amis's *Money*. Her idealism for a new science, if displaying an 'American' ingenuousness, seems nevertheless offered as a hopeful vision of: 'the mystic's experience of timelessness, the chaotic unfolding of time in dreams, the Christian moment of fulfilment and redemption, the annihilated time of deep sleep, the elaborate time schemes of the novelists, poets, daydreamers, the infinite, unchanging time of childhood' (p. 120).

In *The Innocent* the allegorical level is at its clearest yet and, despite its ghoulish murder and disposal of the corpse, the 'snot and pimples' world of his early stories is left most fully behind. Postwar, post-partition Berlin is the setting for the novel which deals directly with the Anglo-American 'special relationship' (a phrase which McEwan considered as an alternative title).

Because of the setting almost everything is specifically marked by national identity. Leonard Marnham, McEwan's innocent, is defined from the start by his Englishness, a quality which was 'not quite the comfort it had been to a preceding generation' (p. 7). In this he is contrasted with Bob Glass one of the 'Americans' who 'don't know a thing . . . won't learn' (p. 1) and 'seemed utterly at ease being themselves' (p. 7). Even the defeated Germans seem to have more self-confidence and swagger in their national identities than Leonard.

The public plot of the novel concerns the Anglo-American cooperation on a top security tunnel dug from West to East Berlin in order to intercept telecommunications behind the Russian lines. The private plot concerns Leonard (still a virgin at twenty-five) and his sexual initiation with older woman Maria Eckdorf ex-wife of German bully and wife-beater Otto, whom Leonard extremely violently, but somehow still rather innocently, murders with a cobbler's last.

One of the most disturbing sequences in the novel concerns Leonard's dismembering of Otto's body and his journey around Berlin carrying the remains in two suitcases, eventually hiding them in the secret tunnel: a task that McEwan describes slowly and meticulously over some four chapters of the book. In the penultimate scene (with a hint of Curtiz's classic wartime airport parting scene in *Casablanca*?) Leonard makes his escape, and he and Maria part, but the resolution is not that of romance. Leonard flies off, leaving Maria in the care of Bob Glass who had fixed his escape. In the ironic final chapter Leonard returns to Berlin thirty years later with a letter from Maria in which he reads that she emigrated to America and became Maria Glass, leaving Leonard with his self-constraining English shyness and gentlemanliness but also the ineradicable suspicion that in the real 'special relationship' he was just the dupe or even the guilt-bearing scapegoat for another romance.

Behind the love and murder story and the evocation of the world of secret intelligence operations there is in *The Innocent* something approaching an allegory of the postwar condition of Britain. Common stereotypes of national character clearly condition the protrayal of Otto, Bob and Leonard but if anything it is Leonard's Englishness (which seems so proper and innocent but gets him into near rape and murder) that is most to blame. Maria writes: 'It was wrong of you to retreat with your anger and silence. So English! So male! If you felt betrayed you should have stood your ground and fought for what was yours' (p. 226). Such a conclusion no longer opposes an image of British or European culture or rationality against American postmodern crisis but rather suggests that nothing needs liberating from inhibiting postwar cultural assumptions more than the British Leonard.

Dynamics of personal and cultural identity condition the use of America as a complex and ambiguous sign in the fictions of Angela Carter, Martin Amis and Ian McEwan. Behind their obvious differences – of gender, of politics and of novelistic genre – we can note some important recurrent concerns. Angela Carter's use of America as a sixties' symbol of emerging female self-consciousness modulates into a fantastic postmodern vision of America as a future self gone wild, thence into a portrayal of aspects of the urban bourgeois self that must transform themselves through an encounter with the magically real and thence into a cross-cultural pageant of the illegitimate forms out of which both cultures are built. The play with stereotypes in Martin Amis's early fictions becomes more complex and inverted, and his fiction develops new types of postmodern experimentation with the structure and psychology of narrative and the forms of selfhood they may imply: a postmodern satire in which no distance is allowed to mystify our complicity with the objects we revile. Ian McEwan describes the indescribability of contemporary California and uses American characters as a way of redefining British national myths in the changing world situation.

All three writers are highly conscious of the role of representation in defining national and cultural identities and the inescapable modulations of representation through which any such identities are necessarily observed. In all three the space between British and American culture provides a space from which their writing can emerge. In none is America simply defined as 'other'. Though each constructs a cultural identity, each does it in the context of what Fredric Jameson has called the 'erosion of difference' itself, characteristic of the postmodern world.[37] In each this 'other' may be recognised by its tendency to become increasingly present as part of the 'self' from which it is supposedly displaced.

NOTES

(Dates given in the text are to the first publication of the novel. Page references in the text refer to the editions below.)

1. Angela Carter, *The Magic Toyshop* (London, 1981), p. 1.

2. Paulina Palmer, *Contemporary Women's Fiction* (Hemel Hempstead, 1989) provides a feminist reading of Carter.

3. Melanie Klein, 'Mourning and its Relation to Manic Depressive States' in *The Selected Melanie Klein*, ed. Juliet Mitchell (Harmondsworth, 1986), pp. 146–174; Jacques Lacan, 'Desire and the interpretation of desire in *Hamlet*', in *Literature and Psychoanalysis* ed. Shoshana Felman (Baltimore, 1982), pp. 11–52.

4. Julia Kristeva, *Revolution in Poetic Language*, in *The Kristeva Reader*, (ed.) Toril Moi (Oxford, 1986), pp. 89–136.

5. Angela Carter, *The Passion of New Eve* (London, 1982).

6. John Locke, *Second Treatise of Government*, section 49, Chapter 5 ('Of Property').

7. Jean Baudrillard, *America*, trans. Chris Turner (London, 1988); Sam Shepard, *Motel Chronicles* (London, 1985); Wim Wenders, dir., *Paris, Texas* (Road Movies / Argos, 1984).

8. John Haffenden, *Novelists in Interview* (London, 1985), pp. 85–6.

9. Baudrillard, *America*, p. 46.

10. Angela Carter, *Nights at the Circus* (London, 1985).

11. Haffenden, *Novelists in Interview*, p. 87.

12. David Gallagher, *Modern Latin American Literature* (Oxford, 1973) and Peter King (ed.) *Latin American Fiction* (London, 1990) offer recent studies of 'magical realism'.

13. Angela Carter, *Wise Children* (London, 1991). Paulina Palmer, 'From "Coded Mannequin" to Bird Woman' in Sue Roe (ed.) *Women Reading Women's Writing* (Brighton, 1987), pp. 179–205.

14. In the 'Circe' episode of Joyce's *Ulysses* (Harmondsworth, 1986), pp. 475–7, Stephen Dedalus believes himself to have smashed a brothel 'chandelier' that turns out to have been only a damaged gas light.

15. J.F. Lyotard, *The Postmodern Condition* (Manchester, 1984, pp. 6–9, and *passim*.

16. Martin Amis, *The Moronic Inferno* (Harmondsworth, 1987).

17. Martin Amis, in interview with Christopher Bigsby, in *New Writing*, (ed.) Malcolm Bradbury and Judy Cooke (London, 1992), pp. 181–3.

18. Martin Amis, *The Rachel Papers* (Harmondsworth, 1984); Martin Amis, *Dead Babies* also published under the title *Dark Secrets* (St Albans, 1977); Martin Amis, *Success* (Harmondsworth, 1985).

19. Malcolm Bradbury (ed.), *The Novel Today* (London, 1991), p. 34. The essays referred to are also included in this selection.

20. Martin Amis, *The Moronic Inferno*, p. 63.

21. Petronius, *The Satyricon*, trans. J.P. Sullivan (Harmondsworth, 1969); *The Kristeva Reader*, pp. 39–40; Brian McHale, *Postmodernist Fiction* (London, 1987), pp. 172–3.

22. Martin Amis, *Money* (London, 1984).

23. Martin Amis, *The Moronic Inferno*, p. 113.

24. Martin Amis, *London Fields* (London, 1989).

25. David Lodge, *Changing Places* (London, 1975).

26. Martin Amis, *Time's Arrow* (London, 1991).

27. Philip K. Dick, *Counter-Clock World* (London, 1968).

28. Ian McEwan, *First Love, Last Rites* (London, 1976); Ian McEwan, *In Between the Sheets* (London, 1978).

29. Edward Soja, *Postmodern Geographies* (London, 1989), pp. 190–248.

30. *The Rolling Stones Complete* (London, 1981), song no. 77 (no page nos).

31. Ian McEwan, *The Comfort of Strangers* (London, 1981).

32. Ian McEwan, *A Move Abroad* (London, 1989).

33. Ibid. p. 40.

34. Ian McEwan, *The Imitation Game: Three Plays for Television* (London, 1981).

35. Ian McEwan, *A Move Abroad*, pp. 106–7.

36. Ian McEwan, *The Child in Time* (London, 1988); *The Innocent* (London, 1990).

37. Fredric Jameson, *Postmodernism, or the Cultural Logic of Late Capitalism* (London, 1991).

FURTHER READING

Malcolm Bradbury and Judy Cooke (eds), *New Writing* (London, 1992).

Lesley Henderson (ed.), *Contemporary Novelists* (5th edn; Chicago and London, 1991).

Alan Sinfield, *Literature, Politics and Culture in Post-War Britain* (Oxford, 1989).

Brian McHale, *Postmodernist Fiction* (London, 1987).

Linda Hutcheon, *A Poetics of Postmodernism* (London, 1988).

Edmund J. Smyth (ed.), *Postmodernism and Contemporary Fiction* (London, 1991).

Alison Lee, *Realism and Power* (London, 1990).

Peter Brooker (ed.), *Modernism / Postmodernism* (London, 1992).

Paulina Palmer, *Contemporary Women's Fictions* (Hemel Hempstead, 1989).

II Literary Relations:
Evelyn Waugh to Alison Lurie

In her pertinently titled novel *Foreign Affairs* (1986) Alison Lurie 'exposes her characters to a variety of intertextual frames, creating comic, ironic or even tragic effects, as characters who have scripted themselves in accordance with one acculturated model undergo slippage into less or more challenging roles'. Lurie's projections of lives 'read' or 'lived' though literature, analysed here by Judie Newman in 'Paleface into Redskin', suggest one logical and disturbing concept of literary relationships. Earlier texts suggest other possibilities, other connections. The theory and practice of American poetry was vital to the 'revival' of British poetry between 1960 and 1975, Eric Mottram argues; while David Seed's essay on Jazz Age fictions demonstrates a spectrum of issues entailed in British–American literary relationships.

First, the issue of influence, here that of shared influence, represented by the British writer Ronald Firbank. Evelyn Waugh and Carl Van Vechten both wrote appreciatively of Firbank and derived from him. Seed cites Waugh's praise for Firbank's combination of apparent inconsequentiality and skill:

> His later novels are almost wholly devoid of any attribution of cause to effect; there is the barest minimum of direct description; his compositions are built up, intricately and with a balanced alternation of the wildest extravagance and the most austere economy, with conversational *nuances*.

The shared literary matrix led both writers to use 'fragmentary and partial views' to give a picture of a social situation: a technique also utilised by Fitzgerald. Second, there is the question of the degree to which existing literary traditions, domestic or imported, are reflected in texts. For the most part the American novelists Seed discusses seem to have functioned in isolation from their nineteenth-century predecessors (though connections have been made: Fitzgerald and James, Hemingway and Twain) and to have perceived themselves as technical innovators, vernacular recorders and privileged commentators. The British writers cited are more conscious of and more prone to employ what has gone before, noting, for instance the ways in which earlier fiction had supplied literary and social trends from which they as postwar British novelists could take their bearings. Aldous Huxley, as Seed observes, 'revives the methods of Thomas Love Peacock wherein the country house supplies the setting within which can be enacted the conflicts between characters' intellectual and emotional pretensions'.

A third comparison concerns the sense of place, the spirit of place (as D.H. Lawrence would have it), a use of place by American and British writers which puts distance between their fictions. The settings utilised by the American writers are not in themselves invented; they are replicas of real salons (Gertrude Vanderbilt Whitney's, Mabel Dodge Luhan's) or, in *The Great Gatsby*, mansions that Fitzgerald knew or which had been documented, named hotels like the Plaza which he had frequented. The American sense of place in these texts is specific and neo-documentary. British texts also exhibit reality of place – there *were* parties in dirigibles – but Waugh renders such parties in terms that are fantastic rather than mimetic; his parties are masquerades in which the participants are conscious masqueraders, Fitzgerald's are functions at which the guests yield to social magic. Indeed, Waugh subverts not just parties but reports of parties and readers of the reports. The British tendency to transform rather than to render is nowhere more evident than in Wyndham Lewis's *Apes of God* (1930), a novel which, as Seed notes, 'brings its satire to a climax in an enormously extended intricate party scene which occupies the last three hundred pages of the novel.'

Contrasting historical circumstances noted by Seed constitute a fourth area of comparison. Prohibition arguably affected not only the society observed but the observing author; similarly, class in England may be seen as a differentiating factor. Hierarchies of various kinds – of generation and value as well as income and origin – are foregrounded in British writing of this period.

The British and American writers discussed by Seed share a realisation of the social significance and the literary potential of party-going but they use strikingly different tonal and, ultimately, conceptual strategies. The Americans see their function as elegiac witnesses and nostalgic recorders; they indulge in pathos, not a term to introduce in describing British attitudes of ridicule and satire. American fictions exhibit romanticism along with a mimetic precision; the British push fragmentation to Cubist extremes.

Peter Egri's essay offers a rare opportunity to look at an unusually close literary relationship: that which developed as Edward Albee worked on his adaptation (1967) of Giles Cooper's *Everything in the Garden* (1962). Egri agrees with John Russell Taylor that the playwrights shared an interest in 'the exploration of strange emotional states on the margin of human experience, sometimes with strongly macabre overtones, and generally on the surface at least in terms of comedy'. Albee expected to make minimal changes, but 'something happened, and by the time I was finished with my work there was hardly a word left of the original'. In terms of content Albee found that as an American and conscious of an American audience's assumptions he had to alter Cooper's presentation of prostitution, of wealth, of stakes and risks. His status as a not unconditioned American playwright (heir of O'Neill, contemporary of Miller and Williams) required the blurring of the boundaries between illusion and reality, the denial of unresolved, merely incidental incongruity (which he chose to counter with a radical absurdity) and the replacement of a closed ending with an open one. Albee contrasts not just with Cooper, but with Beckett, Pinter and N.F. Simpson, the British absurdists. In *The Theatre of the Absurd* (New York, (1961; revised and enlarged, Harmondsworth, 1968) Martin Esslin suggests that the American absurdists can't bring themselves to be thoroughly absurd; they always have to introduce a – national? – element of affirmation. That would perhaps account for Albee's refusal to rest in Cooper's irony and would in part explain the almost mandatory up-beat endings of many American plays, though this is an audience-orientated phenomenon, too.

Ruby Cohn finds Sam Shepard (not unlike Pinter in his juxtaposition of alien forces and closed spaces: there is a line of influence too that runs from Hemingway to Pinter to Mamet) closely related to Edward Bond. Comparing the artist-protagonist plays she concludes that the target for each man is his 'moribund' country. They adopt comparable scenic techniques and employ similar stage properties. But Bond's base is in social history and Shepard's in American myth. This leads Bond to create texts around his versions of Shakespeare and Jonson, John Clare and Mary Lamb, and Shepard to create self-inventing present-day musical artists. Shepard's invention represents a strand in American writing that is related to an American sense of the past that posits either the West (space, possibility) or the East (enclosure and the finite). Both are mythical areas, neither satisfactory; both to be played off against a present which seeks to disassemble the past and, through reselection, project a future. Bond grounds the British present, cultural and political, in strongly socialistic readings of the British past, mercilessly caricaturing iconic figures, presenting Shakespeare as a man who would diagnose suffering but was unwilling to act on his diagnosis.

Bond and Shepard both experiment with idiomatic language, differentiating the idiom through type, class and regional filters. While their polyphonic texts are unmistakably national, national languages do not destroy the closeness of their literary relationship. What distance there is between these two autodidacts is effected by the kinds of protagonists they foreground and by the fact that while both create texts which call the present into question Bond does so by referring to the historical past, Shepard by referring to myths of the past and adumbrating myths of the future.

Eric Mottram's essay poses canonical questions about the development and the relationship of the literatures. It suggests that prior to the revival of 1960–75 British poetry was held back by a school of publishing and critical thought which disdained the contemporary and the innovative and which believed in a British school, indigenous, isolated, traditional. He argues that if the writing of, say, Eliot, Pound, David Jones, Hugh MacDiarmid and Dylan Thomas had been offered to wealthy presses at that time (Jonathan Cape was a notable exception), the chance of publication would have been nil. How far do publishers' readers, editors, bookstores, wholesaling, retailing, publicity and promotions policies, writers, reviewers, prize committees, critics and teachers determine the canon? Can we as readers do any more than choose from a limited menu of texts? (For good examples of the way in which tastes are shaped, consider the diet of women's and ethnic writing that currently fills Western bookstore shelves and the unavailability in Britain of the writings of the American-Jewish writer Cynthia Ozick and in America those of the British-Jewish Clive Sinclair.) In a later essay in this volume Keith Tuma argues that as far as Modernist poetry is concerned the issue has been less one of the general availability of texts and more of the resistance writers and critics have shown to differing transatlantic practices.

Mottram submits that in a country like Britain, often suspicious of novelty, the role of small presses and journals, poetry readings and fringe bookstores is crucial. *Tri Quarterly* No. 216, 1972, edited by John Matthias, was one of the pioneer places where contemporary British poetry was published. And what was just as important to British poets in search of activating forms as alternatives to those known and those rejected was access to poetry in English published in a country arguably as debilitatingly committed to novelty as Britain was hostile to it: America. In the sixties such outlets as Bill Butler's Better Books in London and Jim Haynes's bookstore in Edinburgh provided marvellous resources for American writing, centres for poetic interface. But the question remains: without the importation of, say, Olson's theories, Beat texts and performance poetry, would British poetry by itself have responded to changes in contemporary music, painting, physics, psychology, philosophy? Would the re-evaluation of poetic discourse and writers–reader, audience–performance relationships have taken place? Basil Bunting's work suggests that there were British poets who had come out of the closet only to be ignored. The British–American relationship was, in this instance, crucial for British poetry. But given the (shared) emphasis, in Robert Kelly's words, on poetry that 'talks to us, in our own speech, our own asymmetrical, nervous, alive, embattled, present *hearing*', as well as the existence of contextualising factors, British and American voices will, to a significant degree, remain distinct.

Judie Newman broadens the discussion of literary relationship by connecting it to the issue of cultural identity. She reminds us that if we define 'text' as a system of signs, a text may extend to include folklore, movies, the language of dress, symbolic systems, and the construction of cultural or even individual identity.

> The 'international theme' may be defined as itself an intertext, a set of plots, characters, images and inventions to which a particular novel refers. Moreover, its central situation, in which characters are physically translated and transformed, as a result of crossing from one culture, one set of signals, to another, itself thematises intertextuality.

Forked Tongues?

She looks at works by Frances Hodgson Burnett, Henry James and Alison Lurie from this perspective. Her primary focus is on Lurie, and Lurie's major heroine, Vinnie Miner, an American who allows herself to be shaped by the reading of British literature. Her *alter ego*, British actress Rosemary Radley, escapes from a range of typecasting by involvement in an equally extreme American strategy: a series of rapid transformations which pass well beyond the predictable bounds of creativity. Literary and cultural intertextuality are projected as inextricable, and since in Anglophone societies the intertextual frames will, for the most part, be Anglophonic, intimate, indeed special British–American literary relationships seem likely to continue.

CHAPTER SIX

Party-going: The Jazz Age novels of Evelyn Waugh, Wyndham Lewis, F. Scott Fitzgerald and Carl Van Vechten

David Seed

Reviewing *The Great Gatsby* in 1925 Harvey Eagleton complained: 'The book is highly sensational, loud, blatant, ugly, pointless.'[1] His basic grounds for complaint were that such a superficial social world should actually find its way into fiction and the fact that he has not been alone in moralistically confusing the quality of characters' behaviour with the supposed quality of the novels helps to explain why more critical attention has not been devoted to the fiction of party-going in the twenties. In the pages that follow party scenes will be compared from two American novelists: – Carl Van Vechten and F. Scott Fitzgerald; and two British novelists: Evelyn Waugh and Wyndham Lewis. Their responses to the decade following the First World War, which functions as a major reference point in this fiction, grow out of contrasting historical circumstances and put quite different emphases. While Van Vechten saw himself as the chronicler of an age which had ended and accordingly applied methods of scenic depiction, Fitzgerald investigates the pathos growing out of the failure of his party-givers. His narrative perspectives are characteristically those of a witness elegiacally recording the passing of these social events. In contrast with both these writers, Waugh, Lewis – and for that matter their contemporary Aldous Huxley – vigorously satirise their party-goers, ridiculing the postures of postwar nihilism and exploring the social ferment taking place in this period.

The relation of parties to social nonconformity in the United States reveals itself in the popularity enjoyed by Greenwich Village salons during the 1910s. Figures such as the sculptor Gertrude Vanderbilt Whitney or Mabel Dodge Luhan established permanent forums for cultural and intellectual debate which could not be found elsewhere. A visitor to the latter's salon reported: 'Every lively topic, movement, and interest of the day has been discussed in her house.'[2] Apart from the free play of ideas a life-style and mode of dress were cultivated as a deliberate protest against prevailing norms. The impromptu evenings recorded by the novelist Djuna Barnes in the studios with 'blue and yellow candles pouring their hot wax over things in ivory and things in jade' frequently became the occasion for parties but parties as such did not attract scrutiny in their own right until the twenties, when the era of the salons had passed. [3] The participants had been dispersed by the First World War and dispersed again after 1920 when the buoyant dollar encouraged a fashion of visiting Paris and other European locations.

At this point we encounter one of the crucial historical factors which distinguishes the American twenties from Britain in the same decade – namely, prohibition. Brought in as a wartime measure, the Eighteenth Amendment (enforced by the notorious Volstead Act) was designed to make prohibition permanent with effect from 16 January 1920. Opposition to the act had been strong in the urban north-east and by the mid twenties it was being so widely ignored that it had virtually become a dead letter in cities like New York. A whole alternative system of business grew up with its own jargon of 'bootlegging' and 'speakeasies' presided over by 'magnates' like Al Capone. Fitzgerald records how the dividing line between legality and criminality blurred to the extent that writing and smuggling alike both became 'rackets'. Whatever the truth of whether America as a whole was drinking more in this period, Fitzgerald had no hesitation in linking alcohol to the mood of the twenties: 'Most of my friends drank too much – the more they were in tune to the times the more they drank.'[4] Jay Gatsby is suspected by his guests of being a bootlegger, but without any loss to his social status; just the opposite. And in *Parties* Van Vechten demonstrates the contact between the underworld and New York high society in the most literal way by having a bootlegger seek refuge in the Countess's apartment and then become her adopted companion. If prohibition reflected a search for what Frederick Lewis Allen has called a 'dry Utopia' the characters of Fitzgerald's and Van Vechten's fiction deliberately resort to drink as a gesture of protest against an institutionalised puritanism and as a flirtation with crime.[5]

Both history and earlier fiction supplied literary and social traditions from which postwar English novelists could take their bearings on the country house party. Aldous Huxley in *Crome Yellow* (1921) and *Those Barren leaves* (1925) revives the method of Thomas Love Peacock where a country house supplies the setting within which can be enacted the conflicts between characters' intellectual and romantic pretensions. In a period when doubts were cast over the possibility of meaningful action it was appropriate for those doubts to be articulated through a fiction which uses place to limit action. My title echoes that of Henry Green's novel *Party Going* (started in 1931, published in 1939) where he varies this method by portraying characters forced to take up residence in a London hotel when fog paralyses transport. As the tensions between these characters emerge Green exploits the double meaning of 'party' as collective and individual. It is essential, however, to note the emphasis in the English tradition on the historical dignity and aristocratic ease of the houses, whether in London or in the countryside, which contrast with the vulgarity of their inhabitants. In *Howard's End* (1910) the eponymous house itself raises central issues of ownership and continuity. Far more ironically Huxley introduces the first party in *Point Counter Point* (1923) by explaining the pedigree of the family giving it. Tantamount House preserves a Roman nobility but the obsessions of its inhabitants fragment the family as a unit and help to fragment the party as a social event. Henry James's *The Sacred Fount* (1901) devotes its entire action to a weekend party in a country house and contrasts usefully with the fiction under discussion here by insistently maintaining the social proprieties. Its narrator voyeuristically attempts to find out exactly what sexual liaisons are being formed, but finds to his frustration that the collective restrictions on behaviour imposed by decorum prevent him from ever learning the truth. The fiction dealing with social life in the twenties on the other hand refuses to leave that decorum intact. Looking back on the decade the novelist Douglas Goldring argued that parties had a key role to play in this process: 'The real interest . . . which the period of "wild parties" retains for the social historian is that it brought into the open tendencies in human behaviour which had previously been politely ignored.'[6] Goldring's contrast between politeness and its implied opposite means that James's tantalising hints of something literally unspeakable going on behind the social façade are replaced with explicit verbal expression and a corresponding devaluation of that façade as mere theatre. 'What a pantomime!' exclaims a guest at Tantamount House, and this sentiment echoes and re-echoes throughout this fiction as social forms are perceived to be empty of meaning.

SCENES FROM AMERICAN LIFE

The publication of Carl Van Vechten's *Parties* in 1930 symbolically signalled the end of a decade of party-going and the culmination of his desire to be a chronicler of his age. His earlier novel *The Tattooed Countess* (1924) was to have been called *Scenes from American Provincial life in 1897*, and the 1930

novel, Van Vechten's last, is subtitled *Scenes from Contemporary New York Life.*[7]
One method used to give a continuity of observation to these scenes is by
introducing a German countess as an excited witness and then participant.
The Gräfin ironically suffers from the same disease as the New Yorkers –
boredom – and goes to America in search of excitement, giving Van Vechten
the opportunity of creating passing comic effects by juxtaposing old world
decorum with the democratic mores of America. The Countess gives an
outsider's view, balanced by that of an American, Mrs Alonzo W. Syreno
(we never know her real name), the 'baby wife of the radish king'. After
successfully penetrating the smart set the latter sets up a salon in her own right
which is described as a combination of self-deception and theatre: 'Mrs
Alonzo W. Syreno's new acquaintances – she believed them to be her friends
– were gathered in her drawing room, seated in a circle, for all the world like
an old-fashioned minstrel show grouping . . .'[8] These throw-away narrative
comments repeatedly puncture the poses struck by the New York party-
goers, reversing their desire for novelty into a series of grotesque resemblances
with things past. We are now at the fag end of the brief tradition of literary
salons which Gorham Munson identified as playing a key role in the cultural
life of Greenwich Village.[9] Mrs Syreno's gathering is only the visible sign of
penetrating a social élite. It has, as it were, no content, cultural or otherwise.
Van Vechten's favourite analogies are with opera, theatre or the visual arts,
so that one person is described as a 'cross between a poster by Chéret and a
caricature by Toulouse Lautrec'.[10] Running through these analogies is a
strong motif of performance. This set, just like Waugh's Bright Young
People, transforms itself into a mutual admiration society where the members
alternately strike postures or assess the postures of others, alternate in other
words between actors and audience.

The leading lights in this glittering world are David and Rilda Westlake,
partly modelled on the Fitzgeralds. Their ironic reflections on themselves
stand as comments on the whole ethos of the novel. David declares:

> We're swine, filthy swine, and we are Japanese mice, and we are polar bears walking
> from one end of our cage to the other, to and fro, to and fro, all day, all week, all
> month, for ever to eternity. We'll be drunk pretty soon and then I'll be off to
> Donald's to get drunker and you'll be off with Siegfried and get drunker and we'll
> go to a lot of cocktail parties and then we'll all turn up for dinner at Rosalie's where
> you are never invited. She won't want you, and I shall hate you, but Siegfried will
> want you. And we'll get drunker and drunker and drift about night clubs so drunk
> that we won't know where we are, and then we'll go to Harlem and stay up all
> night and go to bed late tomorrow morning and wake up and begin it all over again.
> Parties, sighed Rilda. Parties.[11]

David's images of enclosure slide consistently into the easy predictions of an
unchanging social pattern signalled stylistically in the repetition of 'and' and

'drunk/er'. Behaviour is reduced to an animalistic level by excluding purpose and feeling. The novel reinforces this claustrophobia by setting up an essentially circular plot. Disgusted with his life in New York David determines to break out, but even his desire to sail for Europe is premised on an eventual return to Rilda. And although he changes his experience geographically by going to London and Paris, socially his world stays the same since he sees familiar faces wherever he goes. The novel opens with the Westlakes locked into a compulsive cycle of parties and closes with them returning to the same routine. When *Parties* first appeared it was praised by Charles Demuth, Alfred Stieglitz and Gertrude Stein for being 'wholly lacking in the photography' perceived in his other novels.[12] And the critic Bruce Kellner rightly comments that the book seems to be 'made up of a series of vignettes, but the total effect is staggeringly cohesive'.[13] This cohesion is achieved by the reader's recognition of a repeated pattern.

The pattern is simultaneously maintained and diagnosed by the Westlakes who demonstrate an ironic self-awareness which blurs the rhetorical distinction between their comments and those of the anonymous narrator. The latter adopts the role of a detached and disenchanted observer. Similarly the Westlakes and a number of other characters display a capacity to stand aside from their own poses and mock them. But much of the claustrophobia of *Parties* grows out of the ineffectual nature of this mockery. Awareness does not result in any change in behaviour and the sequence continues implicitly beyond the ending of the novel. In that respect *Parties* looks forward to Thomas Pynchon's jaundiced view of New York party-going in the fifties.[14] For all the expert Freudian jargon Van Vechten's characters use about their own compulsions, they have no control over their own social habits because, as the narrator points out, 'it is impossible to persuade people not to go to a party in New York'.[15]

Van Vechten's main emphasis in this novel is on the dramatic potential of parties, on the conflicts and oppositions which emerge. These parties would therefore contrast strikingly with those of Hollywood which Van Vechten described in an article for *Vanity Fair* in 1927. He took pains to stress that, contrary to popular belief, there were no orgies, and insisted: 'there is a noticeable air of studied reserve observable at public functions'.[16] By the time he wrote his novel Van Vechten depicted a strikingly different world of social gossip where the parties are certainly not characterised by restraint. On the contrary, the general pursuit of excitement leads invariably to conflict. At one party, for instance, David's absence sharpens sexual jealousies between the women. Rilda expresses annoyance at Mrs Alonzo W. Syreno:

The woman is maddening, cried Rilda, maddening!
At least, Rosalie reminded her, she was invited to my house.

Steady, Rosalie, Siegfried adjured her. Rilda came with me.

What's up about David? inquired Simone Fly casually, sauntering up, cocktail in hand.

I think you all must be crazy, Mrs Alonzo W. Syreno cried, quite crazy. If I knew anything about David I wouldn't tell you. He wouldn't want me to, was her added inspiration.

Roy Fern emitted a growl of rage at this.

David is my friend, he protested.

He's everybody's friend, was Rilda's emendation.

My dear . . . The Gräfin offered Rilda her sympathy and her hand while Siegfried silently pressed her other hand.[17]

The alternation between conflict and a precarious maintenance of social decorum is typical of the party scenes in this novel. Here Van Vechten draws on the reader's memory by allowing the oppositions to play themselves out between wife (Rilda), would-be lover (Rosalie), actual lover (Mrs Alonzo W. Syreno), and male admirer. Ironically the only sarcastic comment made against David comes from his wife, and Van Vechten underlines the point by positioning Rilda between the Countess and her German lover. By suspending narrative comment, by playing one character's speech off against another's, and by using physical detail to give hints of sexual liaisons, Van Vechten succeeds in creating what one critic has called a 'modern tragedy of manners'.[18]

These group scenes reveal a constant dialectic between the individual and his or her social context. Houses in this novel are not important as homes or even really as visible testimony to their owner's wealth, but rather as potential minimal salons, as the settings for parties. The last gathering in the novel is an impromptu party which takes place at the Westlakes' apartment. David has obligingly left recipes for cocktails on his bar in anticipation of his visitors, the apartment being designed as a communal meeting-place at the expense of its domestic value. It is no accident that the Westlakes' son should emerge at this point in the novel – his only appearance – to plead via the guests for his parents to stop drinking, in other words to plead for the reestablishment of a family unit which has been lost.

Drink in a sense is the protagonist of *Parties*, manifesting itself in a whole range of ways as the novel progresses. It creates drunkenly surreal memories of an evening spree in the opening pages; it muffles the superego, allowing theoretically at least – far more open and impulsive behaviour; and it creates a new chic of cocktails. The more elaborate the drinks, the more successful the party. Van Vechten, however, never allows us to forget the economic and political system standing behind drink. Chapter 3 opens with a potted biography of Donald Bliss, the 'handsomest bootlegger in New York'. Ironically it follows a rags-to-riches pattern, but at every stage in this character's career he is involved in corruption. Unfortunately Bliss's appetite for women slows down his meteoric rise and he is moved out of politics into dealing in liquor. This information suggests a cynicism so endemic in the American political system that the reader is left no room to censure Van Vechten's characters. They are simply the product of conditions, the members of a city with a uniquely fluid population (pun intended), and perhaps for that reason compelled to live in an extended shifting present. Although Van Vechten's acquaintance Eleanor Perenyi claims that for him 'a party was like a chemical experiment in which the elements of the human personality can be observed in varying forms of action' the perspective in his novel is not quite as dispassionate as this suggests.[19] Van Vechten, like Waugh, locates a self-destructive impulse in his characters' life-style. *Parties* begins with David Westlake claiming to have killed a man. Fantasy turns real when this very man is shot in a Harlem dance-hall, after which David once again takes upon himself the burden of guilt.

Unlike their English counterparts, for Van Vechten and Scott Fitzgerald alike one importance of party scenes is defined by introductory lists of the consumables which reflect the parties' scales. Oddly in view of his reputation as a chronicler of the Jazz Age, Fitzgerald scarcely uses parties in his fiction before *The Great Gatsby* (1926). Early stories like 'May Day' (1920) and *The Beautiful and the Damned* (1922) concentrate on the impromptu gatherings at fashionable New York restaurants such as Child's or Delmonico's. In the latter novel these parties become a 'source of entertainment' for Anthony Patch and his wife, offering relief from the boredom of their married life. But *The Great Gatsby* refracts its party scenes through the novel's wide-eyed Midwestern narrator, Nick Carraway. It is the scale of his neighbour's social functions which fascinates him:

> Every Friday five crates of oranges and lemons arrived from a fruiterer in New York – every Monday these same oranges and lemons left his back door in a pyramid of pulpless halves . . .
> At least once a fortnight a corps of caterers came down with several hundred feet of canvas and enough coloured lights to make a Christmas tree of Gatsby's enormous garden. On buffet tables, garnished with glistening hors-d'œuvres, spiced baked hams crowded against salads of harlequin designs and pastry pigs and turkeys bewitched to a dark gold.[20]

Van Vechten stresses the exotic mixtures of drinks to reflect his society's pursuit of novelty. For Fitzgerald, however, the emphasis falls of course on quantity ('pyramid', 'corps', etc.) which has its own impact on the impressionable Nick. But there is also a qualitative change, as if Gatsby's parties are magical.

There are three main party scenes in *The Great Gatsby* which mark the phases in the growing acquaintance between narrator and hero. Nick

Carraway distinguishes himself from the majority of Gatsby's guests by stressing that he received an invitation. Usually 'people were not invited – they went there' and 'once there . . . they conducted themselves according to the rules of behaviour associated with an amusement park'.[21] The slightly formal language suggests that Nick is tacitly acting as a spokesman for disappearing social values. Where Van Vechten would not mention 'rules of behaviour' at all, Nick sadly notes the traces of a decorum (chauffeur's uniform, etc.) which has all but vanished, the sort of decorum codified in Emily Post's *Etiquette* (1922) which insists that 'a real garden party is as formal as a dinner of ceremony or a ball'.[22] Nick demonstrates his sense of formality by dressing carefully and apologising to Gatsby when he fails to recognise him. The dialectic between the individual and the group emerges here as a distinction Nick draws between his personal knowledge of Gatsby and his generic descriptions of the typical parties where many guests do not even meet the host. The second party scene at the beginning of Chapter 4 is one such passage, less a description than a list of guests which can only be composed retrospectively because Gatsby keeps open house. This list ironically blurs any clear distinctions between honest and criminal wealth and implies the collapse of the so-called 'code of a gentleman' which Emily Post devoted herself to prolonging. Gatsby's last party (described in Chapter 6) gradually foregrounds Daisy as a possible protagonist in a revived romance, and Gatsby's guests recede into irrelevance at this point.

If these parties form an enormously elaborate and expensive prelude to Gatsby's reunion with Daisy then his house could be taken as a carefully composed romantic setting. Nick implies as much in his excited expectations of drama when present at the parties. But then the house is described as a 'factual imitation of some Hotel de Ville in Normandy', i.e. as an imitation of public building, and throughout the parties there is a constant alternation between the public and the private, between group scenes and scenes containing two characters.[23] Gatsby's car becomes an 'omnibus' shuttling guests to and fro. Nick lists the names of these guests on an old railway timetable, stressing the fleeting nature of these parties. Gatsby's guests drop him as quickly as they take him up. The flux of these parties contrasts sharply with what Fitzgerald's narrator glosses as a Keatsian desire on Gatsby's part to snatch a romantic moment. Indeed this desire enables Nick to balance contradictory views of Gatsby (the personification of social grace as against the criminal, for instance) without attempting to reconcile them. *The Great Gatsby* repeatedly questions the interaction between host and guests, implying that Gatsby is treated as a convenience, a temporary source of social entertainment. It was not until *Tender is the Night* (1934) that Fitzgerald explored the elusive relation of host to guest in its full complexity, a relation so delicate that he presents it as an exercise in social magic.

WAUGH IN THE WASTELAND

When we turn to Evelyn Waugh we encounter a strikingly different con-
textualisation of the party scenes in *Vile Bodies* (1930) which embeds these
episodes in the historical circumstances of Britain during the twenties. Thus
there are unmistakable allusions to the working of the Defence of the Realm
Act, to the power of newspaper barons such as Lords Northcliffe and
Beaverbrook, and to the fashion for flying. These details distinguish the
novel's historical situation from that of the American fiction already considered. While the First World War is used as a point of reference in *Tender is
the Night* (although it does not justify the characters' nihilism as immediately
as Hemingway's *The Sun Also Rises*), it stands crucially behind the ethos of
Vile Bodies. While he was working on that novel Waugh wrote an article
diagnosing the predicament of his contemporaries. 'The War and the Younger Generation' (1929) explains: 'The real and lasting injury was caused, not
by danger, but by the pervading sense of inadequacy. Everything was a
"substitute" for something else, and there was barely enough of that. The
consequence is a generation of whom 950 in every thousand are totally
lacking in any sense of qualitative value.' The new-found freedom of the
postwar years meant that 'there was nothing left for the younger generation
to rebel against, except the widest conceptions of mere decency'[24] If this war
was a watershed to Waugh, the perception feeds into the novel unusually in
a series of fatalistic predictions that a Second World War will take place and
Vile Bodies concludes with a 'Happy Ending' set in the 'biggest battlefield in
the history of the world'. This spectacle of worldly destruction (we should
remember that in 1930 Waugh was received into the Catholic Church)
obviously draws on the Flanders trenches but to set up a summative image
of global emptiness. It is Waugh's wasteland, metaphorically drawing out the
gloomy implications of his preceding narrative.[25]

Waugh's 1929 article stresses a second major factor which finds expression
in his novel: the clash of styles between generations. Fitzgerald had noted a
similar process taking place in America. His obituary on the twenties, 'Echoes
of the Jazz Age' (1931) describes the hegemony of the 'generation which had
been adolescent during the confusion of the war' over those older and
younger than themselves: 'the sequel was like a children's party taken over
by the elders'.[26] In *The Great Gatsby*, however, the main struggle turns out
to be not a generational one, but a doomed attempt to halt the march of time.
And Van Vechten simply takes for granted that older characters might learn
from younger ones. Waugh stays with the generational issue because it gives
him a comic means of ridiculing the representatives of social status and
political power. Chapter 4 of *Vile Bodies* opens with a list of inherited titles
which collapses into bathos as their bearers are identified as gossip columnists.

In the same chapter Jane Brown gives an impromptu party for her new friends from the 'smart set' and it is only the next morning that we realise that it was held at 10 Downing Street. Withholding this information comically diminishes the setting to any old house and reduces the Prime Minister to a 'sweet old boy'. Assumptions of position and dignity are repeatedly undermined, as we shall also see in Wyndham Lewis, and Waugh constantly plays events off against official titles. Indeed the names of his characters (Lady Circumference, Miles Malpractice, etc.) implicitly locate his novel within a tradition of social comedy stretching back from Wilde to the Restoration dramatists. Lady Metroland offers a special case in that the *form* of her title suggests aristocratic estates while her actual name derives from a London Transport campaign to advertise the newly extended Metropolitan line on the London Underground. This incongruity recurs in all the relations between the younger and older characters who are separated by differences in dress, verbal idiom and lifestyle. As Malcolm Bradbury notes, 'the action happens largely among the younger generation, who bear the brunt of the new tension and are shown as intrinsically different from their parents . . . the divided generations form two sectors of value, separated in understanding and purpose'.[27] And this division further issues in a collapse of social hierarchy which is highlighted in the parties of Waugh and Wyndham Lewis. By contrast the endemic social fluidity of American society means that to a degree there is no hierarchy to collapse.

Vile Bodies opens with a ferry crossing the Channel which Martin Stannard has taken to represent a microcosm of English society, rightly identifying an area of reference broader than anything we have seen in Van Vechten or Fitzgerald.[28] After the passengers have cleared customs Waugh places the members of the 'Younger Set' in one railway carriage and gives them a collective voice. This is a crucial stratagem because, although Adam Fenwick-Symes and his girlfriend Nina appear to be the leading characters of the novel, the true protagonist is a volatile group, the younger social set. The method Waugh uses to represent the parties in this novel reinforces this point. In Chapter 6 Lady Metroland's soirée is the chief social event of the day and is depicted through a series of brief fragments which concentrate on a specific groups. As in Van Vechten, the effect is to deny any one group or character priority, and a montage is built up as if from fragments of overheard conversation. Waugh reduces narrative comment mainly to the clarification of gesture, movement and expression.[29] By juxtaposing different scenes – and therefore different perspectives – he allows an irony to emerge silently. The social business of this party, as distinct from Van Vechten's, is not drinking but observation. It is not enough to be simply present; one must be noticed. And Waugh weaves comic variations on this theme. For instance an 'unobtrusive man' with a black beard impresses two women with his bearing but arouses suspicion in Father Rothschild, the Jesuit observer and commentator. He jumps to the paranoid conclusion that he is a spy and unmasks him, only to discover that he is a gossip columnist in disguise. There is in effect a chain of observers who are themselves under observation and this is identified through the apparent discontinuity of one fragment from another. The writer who suggested this method to Waugh was Ronald Firbank, and influence too on Carl Van Vechten. Both novelists wrote appreciations of Firbank, Waugh particularly praising his combination of apparent inconsequentiality and skill: 'His later novels are almost wholly devoid of any attribution of cause to effect; there is the barest minimum of direct description; his compositions are built up, intricately and with a balanced alternation of the wildest extravagance and the most austere economy, with conversational *nuances*.'[30] Waugh praised Firbank for diverging from Victorian plot patterns and he too assembles fragmentary partial views to give a picture of a social situation.

· He does not, however, leave narrative sequence behind. A character near the beginning of the novel comments that 'everything's getting rather broken up' and scenic discontinuity helps to establish this condition of fracture. Chapter 8 juxtaposes an old-style town party with a party in an airship, extending the disparity between perspectives noted above. Because there is no communication between the two generations, the guests at the former envy the young, unaware of the total lack of gaiety in the dirigible. It is at this point that Waugh inserts a choric comment on a central theme of the novel:

> (. . . Masked parties, Savage parties, Victorian parties, Greek parties, Wild West parties, Russian parties, Circus parties, parties where one had to dress as somebody else, almost naked parties in St John's Wood, parties in flats and studios and houses and ships and hotels and night clubs, in windmills and swimming-baths, tea parties at school where one ate muffins and meringues and tinned crab, parties at Oxford where one drank brown sherry and smoked Turkish cigarettes, dull dances in London and comic dances in Scotland and disgusting dances in Paris – all that succession and repetition of massed humanity . . . Those vile bodies . . .).[31]

The comment within parentheses glosses a pursuit of novelty which incorporates the past and the present into a prolonged masquerade attempting to mask its sameness with novelty.[32]

This cycle of 'succession and repetition' is reinforced by the press and it is relevant to remember that Waugh numbered among his friends Tom Driberg who wrote a famous gossip column for the *Daily Express* (or *Daily Excess* as it appears in *Vile Bodies*) under the name William Hickey. In Waugh's novel these columnists have a crucial role to play in witnessing and then publicising the parties. Jane Brown's, for instance is reported under the title 'Midnight Orgies at No. 10': '*What must be the most extraordinary party of the little season took place in the small hours of this morning at No. 10 Downing Street*.[33] The superlatives in these accounts are obligatory and, although the reports are sometimes dictated over the telephone while the events are still in progress, they bear only a distorted relation to actuality. Waugh's ironies, a good deal more comprehensive than those of American contemporaries, here cut in at least three simultaneous directions: against the parties themselves, against the idiom of the reports; and against those readers who eagerly lap up those reports. The gap between press accounts and reality widens as one columnist reports all the actions the guests would not perform before he sticks his head in a gas oven. Adam takes over his role as 'Mr Chatterbox' and transforms his column into an increasingly bizarre series of fictions. The priority of event over report is completely reversed and Adam briefly becomes a capricious arbiter of social fashion, producing pieces on cripples and lunatics, and actually inventing characters like Imogen Quest, the 'most lovely and popular of the young married set': 'One day Imogen gave a party, the preparations for which occupied several paragraphs. On the following day Adam found his table deep in letters of complaint from gate-crashers who had found the house in Seamore Place untenanted.'[34] Absurdly the world of social gossip develops its own internal momentum and becomes a ludicrous system in its own right with 'producers' and 'consumers'.

Waugh's attitude to the party-going set is twofold. On the one hand he recognises their disgust at the inauthentic (hence their favourite epithet 'bogus'); on the other he mocks their capacity for delusion, fed by the press. In a 1932 article 'Why Glorify Youth?' he explained his purpose as follows: 'In the last year of that decade (the twenties) I wrote *Vile Bodies*, in which I attempted to summarise the chief features of those topsy-turvy years in which the younger generation succeeded in knocking the nonsense out of the attempts to sentimentalise them.'[35] Here he understates the extent to which the young are the victims of the novel's ironies, since *Vile Bodies* presents their social world as a closed cycle where inventions take on as much currency as reality, indeed become indistinguishable from it.

In contrasting Evelyn Waugh's fiction with that of Van Vechten and Fitzgerald it would be a gross mistake to ignore the ways in which American culture permeated British life in the twenties. *Vile Bodies* recognises this influence from American movies and revivalism, to mention only two examples. The religious leader Aimee Semple McPherson is parodied as Mrs Melrose Ape, and even the title of the novel was used as the heading of Waugh's review of Edward Van Every's *Sins of New York* (1930) – a series of selections from the *Police Gazette*.[36] Waugh did not discover Fitzgerald's novels until after the Second World War but he actually met Van Vechten in 1930 at the Eiffel Tower restaurant in London. He contributed eagerly to the latter's autograph collection, describing him none too originally as a 'playboy of the western world'.[37] Indeed there is an implication in Waugh's diary entry of a certain familiarity with Van Vechten's fiction.

PERSPECTIVES ON DISORDER

The Eiffel Tower was also a popular restaurant with the fourth of our main novelists – Wyndham Lewis. One measure of Lewis's importance is the fact that by the late twenties he had worked out a consistent theory of the comic which applied in his fiction of the same period. The 1917 essay 'Inferior Religions' sketches out a connection between an observer and the spectacle under observation, a spectacle which will estrange other human figures so strikingly from the registering consciousness that they will become 'puppets'. 'The Meaning of the Wild Body' (1927) further draws out the implications of this position: 'The root of the Comic is to be sought in the sensations resulting from the observations of a *thing* behaving like a person. But from that point of view all men are necessarily comic: for they are all *things*, as physical bodies, behaving as *persons*'.[38] In Part III of *Tarr* (1918, revised 1928) Lewis introduces the German artist Kreisler into a party held in the Bonnington Club, Paris. Kreisler supplies an external and hostile perspective on the event from which he feels excluded by humble social origins but Lewis also reverses the perspective on to him creating a comedy of mutual incomprehension. Kreisler brings about a sexual and anarchic disruption of the scene – for that reason he is a 'satyric form' in more senses than one – and he tries unsuccessfully to force the event to a violent climax. He has a cutting edge that Van Vechten's German outside, the Gräfin, lacks, and that Van Vechten's 'so-it-goes' text eschews.[39]

This party only plays a relatively minor part in *Tarr* whereas *The Roaring Queen* (written around 1930, set up in proof in 1936, but not published until 1973) takes a weekend party as a means of satirising the London literary world. The ruler of this world in little (he is called 'dictator', 'Destiny' and less flattering terms in the course of the novel) is Samuel Shodbutt, a thinly disguised version of Arnold Bennett, and his party reflects a kind of feudal hierarchy where power converges on his unique privilege of deciding which work shall receive the Book of the Week award. This time Lewis does not refract the action through a specified character but still uses an alienating method when describing Shodbutt's house guests:

> Soon Beverley Chase was full of a portentous crowd enough, to be sure, as to the outward man – shuffling exotics and high-stepping stockbrokers it would seem to any Plain Reader brought there to gaze her fill. It was a mixed crowd of great critics

and great authors, leering at the sight of each other as if each and all had been
somewhat improper jokes, and moving up and down in animated knots; congrat-
ulating each other upon everything. . . .[40]

Lewis refuses the tradition of the country house party by denying Beverley
Chase any historical grandeur, and carefully contrasts his perspective with that
of an impressionable 'Plain Reader', stressing externalities of style as if they
masked an inner void. As the crowd implicitly emerges as a mutual admiration
society, the respect notionally signalled by the epithet 'great' drains off into
ridicule. The party gives Lewis an opportunity for summarising a whole
section of London society, which he does partly through such ironic
generalising comment as in the passage above and partly by segmenting the
action into little scenes where the guests' antagonisms break through social
decorum. We have already encountered cases of the latter method; Lewis's
application exploits to the full the oppositions between and within such scenic
fragments. A similar technique is used for more complex effects in Lewis's
satirical masterpiece *The Apes of God* (1930).

This novel brings its satire to a climax in an enormously extended and
intricate party scene which occupies the last 300 pages of the novel. Two
preliminary parties have specific functions in the preparations for this major
set piece. In the first of these a tea-party attempts to recapture the aristocratic
decorum of the prewar period, but Lewis establishes a perspective through
Dan Boleyn which dehumanises the guests into mechanical playthings: 'And
as he looked at Jimmie he might have been regarding one of those life-size
dolls, with mechanically revolving eyes, made for the children of the rich.'[41]
Before Dan's perspective can carry too much authority Lewis makes it clear
that the former was in fact worrying about his aching feet and then has the
host ask Don if he is a manufactured doll.

Lord Osmund's Lenten Party, or 'Lenten Freak Party' as the gossip
columnists call it, is held in Osmund's country house (a hastily converted
Norman grange) and represents a gathering together of the London art world
in an enormously elaborate masquerade. It is thus a summative episode marking
the climax of the novel and the culmination of Boleyn's apprenticeship. It is
also demonstrating the last stages of an aristocratic tradition in decline. The
Osmunds represent the attenuated final generation of their family and their
house reflects their doomed attempts to straddle the past and the present where
the spoils of empire (African masks, etc.) jostle for wall-space with Modernist
paintings. Because the festivities work on such a large scale Lewis exploits the
spatial divisions of the house to separate off different scenes as if they were
taking place in a drama. The analogy is made quite explicit (the second section,
for instance, is called 'The Players Solus') and it differentiates Lewis's method
from that discussed in Van Vechten and Waugh. There the rapid cutting

between details or individuals within the larger scene carried its own ironies of fragmentation. Now Lewis uses each scene not merely to show a part of the whole, but to show the whole in a different light. Although the scenes are sometimes linked by narrative connections (a character going from one to the other, an event in one having consequences in another, etc.), the sequence is cumulative rather than narrative in impetus, applying a Cubist principle of assembling different perspectives on British society as a whole within the same work of art – perspectives which in this case reverse the conventional priorities of surface and inner substance.

Late in 1930 Lewis published *Satire and Fiction*, partly an ironic view of the reception of *The Apes of God* and partly an exposition of the method underlying the novel. He declares: 'In writing the only thing that interests me is *the shell*. It's the actions and the appearance of people that I am concerned with, not the "stream of consciousness" of any "mysterious" invisible within.'[42] Waugh enthusiastically reviewed this book, emphasising that 'no novelist and very few intelligent novel readers can afford to neglect this essay'.[43]

The Apes of God creates characters who seem to be *all* shell, but Lewis also uses appearances as a springboard for speculative comment. Thus the kitchen is presented as the hellish underbelly of the party and the leavings from the food triggers off an analogy between the guests and maggots crawling through a 'world of bowels'. Lewis repeatedly takes bearings in these sections from Pope and Swift, and like them exploits grossly physical imagery to insist on the inseparability of art from its social context. So in the library Blackshirt (a man dressed as a Fascist) dissects contemporary novels, attacking the contemporary taste which welcomes them. In an earlier scene Lewis mimes the social élitism of the party as the aristocratic hosts try to shut out plebeian masses pressing to gain entry: 'A picture of a world swarming with the coarse hordes of Demos was at once evoked, with side by side, in dazzling contrast, another picture – that of an intensely exclusive, aristocratic family – shrinking from publicity.'[44] This political symbolism echoes in the arguments between Zagreus and Blackshirt who fascistically announces the former's obsolescence: 'we will have no more "geniuses" '.[45]

An entropic collapse of hierarchies takes place throughout the party. The Osmunds' claim to aristocratic status is presented as a collective delusion; the military caste is mocked out of existence with the exposure of a bogus naval commander; and the cherished national figure of John Bull is burlesqued. Indeed, so many national references are parodic that Lewis implies the rupturing and therefore irrelevance of tradition to the postwar world. All potential authority figures are undermined: even Zagreus, whose final conjuring tricks are disrupted by the Blackshirts. There is a recurring motif of references to falling, a collapse into uniformity, and decadence; and the novel's stress on violence culminates in a coda briefly depicting the national strike as a final breakdown in social order. Indeed, there is a general drift in all the party scenes discussed here towards disorder. The narrator of Aldous Huxley's *Antic Hay* (1923) declares at one point 'the party disintegrated', using the term 'party' in the Peacockian sense of a group rather than a social event, and equivalent breakdowns occur in the fiction of Huxley's contemporaries, whether it is a climax of drunkenness (Van Vechten) or a 'many-keyed commotion' (Fitzgerald). [46] It was Evelyn Waugh who actually stated the tendentious relation of their fiction to the times. In his article 'Fan-Fare' (1946) he argues that because satire depends on a relatively stable society with homogeneous standards it has become irrelevant to contemporary fragmentation: 'The artist's only service to the disintegrated society of today is to create little independent systems of order of his own'.[47] It is because of this perceived predicament that these novelists, each with their own national emphasis, deny the reader any fixed view or perspective.

The only certainty appears to be death, which is constantly present at the masquerade. Henry Green's Miss Fellowes carries with her a dead pigeon, wrapped in brown paper, as a grotesque *memento mori*. Van Vechten's Simone Fly, whose chalk-white face resembles a 'gay Death', drifts languidly through the novel reminding the party-goers of their ultimate fate. Gatsby's final party sets in train a series of events which will lead to the violent killing of Myrtle Wilson by Gatsby's car and the equally violent death of Gatsby himself, after which point a symbolic dust settles on his house. Waugh's title *Vile Bodies* derives ultimately from the service for the Burial of the Dead where death is a transformation from the earthly 'vile body' into the 'glorious body' of Christ. However, because his novel blocks off spiritual transcendence, the allusion ironically empties the worldly of value without implying an alternative. Most grimly of all, Lewis's *The Apes of God* concludes with the rattle of Death the Drummer echoing along the London streets in a final choric comment on the novel's earlier 'festivities'.

NOTES

1. Jackson R. Bryer, (ed.) *F. Scott Fitzgerald: The Critical Reception* (New York, 1978), p. 224.

2. Lois Palken, Rudnick, *Mabel Dodge Luhan: New Woman, New Worlds* (Albuquerque, 1984), p. 75.

3. Djuna Barnes, *New York*, (ed.) Alyce Barry (Los Angeles, 1989), p. 242.

4. F. Scott Fitzgerald, *The Crack-Up* (Harmondsworth, 1986), p. 28.

5. Frederick Lewis Allen, *Only Yesterday* (New York, 1959), p. 175.

6. Douglas Goldring, *The Nineteen Twenties* (London, 1945), p. 225.

7. Bruce Kellner, *Carl Van Vechten and the Irreverent Decades* (Norman, Oklahoma, 1968), p. 158.

8. Carl Van Vechten, *Parties* (New York, 1977), p. 194.

9. Gorham Munson, *The Awakening Twenties* (Baton Rouge, 1985), pp. 71–2.

10. Carl Van Vechten, *Parties*, p. 79.

11. Ibid., p. 79.

12. Bruce Kellner (ed.), *Letters of Carl Van Vechten* (New Haven, 1987), p. 118.

13. Ibid., p. 246.

14. His chosen analogies for the activities of the Whole Sick Crew in *V.* (1963) are mechanical: 'The lights in the living room would go out one by one, Schoenberg's quartets (complete) would go on the record player / changer, and repeat and repeat.' (Thomas Pynchon, *V.* (London, 1978) p. 57).

15. Carl Van Vechten, *Parties*, p. 59.

16. 'Hollywood Parties', *Vanity Fair* (June 1927), p. 47.

17. Van Vechten, *Parties*, pp. 151–2.

18. Kellner, *Carl Van Vechten* pp. 245–6.

19. Eleanor Perenyi, 'Carl Van Vechten', *Yale Review* 77, iv (1988): p. 53.

20. F. Scott Fitzgerald, *The Great Gatsby* (Harmondsworth, 1968), p. 45.

21. Ibid., p. 47.

22. Emily Post, *Etiquette* (New York, 1941) p. 232. Between 1922 and 1937 this work went through an astonishing forty-three editions.

23. Scott Fitzgerald, *The Great Gatsby*, p. 11.

23. Scott Fitzgerald, *Tender is the Night* (Harmondsworth, 1982), p. 44.

24. Donat Gallagher (ed.), *The Essays, Articles and Reviews of Evelyn Waugh* (London, 1983), p. 62.

25. Rebecca West perceptively places *Vile Bodies* within the 'literature of disillusionment' since the First World War (Martin Stannard (ed.), *Evelyn Waugh: The Critical Heritage* (London, 1984, p. 107).

26. Scott Fitzgerald, *The Crack-Up*, p. 11.

27. Malcolm Bradbury, *Evelyn Waugh* (Edinburgh and London, 1964), pp. 46–7.

28. Martin Stannard, *Evelyn Waugh: The Early Years 1903–39* (London, 1986), p. 197.

29. In 1930 Waugh contrasted the economic use of dialogue by the moderns, where excerpts take on significance in relation to the structure of the plot, with the more wasteful practices of the Victorians (' "Tess" – As a "Modern" See it', *Evening Standard*, 17 January, 1930, p. 7).

30. Gallagher, op. cit. pp. 57–8.

31. Evelyn Waugh, *Vile Bodies* (Harmondsworth, 1951), p. 123.

32. The socialite Polly Cockpurse in *A Handful of Dust* (1934), however, designs her party to be an 'accurate replica of all the best parties she had been to in the last year' (London, 1979, p. 55).

33. Waugh, *Vile Bodies*, p. 59.

34. Ibid., *Vile Bodies*, pp. 114, 115.

35. Gallagher, op. cit., p. 126.

36. Ibid., pp. 99–101.

37. In his autobiography, *A Little Learning* (1964), Waugh records his interest in *The Great Gatsby*; Michael Davie, *The Diaries of Evelyn Waugh* (Harmondsworth, 1986), pp. 316–17.

38. Wyndham Lewis, *The Complete Wild Body*, (ed.) Bernard Lafourcade (Santa Barbara, 1982), p. 158.

39. Wyndham Lewis, *Tarr* (Harmondsworth, 1982), p. 153.

40. Wyndham Lewis, *The Roaring Queen*, (ed.) Walter Allen (London, 1973), p. 58.

41. Ibid., p. 214.

42. Quoted in Jeffrey Meyers, *The Enemy: A Biography of Wyndham Lewis* (London, 1980), p. 159.

43. Gallagher, op. cit., p. 102.

44. Wyndham Lewis, *The Apes of God*, p. 506.

45. Ibid., p. 496.

46. Aldous Huxley, *Antic Hay* (Harmondsworth, 1960), p. 66.

47. Gallagher, op. cit., p. 304.

FURTHER READING

Ronald Blythe, *The Age of Illusion* (London, 1963).

F. Scott Fitzgerald, *The Great Gatsby* (New York, 1925).

Douglas Goldring, *The Nineteen Twenties* (London, 1945).

Frederick J. Hoffman, *The 20s* (revised edn; New York, 1965).

Wyndham Lewis, *The Apes of God* (London, 1930).

Gorham Munson, *The Awakening Twenties* (Baton Rouge, 1985).

Carl Van Vechten, *Parties* (New York, 1930).

Evelyn Waugh, *Vile Bodies* (London, 1930).

CHAPTER SEVEN

American Variations on a British Theme: Giles Cooper and Edward Albee

Peter Egri

Edward Albee's reworking (1967) of Giles Cooper's play *Everything in the Garden* (1962) was given diametrically divergent interpretations. While it was called 'one of the. . . . most outrageous cop outs in recent theatrical history',[1] it was also referred to as 'the first important American play of the season'.[2] For Michael E. Rutenberg, the author of a full-length monograph on Albee, '*Garden* will probably be the most successful of the Albee adaptations . . . Albee has added and changed just enough of the structure to warrant the new play's examination.'[3]

Albee himself at first simply considered the Americanisation of Cooper's work as a commercial commission, and did not even wish to have his name put on the theatre bill. But in the course of remodelling the play he caught himself in the act of recomposing, rather than simply adapting, the drama. In his own words, 'Something happened, and by the time I was finished with my work there was hardly a word left of the original . . . Cooper's play became a catalyst and set me to working my own variations on his theme . . . the play . . . is not an adaptation of another man's work but a much more intense collaboration.'[4]

A comparative close reading of Cooper's and Albee's versions may show that the American dramatist has not only transplanted but has also considerably transformed the British playwright's work. In composing his American variations on a British theme, Albee has also achieved a thorough-going reinterpretation of his model. His transformation of the original – despite parallel details of incident and accident – affects not only external circumstances but also internal qualities: the very focus and form of the play. His reassessment is, in fact, an Americanisation.

He has kept the framework of his model – as he has in his dramatisations of Carson McCuller's novella *The Ballad of the Sad Café* (1963), James Purdy's novel *Malcolm* (1965) or Vladimir Nabokov's novel *Lolita* (1980–81)[5] – but his idiosyncratic fingerprint is nowhere more recognisable than in retouching and reshaping Cooper's *Everything in the Garden*, where Albee did not have to leave his own dramatic medium, and so could use directly his own theatrical experience ranging from *The Zoo Story* (1958), *The Death of Bessie Smith* (1959) and *The Sandbox* (1959) to *The American Dream* (1960), *Who's Afraid of Virginia Woolf?* (1961–62), *Tiny Alice* (1964) and *A Delicate Balance* (1966).

Though no part of the *oeuvre* of a world-famous dramatist, Cooper's *Everything in the Garden* is more than a mere springboard for Albee; it is a remarkable play in its own right. It was first presented by the Royal Shakespeare Theatre Company at the Arts Theatre in London on 13 March 1962, and it was shown by Michael Codron at the Duke of York's Theatre in London on 16 May 1962. First performed at the Plymouth Theatre in New York City on 16 November 1967, and published in 1968, Albee's version was not only based on Cooper's play; it was also dedicated to the memory of the British playwright. The printed acknowledgement is not simply a statement required by law; it is also an expression of personal warmth prompted by appreciation of a playwright who, by British standards, was experimental, specialising as he did in 'the exploration of strange emotional states on the margin of human experience, sometimes with strongly macabre overtones and generally on the surface at least, in terms of comedy.'[6] The comments of John Russell Taylor could apply to Albee, and demonstrate the common ground between the two playwrights. The commonality makes all the more striking the fact that Albee, as American, was impelled radically to alter Cooper's text.

THE AMERICANISATION OF LOCALE; FUSION OF THE REAL AND UNREAL

The first set of differences between Cooper's and Albee's versions appears with description of the stage set. Cooper's representation of the sitting-room of a British suburban house is relatively long; Albee's presentation of its American counterpart is considerably shorter. Cooper lists a number of objects (a television set, magazines, just a few books, the absence of pictures in the room and the presence of playing-fields at the bottom of the garden) which constitute a milieu determining and characterising people; Albee cuts these out and concentrates on dramatically functional detail (a lawnmower, empty packets of cigarettes, etc.). Cooper's emphasis on the environment sometimes leads to a kind of phrasing which not only speaks to an actor or director but also to a potential reader: '*It is a fine evening in late April though cool enough for a fire to be burning in the grate.*'[7] Albee has deleted the fire, the grate and the narrative turn of '*though cool enough*', and has restricted his stage instructions to a dramatically necessary minimum.

The practical lack of stage directions in Sophocles and Shakespeare indicates autonomous characters who create their conditions and dominate their surroundings even if in the last resort, at the peak of the tragic or comic conflict, they cannot disregard and avoid what makes them fall or err. The abundance of factual detail in the scene descriptions of the Ibsen – Shaw – Hauptmann – O'Neill period suggests the domination of circumstances over characters even if they make an effort to oppose them. While Cooper's initial description of an aggressively normal set links him with the naturalist – realist tradition Albee's sketchy set signals a provisional, playful and imaginative disregard of heavy determinism which the characters are exposed to but – from moment to moment – try to dodge and to suspend. The dramatic situation in Albee is an inheritance from Cooper. Its treatment, however, is different.

The difference is dramatically expressed not only by the substantial extenuation, the breaking up and thinning down in Albee of the thick crust of the objective environment, but also by the reinterpretation of whatever has been left of that environment. Albee not only excises a number of objects but also changes their character. A case in point is the lawnmower which in Cooper's description is a motor-mower heard going to and fro on the grass of the garden, but in Albee's presentation is a hand-mower heard *and* seen through the glass door of the sunroom. Since the protagonists of Albee's drama, Richard and Jenny (called, with American informality, by their first names even when they first appear), are obviously better off than are the main characters of Cooper's play, Bernard and Jenny Acton (introduced to the audiences and readers, with British reserve, by their forenames and surnames), it is unlikely that the American couple could not afford what the British couple could, and that Richard should only dream about a power mower (neatly ironised by the mumbling nursery rhyme of its name), while Bernard is day-dreaming about a king-size motor-mower, a real Monarch (also ironised by the royal connotations of its trade mark). Richard, in fact, complains that he is the only natural-born citizen east of the Rockies who has not got a power mower.[8] Cooper builds his world on actual reality. Albee, in the American tradition – O'Neill was the first examplar – anchors his on the border-line between what is likely and unlikely, and what is real and unreal.

The reality and unreality of Albee's initial scene is simultaneously increased by doubling, as it were, the visible space of the stage. The audience is watching Jenny in the foreground frame of the stage, while Jenny is watching Richard in the background frame of the glass doors which serve as a 'picture window'.[9] She is in an immediate theatrical space, he is in a mediated, withdrawn region. As Richard passes the picture window, mows, stops, mops, mows again, and cannot hear what Jenny tells him, he gains a queer, mechanical and mario-nette-like quality. Communication is difficult. Communion is doubtful.

The fusion of the real and unreal is a characteristic feature of Albee's plays written both before and after *Everything in the Garden*. If a work of art is basically a sensuous value judgement, then 'the substitution of artificial for real values'[10] may logically lead to the absurd merger of the real and the unreal (Mommy's beige or wheat-coloured little hat, Grandma's neatly wrapped and tied boxes and Day-Old Cake, a bundle or bumble of joy in *The American Dream*; the death of the fantasy child in *Who's Afraid of Virginia Woolf?*; the implications and consequences of Harry's and Edna's fear in *A Delicate Balance*; the cube in *Box* and the incongruously patterned yet ingeniously counter-pointed stylistic stereotypes in *Quotations from Chairman Mao Tse-tung*). Richard's hand-mower in *Everything in the Garden* is a link in this chain. Bernard's motor-mower is just a tool.

EXPOSITION: THE AMERICANISATION OF STAKES, RISKS AND DIMENSIONS. PROSTITUTION AS A SYMBOL OF SOCIAL STATUS

As the plays progress, differences increase. The exposition in Cooper's drama ranges over the whole of the first act, while in Albee's play it only covers the first scene of the first act: Cooper presents the milieu in more minute detail, whereas Albee builds the plot more dynamically.

The first section of the exposition reveals the narrow financial position of the protagonists. Jenny in Cooper, with a touch of sentimentality, saves the silver paper in cigarette packets in order to decorate her room with it at a party or a ball, while Jenny in Albee, with American practical common sense, collects coupons to save money.[11]

The second section of the exposition concerns Jenny's meeting a procuress for a high-class brothel. In keeping with his emphasis on the psychic gravitational pull of the environment, Cooper throws into relief the easy stages through which Jenny is transformed from a respectable housewife into a part-time prostitute. Being short of money and a keen gardener, and wishing to help her husband who is also a passionate gardener, she puts an advertise-ment in the local paper indicating that she is ready to take a part-time job. She gives her phone number, and Leonie Pimosz, the Polish pander, loses no time in phoning her and calling at her flat. After all, as her name may suggest, she has the relentless force of a lion, she is shrewd, secretive, and sufficiently impudent to claim that 'Nothing is disgusting, unless you are disgusted'.[12] Since it is Bernard who answers the phone when Leonie is telephoning, and Jenny knows that her husband is opposed to her taking any job, she lies to Bernard that a dressmaker is giving her a ring, and so she becomes Leonie's accomplice before she has even met her. When she does meet her, Leonie offers Jenny fifty pounds. Jenny refuses to take the money, and Leonie, with the gesture of Nastasya Filippovna in Dostoevsky's *The Idiot*, throws the bills into the fire. While, however, Nastasya thus refuses to be bought, Leonie's strategy is to try to buy Jenny. At first Jenny suggests that Leonie had better leave her home, but when Leonie starts flinging another bundle of notes into the fire, Jenny is tempted to take the money as an advance of salary. The job is not difficult at all, Jenny is only supposed to work in the afternoons, the place (in Wimpole Street) seems to be respectable, the fee (twenty-five guineas each time) generous, and the clients are all gentlemen. For some time the nature of the job is unclear, but then the penny drops and Jenny orders Leonie out of her home.

Leonie, however, is not offended, tells her that one of Jenny's friends has already undertaken the job, offers Jenny a cigarette which she badly needs and automatically accepts, though immediately throws away. Jenny's resistance is gradually weakening. She may tell the police but then Leonie would have to admit how Jenny has approached her through advertisement. So Jenny does not summon the police. Leonie gives her time to think the matter over, asks her to telephone her, establishes her superiority by warning her not to call her before ten o'clock in the morning, leaves Jenny's home peacefully, and Jenny picks up the bills from the floor. After all, it is money. She locks it up in a drawer, and takes her husband out to dinner.

The *chief* motive underlying Jenny's choice is not voluptuous inconstancy or capricious coquetry or inexperienced levity as is the case with Cressida in Shakespeare's *Troilus and Cressida*. Nor is it poverty, the plight of Mrs Warren in her early years in Shaw's *Mrs Warren's Profession* and the predicament of Anna in O'Neill's *Anna Christie*. Nor is it greed, the propelling force in Mrs Warren's later career or in Leda's attitude in O'Neill's *The Calms of Capricorn*. Nor is it the momentary excitement of a cheap, if lucrative, adventure as it is with the nameless Woman in Miller's *Death of a Salesman*. It is not even pathological disintegration of the personality as it appears to be in the case of Blanche in Tennessee Williams's *A Streetcar Named Desire*. Jenny's decision is fundamentally motivated by the garden as a symbol of social and financial status.[13] This is where Cooper's originality lies in the conception and elaboration of *Everything in the Garden*; and this is the leitmotif which caught Albee's ironic attention.

In the exposition of his play, however, Albee traces Cooper's dramatic blueprint with a difference. He removes Leonie's Jewish background, deletes her concentration camp experience, obliterates her Polish nationality, does away with her uneducated, racy and foreign accent, makes her English, and rechristens her Mrs Toothe, a tag-name with a different connotation. In this way Mrs Toothe's profession ceases to be a matter external to middle-class life, and the conflict becomes internalised, generalised and sharpened. Accordingly, she is no longer Cooper's *'squat, square figure'*, *'an extraordinary creature'*[14] but 'an elegantly dressed, handsome lady, 50 or so', [15] as she would usually appear. She would appeal to people of good society where everybody is 'pleasant-looking' (like Richard and his neighbour, Jack), 'nice-looking' (like Roger, Richard's son), and 'attractive' [16] (like Jenny), to the repeated point of patterned parody. Where Cooper had made the madam a bizarre figure, Albee made her a disturbingly homogenous part of society. The Anglicisation of the character amounted to an Americanisation of theme. Albee himself offered an additional reason for changing Polish Leonie Pimosz into British Mrs Toothe: 'I wanted a symbol of something that Americans would be terribly impressed by. Since Americans *are* terribly impressed by money and by the English, it seems that the offering of money should come from the British.'[17]

The Americanisation of Cooper's theme involves not only a change of place (from the outskirts of London to the suburb of an American city) but also a raising of the stakes: Mrs Toothe throws on the burning logs of the fireplace a thousand dollars rather than fifty pounds; Jenny is supposed to get a hundred dollars rather than twenty-five guineas for an afternoon, Richard is a research chemist, while Bernard, his counterpart in Cooper, is employed as a clerk at a firm making office furniture. In Albee, Jenny's admirer, Jack, is a rich painter who is going to leave more than three million dollars to the couple and can afford making irreverent, if irrelevant, remarks about the colours of Jenny's panties, while Jack in Cooper makes his living by contributing to fashion magazines and drawing strip cartoons.

In Albee's drama Jenny's trapping by the brothel-keeper is a less transitional and more abrupt matter than it is in Cooper's play. The American dramatist has cut out much of the British playwright's circumstantial evidence (including references to the pimp's past and drinking habits as well as to Jenny's advertisement), and has replaced Cooper's often understated conversations by more direct, incisive and dynamic dialogue. [18]

Albee also makes the dramatic texture more closely-knit by focusing the leading motif of the garden as a symbol of social status more emphatically, and finishes his exposition with Richard wondering about the cost of a greenhouse.

THE AMERICANISATION OF FORM; FROM INCONGRUITY TO ABSURDITY

The imbroglio or intrigue phase of the plot presents the arrival by post of a package (containing £198 in Cooper and $4.900 in Albee) which leads to the husband's discovery of the wife's profession (Act II in Cooper and Act I, scene ii, in Albee), and a big celebration and party which reveals the fact that all the wives are involved in the business with the connivance of all the husbands, [19] who, when the police have found out about the brothel, cooperate with the madam in finding a no less lucrative but safer and more appropriate place (the bulk of Act III in Cooper and of Act II in Albee).

The culmination or crisis point of the action comes when Jack, who knows too much and, when drunk, talks more than desirable, is murdered in the room and buried in the garden (*Everything in the Garden*). In Cooper's play it is Jenny whose warning 'Don't let him go!'[20] triggers a series of unavoidable actions leading to Jack's death. In Albee's drama it is the madam's 'Stop him' [21] which starts the fatal act. In Albee the conflict is sharper: it is in the madam's presence that Jack identifies Mrs Toothe as a brothel-keeper he knew in London, and her 'He'll talk' is 'a *command*',[22] just as her 'You must make him be quiet' is the order of '*a commander*'.[23]

The denouement or solution section of the plot shows the way in which the members of good society, after the shock of the murder, are reconciled – albeit sulkily – to the state of affairs (the rest of Act III in Cooper and of Act II in Albee).

It is remarkable that before finally resigning themselves to having participated in an act of murder, both Bernard and Richard suggest that the police ought to be informed. In Cooper's play Jenny rejects her husband's idea with her 'Don't be absurd'.[24] It is at this point that Cooper's sense of incongruity comes closest to Albee's view. Cooper's casual insight is, in fact, the American dramatist's starting point and vantage point. It is the recognition of the fact that in a world where artificial values are substituted for real ones, absurdity prevails.[25] But exactly because Albee takes this reverse situation for granted, he does not need to formulate its absurdity in a single admonishing sentence (which, absurdly enough, makes the right appear absurdly wrong). It is the entire form of his whole play which conveys the sense of absurdity. So in the course of rewriting Cooper's drama, Albee cut out Jenny's absurd reference to an alleged absurdity and made Mrs Toothe prove to everybody present how dangerously unfeasible Richard's idea to call the police was.

A play of this kind is very difficult to finish. Cooper, in fact, experimented with two endings. His first idea was to make the actor playing the part of Bernard revolt against his role. This 'Pirandellian dodge'[26] openly confronted ideal with reality, but later Cooper found this solution was disturbing and discarded the idea. In Cooper's second (and final) ending Bernard and Jenny sink back to their ordinary life and bury their remorse in a routine conversation about pipe-cleaners and keeping up the garden of the new brothel. 'Ours must look like all the others',[27] Jenny concludes. This is a fine and convincing ending which corresponds to Cooper's general concept about the deterministic power of external circumstances. It makes the author's indictment indirect.

Albee seems to have adopted, adapted, developed, changed and reversed both of Cooper's solutions. His first ending is Cooper's quiet acquiescence. What Mrs Toothe has to say to Jenny and Richard about the place in the garden where – along with the cesspool line – Jack has been buried can be considered the equivalent of Cooper's second conclusion: 'The grass will grow over; the earth will be rich, and soon – eventually – everything in the garden . . . will be as it was. You'll see.'[28]

Albee, however, appears to have been dissatisfied with such a peaceful, if ironical, solution at the end of such a violent play, and makes the otherwise dead Jack return in dirty clothes and with sod in his hair to draw the conclusion, speaking about himself as somebody who *was*, in the past tense. At this point of the plot he is an 'Absurd Person Singular', to quote and adapt the title of Alan Ayckbourn's play. Since Jack now is neither alive nor a ghost but a *persona* standing for the author's idea, ideal and ironical position, he clearly corresponds to Bernard rebelling against his part. Is Jack's resurrection dramatically acceptable?

The answer to the question cannot be given in terms of everyday likelihood. The problem is a matter of artistic plausibility, of how far Albee has been able to create a dramatic medium in which such a solution is organic. Not only has Albee used the traditional dramatic structure of exposition, imbroglio, culmination and denouement, crystallised by Sophocles, dynamised by Shakespeare, crossbred with an analytical research of the past by Ibsen and Shaw, embedded and blurred in a more or less deterministic milieu by Hauptmann and O'Neill, and pointed and simplified in their well-made plays by Scribe, Sardou, Pinero, Jones, Boucicault and Belasco. Albee has also *relativised* this structure. Jack's return after his death is no less a corroboration and relativisation of the dramatic climax of his murder than is George's announcement of the death of the imaginary son in *Who's Afraid of Virginia Woolf?* The simultaneous use, misuse and abuse of the dramatic tradition results in an ingenious fusion of a realistic framework and an absurdist texture which characterises Albee's dramatic form[29] and, arguably, has something to do with classic American literary-critical assertions that American texts are more often than not open-ended. Hence Cooper's importance for Albee: Cooper has provided his with the traditional frame which he could adopt and adapt, use and change, follow and reinterpret at the same time. Albee's difficulties in weaving a dramatic plot and building a firm structure in the traditional sense *after* his adaptations (in, for instance, *All Over* 1975, *Listening* 1976, *Counting the Ways* 1977 or *The Lady from Dubuque* (1978–79) point in the same direction.

For all these reasons, the dramatic validity of Jack's unexpected and grotesquely absurd resurrection at the end of Albee's *Everything in the Garden* largely depends on how persistently the American dramatist has been able to combine the adoption and relativisation of dramatic tradition as he found it embodied in the British playwright's work. Scenic and reading evidence shows that Albee has, in fact, been doing this throughout his play.

A comparison of dialogue in Cooper and Albee points this up. In Cooper's play Jenny defends her wish to take a job by a timid reference to Strindberg. She says she would like to be a useful person rather than a mere slave in the house like 'that woman in that play'[30] by Strindberg. This is no more than a thematic element in a casual and natural conversation. With Albee the corresponding dialogue also seems to be real and actual, but at the same time is also repetitively ritualistic,[31] it expresses quick and abrupt changes of mood from tender feelings to savage disagreement, and it may lead to sheer absurdity, as it does in Richard's emphatic statement to Jenny: 'You're up to hock in your eyebrows . . . (*Realises what he has said, tries to fix it, retaining dignity*) . . . *up* in hock to your . . . *in* hock up to your eyebrows, and why!'[32] Undercutting pathos by bathos and quarrelling in patterned 'rounds' relativises the difference between sense and nonsense, raises the Strindbergian element from a thematic to a formal level, and creates a dramatic atmosphere of conversational absurdity which is latent in Strindberg's *The Dance of Death* and becomes overt in Durrenmatt's wittily parodistic *Play Strindberg* or Albee's *Who's Afraid of Virginia Woolf?* The dialogue in Albee's *Everything in the Garden* uses the element of absurdity not to destroy but to modernise Cooper's traditional style and the naturalistic–realistic tradition in general. In this it is different from Beckett's grimly grotesque and ingeniously patterned buffoonery.

The simultaneity of maintaining and transforming naturalistic–realistic tradition can also be observed in the relationship of Cooper's and Albee's stage directions not only at the start but throughout the two plays, and especially in the later phases of presenting the conflict. Cooper, as a rule, uses descriptive stage instructions. His procedure corresponds to the deterministic importance he attributes to the external conditions of human action. Albee, to a certain extent, keeps the descriptive element, but, to a considerable degree, relativises and modifies it. His technique is in keeping with his dramatic concept of tantalisingly delayed determinism and playful absurdity. Accordingly, Albee's stage instructions are sometimes short key phrases indicating a change of attitude by a playfully pretended change of person. When Richard feels he is going to hate the party, he is simply referred to as 'Little boy'.[33] The instruction plays a part here. It can speak and warn ('*Not in front of Roger*'),[34] it can combine an emotional state and a colloquial inference ('*Naked and embarrassed, but if you're in a nudist colony* . . .'),[35] and on occasion it can be a spoken line removing completely the difference between description and dialogue ('*What else?*').[36] Quite often Albee even provides experimentally optional stage directions leaving it to the actor or director which alternative to take.[37]

In a consistently composed play each constituent part or particle is an Archimedean point. In Albee's drama even an 'aside' *is* and at the same time *is not* an 'aside': Roger's is heard by Richard from whom it is supposed to be concealed.[38] Is it not natural then in this play that Jack, who in a sense is a continuous 'aside' and a running commentary, could be raised from the dead to return for a final comment? Throughout Albee's drama he steps into and out of the action; his remarks are sometimes heard by the other characters in the play, and sometimes only by the audience. In Cooper's drama his resurrection would be unimaginable and unacceptable. The fact that his return is imaginable, imaginative and acceptable in Albee's play is indicative of the fact that the Americanisation of a British drama in this case is a special and complex phenomenon. It certainly includes a change of locale from British to American (as it does in the American play and film version of Brian Clark's *Whose Life is it Anyway?*).[39] It also involves an expansion of dimensions (as it does in the Hollywood film adaptation of Peter Shaffer's *Amadeus*).[40] At the same time, however, it also implies a thoroughgoing reinterpretation of the original work both in matter and manner. If Jack's reappearance after his death relativises, though does not annihilate, the validity of the dramatic climax in Albee's version of Cooper's play, then it is only the last link in a well-forged dramatic chain where *each* element performs the theatrical miracle of simultaneously upholding and undermining its own sense and significance.

Yet even if Jack's resurrection in Albee's play is dramatically organic and defendable, his drawing a conclusion, teaching a lesson and preaching a sermon are disturbing. Perhaps he exhibits a passion, a polemical impulse which suggests he challenges rather than ironically accepts the life he portrays. Cooper is more content to rest in ironical protest.

To embarrass his audience, to make it feel uneasy, to tip it out of its habitual expectations, to jolt and shock it out of its traditional complacency have invariably been Albee's characteristic dramatic gestures. In his wittily worded paper 'Which Theater Is the Absurd One?' he claims in no uncertain terms that

> The Theatre of the Absurd, in the sense that it is truly the contemporary theater, facing as it does man's condition as it is, is the Realistic theater of our time; and the supposed Realistic theater – the term used here to mean most of what is done on

Broadway – in the sense that it panders to the public need for self-congratulation and reassurance and presents a false picture of ourselves to ourselves, is, with an occasional very lovely exception, really and truly The Theater of the Absurd.[41]

Albee's dramatic practice often cuts across and goes beyond the scope of this witty paradox. Unlike Beckett, who in *Waiting for Godot* has created an openly absurd universe in which the dramatic principle is ingeniously saved by making the plight of inaction promote the need of action, and unlike Pinter, who in plays like *The Birthday Party* has brought about a pseudo–naturalistic world where behind the seemingly solid crust of external reality absurdly irrational violence proves human action senseless and futile, in several of Albee's plays, including *Who's Afraid of Virginia Woolf?* and *Everything in the Garden*, a cross-breeding of realistic and absurd drama is achieved in a characteristically American fusion. In these cases, however, realistic drama is not a well-made Broadway farce, melodrama or musical, but serious drama with a critical intent and cathartic action. In twentieth-century American drama it has been a well-established procedure and a long-standing practice to modernise traditional realism by cross-breeding it with aspects of other trends. Thus O'Neill in *The Hairy Ape* fuses realism and grotesque expressionism; Miller in *Death of a Salesman* uses modern simultaneity and expressionistic–surrealistic treatment of time; and Williams in *A Streetcar Named Desire* combines realistic characterisation with symbolistic effects. In uniting realistic and absurdist aspects, Albee continues this achievement of modern American drama, and places his dramatic art in the mainstream of the dramatic movement. In this fusion the traditional realism of Cooper's *Everything in the Garden* proved a reliable factor.

At first, when Albee simply set out to retouch Cooper's play as a routine venture for the commercial stage, he no doubt cherished the idea of starting his task in terms of his parodistic paradox. Later, when he saw that Cooper was a more serious, original and innovative playwright, challenging the spectators' complacency by treating prostitution as a status symbol, Albee's imagination was captured, and the process of adaptation – external Americanisation – also became a more serious matter. 'If you find something congenial to your own point of view', Albee observed, 'then your adaptation of it becomes far closer to what you would have done'[42] and what he did was certainly to increase the grotesque elements in the plot. When in the course of recomposing his British predecessor's drama Albee realised that the adaptation had given way to a real collaboration, the enhancement of the grotesque aspect in the original reached the point of absurdity. By using and relativising the dramatic means, the structure, indeed the entire form of Cooper's play, Albee has generalised and intensified the aura of incongruity, already inherent in Cooper's theme, into a sense of absurdity. In the context of the Cooper–Albee relationship it is in this sense that Albee's Americanisation[43] has achieved its internal stage and ultimate degree of modernisation and revaluation. This is the way Albee has composed his American variations on a British theme.

COOPER AND ALBEE: A CONTRASTIVE SUMMARY

COOPER	ALBEE
(1) Stage directions tend to be long.	They are much shorter: the field of play for individual initiative is broader.
(2) The dramatic action is embedded in an epic milieu.	Descriptive detail is dramatically functional: the gravitational pull of circumstances is challenged.
(3) The viewers of the play are also considered to be potential readers of the text: a Shavian inheritance (cf. *Pygmalion*).	The spectators have only been assigned the role of an audience: the dramatic edge is sharper.
(4) External determinism is heavy.	It is, for a long time, playfully suspended: the possibility of a personal choice, or at least the illusion of an alternative is suggested.
(5) Characters are introduced with British reserve and a measure of formality.	They are presented with American informality (first names, more common names).
(6) The action of the play takes place in a real world; the reality of the actual is taken seriously even if it is ironised.	The dramatic action unfolds in a belt between the real and the unreal; the actual is reduced to a mere semblance of the real.
(7) The theatrical space is immediate and calls for a direct emotional relationship.	It is often distanced and alienated; sometimes it is doubled. Alienation, certainly not unknown in European drama, is one of the central concerns and formative principles of the American dramatic tradition from O'Neill through Miller and Williams to Albee.
(8) The plot evolves relatively slowly.	The action develops energetically; people take risks with less hesitation.
(9) The procuress is socially and racially an outsider. The conflict	She is within the social sphere of 'good society'. The conflict has been

between her principles and those of middle-class society is external.

(10) Anti-Semitic views are voiced in Jenny's party; they are obviously not shared by Cooper. He also rejects outdated colonial consciousness.

(11) The setting is emphatically British (the outskirts of London).

(12) The prices of people, the stakes of the game are moderate.

(13) The conversation of characters is interspersed with understatement; it is sophisticated, urbane and suave. Only the madam speaks a coarse and curt language.

(14) The recourse to prostitution for the sake of a status symbol is basically a thematic element. The 'garden' is an umbrella term and a figure of speech.

(15) The contrast between expected and actual standards leads to incongruity.

(16) Cooper's sense of incongruity is summarised in his ending the play in ironic acquiescence (after what he later considered was a false attempt at revolt).

internalised and sharpened.

Anti-Semitic opinions and anti-black prejudice are ridiculed by Albee. The thrust, focus and concern are unmistakably American.

To meet the requirements of an American audience, it has been transferred to the suburbia of an American city.

They have been substantially raised to suit American conditions. Dimensions are greater in the United States both outside and inside the theatre. So are the expectations of the audience.

The dramatic dialogue is straightforward, incisive and dynamic; it is more jerky, rough and rugged, hitting harder and cutting deeper. It is part and parcel of the emotional range and passionate charge of American drama from O'Neill to Albee.

The status symbol is a fundamental principle of form, and so it is generalised. The 'garden' is a leading motif, a structural element, a point of reference and a linguistic unit of tightly controlled recurrence.

The substitution of artificial for real values results in absurdity.

Albee's absurd vision made him contrive a double conclusion, one of realistic resignation and one of grotesque rebellion. Cooper's more traditional approach is thus both understood and undercut, adopted and relativised, continued and revalued, appreciated and Americanised in Albee's pattern of cross-breeding acute social criticism with an awareness of absurdity.

What is true of the work (*Everything in the Garden*) also holds good for the life-work: Cooper and Albee developed in opposite directions. Relying on his life-experience gained during the Second World War when he served in Burma as an infantry officer, and depending on his professional experience obtained as actor and as author of radio and television scripts, adaptations and full-length plays for the theatre, Giles Cooper, as John Russell Taylor suggests in *Anger and After*, developed an ever keener eye for external facts and underlying truths. He had an increasingly firm grasp on theme, character and plot.

By contrast, in Albee's case it is the plays of his early period written before his Americanised version of *Everything in the Garden* (*The Zoo Story*, *The Death of Bessie Smith*, *Who's Afraid of Virginia Woolf?* or *A Delicate Balance*) which are characterised by a marked theme and a firm plot, and it is the later plays composed after *Everything in the Garden* (*All Over*, *Listening*, *Counting the Ways* or *The Lady from Dubuque*) in which patterned variation and stylistic orchestration seem to carry more of the sense and significance of the drama than stating and developing a theme do. Hence the importance of Cooper's *Everything in the Garden* for Albee: the Anglo-Irish playwright provided the American dramatist with a theme which was sufficiently compact and weighty to survive its own relativisation in Albee's treatment and to support the American variations that made it increasingly memorable. This is the way in which aspects of the premodern and the postmodern can invigorate and reinforce one another.

NOTES

1. Cf. M.E. Rutenberg, *Edward Albee: Playwright in Protest* (New York, 1969), p. 172.

2. Ibid.

3. Ibid. Cf. pp. 180, 181, 229.

4. Ibid. p. 171.

5. The place of Albee's theatrical adaptations and dramatic remouldings in his *oeuvre* has been analysed in: C.W.E. Bigsby, *Albee* (Edinburgh, 1969), pp. 71–95; R.E. Amacher, *Edward Albee* (New York, 1969), pp. 109–29; R. Hayman, *Edward Albee* (London, 1971), pp. 45–51, 64–7, 80–4; C.W.E. Bigsby, *A Critical Introduction to Twentieth-Century American Drama 2: Tennessee Williams, Arthur Miller, Edward Albee* (Cambridge, 1986), pp. 278–9, 287–9.

6. John Russell Taylor, *Anger and After* (Harmondsworth, 1963), p. 26.

7. Giles Cooper, *Everything in the Garden*, in *New English Dramatists 7*

(Harmondsworth, 1963), p. 143.

8. Edward Albee, *Everything in the Garden*, in *The Plays IV* (New York, 1982), p. 8.

9. Ibid., p. 3.

10. Albee, 'preface', *The American Dream*, in *New American Drama* (Harmondsworth, 1966), p. 21.

11. Cf. Rutenberg, op. cit., p. 172.

12. Cooper, *Everything in the Garden*, p. 156. It may be merely coincidental, yet worth noting, that 'pimasz' in Hungarian, if not in Polish, means impudent, cheeky. If, for an English-speaking audience, Mrs Toothe is a more natural name than Leonie Pimosz, similarly, Richard is also a more common name than Bernard.

13. Cf. Rutenberg, op. cit., p. 173

14. Cooper, *Everything in the Garden*, p. 152.

15. Albee, *Everything in the Garden*, p. 1

16. Ibid.

17. In an interview (7 August 1968), M.E. Rutenberg, op. cit., p. 228.

18. Cf. Albee, *Everything in the Garden*, p. 38.

19. Rutenberg, pp. 175–6, refers to 'a similar operation blossoming in Long Island's suburbia but he thinks that the denouement in Albee's play is contrived in that 'all of Jenny's friends turn out to be part of the same prostitution ring. Had Mrs Toothe given the party and invited Richard and Jenny, the ending would have been more convincing. It is simply too coincidental that every friend of Jenny's is a whore – unless Jenny knew who the other members of the ring were and invited only them'. Such coincidences, freaks of fortune, accidental events, however, are dramatic means of concentration and generalisation. Without them neither Shakespeare's *Romeo and Juliet* nor Gogol's *The Inspector General* and Durrenmatt's *The Visit* could have been written. Artistic plausibility differs from everyday probability. The same applies to 'Jack's recognition of Mrs Toothe', which in Rutenberg's opinion (p. 178) is 'too coincidental'

20. Cooper, *Everything in the Garden*, p. 211.

21. Albee, *Everything in the Garden*, p. 183.

22. Ibid., p. 184.

23. Ibid., p. 185.

24. Cooper, *Everything in the Garden*, p. 214.

25. Albee, *Everything in the Garden*, pp. 123–5.

26. Cf. J.W. Lambert, 'Introduction', *New English Dramatists* 7 (Harmondsworth, 1963), p. 12.

27. Cooper, *Everything in the Garden*, p. 221

28. Albee, *Everything in the Garden*, p. 197.

29. For the relationship of Pinter, Beckett and Albee compare: R. Dutton, *Modern*

Tragicomedy and the British Tradition: Beckett, Pinter, Stoppard, Albee and Storey (Brighton, 1986), pp. 114, 123. For a graphic 'distinction between the European absurdist stance and Albee's' see C.W.E. Bigsby, *A Critical Introduction to Twenti-eth-Century American Drama 2*, pp. 260, 263. As Cooper's example also suggests, the dilemma of ending a play idealistically or realistically is not unknown in Europe either. But the duality became especially acute in the twentieth-century American drama. In O'Neill's *Days Without End* – a play which has eight draft versions and a number of different endings – the question of how to finish the work is the central problem both for the protagonist and the author. The final solution makes the ideal stand out victoriously with a loud gesture. In O'Neill's greatest play, *Long Day's Journey Into Night*, the conclusion is quiet, and the ideal is realistically mediated by a tragic situation which renders its manifestation indirect. At the end of Tennessee Williams's *The Glass Menagerie*, the ideal appears directly in Tom's sentimental and nostalgic reminiscence. By contrast, in the 'Requiem', section of Arthur Miller's *Death of a Salesman*, Happy's sentimental pledge is effectively counterpointed by Biff's realistic position.

30. Cooper, *Everything in the Garden*, p. 150.

31. Albee, *Everything in the Garden*, p. 18.

32. Ibid., p. 16. Cf. pp. 18, 19, 22, 111–13, 118, 135, 143.

33. Ibid., p. 128.

34. Ibid., p. 127.

35. Ibid., p. 160.

36. Ibid., p. 195

37. Ibid., pp. 66–7, 90, 101, 103, 117, 145, 155, 160. Cooper's instructions offer a choice only once: *Everything in the Garden*, p. 212

38. Albee, *Everything in the Garden*, p. 128. Cf. p. 20, where Jenny speaks '*Sniffling; the whole act which is not an act*'.

39. For the Americanisation of locale, cultural context and language in the Broadway version of Brian Clark's *Whose Life is it Anyway?* compare A.R. Glaap, '*Whose Life is it Anyway?* in London and on Broadway: a contrastive analysis of the British and American versions of Brian Clark's play', in H. Scolnicov and P. Holland (eds), *The Play Out of Context: Transferring from Culture to Culture* (Cambridge, 1989), pp. 214–23.

40. The filming of a play has the potential of increasing visual dimensions, replacing accents and focuses anyway. The American movie used this potential to a very great extent. Yet, as Milos Forman, the director of the film version of *Amadeus* has pointed out to Peter Shaffer, the novelty which the translation of play into film achieves is, in fact, 'another fulfill ment of the same impulse which has created the original', P. Shaffer, 'Postscript: The Play and the Film' in *Amadeus* (Harmondsworth, 1985), p. 109.

41. E. Albee, 'Which Theater Is the Absurd One?', in A.B. Kernan(ed.), *The Modern American Theater: A Collection of Critical Essays* (Englewood Cliffs, New Jersey, 1967), p. 173. Albee's interest in an updated version of realistic drama is also revealed in his appreciation of Chekhov. Cf. Ch. S. Krohn and J.N. Wasserman,

'An Interview with Edward Albee, March 18, 1981', in J. Wasserman (ed.), *Edward Albee:An Interview and Essays* (Houston, Texas, 1983), pp. 1, 4, 18, 22. For Albee's description of himself as an American dramatist, cf. ibid., pp. 12–13.

42. Ibid., p. 17.

43. Albee himself named the process as writing 'the American version of that particular English play'. Cf. Rutenberg, p. 229.

FURTHER READING

Edward Albee, *Everything in the Garden*, in *The Plays IV* (New York, 1982).

C.W.E. Bigsby, *Albee* (Edinburgh, 1969).

——*A Critical Introduction to Twentieth-Century American Drama 2: Tennessee Williams, Arthur Miller, Edward Albee* (Cambridge, 1986).

Giles Cooper, *Everything in the Garden*, in *New English Dramatists 7* (Harmondsworth, 1963).

——*Happy Family*, in *New English Dramatists 11* (Harmondsworth, 1967).

——*The Object*, in *New English Dramatists 12* (Harmondsworth, 1968).

——*Six Plays for Radio (Mathry Beacon, The Disagreeable Oyster, Without the Grail, Under the Loofah Tree, Unman, Wittering and Zigo, Before the Monday)*, (London, 1966).

Martin Esslin, *The Theatre of the Absurd* (Garden City, New York, 1969).

John Killinger, *World in Collapse: The Vision of Absurd Drama* (New York, 1971).

Michael E. Rutenberg, *Edward Albee: Playwright in Protest* (New York, 1969).

John Russell Taylor, *Anger and After: A Guide to New British Drama* (Harmondsworth, 1963).

Julian N. Wasserman, *Edward Albee: An Interview and Essays* (Houston, Texas, 1983).

CHAPTER EIGHT

American Poetry and the British Poetry Revival 1960–75

Eric Mottram

The title is taken from an essay in the programme for the Modern British Poetry Conference held in June 1974 by the Polytechnic of Central London's Centre for Extra Mural Studies, organised by Christopher Brookeman, Roger Guedalla and Eric Mottram. This present essay is an account, as detailed as possible here, of the British–American poetry relationships which this conference and the second one, in augmentation, held in June 1977, in great part represented. More than twenty-five poets and a substantial audience filled the halls; the conference books included collections of the poets' work as well as two extensive essays on the British poetic field they constituted.[1] The present essay is designed as a set of necessary information towards accurate literary history, and a counter to the panic fears of the literary establishment – including university English departments and the big publishing houses – at least since 1950, that British poetry had moved away from the narrow limits of some parochial Little Britain enclosure.

CONDITIONS FOR CHANGE

Even Stephen Spender stated forthrightly in 1973 that 'English literature since 1945 has become provincial – not just in relation to American but in relation also to the English past, perhaps even in relation to Europe.' In fact, the condition of British official poetry then participated in the increasing staleness of British literature and culture in the decades leading to the present time. After a spell in America – the present writer spoke with him on these matters while he read for his recently dead friend W.H. Auden at Kent State University – Spender wrote in *Partisan Review* that the attraction of America lay in 'its being the centre of energies which are entirely contemporary. . . . These show themselves in the arts – painting, fiction and poetry – when these express the American total sum of present-day consciousness, not of a civilisation confined to one class or to an élite.' He referred – unusually for any established British poet at that time – to Charles Olson's influential 1950 essay 'Projective Verse.'[2] 'The American writer seems open to everything that happens in his country. His attitude is summed up in the idea of "projectiveness". He is open to the whole surrounding experience which pours through his senses and realises itself almost spontaneously, and in forms mostly free, in his work.'

This is as good a summary as any of the reasons why a number of younger British poets needed to respond to contemporary American poetry in order to engage in the enterprise of new poetics and responses to their culture in order to produce, and certainly without any separatist 'school' in mind, poetry contrary to the deadly dullness of 'Oxford Poets', repetitions from the thirties, and those repetitions of parts of Hardy, Edward Thomas and even Browning that rapidly became the self-styled Movement poets.

The neglect of Basil Bunting is a central issue here. He could have become an essential bridge between British and American poetry long before his entrances into the New British Poetry in the sixties, while living just outside Newcastle in relative retirement. His impact was due largely to Jonathan Williams – an American poet who published the first ten of Olson's *Maximus Poems* in 1953, in Stuttgart; Tom Pickard – a Newcastle poet and cofounder of the Mordern Tower poetry readings; and Stuart Montgomery – then a young doctor from Zimbabwe (at that time Rhodesia), who became a major poet and a poetry publisher through his Fulcrum Books which included Bunting's work. Bunting had exactly the range, depth, variety of poetics and ambitious dignity that mainstream British poetry resisted and lost. He knew and worked with Yeats, Pound and Louis Zukofsky, while his poetic respects were for certain local Northumberland poets, a detailed reading of Wyatt, Wordsworth, Swinburne as well as Dante, Malherbe, Ferdosi, Machaut and Villon, and among Americans, besides Pound and Zukofsky, Walt Whitman. He lived and worked sporadically in America throughout his life (between 1928 and 1976) and there contacted William Carlos Williams, Kenneth Patchen and Charles Reznikoff, and worked in the State University of New York at Buffalo and the University of California at Santa Barbara (through Pound's biographer, Hugh Kenner). *Poetry* (Chicago) published his long poem *The Spoils* in 1951 and his last major work *Briggflatts* in 1966, long before he began to receive limited recognition in Britain. (T.S. Eliot turned down his work in 1951.) Bunting's first reading of *Briggflatts* took place at the Institute of Further Studies, founded by Charles Olson at SUNY, Buffalo, in 1966. He passed on some of his skills directly to Barry MacSweeney and Tom

Pickard in his own part of Britain in the sixties. When Oxford University Press at last recognised his excellence in 1978, there was no proper acknowledgement of the support of little presses and journals that Bunting had received over the years – only a terse statement on the jacket that the book was a reprint of Stuart Montgomery's edition of 1968, and Bunting's own brief general statement of gratitude to his editors, who 'printed my poems from time to time'.

The wider issue is the usages of American poetics in developing the work of modern British poets, and this in turn is part of a recognition that in the sixties and seventies official poetry and current academic criticism limited and dulled any enterprise to recognise the European and American range in twentieth-century poetics. To put it tersely, if the work of Eliot, Pound, David Jones and Hugh MacDiarmid, and of the nearly forgotten Dylan Thomas, had been offered to the wealthy presses at that time, their chances of publication would have been nil. These poets, along with David Gascoyne and F.T. Prince, raised standards of excellence without the least sense of a British School of poetry. Theirs was an international sense of poetry, including recognitions of American work.

By 1960 American Literature had become part of university courses in some British universities, sometimes as part of American Studies courses, more frequently as part of English department teaching. In 1961 the British Association for American Studies published *A Guide to Manuscripts Relating to America in Great Britain and Ireland*[3] this was the year that the first University of London post in American literature was established at King's College, (and welcomed in a *Times'* leader). The major sixties' poetry event in London, *Wholly Communion*, held at the Albert Hall in 1965 in front of a packed audience, and recorded on film and in a book, was stimulated by the success of public poetry readings in America during the sixties. *Wholly Communion* was an international poetry evening – American, British, Russian and Dutch – and the occasion exemplified Zukofsky's 'test of poetry' in 1928: 'the range of pleasure it affords as sight, sound and intellection'.[4] It amply rebuffed David Wright's ridiculous inaccuracy in *The Mid-Century: English Poetry 1940–60* (1965) that American poetry was a university-influenced industry rather than an art, and 'a Chinese box of semantic ingenuities'.[5] The establishment boycotted, and, where it did notice, scorned major events in London that demonstrated the power of American poetry, the kind of strength signalled in a full essay in *American Literature since 1900* (edited by Marcus Cunliffe in 1975) entitled 'American poetry, Poetics and Poetic Movements since 1950'.[6] A conference organised by the Centre for Extra Mural Studies of the Polytechnic of Central London (hereafter PCL) in 1973 featured Robert Duncan, Jerome Rothenberg, George Oppen and Ted Berrigan (then the latest in Essex University's American Poets invitations) in readings and seminars of a high standard, providing primary and informational materials hitherto unknown in this country. The enthusiastic audiences were drawn into the nature of modern poetics and the life of the poet in exemplary ways. A second PCL conference later that year included Jonathan Williams, who was unable to attend the first; tapes supplied the work of Paul Blackburn, Leroy Jones, Frank O'Hara, Charles Olson and others. In 1975 the Cambridge Poetry Conference included readings and seminars from John Ashbery, Edward Dorn, Robert Duncan and a very wide range of British poets.

The programme for the second PCL poetry conference contains an essay – 'Inheritance Landscape Location: Data for British Poetry 1977' – which drew some attention to poets' perceptions of American work: Tom Leonard's placing of his Glasgow poetry in an experience of William Carlos Williams, Iain Sinclair's *Kodak Mantra Diaries* (1971) as responsive to Ginsberg's presence in England, etc. (It should be mentioned here that the Cambridge poet J.H. Prynne wrote excellently on Olson's *Maximus IV, V, VI*, published by Goliard, in Richard Grossinger's superb American magazine *IO*.) An exemplary and key figure was the poet, and editor at Cape, Nathaniel Tarn. Poems in *The Beautiful Contradictions* (1969) concern the confluence in his life as poet and anthropologist (working in Guatemala) of involvements in Latin American cultures, Mahayana Buddhism and the Kabbalah. *A Nowhere for Vallejo* (1972) draws on South American, mainly Peruvian, experiences. His poetry is deeply inventive in measure and structure; his work for the Cape Editions series included books by Olson (*The Mayan Letters* and *Call Me Ishmael*), Barthes, Hikmet, Paz, Nicanor Parra, Fidel Castro, Neruda and Holub; at the 1975 Cambridge Poetry Festival he spoke on relationships between ethnic cultural studies and poetry, reporting the ethnopoetics conference held recently at the Centre for Twentieth-Century Studies at Milwaukee University. A third PCL conference, *Poetry of the Americas* (in 1975), included, besides Latin American poets, Michael McClure and Jerome Rothenberg from the United States. This time the conference book contained an essay on the issues of translation, which are always between cultures, as well as between languages.[7]

Something of this diversity began to appear in the revived *Poetry Review*, journal of the Poetry Society and, as it became under powerful new management, elected in 1970, the National Poetry Centre. Part of the significance is reported in Abby Arthur Johnson's article 'The Politics of a Literary Magazine: A Study of the Poetry Review 1912–72', in the *Journal of Modern Literature*, No. 3(1973–74).[8] The changes in *Poetry Review* were radical: 'Edited by Eric Mottram. . . . the journal features writers exploring the possibilities of poetry, both in subject matter and style.' Johnson cites the Winter 1971 / 72 issue which contained work by both American (Robert Nichols, Jonathan Williams, Ashbery, Gary Snyder) and British (Bob Cobbing, Pickard, J.P. Ward) poets. Before this, the *Review* was 'a mainstay of poetic conservation for five decades'; its readers 'disliked challenges to their intellect and emotions and changes in the arts or in the broader culture. As the audience for the journal they successfully urged the editors to keep their eyes focused backwards' and in opposition to *Poetry* (Chicago) and the *Criterion* and the kind of work today academically termed 'Modernist'. Between 1970 and 1976 the *Review* published British and American poetry, and work in translation, together, and gave short shrift to Movement adherents. Assault from the Establishment of journalists, reviewers, academics and the Arts Council began almost immediately, and continued until the Council's successful coup that destroyed both the *Poetry Society* and *Poetry Review* and returned them to the conventionalists of backwards focusing. One of the attacks on the editor of *Poetry Review* by the tribunal appointed by the Council, headed by a lawyer named Sir John Witt, was that too much American poetry had been published. But the New British Poetry had been successfully represented in nineteen issues of the *Review*, work reflected in the third and fourth sections of the first representative collection published in Britain, *The New British Poetry* (1988).[9] The title deliberately, if ambitiously, suggested Donald Allen's *The New American Poetry 1946–60*, published twenty-eight years earlier. The range is large, and includes the kind of poetry better represented in *A Various Art* (edited by Andrew Crozier and Tim Longville, 1987),[10] poets associated with Longville's *Grosseteste Review* and with the earlier *English Intelligencer* (1966–67), edited by Crozier and Peter Riley and with Ferry Press – including Americans Fielding Dawson, Tom Clark and Stephen Jonas, and from Britain Chris Torrance, Douglas Oliver, David Chaloner with Crozier and Riley themselves. In 1965 Crozier had edited, at Buffalo, the fifth issue of *Sum* as 'Thirteen English Poets', who included Raworth, Roy Fisher, John James, Prynne and Longville.

From the standpoint of 1993, these events and others around them appear to be major intensifications for which there were a number of preparations. In the early sixties, the American poet Bill Butler managed, in London, Better Books, a centre for international poetry, as well as for other good writing, and an astonishing resource for American poetry. He and Eric Mottram organised a reading series at the old ICA premises in Dover Street, London – a series which included a number of Americans, including Ginsberg, and there were readings at Better Books when Bob Cobbing took over the management, with Paul Selby. In 1962, Alan Ross's *London Magazine* published an essay called 'A Pig-Headed Father and the New Wood',[11] a recognition of Donald Allen's useful anthology *The New American Poetry 1945–60*,[12] which enabled its youthful and inexperienced but eager author to draw attention to poetry beyond 'the saints of 1915–25' – Eliot, Pound, Stevens, Marianne Moore, etc. – to work by the Beats, from the San Francisco scene, of writers associated with Black Mountain College under Olson, and much else. And there was a bibliography. In 1966, the same author went on to publish, in *The Review*, 'American Poetry in the Thirties',[13] providing news of major American poetic issues, still valid, raised by Crane's *The Bridge*, Williams on Lorca and his own *Spring and All* (1923), Sandburg and Jeffers, the Objectivists (1931 onwards, but without a proper consideration of Zukofsky because his work was largely unavailable here), and – briefly referred to – Muriel Rukeyser, Kenneth Patchen and Robert Creeley.

American stimulus to new British poetry at this time came from a number of sources. Exceptionally among British universities, Essex invited American poets for residence in these years: Robert Lowell, Tom Clark, Edward Dorn and Ted Berrigan with his wife Alice Notley. Although the American Embassy ceased to be a cultural force after the sixties, earlier, Louis Zukofsky and Kenneth Koch among others, read there, and the library published a booklet on contemporary American poetry by Eric Mottram (newly appointed lecturer in American literature at King's College, London), entitled *American Poetry in 1963: A Diagram of Health*; it included a short bibliography and photographs of Levertov, Creeley, Zukofsky, Olson, Williams and Jonathan Williams, who contributed an elegy for William Carlos Williams who died in that year.[14] Jonathan Cape published *A Kenneth Rexroth Reader* in 1972 (edited by a British poet) and two volumes of Zukofsky's *A* in 1966 and 1969 (not available at that time in the United States).[15] And besides Better Books, others began to provide regular resources for American poetry; Butler's Unicorn Book shop and Richard Cupidi's Public House Bookshop, both in Brighton, and Nick Kimberley at Compendium Books in London (he also published a series called *Big Venus* which included Ashbery, Eigner, Kelly, Eshleman and other Americans) and others. This, then, was the news needed by British poets as initiatives to explorations and inventions towards their own variety of processes and forms. Significantly, in 1971, *Tri-Quarterly No 21*[16] offered a large collection of contemporary British poetry edited by John Matthias. It constituted the first substantial recognition of the New British poetry, and was published in America (various copyright and other problems prevented its publication here). But it would be absurd to separate this from the effects of Surrealist and Dada poetry, and from the huge international range of concrete and sound-text poetries, especially since the American poets themselves inherited these areas of European and international writing.

Anthony Burgess exaggerated when he said in *Occident* (1973) that Pound 'created modern literature. None of us could have written without him.' But it is certainly clear why he believed this. Poets study and write within fields that are part of their lives. The New British Poetry is as indigenous *and* as part of the century as the music of Peter Maxwell Davies, Harrison Birtwistle, Robert Saxton, Brian Ferneyhough and the rest of the current magnificence. (The difference is that the poets have had nowhere near the opportunities for publication and performance that the music has had.) However, one of the differences between British and American poetry is that while the former hungrily sought news of the latter, American ignorance of British poetry remained widespread. Symptomatically, Hugh Kenner's *A Sinking Island* (1988)[17] is alleged to concern 'the modern English writers'. Given his demonstration of ignorance of the New British Poetry, the book's dedication to Basil Bunting, who died in 1985, and who stood for inventive imagination and against academic criticism, is abusive. Kenner omits the great Scots poet Hugh MacDiarmid, has one small slighting reference to the great Anglo-Welsh poet David Jones, and entirely ignores most of the material on which this essay is based. But it must be said that American ignorance of our poetry is widespread. The exception was the Festival of British Poetry held in New York by the Committee for International Poetry in 1982. British poets – Wendy Mulford, Denise Riley, Douglas Oliver, Allen Fisher, Tom Raworth, Eric Mottram and others – were introduced by American poets – Anne Waldman, Alice Notley, Ted Berrigan and others.

THE IMPACT OF AMERICAN THEORY AND PRACTICE

One way of ascertaining what could be available to a British poet in search of activating forms as alternative to the stale imitations of nineteenth-century verse and those limited styles debilitatingly imitated from the Southern Fugitives and Robert Frost, with a little from Lowell's *Life Studies* thrown in, would be to investigate the issues of *Poetry Information*, a major magazine begun by the revived Poetry Society and edited with great skill and persistence in the seventies by Peter Hodgkiss (publisher of new British poetry through his *Galloping Dog* press). No. 17 (summer 1977) contained a detailed essay based on a 1974 paper for the National Poetry Centre's series investigating contemporary poetics: 'Open Field Poetry'.[18] Beginning with Williams's 'The Poem as a Field of Action' (1948), it delineates the structures of poetic discourse in major American poets. Williams incorporated part of Olson's seminal 1951 'Projective Verse' essay in his *Autobiography*, and the British poet Elaine Feinstein had written to Olson about it – the response is in Olson's *Human Universe and Other Essays* (1965 – 'Letter from Elaine Feinstein', May 1959). Poets like Prynne and Crozier also kept Olson's work within British poetics. Some younger British poets found use in exactly those passages in 'Projective Verse' Williams quoted: 'certain laws and possibilities of breath, of the breathing man who writes as well of own listenings'; 'composition by field, as opposed to inherited line, stanza, over-all form'; the poem as 'high energy construct and, at all points, an energy-discharge'; Pound's 'musical phrase' rather than metronomic (mathematical) repetition; form 'never more than an extension of content'; the process of the kinetics of energy in the poem as 'one perception [which] must immediately and directly lead to a further perception'.

Forty years before, Pound (in 'Credo') *Poetry Review*, (1912), spoke of the use of 'absolute rhythm' in which poetry 'corresponds exactly to the emotion or shade of emotion to be expressed. A man's rhythm must be interpretation, it will be, therefore, in the end, his own, uncounterfeiting, uncounterfeitable'. Pound developed an astonishing formal variety in his *Cantos* (first published by Faber in London) – lyrics, many kinds of speech, images, ideograms, paratactical formations, collages of information. A number of poets learned from Cubist procedures – for example, Williams in *Spring and All*, and classically in a poem later called 'The Rose', in which each unit operates as a place juxtaposed to or overlapping another place, and organised into a synchronising design. In Williams' words: 'Poetry has to do with the dynamisation of emotion into separate form. This is the force of imagination . . . new form dealt with a reality in itself.' Rexroth's introduction to his translations of Pierre Reverdy developed such issues for the poetic scene. In Britain, Hugh MacDiarmid had developed a poetry partly drawing on his wide knowledge of European twentieth-century poetry. But his work was neglected on both sides of the Atlantic.

Americans had also worked at developments of Mallarmé's *Un Coup de Dés* towards managing inscription using the page and the possibilities of black typographies on white space, of measure–notation relationships, and multiple margins. Larry Eigner spoke, in Leary and Kelly's *A Controversy of Poets* (1965), of poetry as 'a matter of getting the distances between words, and usage of marks to conform as well as might be to say what there was to say as spoken, then these typographical devices entering themselves into the discovery and the initiation of attention'.

The *Poetry Information* essay went on to offer a wide range of American examples, too extensive to list here, but including Ginsberg's 'Wichita Vortex Sutra' (1967) as a credo of language–politics relationships any young poet might well recognise; Williams in Book 5 of *Paterson* speaking of measure as 'to dance a measure contra-puntally'; Zukovsky's 'The Mantis' saying 'Our world will not stand it the implications of a too regular form'; and Olson's powerful challenge of poetic responsibility in 'Equal, that is, to the Real Itself':

> What is measure when the universe flips and no part is discrete from another part except by the flow of creation itself, in and out, intensive where it seemed before qualitative, and the extensive exactly widest, which we also have the power to include? Rhythm, suddenly, which has been so long the captive of metre, no matter how good . . . was a pumping of the real so constant art had to invent measure anew.

Political responsibility fused with the responsibility for imaginatively inventive poetics is the subject of Robert Duncan's *The Truth of the Life of Myth* (1965) and the poetics of *Passages*, the turning point in his poetic career, receiving its first public performance at Berkeley in 1966 as a momentous statement within a country engaged in imperialist war and the civil rights movement. This was part of a possible action of 'a given property of the mind / that certain bounds hold against chaos' – lines from 'The Opening of the Field' in 1960. Duncan, a major force at the PCL conference in 1973, offered a cultural power and responsibility for the poet almost totally neglected in establishment British verse. A passage from his *HD Book* may suggest the range of this case and its remoteness from British commonplaces: 'The work itself is the transformation of the ground. In this ground the soul and the world are one in a third hidden thing in imagination of which the work arises ... The plot we are to follow, the great myth of work, is the fiction of what Man is.' Duncan's exhilarating ambition, fulfilled in his poetry and in his fervent readings – fortunately then fairly frequent in this country – was related to changes in contemporary musical composition (Cage, Boulez, Stockhausen) and to contemporary physics; to his place, together with Olson and Williams, within the field of Wolfgang Köhler's *The Place of Value in the World of Facts*,: artists' forms as part of the Gestalt psychology of the body's field; to the biological philosophy of Sherrington's *Man on his Nature* (1940); and to Whitehead's philosophy of processes.

Elsewhere in American poetry, Jackson Mac Low's chance-operational actions – in the same area as Cage's – also relied on a secure apprehension of the human body–mind, as well as international concrete and sound-text poetics, to create 'meanings & connections' within levels of consciousness and intention, so that the poem's field and the reader's 'interpenetrate with a minimum of interference by the poet, whose own action consists of inventing the chance-operational system used, making what choices are necessary to initiate its actions, and carrying thru the actions required by it to produce the poem ... the poet and the word-sources, the audience and the world (as chance in action and as environment) are transparently and unobstructively interpenetrating'. This kind of project deeply interacted with the work of British poets – for example, of Bob Cobbing, Paula Claire, Peter Finch and Clive Fencott.

There were also connections to be learned from American poets' recognitions of Abstract Expressionist painters. In 'Notes Apropos "Free Verse" ' (1969), Robert Creeley offered pointers towards this work (which had begun to penetrate observant British artists, including poets, through the Tate Gallery exhibition of 1956, 'Modern Art in the United States', a selection from the Museum of Modern Art, New York):

. . . the literal root of the word verse . . . a line, furrow, turning – *vertere*, to turn .
. . [The poem] turns upon the occasion intimate with, in fact, the issue of, its own
nature rather than to an abstract decision of 'form' taken from a prior instance . . .
[Franz Kline] said 'if I paint what I know, I bore myself. If I paint what I know, I
bore you. So I paint what I don't know.' I write what I don't know. I feel the
situation parallel to what [Jackson] Pollock suggests by his statement, 'when I am in
my painting . . .'.

Creeley also notes his interest in Charlie Parker's 'intense variation' on the
patterns within numbers known in the jazz world as 'standards' (and certainly
post-swing jazz was not unknown to British poets). MacLow, too, was
committed to the investigation of the frontiers of 'chance' and 'coincidence',
and the relationships of 'synchronicity' and 'meaningful acausal
interconnection': 'absolutely unique situations may arise during performances
of such work, and the experiences of those participating in them (whether as
performers, audience or both) cannot help but be of new *aesthetic* (experiential) meanings. That is, not only do the works embody and express certain
metaphysical, ethical and political meanings, but they also bring into being
new aesthetic meanings.' The contrast with Robert Lowell, writing so
carelessly in 1969, in the same volume as Creeley, goes some way to explain
why so much of his work is flaccid, which in turn suggests his attraction for
certain British poets: 'In writing free verse . . . I am conscious that rhythm is
usually made up of iambics, trochees, anapests and spondees . . . the joy and
strength of unscanned verse is that it can be as natural as conversation and
prose, or can follow the rhythm of the ear that knows no measure.' Robert
Kelly's 'Postscript' to *A Controversy of Poets*, in which the MacLow statement
also appeared, has this to say on the opposition:

> The so-called academic poet, whatever the urgency of his own convictions, chooses
> to write in time-worn, pre-existent patterns and often enough in outworn language,
> as if he himself did not take himself or the poem seriously enough to want to make
> it heard *now* by all those in the midst of whom he must spend his life . . . [The
> alternative poetry] makes extreme demands upon the reader . . . demands everything
> the reader has; it demands that the reader brings himself to the place of the poem .
> . . the traditional metres and stanzas and 'forms' are always available for *tours de force*,
> for training or chaining infant ears. But they do not, cannot, talk to us in our own
> speech, our own asymmetrical, nervous, alive, embattled, *present* hearing . . . craft
> is now exactly what it has always deeply been: perfect attention . . . the true tradition
> (is that) of the poet bold enough and vulnerable enough to elicit the forms of inherent
> in the marriage of himself and his material.

There were many other stimulating statements made by American artists on
their work available to us. The effects of awareness of American poetry were
eminently clear in statements and interviews from British poets themselves –
space prevents a larger selection here. *Poetry Information*, especially, printed a

good number of them until the final 1979–80 issue. Chris Torrance acknowledged his interest in Jack Spicer (also carefully read by Allen Fisher and Robert Miller) and Barbara Guest, and Jeremy Hilton in Robert Duncan. Barry MacSweeney wrote on Michael McClure; Eric Mottram on Clayton Eshleman, John Wieners on John Ashbery; Jim Burns on the Beats, Bukowski, Kerouac and Fielding Dawson; Allen Fisher on Larry Eigner; Colin Simms on Creeley and Levertov; Lee Harwood on Paul Blackburn. The title *Poetry Information* originated in the American poet Anne Lauterback's ICA series of 'weekly colloquies' on contemporary European and American poets in the summer of 1971. She and Eric Mottram agreed to call it *Poetry Information*, and this became the title of the series at the National Poetry Centre between 1972 and 1973, which included public conversation with poets, some of which were taped and transcribed for Hodgkiss's journal.

In his interview,[19] Lee Harwood acknowledges learning from Ashbery a denial of 'interest in writing about his personal life', and from Jack Spicer a sense of the poet as 'receiving set, and if he is a good poet he has his valves all clean and it comes through loud and clear'. In 1963 Harwood published *Night Scenes*, containing American work as well as British and his own Tristan Tzara translations. In the Donald Allen collection, he had read Frank O'Hara. In 1965 he went to New York. In 1965–66, his *Tzarad* magazine contained Tzara, Max Jacob, Ashbery, Gerard Malanga (a member of Warhol's Factory), Ted Berrigan and other New York poets. In *Collection*, published with Peter Riley (1969), appeared Cendrars, Reverdy, Hugo Ball, Raworth and the Americans Anne Waldman, Rod Padgett and Tom Clark. Robert Duncan taught Harwood 'not to go search for the perfect poem, but to let your way of writing at the moment go along its own path, explore and retreat, but never be fully realised (confined) within the bounds of one poem'. But Kerouac and Ginsberg still remained useful: 'to realise that the way you talk is far more fine than any poetry . . . the rhythms change according to the subject and the emotion. You try the best you can to lay up the lines to suggest that rhythm.' And lastly: the new British poems 'are not just trying to produce something that has effect. Even at the expense of being serious, which is a bad word in England!'

Barry MacSweeney recalls reading Ginsberg in the Penguin collection with Ferlinghetti and Gregory Corso, and hearing him read at the Mordern Tower series in Newcastle; and visiting Bunting at Wylam with Tom Pickard, Robert Duncan and Edward Dorn. This,he said, was 'my education'. While on a journalism course at Harlow, he visited Cambridge and contacted Prynne, Crozier, John James, Tim Longville and Peter Riley. Prynne played a tape of Charles Olson at Sparty Lee, a now almost legendary meeting of British poets MacSweeney organised at Allenheads, Northumberland, thirty-five miles from Newcastle. As he says: 'Prynne had a direct link with Olson for quite a few years.' MacSweeney grasped the principles of 'projective verse': 'For me it was like flinging language out beyond the self . . . not using sentences, breaking up, working with the breath, which I'd never realised.' He had already learned from Williams, Zukofsky and Levertov while at Harlow and through meeting Dorn, then at Essex University. The formative pattern of this period was vital: 'I wanted to learn about language, and I was willing to listen to anybody.' But Hutchinson wanted him to continue with what they called 'your little lyrical stuff, out of Carlos Williams' and 'what *sells* best', proved by the earlier volume they had brought out.

In Tom Pickard's case it was through Bunting that he read Zukofsky and Williams – 'formative influences on me when I was about sixteen, seventeen or eighteen years old. I felt these were people I could turn to.' *Paterson* became a model for his own use of industrial materials, and Kerouac's writing with current language helped him to realise his own use of local English. With his wife Connie he co-founded the Mordern Tower readings and brought into his bookshop in Newcastle *Kulchur*, (an outstanding New York publication), City Lights books and Jargon Press books, through their editor, the distinguished American poet, Jonathan Williams, who had been living in England for some years, and who mentioned Bunting to him. His local sense had to remain strong: 'I wanted to create a form within what we had, which would be accessible both in and out of the area.'

The Yorkshire poet Ken Smith went from his small childhood village to Leeds University and in the mid-sixties became coeditor at *Stand* magazine with Jon Silkin. When he left for America in 1969, he had thoroughly rejected the dominant New Poetry crowd – Robert Conquest, Kingsley Amis, John Wain and the rest of the predominantly middle-class crew: 'It's a class thing, I think, based on established educational institutions' and the repression of feelings and emotions. He had taught at primary school and at Dewsbury Technical Art College, but had published his first hardcover poems, *The Pity*, while in Pennsylvania. He had read Lorca and Machado. Then: 'I lined up some reading, decided to cash in on all the contacts I had, and . . . find out what was there and enquire.' He toured, found enough money to live on, found a job at a small state college in Slippery Rock, and began to discover contemporary American poetry, so unlike '*English* poetry, officially':

> You were supposed to leap about . . . to use ungrammatical or cut-up language forms . . . to follow speech the way it went . . . The general example, the fact that they had these things, the fact that Pound . . . talked about his vision, . . . at any rate, of the whole of western history. English poets seem so timid . . . I got into it very slowly – but [found it] liberating because it enlarges the world.

He appreciated the sense of opportunity to begin afresh, and the sense of space: 'I could get away. I could get into some of that wilderness.' And his

British identity modified: 'One of my problems with my accent, which shifts all the time, is part of the identification: I stopped fighting the idea of being British, and just forgot about it . . . I just wanted to be *there* and to get into *that* culture, and so I adopted *this* accent rather easily, and it's hard to get out of it now.' Through meeting Native American people, he became aware of the problems of having to live in two cultures, carrying their environments in one's self. Taking peyote 'several times' enabled a suddenly induced 'crashing through into other conceptions of human behaviour, other conceptions of reality where distances shift, where perspective changes, and so on, and which may not be illusory'. He could now play this into his own sense of growing up with a culture being both restricting and sustaining. 'We live, I think, within a series of decaying cultures, and I receive, or have some idea about, the decay of the tribe, the decay of my own tribe. Shifting those cultures about, it seems to me, is a way of being able to deal with the world more effectively, and has to do with the speed that I *think* we are going to have to learn in order to deal with less space . . .' He lived in Worcester, Massachusetts, where Olson was born, and taught at two universities in that state,confronting the problems of both teaching and writing poetry (virtually impossible in most British universities). The American scene in the sixties also gave him opportunity for a large number of readings, and that training has stood him in good stead ever since. In no way did he suscribe to American confessionalist poets and their criteria:

> I object to the notion that by Robert Lowell or Sylvia Plath or Anne Sexton charting their nervous breakdowns and their attempted suicides and so on . . . and other people doing it for them as well . . . that they are playing some kind of 'son of God' role, whereby they take upon themselves the sins of the world. That is just another version of the same old Christian culture, it seems to me . . . a very narrow understanding of what human beings are . . . it charges the ego with enormous importance: Look at me, Robert Lowell, suffering . . . Robert Lowell is popular in America; but then, in America, they like Larkin too.

Tom Raworth has given regular readings in America since the sixties, and has been supported in his work by Edward Dorn for many years. Dorn printed his letter on his reception of American poetry in *Wild Dog* (No. 3).[20] His reading of *Evergreen Review* (No. 2), the San Francisco issue, had been salutary, as it was to many other young poets in 1961. It contained Duncan, Rexroth, Ferlinghetti, McClure, Spicer, Snyder, Whalen, Kerouac, as well as Ginsberg. This helped Raworth to understand his position.

> *Howl* and all . . . started me off reading more Americans . . . Maybe America some day . . . I don't know. It's the fare . . . There are English poets still, over here, but 'English' and 'poets' . . . you know the sort of thing. It's odd . . . poetry over here is, I think, still a 'class' thing . . . don't know why. There's no flow; no use of sort

of natural language. The whole is so artificial and contrived. I mean you read the stuff and it's just *reading*. Does absolutely nothing . . . Nothing has the power to MOVE.

The final issue of *Poetry Information,* No. 20 / 21 (1979/80) contained essays by British poets and writings of Creeley, Dorn, Ashbery, James Koller, Kukofsky and Olson. Editor Peter Hodgkiss had admirably charted current British – American relationships.

BRITISH VOICES

In the October – December 1990 season of *Literature on the South Bank*, the Voice Box – the poetry centre for a largely establishment cultural structure – organised a series entitled *Brave New Worlds: 1945–68.* The publicity for a talk on 'The Movement' stated that 'In the post-war rejection of the modernist generation, the most significant group was the Movement, which included figures like Kingsley Amis and Philip Larkin, ostentatiously anti-aesthetic.' Certainly the last and damning phrase is accurate: the aesthetic interests of Movement poets is practically non-existent. But who in their right mind would reject so-called Modernist poetry, and for whom was the Movement most significant? Arguably, the reviewers, academics, teachers, the Arts Council and those they perpetually mislead. For 'anti-aesthetic' and anti-Modernist read deliberate ignorance of the main developments of international poetry in this century, and a determination to restrict attention to a peculiar definition of British poetry which can only be termed provincial. But one South Bank talk dealt with 'American Poetry and its Influence'. It was well-attended and followed by a further hour's interested discussion. There were also two discussions in connection with an exhibition organised for the South Bank by the distinguished librarian of contemporary British poetry for University College, London, Geoffrey Soar: *Little Magazines and How They Got That Way.* Speakers included poets who distinctly reject the Movement and all it stands for, and whose experience of American poetry has activated their work: Allen Fisher, Lee Harwood, Gael Turnbull and Ken Smith. The exhibition forcibly indicated the intercultural nature of the New British Poetry, to use the title now of the Paladin anthology published in 1988, the first of its kind in this country.

In fact, the exhibition 'guide' provided accurate information, opening with Pound's essay on 'Small Magazines' in 1930: 'This history of contemporary letters has, to a manifest extent, been written in such magazines' – that is *not* in the big market presses. Soar's exhibition contained major Anglo-American artefacts and influences: from *Blast* (1914–15) and *The Egoist,* through Pound's *The Exile* (1927–28), Peter Russell's *Nine* (1949–56 – one of the few to publish Bunting) and into the sixties with Lee Harwood's magazines, Raworth's *Outburst*, Jeff Nuttall's *My Own Mag*, *Agenda*, *New Departures*, *The Wivenhoe Park Review*, and many more. Soar quotes the absurd Movement-biased *Penguin Anthology of Contemporary British Poetry* (1981): in 'much of the 1960s and 70s . . . very little – in England at any rate – seemed to be happening'. He comments: 'the 1960s can, in fact, be seen as a period of the most intense activity, and this was manifested in the magazines' – and, it must be added, the small presses and one small press backed by a market press, Cape Goliard. This was the period when Anglo-American poetic relations were for the first time strengthening, and the mutuality was excellently signalled by Fulcrum Press, Asa Benveniste's Trigram Press and Tom Pickard and Barry Hall's Goliard Press. The key organisation, the Association of Little Presses, has recently celebrated its twenty-fifth anniversary.

In March 1991 Paula Claire gave a 'celebratory performance' at the Royal Festival Hall's 'Voice Box' for her thirty years of poetry performances and to launch her collected texts, *Declarations: Poems 1961–91*.[21] Her works, also on cassette and CD, usually include a large range of acoustic transformations of voice and environment; she is an internationally celebrated sound-text poet, and heads the International Concrete Poetry Archive in Oxford. 'Branded' (1986) consists of 'improvisations on cattle brands'; some of track 3, as its CD cover notes, is 'based on coded telegrams sent by the Matador Land & Cattle Co from Dundee, Scotland, to its agents in North America early this century'. The piece generates themes on land exploitation and the aggressive assurance of businessmen and their jargons of which a song is made from a recurring lyrical phrase of coded information intercepts. Paula Claire also performs 'Leonardo's Lists' (1985), based on the artist-scientist's celebrated jottings, and organised with the Paxton Group's electronic and instrumental transformations. Track 9 of the CD, 'Fourzero' (1985) is a sombre piece on 'the 40th anniversary of the bombing of Hiroshima'. Paula Claire, as the introduction to *Declarations* states, 'invents poetry as endless creative discovery, with an ease that thoroughly disguises the effort, while leaving us to appreciate methods' – which are astonishingly inventive. But she is part of the development in poetry performance in Britain, stimulated by American example, among others.

An essay in Cris Creek's *Raws* magazine in 1977, 'Declaring a Behaviour: The Poetry Performance' argues the issue that a poem is alive when it is performed, that no poem is performed by critical analysis, let alone written by it.[22] The poem exists as a Gestalt of visible and invisible energies and takes place as an event that includes language capacity, language system, and speech or the actual practice of words, the human body producing sounds, in various public spaces, large and small. A poem is part of writing in a broad sense:

tone, delivery, purpose, ethos, expressive desires, desire for fame, choice of occasion, the need to make a gift of words and other sounds. The increase in discs, tapes and videos, largely from the fifties onwards, in America, has made performances, dramatically more available. Expansion has taken place in Britain too, but with nothing like its American incidence.

Poetry readings began to develop in America precisely when, during the 1950–70 decades, the poet could be a representative commentator and protester against official culture, especially within anti-war and pro-Civil Rights movements. The *Raws* essay describes in detail a performance by Edward Dorn at the National Poetry Center in February 1974, as an exhilarating and exemplary visual and sound presence. By this date the poet's voice had become part of the poetry text. We had recorded readings by many American poets – Sandburg, Pound, Stevens, Olson, Duncan, Ginsberg, Lowell, Plath and Creeley among them. Tapes of British poets and a very few discs, notably from Stream Records, had begun to circulate. We could readily enjoy the voices of Bunting, Cobbing, Pickard, Stuart Montgomery, Harwood and Allen Fisher; we could recall F.T. Prince's memorable reading of his 'Drypoints of the Hasidim' at the Poetry Society in 1974 and Thomas A Clark's meticulous Clydeside accents and the wit and precision of his delivery. Such visual and acoustic actions in a space which holds together poet-speaker and audience-receptor are among the crucial facts of the British poetry revival and its relationship with the theory and practice of American poetry.

NOTES

1. *Modern British Poetry Conference May 31–June 2, 1974*, and *Modern British Poetry Conference October 18–21, 1977* (Cultural and Community Centre Unit, Polytechnic of Central London).

2. Stephen Spender in *Partisan Review*, Vol. XL, No. 3 (1973).

3. Marcus Cunliffe, 'The Growth of American Studies in British Universities', *The Guardian* (2 February, 1963); Howard Temperley, 'American Studies in Britain', *American Quarterly*, Vol. XVIII, No. 2, part 2 (Summer 1966); *Times Educational Supplement* – American Studies Special Issue (2 January, 1976); Bernard Crick and Miriam Alman, *A Guide to American Manuscripts Relating to America in Great Britain and Ireland* (Oxford, 1961).

4. Louis Zukofsky, *A Test of Poetry* (1928; New York, 1964).

5. David Wright, *The Mid Century: English Poetry 1940–60* (London, 1965).

6. Eric Mottram, 'American Poetry, Poetics and Poetic Movements since 1950',

(ed.) Marcus Cunliffe, *American Literature Since 1900* (London 1975; rev. edn 1987).

7. *Modern American Poetry Conference May 25–27, 1973* and *Poetry of the Americas Conference, October 27–November 1, 1975* (Cultural and Community Centre Unit, Polytechnic of Central London).

8. Abby Arthur Johnson, 'The Politics of a Literary Magazine: A Study of the *Poetry Review* 1912–72', *Journal of Modern Literature* No. 3 (1973–74).

9. Gillian Allnutt, Fred D'Aguiar, Ken Edwards and Eric Mottram (eds), *The New British Poetry 1968–88* (London, 1988).

10. Manchester, 1987.

11. Eric Mottram, 'A Pig-Headed Father and the New Wood', *London Magazine*, Vol. 2, No. 9 (December 1962).

12. Donald Allen, *The New American Poetry 1945–60* (New York, 1960).

13. Eric Mottram, 'American Poetry in the Thirties', *The Review*, No. 11–12 (1974).

14. Eric Mottram, *American Poetry in 1963: A Diagram of Health*, USIS, United States Embassy (London, 1963).

15. Eric Mottram (ed.), *A Kenneth Rexroth Reader* (London, 1972).

16. John Matthias (ed.), 'Contemporary British Poets', *Tri-Quarterly* No. 21 (Spring, 1971).

17. Hugh Kenner, *A Sinking Island* (New York, 1988).

18. Eric Mottram, 'Open Field Poetry', in Peter Hodgkiss (ed.), *Poetry Information* No. 17 (1977). All the quotations that follow on pp. 158–61 are taken from this essay.

19. Lee Harwood with Eric Mottram, 'Interview', *Poetry Information* No. 14 (Autumn–Winter 1976). The quotations from other interviews are from subsequent issues of *Poetry Information*.

20. Edward Dorn (ed.), *Wild Dog* No. 3 (Pocatello, Idaho).

21. Paula Claire, *Declarations: Poems, 1961–91*, International Concrete Poetry Archive (Oxford, 1991).

22. Eric Mottram, 'Declaring a Behaviour: the Poetry of Performance', ed. Cris Creek, *Raws* (London, 1977); see also Eric Mottram, 'Transformations of Music and Poetry', (ed.) Allen Fisher, *Speech Poetry* (London, 1980).

FURTHER READING

See Further Reading to Chapter 12, pp. 250–2.

CHAPTER NINE

States of the Artist: The Plays of Edward Bond and Sam Shepard

Ruby Cohn

Now, if you'll notice, there's four main bundles in the wheel. One for each point on the compass. . . . In the West is the sign of the bear. The West is the 'Looks-Within' place and its color is black. . . . It's a very dangerous medicine bundle.

(Rabbit in Angel City by Sam Shepard, 1976)

[The dramatist] should dramatise not the story but the analysis. . . . The changing of the bundle by the river from a baby in scenes one and four to rifles in scene eight (b) is a dramatisation of the analysis.

('A Note on Dramatic Method' in The Bundle by Edward Bond, 1977)

By their bundles shall we know them. Tied to Shepard's Rabbit, who is a self-proclaimed artist, odd bundles envelop smatterings of Indian lore which are mysteriously culled from their land for the enrichment of the contemporary lone soul. Bond's bundles punctuate his drama about a child abandoned by a poet, who grows up to be a rebel leader. Shepard's *Angel City* is Hollywood on the brink of bankruptcy, whereas Bond sets his *The Bundle* in a vaguely designated Asian country on the brink of revolution. By the end of Shepard's play the dangerous 'Looks-Within' bundle oozes green liquid, *'the color of the faces'* of a movie mogul and a subservient artist. By the end of Bond's play the poet who brought the haiku to perfection, but who served reactionary landowners, is so shrunken that he himself resembles a bundle. Visible on stage, the several bundles are emblematic images.

Edward Bond preaches a Rational Theatre, and Sam Shepard explores an inner landscape. Prophets little honoured in their respective countries – Bond accrues more royalties abroad than home in Britain; Shepard is acclaimed as an American film star rather than as a dramatist – they have broadened and deepened dramatic literature. Shepard is hailed (or condemned) as quintessentially American far more often than Bond is cited as typically British, but both are rooted in their native soil. I would not want to foist narrow nationalism on either playwright, and even less to name them as spokesmen for their countries, and yet a comparison of their plays illuminates differences between the contemporary drama of Britain and that of the United States, pre-eminently Bond's base in social history and Shepard's in American myth. The Briton dramatises geographical history, and the American theatricalises a quasi-historical geography of the United States.

White males born a decade apart, Edward Bond (1934) and Sam Shepard (1943) are autodidacts of remarkable range and culture. Both men began playwriting in climates of theatre excitement of the sixties, and both, having produced a sizable body of literature, continue to write into the nineties. Both have written not only plays but other genres – Bond his verse, stories, librettos and polemics; Shepard his song lyrics, film scripts, rock log and autobiographical vignettes. Their protagonists tend to be men, and yet both dramatists have created tender and brain-damaged women – Bond's Ismene and Shepard's Beth. Both authors have written dialogue for films of Antonioni – Bond for *Blow-Up* of 1967 and Shepard for *Zabriskie Point* of 1970. Both men have jealously guarded their privacy – Bond more successfully than Shepard – and both men are increasingly chary of interviews. Perhaps they have been misquoted, but their comments on their work are only minimally helpful towards interpretation, and one must of course ignore journalistic tags with which both have been labelled – obscene and violent. Without trumpeting self-justifications, Bond and Shepard stubbornly pursue their individual dramatic paths, and both occasionally direct their own plays. They have never met, and I can see no cross-reference of one to the other. Bond is the most stubbornly socialist of British political playwrights, whereas Shepard's recent plays centre on that archetypical American theme of the nuclear family.

Edward Bond has divided his plays into three groups: (1) descriptions of his familiar world, ending with *The Sea* (completed 1972); (2) analyses of the problems in that world, ending with *The Woman* (completed 1977); (3) answers to some of those problems (all subsequent work). However Bond may displace his settings to feudal Japan or Jacobean Stratford, his own world – and ours – is at stake. In some two dozen plays – the majority set in his native England – Bond dramatises ideas through pithy dialogue, decentred scenes, coherent characters, and complex fables. He coined the word 'aggro' for his attitude towards the bourgeois audience he intends to disturb. Although he designates his drama as Rational Theatre, he does not hesitate to introduce such irrational elements as ghosts, dreams and fantasies.

Sam Shepard rarely looks back at his *oeuvre* of some fifty plays, but critics have grouped: (1) early collages through *The Holy Ghostly* (1969); (2) fantasies about art or power through *Suicide in B♭* (1976); (3) family plays of surface realism. There is, however, seepage between the groups. Almost without exception, Shepard's plays are set in one of the regions of contemporary

United States.[1] He has declared: 'I'm pulled toward images that shine in the middle of junk', and he forages in a refuse dump of drugs, sports, rock music, astrology, science fiction, old movies, Western lore, detective stories, and races of cars, dogs, horses. Long before the French culture critic Jean Baudrillard hymned American – and especially Western – junk, Shepard dramatised it from within.

What the self-styled English rationalist and the intuitive American irrationalist share is a keen eye for peopling stage space and a keen ear for composing the unique idiom of those people. Bond and Shepard suit their dialogue to the characters they invent, and they do so with greater variety than their skilful compatriots Harold Pinter and David Mamet. Although a number of contemporary playwrights risk setting an artist centre-stage, Bond and Shepard do so with some consistency, and the portraits reveal aspects of their respective countries.

STAGING THE ARTISTS: EARLY SCENES

'Musical artists' inhabit Shepard's *Melodrama Play* of 1967, and my quotation marks signify a playful as well as literal sense of the phrase. In an analogy with musical chairs, successive characters – Duke, Drake, Cisco and even Peter – are composers of songs, as are Bob Dylan and Robert Goulet, whose giant eyeless photographs dominate a rudimentary recording studio. In this play (it was Shepard's first play about contrasting brothers), Duke has stolen the song composed by his brother Drake, but the businessman Floyd is indifferent as to the identity of the artist; what he wants is another commercially successful song, and he is prepared to go to any lengths to get it. His hired thug, Peter, shoots Duke's girlfriend, clubs Duke and Cisco unconscious, and menaces Drake: 'In this particularly unique circumstance I have everything in my control simply because I was once in a position exactly like yourselves.'

Shepard's 'Note' cautions that *Melodrama Play* should 'change from the mechanism of melodrama to something more sincere'. Perhaps Shepard includes satire in 'the mechanism of melodrama', ridiculing a money-minded Floyd and Peter, an intrusive sociologist, and performers obsessed with their image – an all-American team. Sincerity enters only sporadically before the dead and unconscious characters stand up and exit in this *play* of melodrama. Sincerity does filter through five songs that comment on the action in Brechtian, rather than melodramatic fashion. Through songs the German Marxist playwright conveyed to his audience the class basis of history, which his characters could not grasp. Similarly, Shepard's songs offer insights of which his characters are incapable; rather than reveal class cleavage, however, Shepard's songs indict the artist for complicity in his own entrapment. The hit song urges repeatedly: 'So prisoners, get up out a' your homemade heads / Oh prisoners, get up out a' your homemade beds.' Artists must resist threats both internal and external.

Rock music is as English as it is American, but Shepard's first rock play is American in the stock types who ricochet away from a narrative line, while the moral dimension of melodrama shrivels into the myth of the beleaguered artist, whoever he may be. Revealing Shepard's facility for pastiche, *Melodrama Play* is a minor work thriving on its songs and visual images – the eyeless giant photographs, the ubiquitous dark glasses, the artist Drake reduced to animality on all fours. For all the play-long confusion about the identity of the artist, our final image of him is the song-writer Drake cowering under Peter's raised club when '*there is a loud knock at the door*'. We will never know whether that knock announces friend or foe of the artist as victim.

Drake scarcely resists his own victimisation, but Shepard's subsequent musicians are more deeply entrapped in success-orientated America. As the producer Wheeler acknowledges in *Angel City*: 'We're immune and contaminated at the same time.' In the fantasy *Mad Dog Blues* (1971) the rock star Kosmo and the drug-addicted writer Yahoudi encounter legendary figures – Mae West, Marlene Dietrich, Waco Texas, Jesse James, Paul Bunyan – with whom they wander on a bare stage over ocean and desert, on island and frontier, past one another though they are close enough to touch; the 'adventure show' arrives at home sweet Midwestern home, to participate in song, dance and celebration '*through the audience and out into the street*'. In a return to a single visible setting, *Cowboy Mouth* (1971), whatever its autobiographical origins, is Shepard's first attempt to blend the legends of the film cowboy and the rock hero – both active outlaws: 'You gotta be like a rock-and-roll Jesus with a cowboy mouth.' But Slim, the Mouth chosen by Cavale, is only sporadically seduced by celebrity, and when a rock duet by Slim and Cavale cracks the shell of a Lobster Man, Slim escapes Cavale's Pygmalion grasp. In spite of Shepard's brilliant evocation of sixties sordid sensuality, replete with 'miscellaneous debris', rock songs, cowboy pictures, and a dead crow 'old black tooth', the cowboy and the rock-star legends do not mesh, as they do in *The Tooth of Crime*, written while Shepard was living in England in 1972 (upon which I momentarily postpone comment).

Angel City (1976) resembles *Melodrama Play* in its proliferation of artists, who are 'immune and contaminated' at the same time. Rabbit Brown is the outsider, the shaman-figure summoned to be the Master of Disaster, who will retrieve movie millions for Lanx and Wheeler. An innocent in appearance, Rabbit soon confesses to us that he is 'ravenous for power'. The only Shepard character to boast of being an artist, Rabbit finally duels with the diseased producer Wheeler: '*They were one being with two opposing parts*' – both turning green, the colour of American money and Los Angeles smog. Early in *Angel City*, however, Rabbit has naive notions of a three-way cooperation of artists. But to what end? Release from coercion of the producers, or command of the movie industry? The other members of the triumvirate are Tympani, hired to find 'the one, special, never-before-heard-before rhythm, which will drive men crazy', and Miss Scoons, a sexy secretary who dreams of being a film star. A shaman, a musician and a would-be actress, the infernal industry of Angel City engulfs them all in shifting – and shifty – roles.

Suicide in B♭ (1976), following hard upon *Angel City*, returns us to Shepard's ambiguous titles, for not only is the suicide questionable, but 'flat' is a three-way pun: a musical key, the upstage flat of the scenery, and the apartment setting of the jazz composer Niles. In that setting someone has apparently had his face blown off, and two Raymond Chandler-type detectives proceed on the assumption that the victim is Niles. However, that artist, accompanied by a domineering but unexplained Paullette, enters on tiptoe, invisible to the others on stage. Niles may have presented someone else's death as his own suicide, thus disappearing from the public eye in order to renew his music and shed earlier identities, particularly a juvenile cowboy image. When Paullette shoots Niles, it is the detectives who are wounded, but they nevertheless handcuff the hapless composer, who wants someone punished for the death of one who 'was alive to the very last moment'. Perhaps it is his music we hear as the lights dim, for there has been an intermittent intimation that Niles the composer is doubled by the onstage piano player.

From the unlocalised recording studio of *Melodrama Play* to the equally unlocalised flat of *Suicide in B♭*, Shepard moves his musicians across an American map, recognisable in the vocabularies of contending powers. *Mad Dog Blues* devours midwestern miles, but *Angel City* disparages a city on one coast and *Cowboy Mouth* on the other. These plays about musical artists lack the geographic specificity of Shepard's later family plays, but collectively they convey an impression of peripatetic American loners, ill at ease within four walls and commercial pressures and yet not free of their blandishments. So loose are Shepard's plots, and so disjunctive is some of his dialogue, that they nourish a notion of national inarticulacy, even though his artists are erratically loquacious.

In what John Orr has called 'ludic drama' and other critics call 'performance-roles' Shepard emblazons contemporary American consumerism upon a mythic landscape.[2] Although his musicians are more distinctive than other characters, Niles resembles Tympani in obsession with music, and neither is a notable improvement upon the lookalike rockers of *Melodrama Play*. In spite – or because – of their gifts, Shepard's musicians are unable to bond with men or women, and their music offers only momentary solace, as do the astonishing verbal riffs which became Shepard's signature. Although critics may interpret these monologues as quests for identity,[3] or yearning for a lost innocence,[4] the arias usually resonate beyond the specific character into the mythic dimension of the play as a whole. Influenced by his early work with the transformation technique of the Open Theatre, Shepard exudes the immediacy of each moment into his plays of the sixties and seventies, and this enhances his portraits of articulate artists.[5]

In contrast to Shepard's moody musicians, Bond from the first dramatises writers. *Narrow Road to the Deep North* was triggered by a seventeenth-century Japanese poet:

> I started to read a book by Basho, the Japanese poet. . . . The poet, Basho sees this child abandoned by the river – and he goes on his way. . . .[6] I just shut the book and I couldn't read it anymore. . . . I more or less forgot about it but from time to time it came up in my mind and when I had this play to produce I just went back to the book and I read it, and wrote a play.[7]

In choosing a setting far from contemporary Britain, Bond the playwright was following Brecht's narrow road of dramatic estrangement. After the fantastic Victorian reign of *Early Morning*, Bond moved his *Narrow Road* to 'Japan about the seventeenth, eighteenth or nineteenth centuries'. On a bare stage Bond's Basho presents himself to the audience and recites his most famous haiku, but Bond alters the tone. Basho's translator writes: 'Breaking the silence / Of an ancient pond, / A frog jumped into water – / A deep resonance.' But Bond writes: 'Silent old pool / Frog jumps / Kdang!' The comic onomatopoeia upsets the tranquillity of old pools. Similarly, Bond subverts Basho's gift of food to the child, which he does not dramatise, whereas he does dramatise the misery of the child's parents. Bond wants us to be critical of a Basho who ascribes the child's suffering to 'the irresistible will of heaven'.

After the initial incident, Bond's intricate plot is his own invention, continually shifting focus between the poet Basho, the tyrant Shogo, and the priest Kiro. Bond's 'comedy' implicitly condemns their different behaviours: Basho writes poems while Shogo establishes a cruel order in the city; Kiro seeks personal fulfilment first from Basho, then from Shogo, but he shrinks from their violence. When British 'justice' overtakes Shogo, Bond splits the stage; on one side Kiro reads Basho's delicate haikus – actual poems by Bond – but on the other side Basho, having recognised in Shogo the child he once abandoned, declares ruthlessly: 'If I had looked in its eyes I would have seen the devil, and I would have put it in the water and held it under with these poet's hands.' Bond's poet can murder a child.

After Shogo is lynched (to the glee of Basho and the British), Kiro knifes himself ritually but silently. From the river a man calls for help. Saving himself unaided, and unaware of Kiro's suicide, the nameless man berates the priest with the final words of the play: 'I could have drowned.' Kiro virtually drowns in his own blood, but the man, as though newly born, will live on in this violent 'comedy'. Of the three principals, Shogo and Kiro are irresponsible because they were victimised as children, but Basho is a villain because he wrote detached haikus while the city suffered its successive tyrants. Unlike Shepard, whose artists are tainted but also homogenised by their dubious response to success, Bond individualises the artist while immersing him in a whole society – priest, general, prime minister, commodore, students, peasants, soldiers, tribesmen, children (represented by dolls). Members of the several classes speak with similar formality in an ahistorical Japan, but the few English characters are mercilessly caricatured.

Bond sharpened and differentiated the stage idioms when, almost a decade later, he revised *Narrow Road* to *The Bundle*. He enriched the revision with escapist verses of Basho, subservient phrases of the Ferryman, questions asked by the once abandoned child, and explosive nouns of the poverty-stricken beggars who turn first to crime and then to a revolutionary underground. From the same opening event Bond conceived a new plot, with new characters. Perhaps influenced by *Fanshen* (adapted by David Hare for Joint Stock, whose work Bond followed closely), he moved the setting to pre-revolutionary China. This time the abandoned child, the bundle of the title, is adopted by a poor Ferryman, then apprenticed to Basho, who has become a judge in a repressive regime. Learning about social injustice by observing Basho, Wang becomes a rebel. When he in turn is faced with an abandoned child, Wang flings it into the river in order not to be deflected from his revolutionary purpose. Although Wang repeats Basho's murder of a child, Bond exonerates the rebel through a striking theatrical gesture: '*As [Wang] hurls the child far out into the river he holds a corner of the white sheet in his hand and it unravels, catches the wind and falls to hang from his hand.*' The baby-bundle unravels into a momentary banner.

While Wang organises an underground network, Basho continues a dual dedication – to delicate haikus and merciless judgements. After Basho condemns Wang's Ferryman foster-father to death, he himself grows old and demented, going into the audience to plead for information about the narrow road to the deep north. At the last Basho, shrunken under his walking stick, resembles the very bundle he cruelly abandoned at the play's beginning, but Wang tells the audience a fable with a lesson: 'That is the worse story. To carry the dead on your back.'

Although Bond claims that the Asian settings facilitated a simple and direct approach,[8] his plots are in fact intricate, and several scenes are oblique. Dramaturgically, Bond's scenes are patterned on Brecht in their self-contained quality, but the scenes occur in sequence rather than montage. It is probable, too, that Bond's corrosive portrait of the evil poet/judge Basho is the obverse of Brecht's good scribe/judge Azdak, and Bond's good Ferryman resembles Brecht's good Grusha of *The Caucasian Chalk Circle*, since both are seduced by a helpless child. More importantly, Bond's first portrait of an artist, the Oriental poet as villain, emboldened him to dramatise fallible English writers in more telling plays.

The first of these is a fictional writer in *The Sea* (1972). Sometimes called Bond's *The Tempest*, written after his *Lear*, *The Sea* is a harmonising comedy after tragedy. The Prospero-figure is an upper class Mrs Rafi in a turn-of-the-century town on England's east coast. Before contemporary critics read ideology into the dominant British culture, Bond created a character who manipulates culture to dominate her subordinates; she writes, directs and produces a pageant for the local Coastguard Fund. Her subject is the Orpheus–Eurydice myth, of which we see only a rehearsal, in the funniest scene of this 'comedy'.[9] Bond etches the town's social hierarchy into the amateur endeavour, where Mrs Rafi's pretentiousness unwittingly subverts her dialogue: 'Eurydice, let me clasp your marble bosom to my panting breast and warm it with my heart.' Unlike the Orpheus whose role she plays, Mrs Rafi charms no one with her lute, and she rescues no beloved from Hell, which she enters to the tune of 'Home Sweet Home'. Elegant and fastidious, she resembles Basho in her escapist art, while in the real world she callously oppresses her social inferiors. *The Sea* gains strength from Bond's renunciation of the political sermons of his Basho plays. Although drowning is a recurrent image in both his Oriental and English plays, the malefic river of the former is aestheticised or abstracted, whereas the sea-salt of the latter quickens the townspeople with human dimension – even Mrs Rafi, an amateur artist and tyrant.

THE TOOTH OF CRIME: END GAME FOR A ROCK STAR

Like Bond, Shepard fleshes his artists more convincingly when he locates them in specific geographies, and nowhere more firmly than *The Tooth of Crime*, written while he was living in London in 1972: 'It wasn't until I came to England that I found out what it means to be an American.'[10] 'What it means' is dramatised in Shepard's most richly textured play, where the reign of Hoss – 'The West is mine' – is challenged by an upstart Crow. Their virtuosic duel is staged as a prize-fight, but they vie for supremacy as rockers.

Mallarmé's 'Angoisse' provides Shepard's arresting title: 'A heart that the tooth of crime cannot wound'. The French sonnet contrasts the vulnerable persona with his invulnerable partner in vice, and Shepard contrasts the ultimately vulnerable Hoss with a seemingly invulnerable Crow. Shepard's subtitle is 'A play with music in two acts', and music takes the form of six songs: 'I wanted the music in *Tooth of Crime* so that you could step out of the play for a minute, every time a song comes, and be brought to an emotional comment on what's been taking place in the play.'[11] As early as *Melodrama Play* Shepard twisted Brechtian estranging songs to his own purpose, but not until *Tooth* do the songs offer emotional understanding of the contending artists.

Like classical tragedy, and totally unlike earlier Shepard dramas, *Tooth* opens close to its crisis: Hoss needs a 'kill' in 'the game'. He fondles an array of guns – 'the gear' – carried in two black satchels by Becky, his servant-mistress-tutor. Like Nancy Reagan after him, Hoss consults astrologers – Star-Man and Galactic Jack – and is reassured: 'A shootin' star, baby. High flyin' and no jivin'. You is off to number nine. . . . You're number one with a bullet and you ain't even got the needle in the groove.'

Becky reports that a Gypsy has been 'sussed', but the chauffeur Cheyenne advises Hoss against 'cruising'. The loner Hoss feels driven to an alliance with Little Willard in the East, only to learn of his suicide. Doc's injection does not tranquillise Hoss, who reveals his full dread only to Becky. Alone on stage, Hoss bifurcates into a dialogue with his father, to whom he complains: 'They're all countin' on me. The bookies, the agents, the Keepers. I'm a fucking industry.' Once Hoss accepts his father's reply – 'You're just a man, Hoss. Just a man' – the aging artist also accepts a duel with the young Gypsy Crow.

In Act II we see Crow, who resembles Keith Richard with an eye-patch. Crow's words sear Hoss: 'Got the molar chomps. Eyes stitched. You can vision what's sittin'. Very razor to cop z's sussin' me to be on the far end of the spectrum.' From Hoss's stellar isolation, he questions Crow about the outside world, and the younger man's replies are implicit threats: 'Image shots are blown man. No fuse to match the hole. Only power forces weight the points in our match.' Seeking supremacy, Hoss imitates a film cowboy, a twenties' gangster, but Crow counters with a song of self-sufficiency:

> But I believe in my mask – The man I made up is me
> And I believe in my dance – And my destiny.

In Round 1 of their bout Crow attacks Hoss with a capsule biography of a coward and a loser (anathema to the American macho image), and Ref names Crow the winner. In Round 2 Hoss accuses Crow of denying his musical origins in the blues of black people – 'You'd like a free ride on a black man's back' – but Crow retorts: 'I got no guilt to conjure! Fence me with the present.' The Ref declares a draw. In Round 3 Crow sneers in rhyme that Hoss's music is obsolete, imitative, impotent: 'Busted and dyin' and cryin' for more. Busted and bleedin' all over the floor. All bleedin' and wasted and tryin' to score.' The Ref calls it a T.K.O., and is shot by an infuriated Hoss.

Having thus violated 'the code', Hoss is himself a Gypsy, and he implores Crow to give him lessons in survival. Crow drives a hard bargain: 'I give you my style and I take your turf.' In the process of adapting to Crow's 'slick cool', Hoss seems to turn into a little boy (but it is for him that Becky enacts a girlhood rape). After Crow instructs Hoss to be 'Pitiless. Indifferent and riding a state of grace', his male retinue sing 'Slips Away', and Hoss himself slips away from Crow. Like classical heroes, Hoss finally prefers death to dishonour: 'It's my life and my death in one clean shot.' Crow's reign begins, but his final song, 'Rollin' Down', casts doubt on its durability.

The Tooth of Crime is Shepard's most tightly plotted play, inscribing his most indelible antagonists on an end-game set, but the themes are familiar and hyper-American – the tenuous position of the artist, his heritage of sound and fury, his susceptibility to popular culture and media greed – 'Somebody bankable'. The manic machismo of the sixties, which Shepard absorbed with his drugs, culminates onstage in violent death. *The Tooth of Crime* is at once a contest between rock stars, a histrionic match of performers, a bout between generations, and a class war between the haves and have-nots, between the recently rooted Westerner and the catch-as-catch-can Gypsy – a class war innocent of Marx. The bitter bite of Shepard's *Tooth* thrives on a syncopation of the imagery of drugs, sports, film, crime, street smarts, gambling, science fiction, astrology and the rock music that is presented and represented. For all the diversity of the lexicon, however, the polyvalent monosyllables 'hit' and 'kill' toll a threnody of American popular culture. 'The image is my survival kit', cackles Crow, but far more trenchantly than the image, which is oversimplified in every production I have seen, it is the amazing all-American idiom that energises *The Tooth of Crime*.

BINGO AND *THE FOOL*: NEW PLACES FOR OLD POETS

Bond's *Bingo* (1973), written a year after Shepard's *Tooth*, is also a threnody, but with an *andante* rhythm. And it also pits one artist against another, but they are playwrights. Bingo is a game of chance, played for money on numbered squares, and so it is in Bond's play, but the game is deadly, as hinted by his subtitle 'Scenes of Money and Death'. In Bond's *oeuvre The Sea* (1972) precedes *Bingo* (1973); its hero Willy turns his back on a moribund English town in order to build a new life elsewhere. Conversely in *Bingo* a dramatist has returned from London to his native English town, but he finds life there intolerable. The dramatist's name is William Shakespeare. Bond's *Bingo*, after his re-view of Lear and a tempest, boldly places the Bard himself centre-stage.

Bond's Introduction to the published text of *Bingo* mentions his modifications of historical fact 'for dramatic convenience'. Set in and around Shakespeare's still extant home at New Place, Stratford, in 1615–16. *Bingo* depicts an old man, his great works behind him, hoping to retire to Stratford in obscurity and security. Bond eschews the national myth of a Merrie England bubbling with creative spirits, for autumn envelops Stratford, as it does the town's best-known citizen: 'It's the last of the sun.'

Like a spate of plays about Shakespeare, *Bingo* first presents him with writing paper in hand. After a few moments we learn that the paper is host not to words but to numbers – Shakespeare's calculations towards his financial security. With that goal in mind, he acquiesces to the land enclosures that starve out poor farmers and force them to migrate. The play's villain Combe guarantees Shakespeare's holdings at the price of his silence in the protest against enclosure: 'It pays to sit in a garden.'

In six scenes the *public* plot about Shakespeare, money and death is balanced by a *private* plot about Shakespeare, money and death, for Shakespeare's (invisible) wife and daughter Judith are the money-hungry monsters he has made of them: 'I loved you with money.' Shakespeare's family, bourgeois British, is paralleled and contrasted with a lower-class family – Shakespeare's wise old servant, her mentally deficient husband and their radical son. The two families literally speak different-dialects – coldly correct English in the one and warmly active East Anglian in the other. The Old Woman loves both her husband and her son, but the latter, turned Puritan, abhors the carnal appetites of his brain-damaged father: 'He hev the mind of a twelve year ol' an' the needs on a man.' Dispossessed by the land enclosures, rebellious against such dispossession, the Son accidentally shoots his father in a wintry confrontation of opposing forces.

Each half of the 6-scene play pivots on an outsider's arrival in Stratford. In Part I it is a nameless, homeless Young Woman, soon sentenced to whipping 'till the blood runs' and afterwards to hanging. She graphically binds the plot threads – given money by Shakespeare and blame by his daughter, fornicating with the feeble-minded Old Man, judged by the landowner Combe in his office as magistrate. Her gibbeted body is visible throughout scene iii. In Part II the outsider is Ben Jonson, stopping in Stratford on his walk to Scotland. Vigorous with lived experience, Jonson confesses his long-standing hatred to his rival, but he is oblivious of the peasant-rebels at the next table – a climactic Bond scene of split focus. Almost incidentally, Jonson shows Shakespeare the poison that he bought 'In a moment of strength'.

Outsiders are gone after scene 4, but Jonson's poison is in Shakespeare's possession throughout scenes 5 and 6. Bedridden, Shakespeare is beset by his hysterical wife, his importunate daughter, and the Puritan son rationalising away his guilt at his father's death. A self-blaming Shakespeare intones: 'Was anything done? Was anything done?' When the land-rich Combe enters his sickroom, Shakespeare asks for the poison as though it were medicine: 'Some tablets. There. On the table. Please.' As Combe and the Son exchange recriminations, Shakespeare swallows tablet after tablet of poison. Alone when he falls to the floor, he is found by his daughter Judith, but she barely tends to him, so intent is she on finding his will. Shakespeare dies on the floor while Judith repeats in disappointment: 'Nothing'. The 'emptiness and silence' at the start of *Bingo* prefigure the death and 'nothing' at the end – at the dawn of British capitalism.

Bond's Shakespeare is a far more socially sensitive writer than his Basho or Mrs Rafi, and yet the most frequent scenic direction in *Bingo* is: '*Shakespeare doesn't react.*' His few words do, however, penetrate to the ubiquitous suffering of the underprivileged. In scene 3 Puritans picnic near the gibbeted Young Woman, and they register no awareness of an abyss between such punishment and their prayers, but Shakespeare associates her fate with London bear-baiting at his theatre. In scene 4 Shakespeare hears the rebellious conspiracy counterpointed against Jonson's drunken confession of hatred. By scene 5, however, Shakespeare stumbles drunkenly through the snow, oblivious of the rebellion against the land enclosures. At Shakespeare's bedside in scene 6 the poet hears the parallel intransigence of the Son and Combe. What the director William Gaskill said of *Lear* seems just as true of *Bingo*: 'I think the main moments are those when more than one thing is happening on stage at once.'[12] In *Bingo* 'one thing' is usually Shakespeare's failure to act against suffering, for all his sensitivity to it.

While the conspiracy is formulated in scene 4, Jonson confronts Shakespeare with the tattered remains of both their careers, which are also the tatters of British culture. Although Jonson disparages Shakespeare's late romances – 'Your recent stuff's been pretty peculiar' – the two playwrights are only obliquely opposed, Jonson more immediately rooted in contemporary experience and Shakespeare reaching for a spiritual dimension. Jonson accuses Shakespeare of being 'serene', although we have been witness to his deep disquiet. Jonson confesses to a hatred not only of Shakespeare but of their common art (as of Bond's own): 'Fat white fingers excreting dirty black ink'. Although Jonson spurns Shakespeare's compliment – 'a very good writer' – he has no qualms about accepting money from the successful dramatist. Then, as now, artists worry about survival and security.

Bond's Shakespeare is too guilt-ridden to write, but Bond situates his own fifth scene in a blizzard on the heath, which is grounded in the heath scene of *King Lear*. As Lear rages against his daughters, Shakespeare expands on the hate that Jonson confessed: 'There's no limit to my hate.' As Lear arrives at self-knowledge – 'O, I have ta'en too little care of this' – Bond's Shakespeare realises: 'Every writer writes in other men's blood. . . . If I wasn't dead I could kill myself.'[13] Back in his room, Shakespeare recalls Jonson's image of the writer: 'White worms excreting black ink'. At the threshold of Shakespeare's own death, the bard debases Jonson's 'fat fingers' to worms.

In the Introduction to *Bingo* Bond writes: 'I wrote *Bingo* because I think the contradictions in Shakespeare's life are similar to the contradictions in us.' What Bond *preaches* is the contradictions of artistic endeavour in a capitalist society, which begins with the land enclosures of the early seventeenth century. What Bond *dramatises*, however, is a hypersensitive artist whose early verbal fluidity is eroded by his witness to widespread cruelty. New Place is not a home, although it was Bond's original title for his play.

Bingo (1973) and *The Fool* (1975) pivot on the same subject – the English writer's response to his time and society. *Bingo* is set in and around New Place, with a timespan of a little over half a year. *The Fool*, in contrast, moves around Northborough, Ely and London; the timespan is some forty years of the nineteenth century, and the eight-scene plot rambles through several peripetias – John Clare avoiding arrest, his refusal to expunge class criticism from his poems, his romanticising of Mary while married to Patty, her acquiescence to his incarceration in an insane asylum, Clare's brief escape from the asylum. Through all events Clare keeps writing: 'Bin scribblin day-in-day-out for years.' Both Bond's poet-protagonists avoid social action, but their social sensitivity drives the one to suicide and the other to the madhouse.

The eight scenes of *The Fool* are only a slight increase over the six of *Bingo*, but they are more liberally peopled – some forty speaking parts against twelve – many drawn from the life of John Clare. Martin Esslin has succinctly summarised the central difference between these two English poets who have attracted the English poet Edward Bond:

> The Shakespeare of *Bingo* is a highly successful artist who becomes enmeshed in society's guilt precisely *because* he is a financial success and has to invest his money, whereas *The Fool* shows the fate of an artist who cannot support himself by his writing. *The Fool* dramatises the life story – and the bewilderment – of an individual of great talent who lacks the self-awareness which would enable him to master his personal destiny, just as he also lacks the historical and political consciousness that would allow him to make rational political decisions. . . . It is this lack of understanding which makes Bond's Clare a *fool*.[14]

Clare is also a fool in his entertainment of the wealthy, but he never acquires the witty wisdom of the Shakespearean fool.

Bond's play delays focus on Clare, for his early scenes offer a panoramic view of England in an age of transition: a squirearchy adjusting to capitalism while demanding feudal servitude from its workers, a clergy with eyes carefully averted from the here-and-now, Christmas alms dissolved into shrunken wages, petty thefts punishable by hanging, prize-fighters maiming each other for professional gamblers, alcoholic Charles Lamb and his mad sister Mary, homeless vagabonds roaming through the country. And for each social stratum of *The Fool* Bond creates a language. The play opens on a naive Mummer's Play enacted by Lord Milton's tenants, but its coda is the lugubrious piety of the parson and the educated clichés of the gentlemen. When Clare becomes the pet of London intellectuals, we hear the pseudo-lyricism of Mrs Emmerson – 'It is my ambition to be at your side when the muse calls' – the gambling slang of the boxer-backers, the sophisticated cynicism of Charles Lamb. Later there are vagabond Irishmen who sound much like today's Cockneys. Bond's most musical language, however, is reserved for Clare and his fellow villagers. Although the play is set in Northamptonshire, the dialect is East Anglian, praised by Bond: 'I use it because of its curious concrete feel, its repetitiveness, it's like a sort of hammer knocking, knocking, knocking. But at the same time it can be very agile and witty. It's language which imitates experience.'[15] Never mired in stiff diction, Clare's compatriots express emotion through repetition of simple words, particularly ' 'on't' which can mean don't, won't can't, shouldn't, wouldn't, am not. 'On'y' and ' 'on't' pulse through John Clare's speech before he is reduced to slavering consonants.

John Clare, sometimes called the Peasant Poet, is Bond's Fool of the title, who is robbed by society of the 'bread and love' of the subtitle. Although Clare probably attracted Bond by his precise witness to the natural world, his pungent colloquial diction, and his unabashed class pride, there is no reference to the poetry until midway through the play, and there are no quotations at all from actual poems. For that poet in that cruel society Bond finds two main images – the prison (the setting of scene 4), and the madhouse (the setting of the final scene). Although these places confine Clare, they house the only cooperative communities in the play. The prisoners join in widespread hysterical laughter, except for Darkie.[16] By the final scene in the asylum, the inmate John Clare speaks gibberish, but his fellow inmate Mary Lamb deciphers his mumblings and translates them into comprehensible English.

At the last, Clare is deprived even of the words that he prized above the bread and love of Bond's subtitle. During the course of the play, we have seen Mary give stolen bread to Clare, a warden give a bread ration to prisoners, the Mary of Clare's fantasy give Darkie bread that he is unable to swallow, and Clare sell Mary to the Irish vagabond for a piece of bread and cheese. Emerging from his Mary fantasy, Clare appreciates the power of bread: 'Bread goo from mouth t'mouth an' what it taste of: other mouths. . . . I am a poet an' I teach men how to eat.' But he does not teach them how to obtain the food to eat; or how to overthrow a system predicated upon slow starvation; or indeed how to survive within the English society of his time. The critics Hay and Roberts argue for the hopeful ending of *The Fool*, which moves from dark early scenes to brilliant flashes of the sun in the final scene, but no amount of theatre wizardry, and no momentary self-awareness, can efface our last view of Clare in a wheelchair, '*a shrivelled puppet*' uttering gnomic gutterals. Like Shakespeare before him, Bond's foolish Clare has contributed to his own destruction, even though class-ridden England is finally to blame.

In *Bingo* and *The Fool* Bond's artist figures are inactive when compared with those of Shepard, whose music we usually hear. Shakespeare's writing days are over, and Clare treats us to none of his lyrics; yet Bond dramatises their colleagues to convey the literary milieu – Ben Jonson in the one play and Charles Lamb in the other. And the milieu is familiar in today's England, with its close-knit group centred in London, from where the *literati* view the rest of the world with disdain. In both plays, Bond locates their self-important perch on a larger social canvas, and it is in the textural specificity and authenticity of that rough English cloth that Bond has no match.

TRUE WEST: THE DOUBLE NATURE OF THE AMERICAN WRITER

The latest in date of the artist plays of either playwright is Sam Shepard's *True West* (1980).[17] The last play of Shepard's family trilogy, *True West* is the funniest and the least intricate of the three. Significantly, it is the only Shepard play in which the artists are writers; they are also brothers, who grew up some forty miles east of Los Angeles, in the suburb where the play is set. A well-groomed and well-educated Austin house-sits for his mother, to prepare his 'project' for a Hollywood producer. His ne'er-do-well brother Lee arrives from the desert, not only intruding upon the project but inveigling the producer into a game of early-morning golf – offstage. Abruptly, the producer accepts Lee's idea for a Western movie, with its 'ring of truth', and Austin is hired merely to write the dialogue.

Offstage the two brothers abruptly exchange identities. Stealing like Lee, Austin has filled his mother's kitchen with '*a wide variety of models, mostly chrome*' toasters, and Lee, baffled by Austin's typewriter, has destroyed it with a nine-iron golf club. Nevertheless, after Austin toasts some bread for them, the brothers labour together over Lee's Western scenario, in which two men chase each other across the prairie: 'What they don't know is that each one of 'em is afraid.' But the two brothers show no fear of their mother who returns unexpectedly to her demolished kitchen: '*the stage is ravaged*'. Each of the brothers probes into the other's identity, as Austin yearns to live like Lee in the desert, and Lee takes his mother's best china because: 'I'm tired of eatin' outa' my bare hands, ya' know. It's not civilised.' While Lee stacks dishes, Austin suddenly wraps a telephone wire around his brother's hands and neck. Their mother makes sure that Austin allows Lee to breathe, and then leaves: 'This is worse than being homeless.' Austin bargains with Lee: 'Gimme a little headstart and I'll turn you loose.' No sooner done than Lee springs up to block his way: '*a single coyote heard in distance, lights fade softly into moonlight, the figures of the brothers now appear to be caught in a vast desert-like landscape*'.

What begins in familiar rival-brothers realism ends in a mythic image. Modulating a line from *Waiting for Godot* – 'Time stands still when you're havin' fun.' – and an Ionescan profusion of objects, Shepard explodes the traditional American suburban kitchen. Shepard himself thinks *True West* is 'about double nature',[18] and most critics read it as the old true West of Lee versus the new consumer West of Austin, but this is to underestimate Shepard's complexity [19] – an underestimation to which Shepard contributes by his mistrust of analysis. As early as *Cowboys #2* (1967) Shepard knew that the wild West – its cowboys and Indians, its heroism and lawlessness, its veneer of male bonding – knew that the myth was a fiction. He was never naively nostalgic but rather spiritually curious as to what elements could be salvaged towards a national lifestyle. By 1980 Shepard knew that the fiction was fostered by rampant Hollywood commercialism, to which he himself was 'immune and contaminated at the same time'. By 1980 it is impossible to know the true West, if there ever was one, but the two brothers – the wild man and the domesticated man – might write their joint fiction, or destroy one another. In *True West* Austin excels at beginnings and Lee prefers endings; however Shepard may pose as Lee, he resembles Austin in his explosive beginnings and inconclusive endings.

Bread is both the staff of life and the symbol of human community in Bond's *The Fool*. Toast is something of a joke in Shepard's *True West*, for Austin to butter and stack, for Lee to crush with feet and teeth. The image may finally differentiate playwrights who resemble each other in their broad brush-strokes, their linguistic versatility, and their divergently serious humour. Bond's bread has to be theatricalised by actor and director; his scenic directions provide opportunities rather than instruction.[20] Bread in ill-gotten toasters is Shepard's culminating image of surplus food in pulverised families – the half-price artichokes of *Curse of the Starving Class*, the armfuls of corn and carrots of *Buried Child*. Linked by stage properties or artist figures, both Bond and Shepard dramatise their moribund countries.

NOTES

1. Each playwright has set minor works in the country of the other: Shepard, *Geography of a Horse Dreamer* (1974) in *The Tooth of Crime and Geography of a Horse Dreamer* (London 1974) and Bond, *A-A-America!* (1976) in *A-A-America! and Stone* (London, 1976; revised edn 1981).

2. Cf. John Orr, 'Sam Shepard: The Tragicomedy of the Active Victim' in *Modern Tragicomedy* (Ann Arbor, 1991); Florence Falk, 'The Role of Performance in Sam Shepard's Plays'. *Theatre Journal* (1981).

3. Richard Gilman, 'Introduction' to *Seven Plays* by Sam Shepard (New York, 1981).

4. C.W.E. Bigsby, 'Sam Shepard' in *A Critical Introduction to Twentieth-Century American Drama*, vol. 3 (Cambridge, 1985).

5. In transformation exercises of the Open Theatre each actor 'transforms' without motive or transition from one character to another.

6. Malcolm Hay and Philip Roberts, *Edward Bond. a companion to the Plays* (London, 1978), p. 15.

7. Philip Roberts, *Bond on File* (London, 1985), p. 22.

8. Ibid., P. 43.

9. In the same year as *The Bundle* (1977) Bond wrote a ballet *Orpheus*, a story in six scenes, in which 'The conventional myth of Orpheus losing Eurydice because he looked back is modified by Bond, so that Orpheus is now caught between two deadening worlds, that of hell and that represented by Apollo. . . . Orpheus smashes his lyre and, with it, Apollo's control.' However, Bond's Orpheus fashions even more beautiful music from the broken lyre, inspiring Eurydice and the hell-dwellers to emerge into life on earth. Thus, Orpheus blends the artistic talent of Basho with the social purpose of Wang in Bond's musical fantasy, which would scarcely lend itself to drama of the spoken word. Although Bond has not published his *Orpheus*, he graciously allowed me to read it. I cite the excellent account of Philip Roberts, 'The Search for Epic Drama: Edward Bond's Recent Work', *Modern Drama* XXIV, 4 (1981): 459–60.

    For a detailed description of the ballet, see Clement Crisp, 'Orpheus', *Financial Times* (20 March 1979). Bond has also written fifteen 'Part Songs for Chorus' entitled 'Orpheus and the Wire', published in his *Poems 1978–85* (London, 1987).

10. Kenneth Chubb, 'Fruitful Difficulties of Directing Shepard', *Theatre Quarterly* IV, No. 15 (Aug.–Oct. 1974): 18.

11. Ibid. Two versions of *The Tooth of Crime* differ slightly. Rich information on Shepard's strategies of song is found in Bruce W. Powe, '*The Tooth of Crime*: Sam Shepard's Way with Music' in Dorothy Parker (ed.), *Essays on Modern American Drama* (Toronto, 1987).

12. G. Dark, 'Production Casebook, No. 5: Edward Bond's *Lear* at the Royal Court', *Theatre Quarterly* II, No. 5 (1972): 25. Alistair Stead has called to my attention the double focus of Shepard's *Suicide in B♭*, but this is rare in his work.

13. For a less sympathetic view of Shakespeare, see Malcolm Hay and Philip Roberts, *Bond: A Study of his Plays* (London, 1980), pp. 179–99.

14. Martin Esslin, 'Nor yet a "Fool" to Fame . . .', *Theater Quarterly* VI, No. 21 (Spring 1976): 44. Shepard has also titled a play for a fool-protagonist – *Fool for Love* (1983) – but the fool is a cowboy, not an artist.

15. Hay and Roberts, *Bond: A Study*, p. 200.

16. According to Hay and Roberts, Bond intended Clare's laughter as 'a wholly natural and spontaneous reaction to an absurd and unjust situation' (*Bond: A Study*, p. 208), but I defy any theatre spectator to understand that. For a nuanced reading of class conflict in *The Fool* see Jenny S. Spencer, 'Edward Bond's Dramatic Strategies' in *Contemporary English Drama*, ed. C.W.E. Bigsby (London, 1981), p. 135.

17. Shepard published *True Dylan* in 1987, but, hilariously revealing as it is of Dylan and Shepard, it is too slight to merit comment in this context.

18. John Dugdale, *File on Shepard* (London, 1989), p. 43.

19. See especially Tucker Orbison, 'Mythic Levels in Shepard's *True West*' in Dorothy Parker (ed.), *Essays on Modern American Drama* (Toronto, 1987). William Kleb, however, writes that 'past and present [West] both dissolve', ('Worse Than Being Homeless: *True West* and the Divided Self' in Bonnie Marranca (ed.), *American Dreams*, New York, 1981). p. 123

20. Bread can, of course, be theatricalised in production, as in stage presentations as different as the Bread and Puppet Theater and the Maly Theater's *Brothers and Sisters*.

FURTHER READING

Most of Bond's plays have been published in the three volumes of the Methuen edition.

Shepard's plays are shamefully underpublished in Britain, the plays in print being limited to the Faber *Seven Plays* and *Fool for Love* and the Methuen *A Lie of the Mind*.

Other than works cited in the notes, the following are useful:
Tony Coult, *The Plays of Edward Bond*, 2nd edn (London, 1979).
Richard Scharine, *The Plays of Edward Bond* (Lewisburg, 1976).
Elizabeth Hale Winkler, *The Function of Song in Contemporary English Drama* (London, 1990).

Other than works cited in the notes:
'Sam Shepard' in Philip C. Kolin (ed.), *American Playwrights since 1945: A*

Guide to Scholarship, Criticism, and Performance (Westport, Connecticut, 1989). This is indispensable for any serious work on Shepard.

Ron Mottram, *Inner Landscapes: The Theater of Sam Shepard* (Columbia, 1984).

Ellen Oumano, *Sam Shepard: The Life and Work of an American Dreamer* (New York, 1986).

Don Shewey, *Sam Shepard* (New York, 1985).

CHAPTER TEN

Paleface into Redskin: Cultural Transformations in Alison Lurie's Foreign Affairs

Judie Newman

A critic once divided American writers into two camps, the Palefaces and the Redskins. The Redskins looked west, toward the frontier, responded to the more physical and natural aspects of life, and often wrote in a style which expressed raw experience rather than literary form. The Palefaces looked east, wrote of those peculiarly elusive areas in American life, society and manners, and were preoccupied with craft and formal brilliance.[1]

With these words, Malcolm Bradbury opens his review of Alison Lurie's *Foreign Affairs*. Following in the footsteps of Philip Rahv, the critic in question,[2] Bradbury designates Lurie as a Paleface, noting the enthusiastic reception of her work by the British (Palefaces to a man) as indicative of her true forte as a novelist of manners in the mould of Henry James and Edith Wharton. Rahv's paradigm of the schizophrenic nature of the American literary artist is also, of course, a close approximation to the conventional opposition between America and Europe, and between nature and culture, as it is commonly expressed in American fiction in the 'International Theme', the encounter in one novel between representatives of the two cultures, which is coincidentally also the plot of *Foreign Affairs*.

Since ideas of what is characteristically American or European, definitions of a national culture, stem as much from literature as from life, the notion of intertextuality is relevant here. In the purely literary sense intertextuality depends upon the idea that 'every text builds itself upon a mosaic of quotations, every text is absorption and transformation of another text'.[3] The relation is not between individual texts but to a totality, creating the sense of a work of art which interacts with an entire tradition. If we define 'text' as a system of signs, a text may extend to include folklore, movies, the language of dress, symbolic systems, and the constructions of cultural – or even, if we accept Lacanian notions of the primacy of language – individual identity. The 'International Theme' may be defined as itself an intertext, a set of plots, characters, images and conventions to which a particular novel refers. Moreover, its central situation, in which characters are physically translated and transformed as a result of crossing from one culture, one set of signs, to another, itself thematises intertextuality.

Transposition from one intertext to another necessarily brings into question the autonomy of the individual. In interview Lurie described the germ of the novel as an idea which 'came to me at the Opera. I noticed that when the scene changed behind someone they looked different.'[4] The theatrical context is appropriate. If individuals are passive to change, altered by a different cultural scene, they may be considered as acting within a social fiction, a text which is socially evolved, playing a role in a story which is directed elsewhere. The term 'intertextuality' can suggest this negative sense of life as repeating a previously heard story, of life predestined by the notions that shape our consciousness. In this sense, human experience may generate literature but such experience has already been filtered through forms of artistic organisation which may militate against – or even taboo – certain forms of experience. As Lurie's own collection of feminist folktales suggested,[5] too many women have waited around for a handsome prince, to the detriment of creative experience. Fifty-four-year-old Vinnie Miner (the *major* heroine of *Foreign Affairs*) risks the opposite fate, giving up all hope of an erotic existence because 'in English literature, to which in early childhood Vinnie had given her deepest trust – and which for half a century has suggested to her what she might do, think, feel, desire, and become – women of her age seldom have any sexual or romantic life'.[6]

Conversely the notion of life as imitating art opens the way for a dramaturgical concept of the self, continually creating itself through role-play. Vinnie Miner's *alter ego*, Rosemary Radley, a British actress, escapes from typecasting only to undergo a series of rapid transformations which pass well beyond the bounds of creative adaptivity and into the realm of madness. Where Vinnie is more attentive to a past script than to present reality, Rosemary risks the collapse of a self which is already shifting and permeable at the boundaries. In translating characters from one cultural frame (America) to another (London) Lurie investigates whether the result is the regeneration of an ossified individual in a creative rewriting of the scripted self, or merely a chameleon adaptation to different defining norms. By employing the International Theme, Lurie exposes her characters to a variety of intertextual frames, creating comic, ironic or even tragic effects, as characters who have scripted themselves in accordance with one acculturated model undergo slippage into less exalted or more challenging roles.

The International Theme has been a staple of the American novel from

Hawthorne's *Dr Grimshawe's Secret* to Twain's *Innocents Abroad* and Edith Wharton's *Roman Fever*. Broadly defined, the situation involves the encounter between the moral consciousness of an American and the rich cultural atmosphere of Europe, with the ensuing clash of values demonstrating either the provincialism of the American, at sea in a European world of established customs and sophisticated manners, or the precarious moral footing of the experienced European. The American innocent abroad may feature (positively) as democratic, spontaneous, natural and sincere, or (less attractively) as crude, vulgar and ignorant, while the European sophisticate is alternatively representative of all that is aesthetic and civilised in culture, or conversely of a decadent world of deceit, artifice and aristocratic corruption. Henry James, past master of the theme, gives it classic expression in *The American* (1877) in which Christopher Newman, thwarted in his love for Claire de Cintré by the machinations of the corrupt Bellegardes (who include a murderer within their aristocratic ranks), nobly eschews revenge, out of the American generosity of his spirit, thus revealing a natural nobility of worth rather than birth, which is opposed to the false nobility of the Bellegardes. It is something of a fixed fight, as highly idealised American virtue does battle with stereotypical European villainy.[7] In less clear-cut fashion, in *Daisy Miller* (1878) the eponymous heroine falls foul of her fellow American expatriates in Rome, her innocence recognisable only to a young Italian. This shift towards the Europeanised American as villain is also marked in *The Portrait of a Lady* (1881) where Isabel Archer becomes the prey of the self-centred expatriate Gilbert Osmond. By *The Ambassadors* (1903) the American himself is culpable. Chad Newsome pursues a love affair with Madame de Vionnet only as a temporary diversion from his business interests. His countryman, Lambert Strether, despatched to fetch Chad home to America, ultimately crosses to the lady's side, transferring his allegiance to the ostensibly corrupting European mistress, whose love for Chad is real. James therefore offers a range of possibilities, from the stereotypical American innocent, corrupted by sinister Europeans, to the vulnerable European, exploited and about to be betrayed by the New World.

Americans do not, however, feature very effectively in James as redemptive of Old World corruption. Ironically, for that particular variation the reader must turn to a less exalted version of the International Theme, by a British writer, Frances Hodgson Burnett's *Little Lord Fauntleroy* (1886). A bestseller in its day, when the distinctions between adult and children's fiction were elastic, the novel was much admired by Gladstone who told its author that 'the book would have great effect in bringing about added good feeling between the two nations and making them understand each other'.[8] Despite addressing her as 'noblest of neighbors and most heavenly of women'[9] James was somewhat jealous of Burnett's success,[10] unsurprisingly perhaps, given that in *Pilgrimage* Dorothy Richardson's heroine recommends that one should read 'as Anglo-American history, first *Little Lord Fauntleroy* and then *The Ambassadors*'.[11]

Although the novel involves a persistent criticism of adult values from the child's standpoint, Burnett is relatively even-handed in her treatment of the two cultures, depicting illness and unemployment among the New York working poor as well as poverty and squalor in Britain. Cedric Errol, a child living in straitened circumstances with his widowed mother, is suddenly transplanted to the home of his rich grandfather, the Earl of Dorincourt, a thoroughly selfish English aristocrat, whose heir he becomes. Little Lord Fauntleroy (as he now is) promptly humanises his grandfather by the force of love, bringing out the good in him simply by assuming that he *is* good, and scripting him into that role. In the comic plot, a false claimant to the title is bested with the help of Mr Hobbs, an American grocer of pronounced democratic views, initially scathing about the aristocracy, who finally becomes ancestor-mad and settles in England. As Alison Lurie notes,[12] the appeal of the book depended upon its combination of the 'long lost heir' plot with the International Theme, and a form of secular conversion story, involving the regeneration of an older person through the influence of an affectionate and attractive child. Cedric is also the embodiment of republican virtue, whereas his grandfather represents England, the past, age, rank and selfish pride. Lurie herself draws the analogy with *The Portrait of a Lady* 'which also features the confrontation between a charming, eager, natural young American and representatives of an older and more devious civilization'[13] – though Burnett, unlike James, provides a happy ending.

NATURE'S NOBLEMAN: THE AMERICAN AS FROG PRINCE

The reader who turns from nineteenth-century fiction to *Foreign Affairs* will discover the intertext of the International Theme firmly in place, as might be expected from a writer whose second (unpublished) novel despatched its heroine, Chloe Newcome, to discover crime, poverty and disillusion in postwar Europe.[14] In *Foreign Affairs* two American academics, on sabbatical in London, provide the focus for an exploration of the special relationship, as it obtains in the present, as created by past literary models and, by extension, as an example of the fashion in which literary models may function for good or ill. When Vinnie Miner, sceptical and worldly wise rather than innocent, and in her devout Anglophilia a close approximation to one of James's

Europeanised Americans, encounters Chuck Mumpson, an Oklahoma 'cowboy', she learns a lesson in morals. In the more mannered companion plot, Fred Turner, an all-American hero, has an affair with an English aristocratic lady of a certain age and experience, and feels as if he has got into the pages of a James novel, though whether *The American* or *The Ambassadors* is a moot point. Any easy binary oppositions of American innocence to European experience are subject to revision in a novel which interrogates the nature of the relationship by setting it within a variety of intertextual frames. Paradigms of innocence are thematised by Vinnie's research topic (children's play-rhymes) and undergo radical transformation in the interplay of drama-turgical and folk motifs, literary texts and intertexts, as the four main characters move from American to British intertexts, from Alcott and James to Burnett, Gay and Dickens, and from literature to folktale.

The characteristic note is struck from the beginning. Vinnie Miner is explicitly signalled as the creation of fiction by a series of authorial asides. The reader is informed, for example, that 'In less time than it takes to read this paragraph' (p. 2) she has installed herself comfortably on the flight to London, an experienced transatlantic traveller. The image of a character creating her own cultural reality, enhanced by the capsule effect of air travel which suspends her between two worlds, also reflects Vinnie's Anglophilia. Her dearest fantasy is that she may one day live permanently in London and become an Englishwoman. In advance of her first visit, England had been 'slowly and lovingly shaped and furnished out of her favourite books' (p. 15) so that when she eventually reached 'the country of her mind' (p. 15) she found it almost akin to entering the pages of English literature. The opening chapter recapitulates the process of approaching England through framing fictions. Entry into a different world is also entry into a series of texts. Vinnie can hardly wait to get away from the aptly named *Atlantic* in which a slighting reference to her research from a critic (Leonard Zimmern) has filled her with fantasies of revenge. Instead she takes refuge in the 'cosily confiding' (p. 8) pages of British *Vogue*, and is calmed by *The Times*, compared here to the 'voice of an English nanny' (p. 11). Finally 'the shadows of war darken over Singapore' (p. 15) as she flies on, engrossed in *The Singapore Grip*. Briskly classifying her seat-mate, Chuck Mumpson, from the semiotic indicators of his tan suit and rawhide tie as 'a Southern Plains States businessman of no particular education or distinction' (p. 11), she fends off his conversational overtures by lending him *Little Lord Fauntleroy*, mentally casting him as the democratic grocer, Mr Hobbs, whom he slightly resembles.

Vinnie's casual dismissal of Chuck rebounds upon her, however. While she is haunted in the London Library by 'the portly, well-dressed spirit of Henry James' (p. 59), and entertains erotic fantasies about writers and critics (starring roles go to Lionel Trilling, M.H. Abrams and John Cheever, *inter alia*), Chuck allows the fantasy of the long-lost heir to take hold. Predictably his quest ends in apparent disillusion when he discovers that his ancestor, the Hermit of South Leigh (a legendary troglodyte clad in animal skins), was in fact an illiterate pauper acting in someone else's fantasy: Old Mumpson was hired to impersonate a hermit in an eighteenth-century aristocrat's decorative grotto. Later, however, Chuck realises that illiteracy need not preclude wisdom: 'There's a hell of a lot of learning that isn't in books' (p. 167). It is a lesson which Vinnie is about to learn. Unwillingly she begins to detect an uncomfortable resemblance between Chuck's fantasy of being an English lord and her own of becoming an English lady. She is slower, however, to recognise that she is as unable as Leonard Zimmern to see the relevance of her field of research – oral folklore – to her own life. While she casts Chuck as Mr Hobbs, he is actually functioning within a very different intertextual frame. With his ancestry, his leathery tan and his garb of animal skins (a cowboy hat trimmed with feathers, a fleecy sheepskin coat and a leather jacket) Chuck figures as the 'animal groom' of folktale. Typically such tales centre on the shock of recognition when what seemed vulgar, coarse or 'beastly,' reveals itself as the source of human happiness.[15] (*Beauty and the Beast* is a representative example.) Originally Vinnie had found sexual activity embarrassing (one relationship foundered on the excessively hirsute nature of her lover) and is now poised to abandon 'the foamy backwash and weed-choked turbulence of passion' (p. 76).

The metaphor is subconsciously revelatory. Chuck's greenish waterproof outer layer (a semi-transparent plastic raincoat of repellent design), his pearl studs and habit of slow blinking, identify him as the Frog Prince.[16] Even his occupation – as a sanitary engineer conversant with drains and wells – fits the bill, though he has now been 'flushed out' (p. 123) by his company's redundancy scheme. Vinnie, like the princess in the story, fails to spot his potential, even when he covers her with green slime (avocado and watercress soup). Eventually, however, she admits him to her table and her bed, and discovers that nature has its points over culture. With the destruction of the loathed outer skin (in favour of a Burberry) Chuck is transformed from frog to prince, revealed as 'One of nature's noblemen' (p. 276). The phrase, used by James in *The American*,[17] and something of a cliché of American literature, is given a fresh resonance by the folklore motif. As a Frog Prince, Chuck does come into his own in Europe, in Vinnie's arms, rather than as heir to a fortune. He also negotiates a more objective and productive relation with the past, using his engineering expertise to drain a sunken archaeological site.

Vinnie had read *Little Lord Fauntleroy* without absorbing its message, that it is never too late for change and regeneration. Through Chuck she too is transformed, realising that she has allowed the defining voices of English literature to overdetermine her existence. Now, 'English literature . . . has suddenly fallen silent . . . because she is just too old' (p. 199). In the world of classic British fiction, Vinnie sees, almost the entire population is under fifty, as may have been true of the real world when the novel was invented, and the few older women are cast in minor parts as comic, pathetic or disagreeable. It is assumed that nothing interesting can happen to them. Influenced by Chuck's transformation Vinnie refuses now to become a minor character in her own life. For years, she has accustomed herself to the idea that the rest of her life would be 'a mere epilogue to what was never, it has to be admitted, a very exciting novel' (p. 199). Now, however, she realises that beyond the frame of fiction life has its own horizons: 'this world . . . is not English literature. It is full of people over fifty who will be around and in fairly good shape for the next quarter-century: plenty of time for adventure and change, even for heroism and transformation' (p. 199). Vinnie, whose research into children's rhymes is largely a product of her own nostalgia for childhood, has also to learn that age and experience have their merits. In a particularly unpleasant encounter with a grasping child, who regales her with obscene verses, she realises that innocence is not the preserve of youth, and that her thesis – that British rhymes are more lyrical and literary than their cruder American counterparts – is untenable.

If the child in question has come a long way from Little Lord Fauntleroy, Chuck, however unprepossessing his initial impression, fulfils the role to a tee. Although he, too, is no stereotypical innocent (driving while intoxicated, he was responsible for a boy's death), Chuck's persistent vision of self-centred Vinnie as 'a good woman' (p. 174) eventually scripts her into the role. Much as the Earl lived up to Cedric's expectations, so Vinnie fulfils Chuck's. Like Christopher Newman, when the opportunity for revenge on the hated Zimmern occurs (by proxy through his daughter) Vinnie allows her better impulses to triumph, attentive to the inner voice of Chuck. Appealed to by Ruth (*née* Zimmern) to deliver a message to Fred Turner which will reunite these star-crossed lovers, Vinnie hesitates. Fred is on Hampstead Heath observing the solstice: 'most people Vinnie knows certainly wouldn't expect her to go to Hampstead Heath. But one person would . . . Chuck Mumpson' (p. 244). At the end of the novel, heroically braving the muggers, Vinnie does bear the message to Fred. Rejecting a false model in classic British fiction, she adopts a better one, the product of the interaction of folklore and children's literature. More importantly she recognises the idiosyncratic, individual nature of human existence, and the potentially coercive nature of literary models. At a symposium on 'Literature and the Child', the lecturer declares that 'The Child's moral awareness' must be awakened by 'responsible literature' (p. 235). Vinnie is now in no mood to look to literature for guidance. 'Vinnie yawns angrily. There is no Child, she wants to shout . . . there are only children, each one different, unique' (p. 235). The realisation cuts two ways. Though Vinnie has shed her passivity to the discourses of literature which previously wrote her, it is in fact to children's literature that she owes that transformation. Moreover, if the stereotypes of age and youth have been comprehensively revised, the novel none the less appears to conform to the paradigms provided by Burnett and James, as a Europeanised American is redeemed by love, and American virtue triumphs with nature over the rigid forms of European culture. Under Chuck's influence, Vinnie concludes that doing things for others may have caused most of the trouble of her life, 'but it has also caused most of the surprise and interest and even in the end joy' (p. 270).

THE REAL THING: THE CHARWOMAN IN THE BASEMENT

The novel does not end, however, on such a potentially schmaltzy note as *Little Lord Fauntleroy*. Although Vinnie finally wakes up to the fact that Chuck loves her and she him, it is very much a case of too little, too late. Because of her dogged attachment to her image as English lady, Vinnie fears cultural redefinition by proximity to Chuck. When she is juxtaposed with him, her British friends are likely to equate them as each 'rather simple, vulgar, and amusing – a typical American' (p. 206). As a result she fails to join him in Wiltshire, where he dies of a heart attack. Vinnie's story is also only part of the novel, doubled, and its implications to some extent reversed, by that of her fellow expatriate, Fred Turner. Lurie's novel practises what it preaches, offering a choice of outcomes to the International Theme, weaving a plot in one direction and then, Penelope-like, unpicking the threads in the companion plot, so that *Foreign Affairs* resists reinforcing any one literary model.

Even more than Vinnie, Fred sees himself within a literary frame, thinking of John Gay's *Trivia* as he walks the streets of London (Gay is his research topic) and imagining himself as a character in a Henry James novel (p. 87).[18] Others, however, envisage him in a variety of less prestigious roles, as the hero of a Gothic romance, as an actor in *Love's Labour's Lost*, a character in an American detective series, or 'the guy who fought the giant man-eating extraterrestrial cabbage in *The Thing from Beyond*' (p. 25). Nobody connects him with light comedy or game shows; his brooding good looks militate against certain parts. Quite the reverse of Chuck, Ivy League Fred, an American aristocratic in terms of 'entitlement psychology' (p. 51), is recognised as her handsome prince by his wife Roo (Ruth Zimmern). The latter, now surnamed March in homage to 'tomboy' Jo in Alcott's *Little*

Women, whom she closely resembles physically (a long chestnut braid) and in character, unwittingly follows the fate of her chosen model, forfeiting her trip to Europe, like Jo, as the result of independence and frankness. Very much a female version of Chuck, Roo is at home in nature and initiates her relationship with Fred outdoors, following a riding excursion. Just as Vinnie found her world transformed by Chuck, so Fred under Roo's influence sees it as 'naked, beautiful, full of meaning' (p. 44). Fred's story, however, is a replay in reverse of Vinnie's, from frankness, sincerity and natural sexuality in America to the constricting European world of manners and culture. Appropriately, as an artist, Roo draws her effects from the juxtaposition of nature and culture, often with satiric results. Her exhibition, 'Natural Forms', includes a shot of two overweight politicians next to a pair of beef cattle, for example. [19] Fred, however, is discomfited by a photograph of his own penis in juxtaposition with a large and beautiful mushroom, and even less delighted by the presence of two unidentified others – even if one is juxtaposed with an asparagus stalk, and the other with a rusty bolt. In the ensuing marital fracas, Fred concludes that Roo 'was not a lady' (p. 49) and exits sharply for Europe.

In Rosemary Radley, however, he appears to have found the real thing. Herself the daughter of an earl, Rosemary specialises in acting high-born ladies, particularly in *Tallyho Castle,* a television series of snobbish appeal, which paints a fake picture of upper-class country life. The contrast between the two cultures is expressed for Fred by his two women. Where Ruth flung herself into his arms, Fred has to court Rosemary in traditional fashion. She is sophisticated where Roo is naive, graceful where Roo is coarse, reticent where Roo is outspoken, 'Just as, compared with England, America is large, naive, noisy, crude, etc.' (p. 81). Fred's revision of his mental image of Roo is a pompously textual operation, an example in his mind of 'retrospective influence. Just as Wordsworth forever altered our reading of Milton, so Rosemary Radley has altered his reading of Ruth March' (p. 81). Roo's previous natural, free behaviour, her rapid sexual surrender, now seem less a warranty of passion and sincerity than 'hardly civilized' (p. 82). Significantly, where he and Roo came together out of doors, he and Rosemary meet at the theatre, in a world of artifice and illusion. Fred, the expert on Gay, ascribes his conquest of Rosemary to eighteenth-century virtues of civility and boldness. By politely remaining at Vinnie's party he was able to meet Rosemary, a congenital latecomer, and he subsequently pursues her as a challenge 'undertaken in the same spirit that makes other Americans expend energy and ingenuity to view some art collection or local ceremony that is out of bounds to most tourists' (p. 79).

In Rosemary's world – specifically, spending a weekend in an English country house – Fred revels in the sensation that 'by some supernatural slippage between life and art, he has got into a Henry James novel like the one he watched on television' (p. 87). In cold fact the televisual metaphor is more apt. Rosemary is not just typecast on celluloid as an English lady, but also in life. Although she complains to Fred that she longs to play the classic parts ('I know what it is to feel murderous, coarse, full of hate', pp. 88–9) he pooh-poohs her, refusing to envisage her in any character other than that of cultured aristocrat. When, however, the assembled house guests play charades, the childish game reveals raw experience beneath its formal surface. Presumably inspired by Dorothy Parker's dictum that 'You can lead a whore to culture but you can't make her think', Rosemary's team chooses to dramatise the word 'horticulture', breaking it down into three component parts, to reveal a coarse subtext beneath the surface cultivation. In the first, to Fred's horror, Rosemary appears as 'whore'. Since her costume is the identical nightgown in which she has just slept with Fred, the distinction between art and life almost dissolves. In the second ('Tit') she is part of a cow, and in the third a sulky schoolchild (reminiscent of Vinnie's ghastly informant) resisting the efforts of a schoolmaster to lead her to culture. The emphasis on language is also significant. Vinnie had previously described Rosemary's conversation as mere musical noise: 'Words don't matter to actors as they do to a literary person. For them, meaning is mainly in expression and gesture; the text is just the libretto' (p. 64). Gleefully Rosemary acts on this assumption, transforming her text in order to act out the parts denied her in life. In the charades, her homosexual friend Edwin actually seems 'more natural as a fortyish matron' (p. 94) than in real life. Role-play reveals the multifaceted nature of the self in creative ways. The arrival of the hostess's husband, however, reveals even more, as her lover has to be whisked into hiding. Faced with the visible evidence of upper-class corruption, Fred's Jamesian frame of reference wavers :

> only an hour ago he thought it was all beautiful, the real thing. James again, Fred thinks: a Jamesian phrase, a Jamesian situation. But in the novels the scandals and secrets of high life are portrayed as more elegant; the people are better mannered. Maybe because it was a century earlier; or maybe only because the mannered elegance of James' prose obfuscates the crude subtext. Maybe, in fact, it was just like now. (p. 101).

Briskly excluding Rosemary from these speculations, Fred readjusts his James, determined to rescue his innocent beloved from these evil influences, and electing himself as 'the sterling young American champion James himself would have provided. For the second time that day Fred has the giddy sense of having got into a novel' (p. 101).

Ironically, however, Fred has once more got into the wrong fiction. To become Rosemary's true champion, he should have been less intent on stereotyping her as a lady, and paid more attention to the subtext, as the reference to 'the real thing' indicates. In James's story of that title a well-bred couple offer themselves as an artist's models on the grounds that it would be good for him to use 'the real thing; a gentleman . . . or a lady'.[20] When, however, the painter employs the lady he finds her so lacking in adaptive plasticity and expression that she is inferior as a model to his servants: 'She was always a lady, certainly, and into the bargain was always the same lady. She was the real thing, but always the same thing.'[21] As a result, the real thing turns out to be less valuable for artistic purposes than the fake; art depends upon the transformation of reality rather than reflecting the thing itself. Ultimately the real thing is the product of the creative imagination of the artist, just as, paradoxically, Rosemary is more herself when she demonstrates the power of her creative adaptation of words to role.

Where Vinnie finds a new role by accepting a 'lower' subtext, in vulgar Chuck, Fred is determined to expunge it in favour of genteel forms, editing out any aspects of Rosemary's behaviour which he considers out of character. He even insists that she set an appropriate scene for their affair, badgering her to engage a charlady to clean up her grubby house. Meeting the pair at the Opera, Vinnie reflects that 'The dusty chaos of Rosemary's house would surely seem to him a most unsuitable backdrop for their love duet' (p. 116), a duet in which, in operatic metaphor, Fred is 'singing the basso part' (p. 116). Indeed, in the outcome it appears that Fred's arguments have carried the day. Rosemary hires Mrs Harris, a cockney char, and as a result creates 'a scene that resembles a commercial for some luxury product: the perfectly elegant party' (p. 137). Surveying his surroundings, Fred congratulates himself that his rush of moral indignation during the country weekend was merely 'priggish and provincial' (p. 131), misled by 'a too-vivid memory of the novels of Henry James into condemning an entire society' (p. 131). Although Roo has now contacted him, and convinced him that she is innocent of adultery and guilty only of bad taste, his standards are now those of European manners rather than American morals: 'in Rosemary's world bad taste is not nothing: it is the outward and visible sign of an inward and spiritual flaw' (p. 134). Unsurprisingly, when Fred meets Chuck at the party he assumes that someone so inappropriate to the elegant occasion cannot be real but must be one of Rosemary's actor friends trying out a role. Commenting on Chuck's origins, he quips that he has never been to Oklahoma, 'but I saw the movie' (p. 138). In contrast, although he has yet to meet her, Mrs Harris 'sounds like the genuine article' (p. 140). With his taste for Gay, Fred welcomes the crudity of Mrs Harris's manners (as reported by Rosemary) as if she were 'a character out of eighteenth-century literature: a figure from the subplot of some robust comedy illustrated by Hogarth or Rowlandson' (p. 142). As the alert reader may already recognise, the joke is very much on Fred, who finds himself starring in a rather different fictional role in the outcome, scripted in part by the character of Mrs Harris.

The party ends in disaster when Fred's friend Joe Vogeler inadvertently reveals Fred's intention to return to America, on schedule, to teach summer school. Rosemary draws the conclusion that 'it was only an act with you' (p. 149) and breaks off the relationship. Fred is less a Christopher Newman or a Lambert Strether than a Chad Newsome. He has encouraged Rosemary to love him unconditionally while intending to love her only as long as it was convenient. Although Fred pleads poverty as his motive for returning, he refuses Rosemary's offer of a loan, on the Victorian moral principle that a man cannot take money from a woman. Although the offer is made on the set of a television historical drama, with Rosemary in full make-up, it is Fred, in her opinion, who is caught in a rigid role: 'You think you're in some historical drama; it's you who ought to be in costume' (p. 181). Accordingly, despite his American accent, Rosemary offers him a film role: 'you could be a silent brooding undergardener or gypsy tramp' (p. 181). Fred, however, can accept nothing less than heroic status. Instead, he swiftly reclaims the moral high ground by redefining Rosemary. The idea that he has fallen into a Henry James novel recurs, 'but now he casts Rosemary in a different role, as one of James's beautiful, worldly, corrupt European villainesses' (p. 194). Like his Australian friends, who describe their convict ancestors as adventurous and risk-taking, 'Moll Flanders not Oliver Twist' (p. 187), Fred is quick to cite chapter and verse of a supportive literary model, making an opportunistic choice of literary frame.

Where Vinnie learned the need to escape from overly constricting models, Fred has gone to the other extreme, and gets his come-uppance as a result of his belief that he can pick and choose freely between them. Rosemary also operates intertextually, with tragic results, breaking out of her role as English lady and shifting the frame of reference once more, from America to Britain and from James to Dickens. Once again truth comes into being through role-play. Sharing a taxi with Vinnie, Rosemary takes the opportunity to complain about Fred; her speech alternates between her own upper-class drawl and an accent so vulgar and coarse that 'if they hadn't been alone Vinnie would have looked round to see who else was speaking' (p. 209). She goes on alternating between being pathetically ladylike and a low comedy voice, slips into tenor to imitate a male friend, and concludes – to Vinnie's horror – by insulting the latter in a caricature of her own intonation and accent. On one level, of course, the scene appears to confirm Fred's estimation of Rosemary's fundamental falsity. Yet, crying over Fred, Rosemary's face is 'distorted in a way it never becomes when she weeps on camera' (p. 211). Rosemary believed that Fred loved her for herself alone, as the real thing: 'He'd never even heard of *Tallyho Castle*. . . . He never even saw the show, he loved me anyhow' (p. 211). Where Vinnie had been chary of introducing Chuck to her British friends, afraid of being redefined as of similarly American character, Rosemary actively sought role revision by contact with Fred. She has been over-defined, as an English lady, and the cultural definition has constricted her life. Ironically, the fate which Vinnie so feared is actually visited upon her by her association with Fred. Gesturing at souvenir shops and hamburger joints, Rosemary accuses: 'I've had it with all you fuckin' Americans. Why don't you stay home where you belong? Nobody wants you comin' over here, messin' up our country' (p. 212). Uneasily Vinnie recognises the low comedy stage character as that of Mrs Harris, whom Rosemary has taken to imitating. For Vinnie the episode reveals that there is 'something unnatural, really, in the ability of certain persons to assume at will a completely alien voice and manner' (p. 213); the practice 'overturns our belief in the uniqueness of the individual' (p. 213). The comment extends also to Vinnie, who has been acting the alien role of English lady and sacrificing her own uniqueness to the scripts of British fiction. When Rosemary uses her histrionic talents to become Vinnie Miner, she indicates that the two have more in common than Vinnie would care to concede.

If Vinnie's encounter with 'Mrs Harris' leaves her shaken, Fred's has even more bruising consequences. Entering Rosemary's house in search of his *Oxford Book of Eighteenth Century Verse*, Fred finds Mrs Harris, a drunken slut, in the darkened basement drinking Rosemary's gin. Upstairs he recoils in horror at the dirt and disorder. Rosemary's bathroom is 'littered and foul – the toilet, for instance, is full of turds' (p. 226). When Mrs Harris makes a pass at him in a drunken imitation of Rosemary's voice, he calls her a 'dirty old cow' (p. 228) and shoves her forcibly aside. Giving an edited account of the scene later to his friends, Fred converts it into comedy, 'a scene from Smollett . . . a cartoon by Rowlandson' (p. 229). But as the alert reader may have guessed,[22] Mrs Harris is not so much an eighteenth- as a nineteenth-century character. In a moment of dreadful revelation Fred recalls the charlady's telltale birthmark, identical to Rosemary's: Mrs Harris and Rosemary are one and the same. While Fred wandered the pages of James, Rosemary has adopted a character from another novel of transatlantic encounter, Dickens' *Martin Chuzzlewit*, in which Mrs Harris features as Sairey Gamp's imaginary friend. 'A fearful mystery surrounded this lady of the name of Harris, whom no one in the circle of Mrs Gamp's acquaintance had ever seen. . . . There were conflicting rumours on the subject; but the prevalent opinion was that she was a phantom of Mrs Gamp's brain.'[23] Thwarted by typecasting, Rosemary has created in life the part denied her on stage. Fred had allowed the idea of her as cultivated, refined and aristocratically English to become so fixed in his mind that anyone who did not conform to the model could not be Rosemary. Although her role-play has now tipped her over into Gothic delusion – her repressed self finally emerging, if not as the madwoman in the attic, at least as the charwoman in the basement – Fred does little to save her, though he nobly offers to see her once more in the *twenty minutes* which he can spare before his flight departs.

Cultural transformations can work both ways. Where Vinnie, the stereo-typical sexless crone of British fiction, is transformed by love, Rosemary evolves from beauty to hag, in the 'loathly lady' motif of folklore.[24] Chuck transforms himself from beast to prince, Fred from prince to brute. The parallels are emphasised in the action. In a reprise of the folklore motif, Fred is seen walking by Regent's canal with the Vogelers. The latter equate his passion for Rosemary with their infant's desire for an old rubber ball, its cracked surface patterned with a dirty Union Jack. (They have been discussing Rosemary's advanced age.) As the ball bounces into the 'frog-green water' (p. 189) 'surrounded by waterlogged crap' (p. 190), the image is associated with the foulness of Rosemary's house and takes the reader back to the starting point of *The Frog Prince*, when the princess's ball is lost and rescued by the frog. Earlier Vinnie had reminisced about her husband, who had married her when, on the rebound from another woman, he had 'like a waterlogged tennis ball . . . rolled into the nearest hole' only to regain his elasticity, 'bounce about' at parties, and 'hop' into the arms of another (p. 74). The ball metaphor (with its connections to an even cruder subtext) suggests that Fred is unable to reconcile the 'beastly' elements of Rosemary's character with his ideal, or to love anyone who is not young and beautiful. It dawns upon him – too late – that his chosen role of Jamesian hero is altogether less convincing than that of a British rogue – Macheath in Gay's *The Beggar's Opera*. If his academic work now appears as a mere patching together of ideas from other people's books, 'his love life is no better. Like Macheath's, it follows one of the classic literary patterns of the eighteenth century, in which a man meets and seduces an innocent woman, then abandons her' (p. 255).

Lurie, however, like Gay, is merciful. At the end the two plots unite on Hampstead Heath. Clad in a romantically draped coat, a gift from Chuck, Vinnie looks like one of the 'Druids' celebrating the solstice, derided by Fred as examples of mummery and phoniness.

> Yes, Fred thinks as the foolish figure drifts nearer, this is what England, with her great history and traditions – political, social, cultural – has become; this is what Britannia, that vigorous, ancient, and noble goddess, has shrunk to: a nervous elderly little imitation Druid (p. 252).

Yet it is Fred, the American champion, who is rescued by Vinnie, braving 'drifters and tramps and thieves' (p. 248) to deliver the vital message which will reunite him with Roo. As the dramatic mummery of the Druids indicates, Fred's rescue and Vinnie's regeneration both depend to some extent on contacts with an artificial world in which a new self can be fashioned. Neither Vinnie nor Fred has survived with their illusions about England intact. Vinnie sees a different, potentially violent, London on her way to the Heath; Fred decides that 'London in Gay's time was filthy, violent, corrupt – and it hasn't changed all that much' (p. 249). In a last, ironic turn of the plot, however, the cycle of illusion reopens, as the Vogelers declare their enthusiasm for the country: 'It's like being in the nineteenth century, really. Everybody in the village is so friendly . . . and they're all such perfect *characters*' (p. 250).

This essay began from a consideration of Lurie as a 'paleface' writer. Whereas the relation to James may appear to confirm Malcolm Bradbury's hypothesis, it is worth noting that in this novel Chuck and Roo – the cowboy and the Alcott girl – come up trumps, while Jamesian Fred and Vinnie are led intertextually astray. Moreover the robustness of the folklore plot, the directness of its crude subtext, impose different conclusions. Teasingly, Lurie includes as the climax to the romantic plot a scene in which Vinnie (pale but not very interesting as the result of a heavy cold) is contrasted with Chuck in the role of redskin. The latter, minus his clothes on which he has spilled soup, is transformed by a fringed, homespun bedspread into 'a comic oversized pink-faced Red Indian' (p. 172), who promptly seduces Vinnie against the backdrop of a singularly inappropriate watercolour of New College, Oxford. Although paleface and redskin – the two halves of the American character – come together for once, the national stereotype does not remain fixed. Confusingly, the couple consume a (British) Indian takeaway, and reference is made to Gandhi.

As these examples of cultural slippage indicate, there can be no real return to nature, nor to some primary state of childlike innocence of language or culture. Culture is textuality. Even Roo is an artist, and in her chosen surname as consciously intertextual as Rosemary. Each of us is always to some extent a role-player; only Fred is so naive as to consider Roo sincere, Rosemary false. Yet although cultural models cannot be ignored, Lurie indicates that wiser choices may be made between them. When Chuck is informed that he is descended from the aristocratic De Mompesson family – of which Mumpson is a contraction – he wisely discards the idea as irrelevant, a sensible contrast to Tess Durbeyfield's papa. *Little Lord Fauntleroy* turns out to be more productive of happiness for Chuck and Vinnie than Dickens and Gay are for Rosemary and Fred. The fact that he is an expert on *The Beggar's Opera* does not prevent Rosemary from beggaring Fred. On the other hand ignorance is never bliss, as Fred's inability to recognise Mrs Harris, and Vinnie's to spot her Frog Prince, amply demonstrate. Although Roo features, like Daisy Miller, as the American Girl, Chuck's daughter Barbie, introduced at the close, acts as a corrective to any anti-intellectual glorification of a state of nature. Barbie commits every form of vulgar Americanism, from describing her father's 'cremains' while shovelling down a cream tea, to subsequently wishing Vinnie 'Have a nice day' (p. 270). So much for the Jamesian heiress of all the ages.

While the novel demonstrates the dangers of looking to literature for guidance, it therefore also indicates the very real advantages of a sophisticated knowledge thereof. Both British and American heroines, for all their differences, are almost equally victimised by literary and cultural stereotypes. Rosemary's English lady reveals depths of feeling, while Chuck, emblematic of 'Oklahoma crude', proves a sensitive lover who enables Vinnie to grow and change. Chuck may be said to civilise Vinnie, whereas Fred comes close to ruining Rosemary altogether. The deconstruction of the fiction of The Child and the stereotype of The Lady is part and parcel of the deconstruction of the stereotypes of national and literary character. As the novel indicates, works of literature are flexibly bound to each other despite national divisions. As a result *Foreign Affairs* is not merely a novel about two cultures clashing, but about all culture as intertextual, changing and created by individuals, and continually undergoing slippage, reversals and revision. Just as its meaning is constructed and revised, built up or shifted by slippage between intertextual frames, the novel's overall structure allows one plot to form a paradigm, a guide through the labyrinth, which the other is simultaneously unravelling. Even as culture is revealed as a continual process of creative transformation, so *Foreign Affairs* is careful to preclude the possibility of establishing a single, normative voice. In its imaginative transformations, it may therefore be characterised as in itself very much the real thing.

NOTES

1. Malcolm Bradbury, 'The Paleface Professor', *The Times* (19 January 1985): 6.

2. Philip Rahv, 'Paleface and Redskin' in *Literature and the Sixth Sense* (London, 1970), pp. 1–6.

3. Julia Kristeva, *Séméiôtiké, recherches pour une sémananalyse* (Paris, 1969), p. 146 (my translation). I have discussed the importance of intertextuality in relation to Lurie's *Imaginary Friends* in 'The Revenge of the Trance Maiden: Alison Lurie and Intertextuality' in Linda Anderson (ed.), *Plotting Change: Contemporary Women's Fiction* (London, 1990), pp. 113–27.

4. Christopher Tookey, 'The witch guide to literary London', *Books and Bookmen* 352 (January 1985): 25.

5. Alison Lurie, *Clever Gretchen and Other Forgotten Folktales* (London, 1980).

6. Alison Lurie, *Foreign Affairs* (London, 1986), p. 75. Subsequent page references follow citations in parentheses.

7. For a comprehensive and accessible discussion of the International Theme in James see Christof Wegelin, *The Image of Europe in Henry James* (Dallas, 1958) and Tony Tanner, *Henry James: The Writer and His Work* (Amherst, 1985). I draw upon both writers extensively here.

8. Ann Thwaite, *Waiting for the Party: The Life of Frances Hodgson Burnett* (London, 1974), pp. 107–8.

9. Ibid., p. xi.

10. Juliet Dusinberre, *Alice to the Lighthouse: Children's Books and Radical Experiments in Art* (London, 1987), p. 30.

11. Ibid., p. 30.

12. Alison Lurie, 'Happy Endings: Frances Hodgson Burnett' in *Don't Tell the Grown-Ups: Subversive Children's Literature* (London, 1990), pp. 136–43.

13. Ibid., p. 140.

14. Private interview with Alison Lurie, Key West, Florida, 19 February 1991. Grateful acknowledgement is made to the British Academy and the University of Newcastle upon Tyne for assistance with travel expenses.

15. Bruno Bettelheim, *The Uses of Enchantment: The Meaning and Importance of Fairy Tales* (Harmondsworth, 1978), pp. 277–310.

16. Maureen Corrigan is the one reviewer who drew attention to this motif, reviewing the novel in *Village Voice Literary Supplement*, October 1984: 5.

17. Christof Wegelin notes that James used the phrase in the New York edition of *The American* (p. 91) as a revision of 'a noble fellow' (Rinehart edn, p. 63). Emerson wrote in his *Journal* of 'Nature's Gentlemen, who need no discipline, but grow straight up into shape and grace and can match the proudest in dignified demeanour and the gentlest in courtesy'. Thoreau, Margaret Fuller, Howells and Melville all make conspicuous reference to the concept of natural nobility (*The Image of Europe in Henry James*, op. cit., p. 178).

18. Readers familiar with Lurie's work will note a further irony. Fred is already a character in a novel – Lurie's first, *Love and Friendship* – a scene from which is referred to in *Foreign Affairs*, p. 43, to establish Fred's obtuseness.

19. Similar juxtapositions were a feature of the British magazine *Lilliput*. See Kaye Webb (ed.), *Lilliput Goes to War* (London, 1985).

20. Henry James, 'The Real Thing' (1892) in Christof Wegelin (ed.), *Tales of Henry James* (New York, 1984), p. 246.

21. Ibid., p. 249.

22. Some of the most alert were Ferdinand Mount, 'The Lonely American', *Spectator*, 26 January 1985: 24; Walter Clemons, 'Lovers and Other Strangers', *Newsweek* 104 (24 September 1984): 80; Lorna Sage, 'Adventures in the Old World', *Times*

Literary Supplement (1 February 1985): 109; Marilyn Butler, 'Amor Vincit Vinnie', *London Review of Books* (21 February 1985): 5–6.

23. Charles Dickens, *The Life and Adventures of Martin Chuzzlewit* (London, 1858), p. 423

24. In which either a hag turns into a lovely lady, or vice versa. See Chaucer's 'Wife of Bath's Tale', *Sir Gawain and the Green Knight* or Spenser's *Faerie Queen*, Book One.

The author is grateful for an award from the British Academy which allowed the first delivery of the paper on which this essay is based, at the American Literature Association Conference, San Diego, May 1992.

FURTHER READING

Frances Hodgson Burnett, *Little Lord Fauntleroy* (London, 1981).
Charles Dickens, *The Life and Adventures of Martin Chuzzlewit* (London, 1858).
John Gay, *The Beggar's Opera* (London, 1968).
Henry James, *The American, The Portrait of a Lady, The Ambassadors*, in *The Novels and Tales of Henry James*, 'New York Edition' (New York, 1907–9).
Alison Lurie, *Foreign Affairs* (New York, 1984 and London, 1985).

III   Generic Perspectives: George Orwell to Raymond Carver

Brian Harding, in the third essay in this section, takes as his point of departure Martin Green's contention that by the seventies a new genre – sub-genre – of fiction had emerged. This new historical novel, now better known as 'historiographical metafiction' since Linda Hutcheon's introduction of the term in her expositions of postmodernist fiction, has proved an immensely popular species of contemporary literature on both sides of the Atlantic. From which fact we may deduce a general rule governing the approach to the question of international comparisons through genre: no nation has exclusive rights to a genre. Today, with the advancing internationalisation of literary and cultural forms, this may appear very obvious. In the past, however, there have been moments when one literary kind has so commanded the cultural space that the national ethos has appeared to be bound up in its fortunes and formulations – consider the hundred years of outstanding drama in England that stretches from the Elizabethan to the Restoration playwrights. But in the twentieth century the contribution to theatre of American writers has challenged any notion of an undisputed British hegemony in the field of dramatic literature in English. Conversely, the Western romance has often been seen as absolutely indigenous to America, taking its formal impulse from European romantic narrative but strikingly adapting to the conditions of the New World (dealing with the opening up and settlement of the land, staging in this symbolic space confrontations and negotiations between configurations of civilisation and wilderness, East and West, settled society and lawlessness).

The Western's translation into popular cinematic and televisual images has played a notable part in the process of 'Americanisation' and, in particular, in what Europeans have sometimes unfairly called the colonisation of Europe's, even the whole world's, unconscious by Hollywood. Yet today's leading writer of Westerns is the Briton J.T. Edson, resident in the English Midlands and prolific author of the 'Rapido' series, and, by courtesy of the intercontinental boomerang, the American film industry has had to receive, assimilate and re-work John Ford-inspired Samurai epics from Japan and Spaghetti Westerns from Italy. Duncan Webster, shrewd analyst of popular culture in Britain and the United States in his spirited *Looka Yonder!* (London and New York, 1988), also usefully relays Cora Kaplan's insight that a genre as an explanatory frame can change its meaning as it crosses international frontiers: the conservative ideology that the American Left deplored in Ford's Westerns in the sixties could function cisatlantically to begin to open up 'the class bound complacency of the Great Tradition of British Culture' (pp. 178–9). Robert Weisbach, in his brilliant examination of American literature and British influence in the Age of Emerson, *Atlantic Double-Cross* (Chicago, 1986), claims that America's prevalent genre is encyclopedic. The observation, provoked by works like Melville's *Moby Dick* and Whitman's *Leaves of Grass*, excites us to speculate on the survival or revival of such a dominant in our period (William Gaddis's *J.R.* and Thomas Pynchon's *Gravity's Rainbow?*). David Peck's comparison of the distinguished reportage of Orwell and Agee in the thirties in the context of the radicalising effect of political journalism on writers in both countries might well prompt speculation about the continuing high prestige of journalism in the United States today, with Tom Wolfe's New Journalism, the non-fiction novels of Truman Capote and Norman Mailer, and the post-Watergate canonisation of the muckraking reporter behind it, and little to correspond to it in British culture. The exception perhaps is Iain Chambers's suggestion in *Popular Culture* (London and New York, 1986) that a 'British way of seeing', predominantly natural-istic, emerges from the Mass Observation researches and Documentary Movement in the cinema of the thirties and forties, and the 'Free Cinema' and 'working-class realist' films of the later fifties and early sixties. But which culture is it that overestimates factuality or what documentary techniques can contribute to imaginative fictions?

One aspect of genre that throws light on how British and American literary cultures tend to differ is the way plays end in popular theatre. Egri's comparison of the closure of plays by Cooper and Albee (the former ironic within realism, the latter double: first plausibly resigned, then improbably rebellious) suggests that conclusions may be culturally determined. This is more obvious in the commercially successful theatre which, for the most part, does not include many of the dramatists analysed in this volume. The popular dramatist in America is much more likely than his British counterpart to be faced with the ultimatum: end 'up', or close down. The clamminess of the American closure has been splendidly ridiculed by Philip Roth in *Reading Myself and Others* (/) Harmondsworth, 1985 expanded edn, p. 178: 'And on Broadway, in the third act, someone says, "Look, why don't you just love each other?" and the protagonist, throwing his hand to his forehead, cries "Oh, God, why didn't *I* think of that!" and before the bulldozing action of love, all else collapses – verisimilitude, truth and interest.'

Ever since the beginning of the century, when an indigenous American theatre was stirring into life, the curse of the upbeat ending and uplifting gesture has impended over the best talents. Thus W.D. Howells was fore-warning Edith Wharton that her first play, Clyde Fitch's dramatisation of *The House of Mirth* in 1906, was too uncomfortable to run: 'Yes what the American public wants is a tragedy with a happy ending.' (Edith Wharton, *A Backward Glance*, New York, 1934, p. 147) Box-office receipts have not been the only determinants; as the century wore on, America's therapy culture, promoting personal growth and the centrality of interpersonal relationships (most bla-tantly by the talking cure of psychoanalysis), boosted Roth's 'theatrical *amor-vincit-omnia* boys'. A serious-minded, ambitious, sometimes tragic the-atre managed to make its mark from the twenties to the fifties in the United States, but popular taste and concentrated metropolitan commercial pressures have tended to distort. When the British playwright David Hare complains that 'the prevalent policy of Official Optimism' has killed his sex-change opera *The Knife* (co-written with Nick Bičat and mounted on Broadway in 1987) because it has offered no affirmative or reconciling gesture, its failure may reflect more than 'the current orthodoxies of American culture' (*Writing Left-Handed*, London, 1991, pp. 136–50). Comparison of the careers of the two most popular dramatists of the British and American stages in the second half of the century (Alan Ayckbourn and Neil Simon) may confirm a longer trend: both writers construct ingenious comic entertainments, the former out of Home Counties suburban inanities, the latter from urban Jewish one-liners (*Bedroom Farce*, 1975; *The Odd Couple*, 1966). Although both have extended their emotional range (*Just Between Ourselves*, 1976; *The Sunshine Boys*, 1973), they have begun to diverge more radically: whereas Simon stays within sentimental bounds in his autobiographical plays (*Brighton Beach Memoirs*, 1984), Ayckbourn takes on the monstrous, waxing increasingly satirical (*Man of the Moment*, 1990), providing conclusions that are grimly ironic (*A Chorus of Disapproval*, 1984) or downright disturbing (*Woman in Mind*, 1985).

The comparison of British and American literary cultures and productions in this section rests on a number of shared genres (reportage, poetry, historical fiction, short story) variously shaped and framed. Particularly prominent in the first two essays (one on prose, the other on verse) is the importance of a specific historical perspective on the genre in question; for both are in good part studies in reception. Peck demonstrates how evaluation of the politicised writings of the thirties suffered disproportionately in America from the need of literary critics surviving the decade to rewrite their participation in it in the light of the anti-Marxism of the McCarthy years; the equivalent British memoirs were under no such powerful pressures. The revision of the revisionists, in which Peck shares, has followed on the new wave of radicalisa-tion that Vietnam and the anti-war movement ushered in and the ending of the Cold War. Keith Tuma in his enquiry into whether there was a British modernist poetry looks back from the nineties to the retrospects on the moderns in both countries which were fuelling the debate in the sixties and seventies on the alleged discontinuity of British and American poetry. Peck endeavours to re-establish, as he discriminates between, the radical literary achievements of such as Orwell and Agee, paradigmatic consonants and dissonants in his study of the 'creative transformation' of the 'hard facts of observation'. In a species of parallel process Tuma redeems from the intricate but cultural-cliché-clouded literary politics of the international debates sub-stantial British modernists like Basil Bunting, Mina Loy, Hugh MacDiarmid and David Jones, and rescues them, either from American appropriation or from British indifference.

Both Peck and Tuma foreground the ways in which our literary histories are constructs, fabricated according to notions of national and cultural identity that have to be sceptically reviewed and tested in detail. So the first corrective to any oversimplifying differentiations is to register how striking are the parallels rather than the contrasts. In Peck, how the socioeconomic conditions of the two countries were so similar, how closely Orwell and Agee resembled each other, in social background, political inclination and literary ambition. In Tuma, how the American modernism of Pound, Williams, H.D., and their epigones had fared as badly in America from the thirties to the early fifties as it had in 'anti-modernist' Britain. Both essays are alert to the chronology. Peck notes, for example, how the decade divides into orientation towards domestic issues early, international affairs late, for the Americans, whereas the British were orientated to both from the start. Tuma gives prominence to 1979, the year of Donald Hall's essay 'Reading the English' which set the seal on the conviction growing steadily on both sides that there were now *two* poetries, British and American: 'American readers must learn to approach English poets *as if* they were reading translations from the Polish.' Both essayists arrive at clearly distinguishing factors. In spite of Tuma's cautious postculturalist views on the validity of a national identity, he proves Americanly resistant to the ideal of 'the Common Reader', since poetry should be innovatory and disturbing; that ideal is fostered by British conservative critics able to look back on moments when it seems as if the ideal could still be realised in their very different history. Peck shows us an American thirties 'doubly Marxist', much more radicalised than the British.

Peck quotes Walter Allen on the American thirties writers: 'they had a stronger resolution to grapple with the political and economic situation and change it' (than the British). This view accords with Ann Massa's perception of the passionately engaged American drama of the same period, and this radicalised and urgent quality survives, it seems, in the new American historical fiction, especially as exemplified by the novels of E.L. Doctorow whose thirties' settings for several of his fictions keep the political continuities in mind. Harding's argument, in the third essay in this section, does not dwell on matters of reception or any retrospective views of the novels themselves, but in attitudes towards the writing of the past embodied in the fictions themselves. In these postmodern works, where history is used simultaneously as a reference to the 'facts' of the past and as a discursive construct, the American writer, unlike the British, maintains a healthy disrespect for the positivist constructions of history and is attentive to the deconstructions of theorists like Hayden White and Dominick LaCapra. There is a demonstrably paradoxical mobilisation of this new understanding of history's essential textuality in order to 'expose the ideological basis of American social myths'. Doctorow's novels, revisiting the early years of the century in *Ragtime* and the Prohibition era in *Billy Bathgate*, compel their readers, as John Fowles's novels do not, 'to re-examine history and recognise the myths embodied in unconventional versions of the past'. Fowles, whom Harding proposes as a typically British composer of historiographical metafictions in works like *The French Lieutenant's Woman* and *A Maggot*, deploys his great gifts for ironic pastiche and postmodern defamiliarisation but still contrives to defer to a sense of ' "real history" as something beyond the province of the fiction writer'. He renders the past in comparatively depoliticised terms, abandoning the class interest of his model, Hardy, and purveying the familiar liberal humanist fable of the emergent modern self, the transcendent individual 'disengaged from the very moral and political issues that have been involved in the construction of that history'. Doctorow's exemplary disrespect and political urgency can be aligned with the stances of, say, Robert Coover, Kurt Vonnegut and Norman Mailer; if it has a British counterpart, it is perhaps in the work of Salman Rushdie (in *Midnight's Children* and *Shame*) which imports a non-British storytelling tradition and approaches the idea of any settled notion of history with radical iconoclasm.

At the other end of the spectrum from the vertiginous metafictions and fabulatory extravagances of Doctorow and Fowles is that species of American neo-realism known as 'dirty realism' since Bill Buford's 1983 issue of *Granta*, the British literary magazine, anthologised under that name new writings by the then comparatively unknown talents of Raymond Carver, Richard Ford, Jayne Anne Phillips, among others. Exposing the underside of middle American life during the Reagan–Bush recessionary years in a spare, uni-llusioned prose, these fictions seem to return us to aspects of the fictions of the thirties considered by Peck in the first essay. But Brian Scobie, in this last essay, focuses on the ambiguous relation of Carver to this vaunted low mimeticism (with which his own extratextual comments seem collusive) and to the specific cultural determinants, as they have sometimes been conceived, of his texts. Although dwelling on the commonplaces (and common places) of marginal and lower-class characters, Carver's blue-collar protagonists are no longer rebels or stoics in the Depression mould, but more inclined to drug themselves with drink and TV against some overwhelming sense of loss. Scobie acknowledges the potential in this for implicit critique of the deprivations and excesses of the eighties, the way the stories reproduce an environment of the 'generic and mass-produced' (as much as any plays by Shepard, say) and point to conspicuous and unsatisfying consumption. But his close analysis of the narrative strategies of the stories themselves throws suspicion on the deceptive superficiality of the 'realism' and the misleading slightness of the 'minimalism' with which his work is often associated.

(Although *Sudden Fiction*, (eds.) Robert Shapard and James Thomas, Harmondsworth, 1986, is an anthology of American very short stories, the minimalist mode is not restricted to the United States; its European avatar is Kafka, its Latin American patron Borges, and the Scottish short story writer James Kelman might be cited.) Far from being quintessentially American, in a local colour tradition, they open up a kind of Beckettian existential space through a subtle perspectivism and concentrate on personal/interpersonal matters in the manner of Chekhov (admired subject of Carver's 'The Errand'). Although the title for this essay, 'Carver Country', echoes that of the 1991 photographic study by Carver's friend Bob Adelman of the milieux and ambience of the fiction, Scobie posits an oblique relation to the actualities and an unexpected Eurocentric orientation through intertextual reference and critical preference (Chekhov, even V.S. Pritchett). It may be that the short story, as practised so superbly by so many American writers from Poe to Flannery O'Connor, is neither a homogenous genre nor one that can be identified exclusively with America, but Carver's contribution recalls the paradoxically expansive contractions of Hemingway at his best and the anti-climactic glimpses of William Carlos Williams in his prose.

CHAPTER ELEVEN

'The morning that is yours': American and British Literary Cultures in the Thirties[1]

David Peck

JAMES AGEE AND GEORGE ORWELL: EMBLEMS OF THE THIRTIES

If there is an historical moment that best captures the literary thirties, it would be some time in 1936. In February and March of that year, George Orwell was wandering through the north of England, on foot and by bus, recording in his diary the conditions under which miners and other industrial workers and their families lived and worked. In July and August, James Agee and Walker Evans were living in rural Alabama, recording in word and photograph the poverty, but inherent beauty, of three tenant-farming families. In these few months of 1936, an ocean apart, three journalists were thus creating essential images of thirties' life, at the same time that they were helping to shape a documentary genre.

The parallels between *The Road to Wigan Pier* (1937) and *Let Us Now Praise Famous Men* (1941) epitomise the thirties' experience for us. Even the lives of their authors followed a definite thirties' trajectory. Neither Orwell nor Agee was working–class, of course, in a decade that venerated proletarian backgrounds, but both had been educated at the best schools their cultures offered, and had been shaped, more than many writers, by these early educational experiences. Both struggled in their careers with false starts in their art and with doubts about their ability to master it. Both wanted to be serious novelists but succeeded, in their own lifetimes at least, at something much more perishable. Agee's novel *A Death in the Family* was published posthumously in 1955; *Famous Men* would not gain critical popularity until after it was republished in the early sixties. Fame in his lifetime would come from essay and review. Orwell's naturalistic thirties' novels were never as successful as – at the one pole – his occasional journalism (*Homage to Catalonia*, for example, in 1938), or, at the other, his forties' fables (*Animal Farm, 1984*). Neither writer had studied the classic Marxist texts (although Orwell's knowledge was surely deeper) but by the end of the thirties they both had made leftist commitments and had serious suspicions of the orthodox Marxisms of their day. Both, in short, were model thirties' writers.

Even after the thirties, their careers dovetail: Orwell's 'As I Please' columns in the *Tribune* between 1943 and 1945, to cite but one example, have much in common with Agee's personal film reviews in *The Nation* at almost the same time. Both died before their full promise was realised, both have been rediscovered after their deaths, and both are still the subject of intense debate over the meaning and value of their work.

What is most striking for those of us trying to recover the thirties today are the parallels between their two books, in history and style. Both works were commissioned by organisations, but with unhappy results. *Fortune* magazine, for obvious reasons, declined to publish the final articles it had assigned, and Agee laboured for years shaping them into a book that Houghton Mifflin finally published in 1941. While the Left Book Club *did* distribute *The Road to Wigan Pier* in January of 1937 – the book would become one of the LBC's most successful offerings and would sell over 40,000 copies – the foreword by publisher Victor Gollancz was riddled with disclaimers, and the revised edition in May lopped off the entire second half of Orwell's book.

Even the structures of the two books are similar. Both fail. Agee's book circles about itself, and, while critics have found justification for the disjointed structure, most readers must still struggle with the circular, almost labyrinthine movement of *Famous Men*. Orwell's book is broken in two – split between the vivid description of the first part and the autobiographical argument of the second – and few readers defend the second half.

Today of course we recognise the full power of the two works. *Let Us Now Praise Famous Men* has been called a sociological masterpiece by numerous critics. *The Road to Wigan Pier*, as Richard Rovere has described it, is 'a basic document in the intellectual history of this century'.[2] And Richard Hoggart has argued that: '. . . Orwell's picture, though not the whole truth, was truer than almost all the other documentary material which came out of the documentary 'thirties. It was true to the *spirit* of its place and time and . . . its people. It was true to the spirit of the misery. . . .'[3]

The problem facing both writers was also the same: how to use their prose to get inside this essential experience, to describe the conditions under which people in the worst of the Depression were living and working. What is most permanent in either work is the creative transformation of these hard facts of observation into imaginative literature. It is this imaginative transformation that links us (through the New Journalism of the sixties and other non-fictional forms) to both Agee and Orwell. There is certainly a more complete – and visual, thanks to collaborator Walker Evans's classic photographs – identification with his subjects in Agee, a more objective detachment in Orwell, but the goals are the same: to get inside outer history, to convey for readers the lived experience of Wigan and Alabama.[4]

The styles of the two books – their particular combination of voice and language – provided the vehicles for their success in this effort. Neither Agee nor Orwell seemed to be writing in the 'official' language of thirties' non-fiction. Orwell came to the colloquial style of *Wigan Pier* (as Peter Stansky and William Abrahams have shown) by his own circuitous, almost hit-or-miss route; he does not seem to have been influenced much by earlier thirties' non-fiction. And Agee was writing what on the surface appeared almost an anti-thirties book: a lyrical hymn to the suffering and dignity of human beings. And yet both were working within the tradition of thirties' non-fiction, particularly the tradition of proletarian reportage that exposed the poverty and unemployment that so concerned Agee and Orwell. As Valentine Cunningham has noted, *The Road to Wigan Pier* 'is sometimes wrongly taken as a wonderfully unique achievement'.[5] Likewise, as Marcus Klein has written of Agee in comparing *Famous Men* to other American documentary journalism, 'the book was not the transcendence of a genre but was rather something closer to being the ultimate statement of the road-writers, with or without photographs'.[6]

The style of *Wigan Pier*, as Rovere has described it, is 'colloquial and sinewy in construction; it aimed at clarity and unobtrusiveness and achieved both'.[7] And yet, as Raymond Williams has noted, there is also 'a saturation of the scene with feeling'[8] closer to Agee's more subjective style. Orwell's dictum that 'Good prose is like a windowpane' ('Why I Write', 1947)[9] can be a disarming and deceptive statement, until we see the ways in which the window panes in *Wigan Pier* have been carefully constructed to give us these particularly intense pictures of conditions in the industrial north.

Both writers were wrestling with similar strategic problems in the same genre: how to create personas to lure readers into the horrific worlds of gritty Wigan and dirt-poor Alabama. Williams has argued that what is created in *Wigan Pier* 'is an isolated independent observer and the objects of his observation'; that we should see all of Orwell's work before 1937, in fact, as 'sketches toward the creation of his most successful character, "Orwell" '.[10] In a more recognisably American manner, one of Agee's main subjects was his own consciousness; it is the New Journalist Tom Wolfe's main complaint about the book: Agee's 'extreme personal diffidence' meant that the book 'uses no point of view other than his own'.[11] In either case, Agee and Orwell found prose voices – Agee's a rich, romantic, often baroque voice – that brought them closer to their readers. For the point is that both Orwell and

Agee get at thirties' experience through *themselves*. *Let Us Now Praise Famous Men* and *The Road to Wigan Pier* are about not only the people suffering these horrible conditions, but also the responses of two middle-class writers to these people and their experiences. Orwell and Agee get between the misery and the reader and thus blunt the pain.

One of the most painful pictures in *Wigan Pier* – to cite an instance from Orwell – is the image of a young woman kneeling at the back of a slum house and 'poking a stick up a leaden wastepipe'. In the book Orwell views the scene from a moving train, but when we open the 'Diary' for *The Road to Wigan Pier* we discover that he was actually 'Passing up a horrible squalid side-alley'[12] close by the freezing woman. Orwell has removed readers to a safe distance from the scene.

Other parallels permeate the two books: Orwell's self-consciousness, for example, his realisation of how 'feeble' mere words are to convey this experience. (He even quotes a review of himself at the end of Chapter 4, as Agee includes an article on Margaret Bourke-White's documentary *You Have Seen Their Faces*, as a contrast to the real job that he and Walker Evans are doing in the South.) Orwell's description of the 'feeling of impotence and despair' that many of the unemployed share, as well as his recognition that 'a change *is* taking place', recall Agee's analyses in similar situations. Finally, Orwell's admiration for these people in Wigan living and working (and *not* working) under impossible conditions reminds us of the three tenant families in *Famous Men*. 'In a working-class home', Orwell writes at the end of Part I of *The Road to Wigan Pier*, 'you breathe a warm, decent, deeply human atmosphere which it is not so easy to find elsewhere.' It is this 'memory of working-class interiors'. Orwell concludes, 'that reminds me that our age has not been altogether a bad one to live in'.[13]

This intimacy and hopefulness may be part of the reason for Agee and Orwell's success: they sanitise these lives enough to make them palatable. And while both Agee and Orwell call themselves socialists, they preach reform, not revolution. Orwell describes the ugliness (and smelliness) of poverty, as he and Agee capture the beauty of its victims, but neither demands that we completely dismantle the system that produced it. Like other writers labelled 'radical' since the thirties, in short, their work seems hardly revolutionary today. Rather, they were writers who identified strongly with the working classes, and this of course was one major movement of the thirties, in both fiction (the proletarian novel, for example) and non-fiction (documentary reportage). It was a plank of the communist literary platform in both countries as well, but it was an identification that middle-class writers like Agee and Orwell came to easily enough on their own in this decade of poverty and unemployment.[14] Writers had only to look about them to see the poverty and suffering, and what they saw became increasingly the subjects of their writing: unemployment (Walter Greenwood's *Love on the Dole*, or Jack Conroy's *The Disinherited*, both 1933); strikes (John Sommerfield's *May Day*, or John Steinbeck's *In Dubious Battle*, 1936); tapestries of proletarian life (Lewis Grassic Gibbon's *A Scots Quair* trilogy, James T. Farrell's *Studs Lonigan*, 1935). The shock of the Depression may have been greater in the United States – as the twenties had been comparatively richer – and this fact may explain something about the different literary responses in the two cultures. But the similarities between the two literatures in the thirties clearly outweigh the differences.

THE DOCUMENTARY DECADE

There were, as we shall see, a number of significant parallels between the two literary cultures, but the human and journalistic efforts that would become *The Road to Wigan Pier* and *Let Us Now Praise Famous Men* can stand as guidons for these other issues raised during the thirties. First, in both England and the United States the 1930s was the documentary decade: as economic conditions pushed artists and writers in both countries into social genres to depict and explain these conditions accurately, visual art became social realism, film the cinematic documentary of John Grierson and Pare Lorentz. Agee and Orwell are only two good examples of this impulse in their respective cultures.

The roots for these particular social-literary forms existed in both countries, of course. In England, the nineteenth-century novel contained a strong tradition of fiction fused to social concerns. Disraeli had written, 'I was told that the privileged and the people formed two nations' (*Sybil*) in 1845, but John Dos Passos's echo – 'all right we are two nations' – came more than ninety years later (in *The Big Money*, 1936). In the United States, in other words, there was a weaker strain of social realist fiction – the tradition of Theodore Dreiser and Sinclair Lewis was after all a contemporary one – but a living history of social journalism, from the Muckrakers at the turn of the century through to the more recent writings of Randolph Bourne and John Reed before and just after the First World War, in *The Masses, The Liberator* and other radical journals. The protests that centred on the executions of Sacco and Vanzetti in 1927 were only preludes to the radical journalism (and fiction) to come in the thirties; Dos Passos's line is in fact from a Camera Eye passage on the death of the two anarchists.

In the late twenties and early thirties in New York, as Depression conditions deepened and as middle-class writers started drifting leftward, editor Mike Gold was urging in the pages of the *New Masses* that workers should write of their lives and writers should turn to the lives of workers for subject and inspiration. Worker narratives would become a mainstay of radical journalism in the early thirties, and not only in the *New Masses* but in more liberal journals like *The Nation* and *The New Republic* as well. But these magazines also published a good deal of what we can call proletarian reportage by professional writers, and some of the best examples of this genre – such as Tillie Lerner, Meridel Le Sueur, John L. Spivak and Joseph North – were clearly influential on other literary forms. It is only recently that we have begun to recognise this separate proletarian form and the ways in which this journalism helped to open up the literature of the thirties.[15] By exposing the underside of American capitalism, and giving voice to its victims, the proletarian reportage of the early thirties provided subjects and materials not only for the journalists (e.g. Agee) but also for the novelists (like Richard Wright) who followed. Some of the best 1930s non-fiction of more established writers like Edmund Wilson, Sherwood Anderson, Erskine Caldwell and others would come out of this new social reportage of the early thirties, culminating in *Let Us Now Praise Famous Men*, or Dorothea Lange and Paul Taylor's *An American Exodus: A Record of Human Erosion* (1939), on migrants driven west by the dust storms of the thirties.

Likewise, some of the greatest imaginative literature of the thirties had a direct connection to this reportage: Steinbeck himself studied the migrant labour camps of California as a journalist (*Their Blood is Strong*, 1938) before transforming those efforts into *The Grapes of Wrath* in 1939. Put another way, a book like *The Grapes of Wrath* was possible only after the ground had been prepared by journalists – Steinbeck among them – who had described the Joads and other disenfranchised Americans of the Depression for mainly middle-class readers. John L. Spivak's 1934 'A Letter to President Roosevelt' in the *New Masses* – to cite but one example – is a poignant confrontation with Depression America from the point of view of one of its victims, in a letter supposedly from an illiterate Mexican girl working in the cotton fields of California's Imperial Valley.

The same thing can be said of the other great imaginative works at the end of the decade; Hemingway's *For Whom the Bell Tolls* and Richard Wright's *Native Son* (both 1940) had been affected in one way or another by this impulse to social reportage, by the desire to get closer to socioeconomic conditions. (Ten years earlier the representative American novel would have been – *A Farewell to Arms?*) Seen this way, the proletarian novel of the early 1930s in the United States was only another response to the campaign for a closer examination of working-class life which we find in the radical journals like *New Masses* at the beginning of the decade, and the best works of the form (Gold's 1930 *Jews Without Money*, for example, or Robert Cantwell's *The Land of Plenty* in 1934) reveal this influence.

In England this documentary impulse came significantly later when, as Samuel Hynes tells us,

> left journals like John Lehmann's *New Writing* and *Left Review* . . . sought out and published stories by coalminers and factory hands and men on the dole. . . . In the mid-'thirties, various efforts had been made to transpose the descriptive function of realistic literature to actual events, and so make realism literally the fact . . . . [as in] the growth of the documentary film movement, and the establishment of the Left Book Club.[16]

One should add to this the growth of journals like *Fact* (1937) and the Mass Observation movement. Montagu Slater's *Stay Down Miner* (1936) was published with a note that 'This is No. 1 of a series of *Reportage* books.' In the fourth and final issue of *Fact*, in July of 1937 when Storm Jameson was looking for the best example of the new socialist 'documents' genre she was defining, she found that 'George Orwell has begun on it in the first half of *The Road to Wigan Pier* . . . a social document as vivid, bitter, and telling as one could have asked.'[17] In addition to *Wigan Pier*, the Left Book Club would produce works like B.L. Coombes's *These Poor Hands: The Autobiography of a Miner Working in South Wales* (1939).

1936: REPRESENTATIVE YEAR

But the year that Agee and Orwell were documenting Depression conditions can also provide other illuminations for both literary cultures.[18] In Great Britain, 1936 was the year of George V's death, and of the Jarrow march; the Spanish Civil War began, and Germany occupied the Rhineland. In the United States, Roosevelt was re-elected President and Eugene O'Neill received the Nobel Prize for literature. Consider the lists below of the major works that appeared and other literary events that occurred in the two countries in 1936.

American

SIGNIFICANT LITERARY EVENTS
Federal Theater Project started
Pare Lorentz, 'The Plow that Broke the Plains' (documentary film)
Science & Society (Marxist journal) started

POETRY
T.S Eliot, *Collected Poems, 1909–1935*
Robert Frost, *A Further Range*
Edgar Lee Masters, *Poems of People*
Marianne Moore, *The Pangolin and Other Verse*
Carl Sandburg, *The People, Yes*

ESSAYS AND CRITICISM
Willa Cather, *Not Under Forty* (essays)
James T. Farrell, *A Note on Literary Criticism*
Joseph Freeman, *An American Testament* (autobiography)
John Howard Lawson, *Theory and Practice of Playwriting*
Gertrude Stein, *The Geographical History of America*

FICTION
Djuna Barnes, *Nightwood*
Thomas Bell, *All Brides Are Beautiful*
Arna Bontemps, *Black Thunder*
John Dos Passos, *The Big Money* (*USA* trilogy completed)
James T. Farrell, *A World I Never Made*
William Faulkner, *Absalom, Absalom!*
Daniel Fuchs, *Homage to Blenholt*
Munro Leaf, *Ferdinand the Bull*
Sinclair Lewis, *It Can't Happen Here*
Henry Miller, *Black Spring*
Margaret Mitchell, *Gone with the Wind*
George Santayana, *The Last Puritan*
John Steinbeck, *In Dubious Battle*
Leane Zugsmith, *A Time to Remember*

British

SIGNIFICANT LITERARY EVENTS
Contemporary Poetry and Prose (journal) started
Victor Gollancz's Left Book Club founded
John Lehmann's *New Writing* (journal) started

POETRY
W.H. Auden, *Look, Stranger!*
A.E. Housman, *More Poems*
Ian Parsons (ed.), *The Progress of Poetry*

Michael Roberts (ed.), *Faber Book of Modern Verse*
Dylan Thomas, *Twenty-Five Poems*
W.B. Yeats (ed.), *Oxford Book of Modern Verse*

ESSAYS AND CRITICISM
E.M. Forster, *Abinger Harvest*
Graham Greene, *Journey Without Maps*
Philip Henderson, *The Novel Today: Studies in Contemporary Attitudes*
G. Wilson Knight, *Principles of Shakespearian Production*
I.A. Richards, *The Philosophy of Rhetoric*
Montagu Slater, *Stay Down Miner*
Evelyn Waugh, *Waugh in Abyssinia*

FICTION
Ralph Bates, *The Olive Field*
Joyce Cary, *The African Witch*
Cyril Connolly, *The Rock Pool*
Graham Greene, *A Gun for Sale*
James Hanley, *The Secret Journey*
Winifred Holtby, *South Riding*
Aldous Huxley, *Eyeless in Gaza*
Storm Jameson, *None Turn Back*
L.H. Myers, *Strange Glory*
Sean O'Faolain, *Bird Alone*
George Orwell, *Keep the Aspidistra Flying*
Anthony Powell, *Agents and Patients*
Siegfried Sassoon, *Sherston's Progress*
John Sommerfield, *May Day*

Any such lists must be in some way misleading; no year could ever be historically representative of an entire decade. As just one example, 1936 saw the publication of three anthologies of poetry in Britain, two of which (the *Faber* and *Oxford*) would become standard collections in the next decades. But discounting such distortion here, the value of the lists is still clear. The first impression is a mixed one, that a decade so often labelled 'Marxist' and 'proletarian' produced such a varied literary output:leftovers from earlier eras (Cather, Santayana, Masters; Housman, Sassoon, Yeats), major modernists still at work (particularly Americans: Eliot, Faulkner, Stein), newer talents emerging (especially British: Powell, Thomas). At the same time, all literary forms in both cultures would be radicalised by history – and by the actors of history urging writers to go left, in review, essay and book. The lists of 'other significant literary events' indicate the breadth of radical literary activities in both countries in the thirties: from poetry and criticism (*Left Review, Science*

& *Society*), to theatre (the Federal Theater Project), film (Lorentz) and publishing (Gollancz).

The 'essays and criticism' category best reveals the mix. In England, one volume of Marxist criticism (Henderson) and one piece of radical journalism (Slater) are overwhelmed by five more traditional volumes of essays and criticism (Forster, Greene, Knight, Richards and Waugh). While more Marxist literary criticism was produced in the thirties in the United States, less of it has lasted, but its influence was probably more powerful within the decade. As Eliot commented in the January 1933 *Criterion*, 'communistic theories appear to have more vogue among men of letters [in the United States] than they have yet reached in England'.[19] The difference was the role of orthodox literary Marxism (e.g. doctrinaire criticism centring on the Communist Party), which can best be represented by the two works of radical non-fiction listed for 1936. Freeman's autobiography, *An American Testament* – one of the truly neglected works of American intellectual history – traces his conversion to communism and along the way describes the evolution of an American Marxist literary criticism in the late 1920s. But Freeman was censored in Moscow for treating Trotsky as a 'person' and helped in killing his own book – although he couldn't stop its distribution through the Left Book Club in Britain, where an ad noted that the work had been chosen as 'the best autobiography of its year' by the American Writers' Congress. Freeman's manuscript on the history of American Marxist criticism, probably the best short work on the subject, was never published.[20]

Farrell's polemical *Note on Literary Criticism* shows just how nasty the internecine critical wars of the thirties in the United States had become by 1936, when critical positions had hardened and criticism dealt less with theory than – as in Farrell – with the enemies of one's particular critical practice. One of the central objects of Farrell's attack was Granville Hicks. In 'The Crisis in American Criticism' in the *New Masses* in 1933, Hicks had argued that critics must demand that literature, 'directly or indirectly, show the effects of the class struggle' and 'that the author's point of view be that of the vanguard of the proletariat'.[21] In contrast, the British Edward Upward's 'A Marxist Interpretation of Literature' four years later also urged writers to side with the revolution – but with a significant difference.

> The writer's job is to create new forms now, to arrive by hard work at the emotional truth about present-day reality.
> He cannot begin to do this until he has in his everyday life allied himself with the forces of the future, until he has gone over to the socialist movements.[22]

Hick's 'vanguard of the proletariat' is of course the CPUSA (the Communist Party of the United States) and the literary activities (proletarian literature, the John Reed Clubs, orthodox Marxist criticism) circling it; Upward's 'socialist movements' is a much vaguer critical category. Neither country contained a monolithic leftist literary culture, but orthodox Marxism certainly had a stronger grip on the United States.

In fact, 1936 was not a very representative year for British Marxist criticism, but in the following year four substantial volumes would be published: Ralph Fox's *The Novel and the People*, Alick West's *Crisis and Criticism*, and Christopher Caudwell's *Illusion and Reality*, as well as the C. Day Lewis collection, *The Mind in Chains*, that included Upward's essay quoted above. British Marxist efforts in general produced a broader range of radical criticism, which is why critics like Fox, Caudwell, West, Upward, Arnold Kettle, T.A. Jackson, Edgell Rickword, Jack Lindsay and others continued to be reprinted and read after the thirties. American Marxist criticism was from its inception more closely tied to proletarian forms (as in Hicks above) and guided by CP policy. While this alliance would reap creative rewards (see the *Proletarian Literature in the US* anthology edited by Hicks and others and published in 1935, for example), it also meant the kind of critical warfare represented by *A Note on Literary Criticism*, between those like Hicks or Gold committed to proletarian forms and other critics, like Farrell or Edmund Wilson, who believed in a less political criticism.

It is in the 1936 fiction lists that we observe the greatest radical concentration: proletarian or socialist novels are a major component of both British (Bates, Hanley, Sommerfield) and American (Bell, Fuchs, Zugsmith) fiction. But on the US side we can also recognise a greater number of well-known writers who have been radicalised in their fiction: Dos Passos, Farrell, Steinbeck. British fiction, on the contrary, shows socialist writers (including Connolly, Jameson, Orwell) still wrestling with bourgeois literary forms. One reason for this difference is the link to orthodox Marxism in the United States. As David Smith has remarked, the American Communist Party 'attracted to it from the start a far larger proportion of the intellectual ranks of the middle class'.[23] In Britain a more rigid class structure meant that it was harder for writers and intellectuals to 'come over' to the workers; in the United States, the leftward movement of artists and intellectuals at times resembled a migration.

Roughly the same number of socialist novels – about seventy – would be published in the United States as in Great Britain during the decade,[24] but more in Great Britain appeared in the second half of the decade. Fifty of the American proletarian novels listed in Rideout appear in the first half of the decade, from 1930 to 1935. British critics have noted what they consider 'the flood of revolutionary literature in the US' compared with 'the sluggishness of this movement' in Great Britain,[25] but they are speaking of the energy during the first half of the decade. 'Again and again American novels were praised for their proletarian vigour' in Great Britain,[26] but the praise was not just for proletarian models; as Walter Allen has argued, most American novels in the thirties, in addition to their 'violence and radical anger', have a stronger 'resolution to grapple with the political and economic situation and to change it'.[27]

The legacy of both the campaign for proletarian literature and the Marxist literary criticism that was its stepfather was a radical political-literary tenor that permeated every corner of the American decade. In Hollywood in the late thirties, to cite but one example, F. Scott Fitzgerald, Dorothy Parker, Nathanael West and other writers were studying Marxism and giving their names and money to radical causes. Zugsmith's *A Time to Remember* represents another consequence of the Marxist atmosphere created in the thirties: a greater number of women writers emerging in the United States. In addition to Zugsmith, Le Sueur and Lerner, already mentioned above, one could name Josephine Herbst, Mary Heaton Vorse, Tess Slesinger, Grace Lumpkin and Fielding Burke. Not all of them appeared merely because of the campaign for proletarian literature, surely, but the radical literary activity at the beginning of the decade helped to open doors for a number of different minority groups (including blacks). British women writers also emerged in the thirties – Jameson, Sylvia Townsend Warner, Stevie Smith, Rosamond Lehmann et al. – but fewer of them had this irreplaceable link with the Left.

American fiction, in short, shows a double Marxist influence, in specific proletarian novels as well as in a broader effect on writers in general. And perhaps as a consequence, radical literary activity in Britain in the thirties produced nothing as comprehensive as *USA* or *The Grapes of Wrath*. On the other hand, no American proletarian novel saw the popularity of Walter Greenwood's *Love on the Dole* and none achieved the lyrical, revolutionary power of Lewis Grassic Gibbon's *A Scots Quair*. Each culture created its own unique achievements.

The American thirties is actually split in two: in the first half of the decade, the focus was on domestic issues; the later thirties, in the 'popular front' period of the Spanish Civil War and other anti-Fascist campaigns, saw American writers become increasingly concerned about international developments, and creative literature also reflected the shift (Hemingway's *For Whom the Bell Tolls* in 1940, for example, or Lillian Hellman's 1941 play *Watch on the Rhine*). British literature – as the 1936 fiction lists reveal – had both concerns from the start. As Valentine Cunningham has written in his study of *British Writers of the Thirties*, ' '30s writing was obsessed by the topography of England'.[28] It is noteworthy that both cultures supported this 'back-to-the-village movement', as writers searched for a simpler, often rural past in the midst of the current crises. At the same time, British writing was also international in focus, for there had been since the beginning of the decade concern about fascism in Italy and Germany. (Cunningham devotes several chapters to

British travel literature in the 1930s, and to English writers heading for both the United States and the Soviet Union; note the Greene and Waugh titles above.) American writers became concerned with the Spanish Civil War after 1936, and several (Hemingway, Dos Passos) participated, but British literature lost some of its brightest lights – Fox, Caudwell, John Cornford and Julian Bell among them – in that conflict.

The point raises another. The perception of any decade is conditioned by those who survive it, by those who live to write the memoirs and the histories. Cornford, Caudwell, Bell and Fox did not; neither, for that matter, did George Orwell. But the writers who did survive to write the stories of the British thirties comprise on the whole a fairly representative group: Claud Cockburn, Cyril Connolly, Stephen Spender, John Lehmann et al.

In the United States, on the contrary, those who have given us their history of the thirties were primarily literary critics who needed to rewrite their own participation in the decade: Granville Hicks, Malcolm Cowley, Edmund Wilson, Alfred Kazin. Most had taken part in the Marxist literary movements of the 1930s and felt a need later to clear their names. Their memoirs, their literary histories, and their collections of primary materials from the thirties carry the virulence of their earlier critical battles but distort our perceptions of that American decade in their staunch anti-Marxism.

Their apostasy raises a larger historical issue. The main difference between the two literary cultures does not even occur in the thirties at all. The difference was the fifties, and the fact that the British did not go through the experience of McCarthyism.[29] The rush by Kazin and Hicks and the others to clear their names in the fifties and sixties can be explained only by citing the inordinate pressure they were under because of the McCarthy hysteria. If critics wanted to save themselves, they would do it by scuttling the 'red decade', and they did. It has consequently been much more difficult in the United States to get a clear view of the thirties, for we have first had to work our way through the distorted accounts written and reiterated in the forties and fifties, and even later, by those bent on saving themselves in a time in which few could.

In addition to his many other talents in the thirties, George Orwell proved prophetic as well. Towards the end of *Coming Up for Air* (1939), Orwell's hero George Bowling has a vision of the nightmare future: 'War is coming. . . . The bombs, the food-queues, the rubber truncheons, the barbed wire, the coloured shirts, the slogans, the enormous faces, the machine guns squirting out of bedroom windows. It's all going to happen.'[30] Simultaneously, Bowling discovers that he can't go home again: that the childhood home he has been seeking since the beginning of the novel – in another example of the English back-to-the-village movement of the thirties – has become a fake Tudor housing tract. Frustrated in his search for the idyllic past ('The old life is finished and to go about looking for it is just waste of time'),[31] George Bowling surrenders to the bland and plastic present and crawls home to his wife in defeat.

Just two months before the publication of *Coming Up for Air* (by Gollancz in June in London), Viking in New York published John Steinbeck's *The Grapes of Wrath*. Steinbeck's novel includes a number of attacks on the capitalist exploitation of both people and land, and presents several socialist alternatives – the government camp at Weedpatch, for example. A typical Steinbeck passage from one of the intercalary chapters:

> And the companies, the banks worked at their own doom and they did not know it. The fields were fruitful, and starving men moved on the roads. The granaries were full and the children of the poor grew up rachitic, and the pustules of pellegra swelled on their sides. The great companies did not know that the line between hunger and anger is a thin line. . . . And the anger began to ferment.[32]

At the end of the novel, Tom Joad leaves his family to become an organiser: 'But I know now a fella ain't no good alone' (p. 570). It is the same message that Hemingway gave in *To Have and Have Not* in 1937 and would repeat three years later in *For Whom the Bell Tolls*. Unlike Orwell, Steinbeck ends *The Grapes of Wrath* not in defeat and frustration, but in another mystical scene of the community of need banding together, with Rose of Sharon nursing the dying old man: 'She looked up and across the barn, and her lips came together and smiled mysteriously.'[33] Perhaps the comparisons between the novels are too obvious, or are just too ingrained in their respective national cultures, to bear comment. But it seems perfectly appropriate that, in the last moments of the thirties, a British writer should be absolutely realistic about what was to happen to his country – and accept it almost in defeat – and that an American writer be so absolutely wrong about the revolutionary promise, and yet so optimistic. A few months after the two novels were published the Second World War would start and the thirties would be finished – at least for the moment.

NOTES

1. The phrase is from Malcolm Cowley's 1937 poem 'Tomorrow Morning', collected in *Blue Juniata: A Life. Collected and New Poems* (New York, 1968).

2. Richard Rovere (ed.), *Poetry of the 1930s* (London, 1967), p. xv.

3. George Orwell, *The Road to Wigan Pier*, edited with an introduction by Richard Hoggart (London, 1965), pp. 41 – 2. (First published in 1937.)

4. The latest Penguin reprint (1989) of *Wigan Pier* has restored the thirty-two photographs which illustrated the first edition (but which Orwell himself did not choose, and which certainly did not have the same immediacy to the text as Evans's photographs).

5. Valentine Cunningham, *British Writers of the Thirties* (Oxford, 1988), p. 239.

6. Marcus Klein, *Foreigners: The Making of American Literature, 1900–1940* (Chicago, 1981), p. 162.

7. Rovere, op. cit., p. xviii

8. Raymond Williams (ed.), *George Orwell: A Collection of Critical Essays* (Englewood Cliffs, NJ, 1974), p. 59.

9. Sonia Orwell and Ian Angus (eds), *The Collected Essays, Journalism and Letters of George Orwell*, vol. I: 'An Age Like This, 1920–1940' (London, 1968), p. 7.

10. Williams; op. cit., pp. 60–1.

11. Tom Wolfe and E.W. Johnson (eds), *The New Journalism* (London, 1975), p. 60.

12. Sonia Orwell, op. cit., pp. 170–214.

13. George Orwell, *The Road to Wigan Pier*, pp. 57, 85–6, 116–18.

14. At the end of 1932, British unemployment stood at nearly three million, or about one worker in five; in the United States, unemployment was closer to fifteen million, or one in four.

15. See my 'Joseph North and the Proletarian Reportage of the 1930s', *Zeitschrift für Anglistik und Amerikanistik* 33 (1985): 210–20.

16. Samuel Hynes, *The Auden Generation: Literature and Politics in England in the 1930s* (London, 1976), p. 218.

17. Storm Jameson, 'Documents', *Fact*, No. 4 (July 1937): 9–18.

18. As Francis Barker and others recognised, at least for the British 1930s, in *1936: The Sociology of Literature* (1979). See also Gustav Klaus's 'Socialist Novels of 1936' in his *The Literature of Labour* (London, 1985).

19. Cunningham, op. cit., p, 32.

20. See Daniel Aaron, *Writers on the Left* (New York, 1961), Chapter 17, 'Never Call Retreat', for details of this controversy.

21. Granville Hicks, 'The Crisis in American Criticism', *New Masses* 8 (February 1933): 5.

22. Cecil Day Lewis (ed.), *The Mind in Chains: Socialism and the Cultural Revolution* (Folcroft, Pa., 1972), p. 54. First published in 1937.

23. David Smith, *Socialist Propaganda in the Twentieth Century British Novel* (London, 1978), p. 53. In fact a larger number overall: while the Communist Party in Great Britain would increase almost fourfold between 1930 and 1936–37 (from 3,200 to 11,700; Cunningham op. cit., p. 53), membership in the CPUSA would grow more than tenfold in roughly the same period (from 7,000 in 1930 to 75,000 in 1938; see Walter B. Rideout, *The Radical Novel in the United States*, Cambridge,

Mass., 1956, pp. 136–7).

24. See appendix in Walter B. Rideout and Gustav Klaus's 'Socialist Fiction of the 1930s', collected in John Lucas (ed.), *The 1930s: A Challenge to Orthodoxy* (New York, 1979).

25. Smith, op. cit., p. 51.

26. Cunningham, op. cit., p. 343.

27. Allen, op. cit., p. 142.

28. Cunningham, op. cit., p. 226.

29. David Caute in *The Great Fear: The Anti-Communist Purge under Truman and Eisenhower* (London, 1978) has expressed the difference most effectively:

> The British of the Attlee era, unlike the British of the Pitt era or of the sixteenth century confrontation with Catholic Spain, kept their heads: teachers and professors were not purged; dismissals in the civil service were few and confined mainly to genuinely sensitive jobs; Parliament did not go witch hunting; there was no Un-British Activities Committee to whip up enmity toward radicals or fellow travellers; no rash of loyalty oaths brought disgrace to the professions; welfare benefits were not denied to Communist veterans or their widows; union officials were not required by law to sign non-Communist affidavits; panels of military officers did not hound industrial workers from their jobs or question them as to how they had voted; seamen were not swept off ships by waves of prejudice; CP leaders were not sent to prison for being Communists; there was no government list of prescribed organisers. . . . Need one go on? Having stumbled through the Cold War with this myopic attitude Britain emerged with just as few Communists as before.
>
> (pp. 20–1. Ellipsis is Caute's.)

30. George Orwell, *Coming Up for Air* (London, 1969), pp. 227–8.

31. Ibid., p. 227.

32. John Steinbeck, *The Grapes of Wrath* (New York, 1967), pp. 387–8.

33. Ibid., p. 619.

The works used in this study give us a clue to the different directions in which thirties' literary scholarship has recently moved in two cultures.

In both countries we have been busy in the last twenty-five years or so recovering some of the best literature left behind in the thirties, and anthologies and reprints are today far too numerous to list. A better barometer to the two decades lies perhaps in what we emphasise in our scholarship. In Great Britain, critics have produced a number of studies of thirties' poetry (Hynes, Maxwell, Rodway, Skelton, Tolley), but there has also been a recent and healthy re-examination of fiction (Hawthorn, Johnstone, Smith, as well as essays in the Barker, Clark and Lucas collections), and a good number of studies of British literary responses to the war on Spain. Finally, Great Britain has seen several comprehensive studies of the relations between literature and society in the thirties. The first, Samuel Hynes's *The Auden Generation*, is limited in its focus, but Valentine Cunningham has produced *British Writers of the Thirties*, an exhaustive study of the literature of the decade from almost every conceivable angle, and a book which, in capturing so well 'the stir, the literary excitement of the 30s' (p. 110), is not likely to be soon replaced as the standard literary history of the decade. Finally, while its focus is on fiction, Andy Croft's *Red Letter Days* is an important corrective to myopic sentiments in both Hynes and Cunningham.

In the United States, critics and historians have produced a good number of studies of the important Federal Arts Projects (including the Federal Theater and Writers Projects) and various aspects of the documentary photojournalism of the decade (Pells, Stott), as well as numerous memoirs and studies of theatre in the thirties. (While there were radical dramatic experiments in both cultures, the American leftist theatre produced more lasting contributions; Odets's 1935 *Waiting for Lefty*, for example, was in fact one of the most popular plays in Britain's left theatre in the later thirties. For a bibliography of writings on drama of the period, see Ann Massa's essay, pp. 73–4.) Unfortunately, Americans still cannot read a literary history as comprehensive as Croft's or Cunningham's. The Daniel Aaron and Walter B. Rideout volumes are dated and crippled by a clear anti-Marxist bias; the best recent study is Marcus Klein's *Foreigners*, for, although it also covers three decades before the 1930s, its insights into that decade are sharp and sympathetic to the contributions of the Left.

FURTHER READING

Daniel Aaron, *Writers on the Left* (New York, 1961).

Francis Barker et al. (eds), *1936: The Sociology of Literature.* (Essex, 1979).

Angus Calder and Dorothy Sheridan (eds), *Speak for Yourself: A Mass-Observation Anthology, 1937–1949* (London, 1984).

Jon Clark, Margot Heinemann, David Margolies and Carol Snee (eds), *Culture and Crisis in Britain in the Thirties* (London, 1979).

Andy Croft, *Red Letter Days: British Fiction in the 1930s* (London, 1990).

Valentine Cunningham, *British Writers of the Thirties* (Oxford, 1988).

Jeremy Hawthorn, (ed.), *The British Working-Class Novel in the 20th Century* (London, 1984).

Granville Hicks et al. (eds), *Proletarian Literature in the United States: An Anthology* (New York, 1935).

Samuel Hynes, *The Auden Generation: Literature and Politics in England in the 1930s* (London, 1976).

Richard Johnstone, *The Will to Believe: Novelists of the 1930s* (Oxford, 1982).

Gustav Klaus, *The Literature of Labour: 200 Years of Working-Class Writing* (London, 1985).

Marcus Klein, *Foreigners: The Making of American Literature, 1900–1940* (Chicago, 1981).

John Lucas (ed.), *The 1930s: A Challenge to Orthodoxy* (New York, 1979).

D.E.S. Maxwell, *Poets of the Thirties* (London, 1969).

Richard Pells, *Radical Visions and American Dreams: Culture and Social Thought in the Depression Years* (New York, 1973).

Walter B. Rideout, *The Radical Novel in the United States, 1900–1954* (Cambridge, Mass., 1956).

Allen Rodway (ed.), *Poetry of the 1930s* (London, 1967).

Robin Skelton (ed.), *Poetry of the Thirties* (Harmondsworth, 1964).

David Smith, *Socialist Propaganda in the Twentieth-Century British Novel* (London, 1978).

Peter Stansky and William Abrahams, *Orwell: The Transformation* (London, 1981).

William Stott, *Documentary Expression and Thirties America* (New York, 1973).

A.T. Tolley, *The Poetry of the Thirties* (London, 1975).

Ken Worpole, *Dockers and Detectives* (London, 1983).

CHAPTER TWELVE

Is there a British Modernism?

Keith Tuma

POETRY AND NATIONAL IDENTITY

In 1979 the American poet Donald Hall announced in the pages of *Parnassus* that 'the poetries of England and America have become discontinuous'. While American readers had heard similar statements coming from both sides of the Atlantic for fifteen years or more, rarely had they heard that such a state of affairs had consequences like those Hall described: 'Because prevailing English modes are as distinct from prevailing American modes as haiku from Icelandic saga, American readers must learn to approach English poets *as if* they were reading translations from the Polish.' [1] Surely, comparing the reading of English poetry and the reading of translations of Polish poetry was a little extreme, a little rhetorical, but Hall knew that if he could convince Americans that English poetry had become truly 'foreign' then he might expect them to read it with an eye towards expanding the possibilities of their own poetic practice, just as in previous decades they had turned to the Spanish of Pablo Neruda or, much earlier, the French of Jules Laforgue for something not quite so readily available in the poetry of American contemporaries and predecessors. To justify an engagement with English poetry in these terms seems odd given the centuries-old relationship of the two poetries, but Hall was only responding to what was in 1979 (and still is) the general sense among American poets that English poetry had not only gone its separate way but that American poets had no more reason to consider its traditions and conventions than the traditions and conventions of any other poetry.

Apparently Hall had been asked to survey recent English poetry in order to introduce unfamiliar English poets and poems to American readers; he was especially qualified for the task, having long been familiar with England and its poets. But the introduction of poets occurs almost as an afterthought in the essay, which instead responds to another essay by the English poet C.H. Sisson, published in a previous issue of the same American journal. In the course of a review essay on an anthology of American poetry Sisson had rather

begrudgingly admitted that six or seven American poets had been important
to him, and in passing he had poked at the reputations of Walt Whitman
('What a lout the man is!') and Emily Dickinson (whom he would have us
measure against Christina Rossetti). Whatever their opinion of Whitman and
Dickinson, few American readers of Sisson's essay would have been able to
take such remarks too seriously, but Sisson's argument about the relationship
of English and American poetry could not be so easily dismissed even by the
most chauvinistic American reader. The 'widely assumed' separateness of
English and American poetry, Sisson wrote, had nowhere been convincingly
argued, and an 'unimpeded conversation' between the two poetries had been
and would continue to be possible. 'A literature is the literature of a language',
Sisson continued, not of a nation, and thus the changing circumstances of
England and America, the 'immense international role of the United States,
and the diminished and dependent role of the United Kingdom', had little
bearing on what was after all still one literature.[2]

It was the assertion of a unified tradition of English literature that Hall set
out to disprove, though it must be admitted not so much by arguing the case
as by pointing to the differences between 'prevailing' English and American
poetic modes. He might have thought that there was something to be gained
simply in seeming to be more generous than the cantankerous Sisson as he
set out to praise the attention to sound and syntax in the work of several
English poets and said that Americans might learn from English examples,
might in reading them recognise certain limitations in current American
poetic conventions. Naming no one in particular, Hall suggested that 'it is a
characteristic flaw among young Americans, however accomplished and
innovative, to lack resourceful sound. . . . Allied is the lack of resourceful
syntax, reliance instead on simple and compound sentences.'[3] Hall must have
known that in raising the issue of syntactical practices he was staking out his
own ground in several related debates concerning the relative merits of
various poetries in this century, debates which have not only been used to
draw boundaries between national poetries but also to distinguish a modernist
from a more 'traditional' poetry. Donald Davie, perhaps the most influential
English advocate of English poetry in America, had on any number of
occasions written eloquently on behalf of the expressive potential of traditional English syntax, defending it against the abnegation of syntax he takes
to be characteristic of Modernist poetry following the examples of T.E.
Hulme, Ezra Pound and others.[4] And just two years before Hall's own article,
Marjorie Perloff had compared one of Sisson's poems with a poem by the
American poet James Wright and concluded that the former's syntax was
'much tighter, more traditional',[5] using that comparison to say something in
general about the divergence of the two poetries. Ultimately, it seems, Hall's
interest in the English depends upon his sense that modernist modes had by

233

1979 reached a point of exhaustion in the United States and that the 'prevailing' anti-modernism of the English might now become a resource. For all of his good intentions, it is clear that Hall was implying that English poets are not 'innovative', that to be an English poet was to feel, as Perloff had said, a 'burdensome sense of tradition'[6] which somehow makes one resistant to experimental energies.

If, like Donald Hall, we want to contest C.H. Sisson's almost archaic idea of a single tradition of English-language poetry transcending national boundaries, it is essential to consider not just individual poets and poems but also the institutions which have differently shaped the reception of poems in Britain and America.[7] Sisson does not deny the existence of competing versions of viable poetic tradition, within or across national boundaries; but he does insist upon what counts for him as a ' "true" English tradition of English',[8] which happens to include the poetry of Americans such as Ezra Pound and T.S. Eliot, though apparently not Walt Whitman. To be fair to Sisson, 'true' here acquires its inverted commas because he is sardonically miming the language of those poets among his English contemporaries who want to leap backwards beyond Pound and Eliot to identify Hardy or some other poet as representative of the essence of a specifically English tradition. (Philip Larkin is only the most famous of the poets Sisson might have in mind.) But a moralising identification of true and that-which-only-pretends-to-be true tradition tells us nothing about the role of competing discourses of tradition in shaping tastes, nor their position at the centre or the margins of British society.

Sisson's sense of tradition is remarkably close to one often attributed to Eliot, and my objection to it is not that it is therefore somehow American or even 'international' but that, like Eliot's ideal order of cultural monuments, it allows us to isolate one preferred literary tradition from the full range of literary practices, and also from the modes of behaviour and the social practices within which we produce and receive poems. If we want to explain the reception of Modernism in Britain or the reason a great number of contemporary British poets might have felt it incumbent upon them to search back beyond Modernism to find models they might wish to emulate, Sisson's prescriptive model of tradition will not serve. One might as well say it straight out. There is almost unanimous agreement in America that there have been in this century very few British poets who have worked in a manner related to or influenced by poets American readers have come to identify as Modernist – Pound and Eliot and also H.D., William Carlos Williams, Gertrude Stein, Marianne Moore, Langston Hughes and others. Moreover, those British poets whom Americans have thought of as Modernists have seemed almost in need of rescue from their fate in Britain: Tom Raworth (indebted to the New York poets) and J.H. Prynne (indebted to the Black

Mountain poets). If we move backwards closer to the era of 'high modernism' there is Basil Bunting,[9] who has lately been represented by both American and British critics as a lone English Modernist poet. Earlier even than Bunting there is Mina Loy – a British woman who chose to spend her entire adult life outside Britain, eventually becoming an American citizen; she is a poet whose longest poem contains an exploration of her British origins as distinctive as Bunting's return to Northumbria in *Briggflatts*. Writing about Bunting and Loy in an issue of the *Chicago Review* dedicated to neglected poets, the American poet Jim Powell proposed that we 'adopt both poets into citizenship in American poetry', and indeed the first full-length critical study of Loy was entitled *Mina Loy: American Modernist Poet*.[10] Today there is an archive at Durham University preserving Bunting materials for poetry scholars, but Loy's work is still virtually unknown in England. No doubt her publishing history is partly responsible for this; her work was not generally available even in America until the eighties, and no British edition of her poems exists.

In insisting that we recognise the current discontinuity of contemporary English and American poetry and in the service of an appreciation of the useful difference of English poetry, Donald Hall appeals to a very different idea of tradition from Sisson's Eliotic 'ideal order' of poetic masterworks. Having proposed that the level of engagement with tradition as such differs in England and America, he offers his alternative understanding of tradition:

> American literature differs from English not only because of the difference between the traditions, but in the extent to which tradition informs the work at all. . . . The tradition that matters most, to a nation's literature, is not the style or the content of its great writers. It is the soil of its history, the bones of its dead ground up in that soil, and the ideas and passions, the battles and revolutions, the glories and defeats of nation and spirit. Our tradition (like it or not) is enlightenment, protestant, industrial, and capitalist. In England tradition is inevitably layered.[11]

While one may wish to contest Hall's description of the essential character of American tradition for the way it inadequately represents marginalised cultural practices, at least his sense of tradition, stripped of its florid poeticisms, seems a little more satisfactory than Sisson's. It seems closer to an anthropologist's sense of 'culture' as 'way of life'. So far from being limited to a body of literary works arranged in an ideal order and manifesting specific characteristics in style and subject matter, tradition is the very ground we stand on, the social, political and intellectual customs we inherit with whatever degree of historical consciousness. In Hall we can hear, instead of Eliot, that other American Modernist William Carlos Williams, and this is not surprising, since among American poets of Hall's generation Eliot was eventually supplanted by Williams. This was mostly not the case among his contemporaries in Britain.

Hall's definition of tradition is still unsatisfactory for the way it mystifies 'nation' and 'spirit'. But if we hold, as I do, that there is no such thing as an essential national identity or 'spirit' but instead only those identities which we create and have created for us in our discursive, aesthetic, social and political practices, then we must suspect claims about a unified national spirit or 'character'. Such claims tend to minimise or ignore cultural conflict to posit a cultural coherence, and depend, as one critic has said, on the 'reification of a shared glorious past and the deployment of this solidified memory in the present as an object of consent . . .'.[12] Hall, though, is not reluctant to sketch a national character in pretty rough outlines, while he is savvy enough to add the proviso that 'no generalization about national character will hold'.[13] Casting Sisson in the role of typical Englishman he writes:

> I am struck [in Sisson's own poetry] with his self-accusation and self-distrust. He displays an emotion or an idea, then sees through himself to report on his own dishonesty or vanity or greed or egotism; distrust has the last word. In the best English poet of all, Geoffrey Hill, this self-distrust is almost the basis of the style, of the grammar, clauses balanced so that the final antithesis contains in a precise doubleness both the statement and an acidulous criticism of the statement. I suppose this is called irony – but I want a more serious word: an ironic American tends merely to display a consistent tonal sarcasm, saying something and denying its seriousness, wearing protective covering. In Sisson and in Hill this irony is deadly serious, not mask nor armor plate but vision.[14]

This is a useful and not inaccurate description of Sisson and Hill, or, more exactly, of the self-distrust and irony evident in their verse. But one cannot assume that Sisson's texts or Hill's are dependent upon a personality that can be defined as English. For the sake of his argument Hall uses Hill and Sisson to define 'Englishness', reading the poetry of the two writers as if it simply reflected something about the character of the two men, as if their poems were the natural expression of some self-understanding previous to their struggle to compose and order a poem. But voice and subjectivity are constructed within the existing discursive practices of the social body. Hill and Sisson write within and against the histories of discursive practices that work to form them in their image. If Hall is right about the predominance of a certain kind of irony, we need to know what accounts for this. Such irony is not a reflection of some essential 'Englishness' but rather one response to a complex field of social and cultural discourse in post-Second World War Britain, a Britain experiencing specific problems such as the devastated economy of the postwar years and the shrinking of its sphere of influence in the world.

A HISTORY OF THE 'TWO POETRIES' DEBATE

In his famous 1962 introduction, 'The New Poetry, *or* Beyond the Gentility Principle' (in his *The New Poetry* anthology), Alvarez identified 'gentility', which for him meant 'a belief that life is always more or less orderly, people always more or less polite, their emotions and habits more or less decent and more or less controllable', as characteristic of the then-dominant modes of British poetry. According to Alvarez, the concept of gentility reigned across class divisions; it could be seen influencing upper-middle-class Tory poets like John Betjeman and the lower-middle-class poets included in Robert Conquest's anthology of Movement poets, *New Lines* (1956). Such an ideal of gentility, Alvarez argued, reflected a wilful denial of the horrors of the modern world, which psychoanalysis had shown us were also the horrors of our individual selves. The cultivation of a British insularity, the denial of our own evil impulses which was encouraged by gentility, was simply no longer an option in a time of world wars, mass destruction and genocide. Alvarez presented his selections for his anthology as evidence that British poetry was ready to move beyond gentility to wed 'the psychological insight and integrity' of D.H. Lawrence and 'the technical skill and formal intelligence' of T.S. Eliot. What was especially noteworthy about those selections was that they included several Americans, placed at the front of the book. Alvarez did not hide the fact that he thought Robert Lowell and John Berryman – a second edition would add Sylvia Plath and Anne Sexton – were showing the way to a new practice that would be 'without evasion'. This was a poetry which showed what Bruno Bettelheim's observations at Dachau and Buchenwald had shown: that 'much of what went on around him expressed what went on inside himself'.[15]

This is not the place to express reservations about this model of an unmediated relationship between the individual psyche and society; the critic Paul Breslin has done this for us.[16] More pertinent to my discussion is the way Alvarez's encapsulated history of twentieth-century English poetry culminates in the suggestion that it is a wedding of Lawrence and Eliot which was needed. According to Alvarez, since the early thirties, when F.R. Leavis had called the work of Eliot and Ezra Pound a 'significant reorientation of literature', British poetry had been 'controlled' by a reaction to the modernism these two writers represented – or were made to represent. Thomas Hardy's prophecy that *vers libre* would come to nothing in Britain had been made into reality; even Leavis had eventually recanted on Pound and Eliot. First there was the rejection of the difficulty and experimentalism of Pound and Eliot in the thirties, when Auden and others reinvented the 'traditional lyric' in order to communicate the urgencies of the political situation. Then there was the reaction to Auden embodied by Dylan Thomas, the reaction to Thomas embodied by the Movement. Now poets were once again coming around to see the value of Eliot, though it was not the Eliot who promoted a classicist ideal of 'impersonality' or the Eliot whom the mostly American New Criticism had used to purge all consideration of an author's personal and social circumstances from the reading of poetry, but the Eliot whose poem 'The Waste Land' 'follows, with great precision and delicacy, the movement of a psyche, not just of society, in the process of disintegration'. Robert Lowell, who had begun in 'Lord Weary's Castle' (1946) under the influence of the New Criticism and the Eliot of 'impersonality', had in *Life Studies* (1959) taken a 'step forward in this new direction' related to this newly understood Eliotic mode.[17] British poets were ready to follow his lead.

Somewhere in this literary history, where change in dominant modes of poetic practice is determined by a series of reactions and misunderstandings largely independent of institutional changes and sociohistorical contexts, poor Ezra Pound vanishes. Apparently Alvarez did not understand his work as providing a viable model. And yet it was Pound, H.D. and most especially William Carlos Williams who would turn out to be the most frequently cited Modernist influences in the work of a new group of poets in America who were already emerging even as Alvarez gathered his poets and introduced his anthology. When Lowell was asked about the work he thought made the new poetry of *Life Studies* possible, he pointed to William Carlos Williams, and Allen Ginsberg's 'Howl' (1956), which had been influenced and introduced by Williams. The various loosely affiliated poets gathered together two years before the publication of Alvarez's anthology in Donald Allen's extremely successful American poetry anthology *The New American Poetry* (1960) had very little use for Eliot, whom they mostly understood as the post-symbolist poet of impersonality safely institutionalised by the New Critics. Not only were Pound, Williams and H.D. still writing and publishing poetry, unlike Eliot, but they had not yet anything like Eliot's status within the canon and the academy. And thus along with the possible compositional strategies one or several of these different models could be seen to underwrite – a greater attention to history, a less exclusively Eurocentric frame of reference (Pound's China, H.D.'s Egypt, Williams's America), a more 'open' or process-orientated poetry, a rejection of the post-symbolist's 'interpretive mind' in favour of the objectivist's 'measuring mind',[18] an emphasis on idiosyncratic syntactical and rhythmical patterns – there was the fact that all of these other Modernists could be used to fuel an assault on a literary academy dominated by the New Criticism and the 'academic' verse the New Criticism was thought to have bred.

The Modernism that mattered to the New American poets had hardly been more successful in America in the thirties, forties and early fifties than it had been in England. Williams had been ignored for decades before being revived in the fifties and sixties, as had been H.D., and even Ezra Pound had nothing like Eliot's status. The Objectivist poets like George Oppen and Louis Zukofsky who extended and revised the strategies of Williams and Pound were almost completely unknown. The 'Modernism' that we now understand to have been triumphant in America and steadfastly resisted in Britain is a relatively recent development. If too often we can hardly come up with a definition of modernist writing any more specific than 'experimental, audience-challenging, and language-focused'[19] it would also seem to be the case that modernism is fragmented at its source. We can hardly agree upon how to read its major contributors, the list of whom has been for thirty years now undergoing revision and rearrangement. Thus we see among the American 'Language poets' of the last fifteen years a great increase in Gertrude Stein, Laura Riding and Louis Zukofsky, and a slight decline in interest in Pound, who together with Williams ruled over the New American poetry.

The transformation of modernism in America certainly cannot be attributed solely to the work of the New American poets or any other group, as the sixties and seventies also saw the expansion of American universities, the introduction of governmental subsidies for writers and scholars, the emergence of creative writing programmes, the boom in the academic study of not just modern but also contemporary literature, and other changes in those institutional practices that bear directly upon the production and reception of poetry. Britain experienced many but not all of these transformations and those it has seen have not always been of the same magnitude. Likewise the United States has seen nothing on the scale of George MacBeth's BBC poetry broadcast *Poetry Now* – originally *The Poet's Voice* – which began in 1957, reaching on occasion an estimated audience of 50,000 plus.[20] Such institutional factors have had an effect on the different reception of modernism in the two nations.

Moreover, we are only now just beginning to understand the degree to which what Hugh Kenner and others have called an 'International Modernism' is a product of Cold War contingencies of value in America, on the need for America to support its new role as economic and military superpower with an assertion of cultural leadership. In a recent essay on Wallace Stevens, Alan Filreis asked 'To what extent is the idea of having transcended the very idea of national style uniquely American?'[21] Sisson's idea of a tradition of English-language poetry might suggest that such an idea is not at all uniquely American, but Sisson is much indebted to Pound and Eliot, and there is little question that American Modernists and their post-Second World War promoters have been especially aggressive and successful in promoting an international style. Pound's 1914 essay 'The Renaissance', where he predicted an imminent American renaissance in the arts and culture, polemically insisted that one requirement of such a renaissance was 'a criticism of poetry based on world-poetry'.[22] Pound thought he had to argue the point in 1914; by the forties even the middlebrow editor of the mass-circulation magazine *Life* knew that Americans were ready and able to contest the European perception of their culture as provincial and 'gadget-minded'.[23] And in 1960 Donald Allen felt that it was important to promote his New American poets just as the modern jazz and abstract expressionist painting some of the poets had learned from had been promoted, as 'a dominant movement in the second phase of our twentieth-century literature . . . already exerting strong influence abroad'.[24] However opposed to American chauvinism individual New American poets often were, there it was rearing its ugly head in the introduction to the book that made many of them famous.

An early essay by Nathaniel Tarn, published in 1968, can serve as representative of the kind of polemic that angered a number of British poets and forced them to justify their 'insularity' and 'little-Englandism' with claims about an essential British tradition and 'character'. Like Alvarez, Tarn positioned himself as an enemy of 'gentility', of 'the miserable timidity' and 'smallness of mind and purpose which keeps us almost totally alienated from our true potential'. He found the bulk of British poetry to be 'relentlessly superficial', a manifestation of the 'immemorial British shyness, a shyness which can, at the drop of a hat, become rabid arrogance when it is suggested we might learn from the outside world'. While the remedies for such a state of affairs were various, and included a need to remain open to poetic, religious and cultural influences from around the world, Tarn insisted that the British needed to pay special attention to the Americans: 'Fifty-first state or not, now or in the future, our local stance is inevitably conditioned by the kind of yes or no we say to the poetry of the United States.'[25]

For Tarn, now an American citizen, 'America was and still is the one place that satisfies the desire for national identity while it assumes that absolute, irrational identity is impossible', as Doris Sommer has written in an essay on his work. It is 'the alienated and self-willed quality of America that made it so attractive and available to Tarn', the fact that Americans 'may sense that their culture is made, whereas other societies may more easily mistake culture for nature, human products for natural givens'.[26] Like de Tocqueville, Baudrillard and other Europeans, Tarn found these truisms about America compelling. He came to represent America as 'a family of nations rather than a single nation',[27] 'England' and 'America' as states of mind and types of cultural practice.[28]

In 'The World Wide Open: The Work Laid Before Us in this Disunited Kingdom' (1968), after reminding his readers that Pound and Eliot were Americans, Tarn nodded in the direction of a British modernism to say that, in his opinion, the only post-Georgian poetry of value 'is not English but Celtic: Yeats, Joyce, MacDiarmid, Dylan Thomas'.[29] Three years later, the

American poet John Matthias edited *23 Modern British Poets*, an anthology designed to prove to Americans that 'there *is* a contemporary British poetry which is modern; for a while that seemed in doubt. Perhaps, in America at least, it's still in doubt'.[30] Then in 1972 in Britain there appeared Michael Schmidt and Grevel Lindop's aggressive anthology of essays on British poetry which included an introduction attacking American detractors of British poetry and much American poetry itself.[31] Also in 1972 Donald Davie published *Thomas Hardy and British Poetry*, a sustained defence of the tradition of Hardy, which he found to be more pervasively influential than had sometimes been recognised in England and certainly more attractive than typically acknowledged in America. Along the way it was necessary to attack Lawrence, especially as Lawrence was understood by Kenneth Rexroth, one of the fathers of the New American poetry. This book, and Davie's work in general, contributed greatly to the idea that the two poetries had become discontinuous. In 1974 Calvin Bedient published a book on eight British poets in which he felt obliged to begin by defending British poetry against its reputation as genteel and trivial. Finally, in 1977 Marjorie Perloff edited a special issue of *Contemporary Literature* which featured her own and Lawrence Kramer's essays on the discontinuities among the two poetries. Of course there were briefer essays in journals too; I mean only to outline the debate here and suggest its level of intensity in the seventies.

A number of critics, including Alan Brownjohn, attributed the success of the New American poetry to its links with a somewhat incoherent counter-culture.[32] By contrast the 'one peculiar and excellent strength of the English creative intellect' was its insistence on 'reasonable' and 'defensible' utterance. One would also do well to remember, he wrote, that 'empirical, critical attitudes *are* the English tradition'.[33] The emphasis in that last sentence speaks volumes;Brownjohn needed to insist upon the essence of what he calls the English – properly the British – tradition. My point is not to quarrel about the importance of empiricism to Britain; that would be like saying that pragmatism did not matter to the United States. But to say that 'empirical attitudes' have historically been central to British thought is quite another thing than saying that they alone have defined British life and must continue to do so, especially when what counts as 'empiricism' or for that matter 'reason' is always open to debate.

Donald Davie's defence of British poetry in his book on Hardy is also a polemic on behalf of contemporary British poetry, though like Donald Hall and unlike many other British and American critics Davie has always worked to improve the conversation between the two poetries. In contrasting the two cultures in general Davie also has recourse to the ready clichés (including the substitution of English for British):

> The Englishman supposes he is trying to operate in some highly specific historical situation, conditioned by manifold contingencies (hence his qualifications, his hesitancies, his damaging concessions), whereas the American poet, conditioned since the Pilgrim Fathers to think in utopian terms, is sure that he is enacting a drama of which the issues are basically simple and permanent, and will be seen to be so once we have penetrated through their accidental, historical overlay.[34]

Even if one agrees that there is a necessary correlation between an awareness of historical contingencies and a fundamental scepticism, or between a moral and utopian consciousness and vatic posturing in poetry, one might want to contest the description of Americans as a less historically conscious people than the British. In his *An Explanation of America*, Robert Pinsky writes of Americans that 'Nostalgia and Progress seem to be our frail / National gestures against the enveloping, / Suffusive nightmare of time'.[35] If he is right, it might be better to suggest that, typically, the historical consciousness of Americans has an element of sentimentality in it; this is quite another thing than saying that Americans simply do not think historically. Moreover, if Davie is mostly right about the Americans and the British and their different attitudes towards history, one would still have to account for the exceptions. To his credit, Davie does attempt to do just this, at least on the British side, by arguing that it is not the ahistorical tendencies in W.B. Yeats and D.H. Lawrence that have won the day in contemporary British poetry but rather Hardy's 'world of historical contingency'. But, like most of the critics we have been following in this debate, Davie needs to represent the 'other' nation as a monolithic entity. Thus we learn that 'diluted Freudianism has been characteristic of American culture'.[36]

In taking up the cause of Hardy and those poets influenced by him – Larkin, Roy Fisher, Charles Tomlinson, the early J.H. Prynne – Davie subtly reverses the valuations of Alvarez's introduction. What is 'gentility', he asks, but civic sense and political responsibility? If a Hardyesque tone and manner has come to dominate British poetry, this is the result of social and political circumstances, namely the triumph of 'scientific humanism' and 'social democracy' in modern Britain. The success of Hardy and his followers is worth celebrating, for Hardy is the poet most in accord with these social and intellectual movements. As for the success of those antidemocratic poets Pound, Yeats, Lawrence and Eliot, that was an academic affair, and it was a fact that the academic critic who 'toys with' the political opinions of these men 'transforms himself into a social democrat as soon as he attends his university senate, voting there . . . .'.[37] But such an argument cannot account for the fact that Hardy's mode has had considerably more success in Britain than America, which has also witnessed the triumph of 'scientific humanism' and 'social democracy'. (It also reduces Pound and Eliot to their political opinions.) So Davie is forced to look elsewhere to explain the divergence between the two poetries and ends up arguing that 'the distinctive quality and the distinctive task of poetry in Britain were defined, and are still to be defined, by the fact that Britain as a whole is the most industrialised landscape in the world'. [38] In her own essay on the two poetries, the American critic Marjorie Perloff correctly pointed out that Britain was no more industrialised than New Jersey, which had been the home of William Carlos Williams and Allen Ginsberg, two poets who had little in common with Hardy, Larkin or Donald Davie. [39] The argument about the two poetries sometimes included claims more far-fetched than Davie's, and to be fair to him it must be said that his best observations on the divergence between the two poetries are not dependent on the blunt determinism evident at times in *Thomas Hardy and British Poetry*, and I will have occasion to refer to other, more useful differences Davie has brought to light as I turn now to sketch my own sense of the reasons the two poetries have gone their (mostly) separate ways.

BRITISH MODERNIST POETRY AND THE COMMON READER

> [E]pistemology, subjectivity, and language, are everywhere the concern of English poetry from William Wordsworth, say, to Arthur Hugh Clough, where they are understood as central to the issue, among others, of the authority of poetry and of the poet. They are the concerns also of the early twentieth-century modernism that hardly happened to poetry in Britain, or that happened only in the works of writers who, precisely because their concerns were the concerns of modernism. . . . Issues like these are nowhere to be found in what many of the most influential institutions of British literary culture represent as the most important poetry now being written. They are kept out by a series of arguments – that they are undecidable and therefore not worth discussing, that they empty poetry of its human content, that they are properly the province of philosophers and not of poets, that they are elitist preoccupations which can never engage a wider public. All these arguments do something to explain why poetry in Britain has become such a trivial affair. [40]

John Barrell's essay, from which I take these remarks, is on the poetry of Tom Raworth, and more especially on the role of syntax in Raworth's poetry (of great interest to any number of American poets who would continue and extend the experimentalist imperative of Modernist poetry). Reading these remarks an American might want to ask Barrell which is the case: did Modernism 'hardly happen' to poetry in Britain or has its reception made it seem more of a marginal phenomenon? The work of Basil Bunting, Hugh MacDiarmid, David Jones and others collected in the John Matthias anthology (including Raworth) would suggest that the latter is the case. Our job would then seem to be to explain what has hampered the reception of Modernism in England along the lines of the reasons sketched by Barrell.

But it might be objected that we would do well first to understand what might characterise English and British Modernist poetry, or distinguish it from the poetry of American Modernists. This kind of work also might tell us something about the importance of national contexts. Even a cursory glance at the manifestos of Vorticism published in *Blast* shows us that the Modernist painter and novelist Wyndham Lewis understood his movement as distinct from the other Modernist and avant-garde movements then current on the Continent, even as he borrowed some of the publicising strategies of those movements, of Italian Futurism in particular. Vorticist pronouncements reflected a not altogether resolved conflict of nationalistic and internationalist impulses, Lewis insisting on the one hand that it was okay to learn from France or Germany and on the other that Vorticism was different from movements there, something responsive to an 'English Character' which was 'northern', 'based on the sea', and more truly a product of a mechanised world 'due almost entirely to Anglo-Saxon genius'.[41]

All in all, it is not hard to see why a critic like Barrell might be tempted to say that Modernist poetry 'hardly happened' in Britain. Ford Madox Ford, D.H. Lawrence, Hugh MacDiarmid. David Jones, Mina Loy, Edith Sitwell and Basil Bunting constitute no group but a collection of idiosyncratic talents. They were less eager than Pound, Eliot or Williams to offer prose explanations of such issues of technique as the importance of the image or the 'ideogrammic method' (Pound), the 'objective correlative' and 'impersonality' (Eliot), the 'variable foot' (Williams). It may be because Modernism came late to Great Britain – Bunting was fifteen years younger than Pound – that its poets felt it less urgent to write extensively on technique and its implications. But even if British Modernism was a 'belated' phenomenon, that does not mean that it 'hardly happened', nor does that fact tell us much about the poems we are concerned with, and what might distinguish them from American Modernist poems.

Any effort to identify an English or a British Modernist poetry will eventually have to confront the possibility that one's claims about the nature of that poetry are the product of the poems chosen to represent it. Thus what Donald Davie says about Basil Bunting, whom he is not alone in singling out to represent British Modernism in poetry, may not pertain to David Jones or others. Here is what Davie has to say about Bunting's Modernism:

> Bunting is undoubtedly a Modernist, in the sense in which Pound is a Modernist, though T.S. Eliot also. Historically this is Bunting's unique importance; for in the present century there is no British-English poet of whom as much can be said. And so Bunting's existence is an embarrassment to the numerous English historians who would have it that modernism in poetry was a temporary American-inspired

distraction from a native tradition which persisted, undeterred though for a time invisible, behind the marches and countermarches of modernist polemics. . . .
In the same year when *Briggflatts* appeared, Bunting's American contemporary George Oppen, who had appeared with him as long ago as 1932 in *An Objectivist's Anthology*, sneered at poems addressed to readers 'who may be imagined to admire the quaintness and ingenuity of the poet, but can scarcely have been part of the poet's attempt to find himself in the world – unless perhaps to find himself as a charming conversationalist'.

And Davie continues on to point to a passage in *Briggflatts* that seems to him 'undoubtedly conversational' and 'not the ruminations of a solitary' one hears so often in Pound's *Cantos* or in many of Oppen's poems. Furthermore, he writes, while Bunting 'strenuously condenses his sentences' (condensation and a hatred for rhetoric being central to Pound's poetic as well) he 'never abandons the subject–verb–object structure of the English sentence, whereas in Oppen and Pound what we read is quite often a series of disjunct phrases pulled free of any syntactical anchorage'.[42] To hear the conversational quality and the syntax of Bunting's work praised by Davie is not surprising, considering that he is the author of *Articulate Energy*, a study of the powers of expression possible in English syntax. But one is obliged to point out that not all of *Briggflatts* is equally conversational, as Davie knows, and that Bunting did in the earlier poem 'Attis, Or, Something Missing' employ sentence fragments and paratactic methods in the manner of Pound and Eliot. Moreover, so far is Bunting from appearing 'conversational' to all readers that the American Language poet Charles Bernstein in his verse essay on 'anti-absorptive' strategies in poetic composition, by which he means strategies which downplay the communicative possibilities of poetry to emphasise the sheer materiality and musicality of language, says of Bunting that his 'primary audience has always been / readers for whom his vocabulary is opaque / & this is inextricable from the poem's power & / particular music'.[43] An opaque vocabulary would hardly seem to make for a conversational poetry, nor for that matter would a syntax as extremely condensed as Bunting's. This is not to argue that Davie is somehow wrong about Bunting but to point out the way in which Bunting's Modernism can be differently appropriated.

The second of John Barrell's points in his essay on Raworth is that if Modernism seems hardly to have happened in Britain, he argues, it is because Modernism there has been marginalised. And I would argue that, if we want to know why the reception of Modernism has been more successful in America than in Britain we have to understand that British literary culture is more centralised than American literary culture. More importantly, we have to understand that the critics at the centre of British culture have been more aggressive in speaking in the name of a 'common' or 'general' reader and against the professionalisation of literature with which the history of

Modernism is entangled, especially in America. The complaint about Modernism from its beginnings has been that it is elitist and difficult, that it has wilfully flaunted its disregard for any audience but an audience of the initiated. Critics responding to such a perceived arrogance have not been in short supply in either nation, from John Middleton Murry to Philip Larkin in Britain, from Karl Shapiro to Robert Richman in America. But there is little doubt that the anti-modernist forces have been more influential in Britain especially over the last thirty years.

If it has long been known in America that the audience for poetry is dependent on the culture of the universities and its margins, the illusion of a Common Reader has died a slower death in Britain.[44] As Frank Kermode has written, we are badly in need of a history of the Common Reader which would take us up into the present day, and I can add that the best history of this sort would acknowledge that the ideal of the Common Reader has met a different fate in different nations. Following Erich Auerbach, Kermode notes that the English Common Reader was in Samuel Johnson's day and throughout much of the nineteenth century a member of 'an élite minority, clearly differentiated from the uneducated on the one hand and the specialists on the other'.[45] In the twentieth century, especially after the advent of radio and television, it has become much harder both to identify such a reader and to locate him, as Johnson did, in a socioeconomic class. Today, writes Kermode, lamenting the irresponsibility of academic literary theorists who write only for one another, the Common Reader is perhaps nobody but our undergraduate student.

What can explain, then, remarks like the following by Philip Larkin? In a passage that has been much derided by American supporters of Modernist and Post Modernist poetry, Larkin wrote:

> All I am saying is that the term 'modern', when applied to art, has a more than chronological meaning: it denotes a quality of irresponsibility peculiar to this century, known sometimes as Modernism. . . . I am sure that there are books in which the genesis of modernism is set out in full. My own theory is that it is related to an imbalance between the two tensions from which art springs: these are the tension between the artist and his material, and between the artist and his audience, and that in the last seventy-five years or so the second of these has slackened or even perished. In consequence the artist has become over-concerned with his material (hence an age of technical experiment) and, in isolation, has busied himself with the two principal themes of modernism, mystification and outrage. . . . [Larkin provides several colorful examples.] [T]here has grown up a kind of critical journalism designed to put it over. The terms of the argument vary with the circumstances, but basically the message is: Don't trust your eyes, or ears, or understanding. They'll tell you this is ridiculous, or ugly, or meaningless. Don't believe them. You've got to work at this: after all, you don't expect to understand anything as important as art straight off, do you? I mean, this is pretty complex stuff: if you want to know how complex, I'm giving a course of ninety-six lectures at the local college, starting

next week, and you'd be more than welcome. The whole thing's on the rates, you won't have to pay. . . . [46]

As Hugh Kenner notes, it is sometimes difficult to establish how much affectation is involved in Larkin's vulgar public persona.[47] I suggest that Larkin, a professional librarian and a talented poet, is speaking in the name of a Common Reader. The huge success of Larkin in Britain would suggest that there was much to be gained by playing to widespread anxieties about the increasing professionalisation of literature in this century and especially in the post-Second World War era. While Larkin is notorious for being hostile to Modernism, the real barbs here are directed at the academic exegetes of Modernist writing.

In what are his most useful comments on the divergence of American and British poetry in this century, Donald Davie writes that 'in our national tradition, in the arts as until recently in sports, it is the amateur who is most admired'. Davie, for all of his attacks on Larkin and his professed admiration for the work of Ezra Pound and Americans who have taken Pound for a model, is not prepared to abandon this tradition, which has a 'continuing validity'.[48] As far as poetry is specifically concerned, it can be argued that the ideal of amateurism and the perceived need to address a Common Reader results in a poetry less ready to violate what that reader has come to expect in the way of subject matter, form and syntax.

If the *ideal* of a Common Reader persists as a more influential force upon poetic production in Britain, this must be because British intellectuals can point to a number of poets who have had a significant popular readership *and* remain worthy of the 'serious' attention these intellectuals bring to poetry. To understand why the British may have developed more faith in theirs, one might go back to examine the popular success of Byron and Tennyson in the nineteenth century, but one need go back no farther than the poets of the Great War – Blunden, Sassoon, Owen, Rosenberg, Graves – or the poets of Edward Marsh's Georgian anthologies. It has been much harder for American intellectuals to agree upon the worth of our popular poets, with Allen Ginsberg being perhaps an exception, and a notable exception in so far as his huge success within the counter-culture seemed to prove that a poet indebted to modernist paradigms might under the right set of circumstances reach an audience beyond the traditional readers of poetry. In this century America has had a few poets roughly contemporary with Sassoon and Owen of comparable popularity – Joyce Kilmer for instance – but American intellectuals have not been able to point to such poets as evidence of the wisdom and judgement of American readers. And here I would remind the reader of what was said above about American Cold War contingencies of value, about the widespread perception among American intellectuals in the decades after the Second World War that it was necessary to assert the vitality of an élite or 'high' culture, which meant that defending the judgements and tastes of a Common Reader received lower priority. In fact it was thought to be the case that such a Common Reader could be formed and manufactured as it were *ex nihilo*. The American Common Reader was not to be appealed to but made; he had no history. And he was to be made entirely in the university.

Thinking about Larkin, Kermode and Davie, and the 'prevailing' practices in British poetry, one may imagine that the Common Reader still exists in Britain, reading poetry outside the university; but I suspect that if such a reader does exist it will not be for long. No doubt his existence today is largely symbolic. Perhaps one day we will mark the late seventies as the era of his disappearance. A timely disappearance? Marjorie Perloff notes that by the mid seventies America had numerous academic journals devoted to theories of modernism and Modernist and Postmodernist poetry. Britain had as yet seen nothing like this number of academic journals of criticism, and for the most part its poetry journals devoted little space to theoretical discussions of modernism. This seemed significant to Perloff; the absence of a thriving and constantly changing critical industry in modernist studies might explain a divergence between the two poetries which was becoming more and more evident on the contemporary scene.[49] It seems to me that she was right.

NOTES

1. Donald Hall, 'Reading the English: The Continental Drift of the Poetries', *Parnassus* 7: 2 (Spring–Summer 1979): 24–5. Hall uses the term 'English', but except where the term is appropriately exclusive and/or appears in quoted material, the author and the editors have preferred the term 'British'.

2. C.H. Sisson, 'Some Reflections on American Poetry' (1978) in Sisson, *The Avoidance of Literature: Collected Essays* (Manchester, 1978), pp. 524–5.

3. Hall, op. cit., pp. 25–6.

4. See especially Donald Davie, *Articulate Energy: An Inquiry into the Syntax of English Poetry* (London, Henley and Boston, 1955).

5. Marjorie Perloff, 'The Two Poetries: An Introduction', *Contemporary Literature* 18 (Summer 1977): 268.

6. Ibid., p. 264.

7. See the introduction to Robert Richman, *The Direction of Poetry: An Anthology of Rhymed and Metered Verse Written in the English Language since 1975* (Boston, 1988), p. xiii.

8. Sisson, op. cit., p. 525.

9. See Hugh Kenner, *A Sinking Island: The Modern English Writers* (New York, 1988), which is dedicated *in memoriam* Basil Bunting.

10. Jim Powell, 'Basil Bunting and Mina Loy', *Chicago Review* 37: 1 (Winter 1990): 24; Virginia Kouidis, *Mina Loy: American Modernist Poet* (Baton Rouge, 1980).

11. Hall, p. 27.

12. Ian Baucom, 'Narrating the Nation', *Transition* 55 (1992): 148.

13. Hall, op. cit., p. 31.

14. Ibid

15. A. Alvarez, 'The New Poetry, Or, Beyond the Gentility Principle' (1962) in Alvarez (ed.), *The New Poetry* (rev. edn Harmondsworth and New York, 1966), pp. 25–32.

16. See Paul Breslin, *The Psycho-Political Muse: American Poetry since the Fifties* (Chicago and London, 1987), pp. 21–9.

17. Alvarez, op. cit., pp. 21–9.

18. These are Charles Altieri's terms. See his 'The Objectivist Tradition', *Chicago Review* 30: 3 (1979): 68.

19. See Bonnie Kime Scott, introduction to Scott (ed.), *The Gender of Modernism: A Critical Anthology* (Bloomington and Indianapolis, 1990), p. 4.

20. See Martin Booth, *British Poetry 1964 to 1984: Driving the Barricades* (London, Boston, Melbourne and Henley, 1985), pp. 87–92.

21. Alan Filreis, ' "Beyond the Rhetorician's Touch": Stevens's Painterly Abstractions', *American Literary History* 4: 2 (Summer 1992): 253.

22. Ezra Pound, 'The Renaissance' (1914) in T.S. Eliot (ed.), *Literary Essays of Ezra Pound* (rpt New York, 1968), p. 225.

23. 'Revolution on Campus', *Life Magazine* (28 November 1949): 7.

24. Donald Allen, preface to Allen (ed.), *The New American Poetry* (New York and London, 1960), p. xiii.

25. Nathaniel Tarn, 'The World Wide Open: The Work Laid Before Us in this Disunited Kingdom' (1968) in Tarn, *Views from the Weaving Mountain: Selected Essays in Poetics and Anthropology* (Albuquerque, 1991), pp. 16–24.

26. Doris Sommer, 'America as Desire(d): Nathaniel Tarn's Poetry of the Outsider as Insider', *American Poetry* 2: 1 (Fall 1984): 14–15.

27. Nathaniel Tarn, 'Child as Father to Man in the American Uni-Verse' in *Views from the Weaving Mountain.* p. 58.

28. Ibid., pp. 57–8.

29. Tarn, 'The World Wide Open', pp. 16–17.

30. John Matthias, foreword to Matthias (ed.), *23 Modern British Poets* (Chicago, 1971), p. xiii.

31. Michael Schmidt and Grevel Lindop, introduction to Schmidt and Lindop, (eds.), *British Poetry since 1960: A Critical Survey* (Oxford, 1972), p. 4.

32. Alan Brownjohn, 'A View of English Poetry in the Early Seventies' in *British Poetry since 1960: A Critical Survey*, pp. 240–9.

33. Brownjohn, pp. 248–9.

34. Donald Davie, *Thomas Hardy and British Poetry* (New York, 1972), p. 186.

35. Robert Pinsky, *An Explanation of America* (Princeton, 1979), p. 54.

36. Ibid., p. 186.

37. Ibid., p. 5.

38. Ibid., p. 72.

39. Perloff, 'The Two Poetries: An Introduction', p. 264.

40. John Barrell, 'Subject and Sentence: The Poetry of Tom Raworth', *Critical Inquiry* 17: 2 (Winter 1991): 388.

41. Wyndham Lewis, *Blast* (June 1914; rpt Santa Barbara, 1981): 84–90.

42. Donald Davie, *Under Briggflatts: A History of Poetry in Great Britain 1960–1988* (Chicago, 1989), pp. 42–3.

43. Charles Bernstein, 'Artifice of Absorption' in Bernstein, *A Poetics* (Cambridge and London, 1992), p. 59.

44. See Charles Bernstein, 'Comedy and the Poetics of Political Form' in *A Poetics*, pp. 225–6.

45. Frank Kermode, 'The Common Reader' in Kermode, *An Appetite for Poetry* (Cambridge, 1989), p. 49.

46. Philip Larkin, *Required Writing: Miscellaneous Pieces 1955–1982* (London, 1983), p. 293.

47. *A Sinking Island*, pp. 238–40.

48. Donald Davie, 'Ezra Pound and the English' in Davie, *Trying to Explain* (Ann Arbor, 1979), pp. 158–61.

49. Perloff, 'The Two Poetries: An Introduction', p. 265.

FURTHER READING

Donald Allen (ed.), *The New American Poetry* (New York, 1960).

Charles Altieri, 'The Objectivist Tradition', *Chicago Review* 30 (3): 5–22.

A. Alvarez (ed.), *The New Poetry* (Harmondsworth, 1966).

John Barrell, 'Subject and Sentence: The Poetry of Tom Raworth', *Critical Inquiry* 17: 2 (Winter 1991): 386–409.

Ian Baucom, 'Narrating the Nation', *Transition* 55 (1992): 144–53.

Charles Bernstein, *A Poetics* (Cambridge and London, 1992).

Martin Booth, *British Poetry 1964 to 1984: Driving the Barricades* (London, 1985).

Paul Breslin, *The Psycho-Political Muse: American Poetry since the Fifties* (Chicago, 1897).

Alan Brownjohn, 'A View of English Poetry in the Early Seventies', *British Poetry since 1960: A Critical Survey*, (ed.) Michael Schmidt and Grevel Lindop (Oxford, 1972), pp. 240–9.

Donald Davie, *Articulate Energy: An Inquiry into the Syntax of English Poetry* (London, 1955).

——'Ezra Pound and the English', *Trying to Explain* (Ann Arbor, 1979), pp. 150–64.

——*Thomas Hardy and British Poetry* (New York, 1972).

——*Under Briggflatts: A History of Poetry in Great Britain 1960–1988* (Chicago, 1989).

James Dickey, *Babel to Byzantium: Poets and Poetry Now* (New York, 1968), pp. 173–5.

Alan Filreis, 'Beyond the Rhetorician's Touch: Stevens's Painterly Abstractions', *American Literary History* 4:2 (Summer 1992): 230–63.

Donald Hall, 'Reading the English: The Continental Drift of the Poetries', *Parnassus* 7: 2 (Spring–Summer 1979): 24–43.

Hugh Kenner, *A Sinking Island: The Modern English Writers* (New York, 1988).

Frank Kermode, *An Appetite for Poetry* (Cambridge, Mass., 1989).

Virginia Kouidis, *Mina Loy: American Modernist Poet* (Baton Rouge, 1980).

Philip Larkin, *Required Writing: Miscellaneous Pieces 1955–1982* (London, 1983).

Wyndham Lewis (ed.), *Blast* (June 1914, rpt Santa Barbara, 1981).

John Matthias (ed.), *23 Modern British Poets* (Chicago, 1971).

Marjorie Perloff, 'The Two Poetries: An Introduction', *Contemporary Literature* 18 (Summer 1977): 263–78.

Robert Pinsky, *An Explanation of America* (Princeton, 1979).

Ezra Pound, 'Patria Mia', *Selected Prose 1909–1965* (New York, 1973), pp. 100–41.

Ezra Pound, 'The Renaissance', Literary Essays of Ezra Pound, (ed.) T.S. Eliot (New York, 1968), pp. 214–26.

Jim Powell, 'Basil Bunting and Mina Loy', *Chicago Review* 37: 1 (Winter 1990): 6–25.

Robert Richman (ed.), *The Direction of Poetry: An Anthology of Rhymed and Metered Verse Written in the English Language since 1975* (Boston, 1988).

Edward Said, 'Opponents, Audiences, Constituencies and Community',

The Anti-Aesthetic: Essays on Postmodern Culture, (ed.) Hal Foster (Port Townsend, Washington, 1983), pp. 135–59.

Michael Schmidt and Grevel Lindop (eds), *British Poetry since 1960: A Critical Survey* (Manchester, 1972).

Bonnie Kime Scott (ed.), *The Gender of Modernism: A Critical Anthology* (Bloomington, 1990).

C.H. Sisson, *The Avoidance of Literature: Collected Essays* (Manchester, 1978).

Doris Sommer, 'America as Desired(d): Nathaniel Tarn's Poetry of the Outsider as Insider', *American Poetry* 2:1 (Fall 1984): pp. 13–35.

Nathaniel Tarn, *View from the Weaving Mountain: Selected Essays in Poetics and Anthropology* (Albuquerque, 1991).

Yvor Winters, *In Defense of Reason* (Chicago, 1947).

CHAPTER THIRTEEN

Comparative Metafictions of History: E.L. Doctorow and John Fowles

Brian Harding

In the winter 1975–76 issue of *The American Scholar*, Martin Green noted the emergence of a new genre – or sub-genre – of fiction and judged it to be the most promising development of the previous decade. The new kind of fiction was the 'historical' novel in which real historical personages were introduced only to be treated like fictional characters; the point of view was not confined to the period in which the action was set; the reader was teased to discover the imaginative status of the characters and events. In Green's opinion, the importance of the new techniques lay in the fact that they challenged the reader 'both generally, to cope with assaults on his rational composure, and, specifically, to relate his modernism to the historical period depicted'. Moreover, they challenged the reader 'in the name of art'[1]. The examples on which Green based his generalisations included John Fowles's *The French Lieutenant's Woman* (1969) and E.L. Doctorow's *Ragtime* (1974).

Although subsequent discussions of 'historiographic metafictions' have deployed more specialised and more refined critical terminology in approaching the new-historical novel, Green's review deserves credit for its insistence that this kind of novel 'challenges' the reader by problematising the status of the characters and events in the story. In other words, it involves a 'defamiliarisation'. Moreover, if we substitute 'ontological' for Green's 'imaginative', we can see that his account is moving towards a definition of postmodernist fiction, while keeping in focus the crucial matter of reader response. The weakness of Green's review, however, is that it overlooks important differences between the representative writers he selects and thus initiates a tendency to homogenise those metafictional works whose subject is history. More recent and lengthier discussions of metafiction, such as Marguerite Alexander's *Flights from Realism* (1990), have almost routinely assumed that all recent fictions in which the distinctions between history and fiction are blurred have the same goals and work to the same effects. A corrective to this tendency was provided by the brief chapter on 'Fabulation as History' in Robert Scholes's *Fabulation and Metafiction* (1979). Bringing together Barth (*The Sot-Weed Factor*), Pynchon (*Gravity's Rainbow*), Coover (*The Public Burning*) and Doctorow (*Ragtime*), Scholes decided that the North American writers were 'obsessed with their own history', and offered a tentative explanation that should – surely – have orientated all future comparative studies. Living in a country which was itself a 'fabulous fiction' in the minds of its discoverers before they discovered it and in the minds of the Founders who 'invented its political and social structures out of their ideals and hopes', the modern American writer shows a concern with history that is an 'atonement'[2] for the nation's guilt at having created a fabulation (the American Dream) and pretended it was real.

In contrast to Scholes, one British attempt to establish necessary distinctions – Bernard Bergonzi's 'Fictions of History', a broad survey of the international literary scene – argues that recent American novelists have treated history as 'infinitely malleable'; as a text lacking interest and organisation. Europeans, he argues, treat history with more respect, perhaps because they have so much more of it.[3] In 1980 Bergonzi seems to have been unaware of Doctorow's work (his Americans are Pynchon, Barth, Vonnegut and Hawkes) but had he known of it he would hardly have been likely to find it more 'respectful' of history. If we discount his value judgement, Bergonzi's distinction may prove useful, for lack of deference towards a supposedly established 'text' of history could well be the distinguishing feature of recent American fictions, though – reversing Bergonzi's conservative prejudice – we may well decide that the Americans show more concern for – or involvement in – the history that they fictionalise. Limiting my discussion to the work of Fowles and Doctorow, I intend to argue that the American writer's sense of the past is more urgent than the Englishman's; that for Doctorow 'American history' is a text that must be continually rewritten if the present is to be understood. Not only does Doctorow's writing reveal a serious concern with the status of the official historical text; it also concerns itself with the creation of texts, and thus with the encoding of ideology. Where Fowles plays with history, using the British past as a way of exploring the present yet showing a deferential sense of 'real history' as something beyond the province of the writer of fiction, Doctorow shows no respect for any history of his country; instead his fictions alert their readers to the myths embodied in all histories.

DOCTOROW, 'HISTORY' AND CLASS

It is not surprising, then, that *Ragtime* (1975) has seemed – to one of its most astute readers – to exemplify a 'crisis in historicity'. For Fredric Jameson the novel is postmodernist in the sense that it resists, or short-circuits, traditional social and historical interpretation. It imposes the kind of reading that makes it impossible for the reader to reach and thematise the official subjects that 'float above the text'. Thus *Ragtime* becomes a monument to 'the aesthetic situation engendered by the disappearance of the historical referent'. In other words, the novel does not represent the past; it can only represent our stereotypical visions of the past. In this it is indicative of our situation: we can only seek history by way of pop images and simulacra of history.[4]

Jameson's metaphors are persuasive but problematic. The historical referent has 'disappeared' in the sense that it comes wearing a mask of costume-history. The costumes are, precisely, conventional interpretations of that history, and these are presented with irony. The history of the 1900s is reduced to the version offered in illustrated magazines when we are told, in the first chapter, that the style of the age was set by 'parades, public concerts, fish fries, political picnics, social outings, or indoors in meeting halls, vaudeville theatres' and other mass entertainments. Yet Harry K. Thaw and Evelyn Nesbit sail for Europe on the *Kronprinzessin Cecile*; Freud returns to Germany on the *Kaiser Wilhelm der Grosse*; Houdini makes the transatlantic crossing on the *Imperator*, 'an immense German vessel' whose figurehead 'was a crowned eagle with its claws embedded in the world'. Imperialistic arrogance and ambition are not limited to the Germanic powers in *Ragtime*. J.P. Morgan responds to Henry Ford's achievement because he senses in it 'a lust for order as imperial as his own'. Morgan is 'a monarch of the invisible transnational kingdom of capital whose sovereignty was everywhere granted', so it is entirely appropriate that Coalhouse Walker should make his defiant gesture at the Morgan Library. Yet it is no less appropriate that Father should sail with Peary to 'conquer' the pole on a ship called the *Roosevelt*, for the Teddy Roosevelt who figures in this story is 'the great conservationist' who destroys vast numbers of animals on his African safari. The age in which men were proud of carrying a 'great stomach' before them is also the age of parades, flags and firework displays. Father, the respectable bourgeois, makes his income from the manufacture of the 'accoutrements of patriotism'. His firm provides the 'patriotic bunting' that enriches the excursion on the *Grand Republic*, and the fireworks which provide a climax to the day's celebrations. When Father dies on the *Lusitania*, this is no playful blurring of fiction and history, for the novel insists on the progression from fireworks to high explosive devices and from flag-waving to dying for the flag. If 'referent' means merely the raw 'facts' of history before they enter historical discourse and become part of its 'story', then we have such a referent in the assassination of the Archduke Franz Ferdinand. The Archduke's encounter with Harry Houdini (in Chapter 13) is both fictitious and farcical. Ferdinand congratulates Houdini on the invention of the aeroplane. This does not make the referent disappear; rather it foregrounds Doctorow's belief that all 'history' is constructed.

Another historical referent, the 1912 textile strike at Lawrence, Massachusetts, is fictionalised in the sense that it is presented as part of the story of Tateh and his daughter. Thus the brutal repression of the workers by the police is rendered vivid as we perceive it through Tateh's innocent astonishment and his anguished concern for his child. Yet, ironically, this incident is crucial in another story, that of the idealistic, socialist Jewish immigrant's (Tateh's) Americanisation: his 'abdication of belief' in the cause of justice for the oppressed and the beginning of his story of success, American style. Doctorow's avowed sympathy for Tateh[5] does not alter the fictional fact that the one-time idealist will achieve wealth and eminence by making movies that mythologise America as a great happy family. The last notes of the tune on the player piano (the ragtime history of *Ragtime*) include Tateh's idea for a very successful film. It will tell the story of 'a bunch of children who were pals, white black, fat thin, rich poor, all kinds, mischievous little urchins' who would constitute 'a society of ragamuffins, like all of us, a gang'. In the fictional world that produces this bland reconciliation of opposites, the black child is part of the newly constituted family because both his parents have been destroyed by white prejudice.

The Coalhouse Walker story, introduced in Part Two of the novel, presents a challenge to the reader not only in its flagrant anachronism (locating a sixties-type black revolutionary action in the ragtime era) but also in its particular kind of literary borrowing. Kleist's Michael Kohlhaas is a close enough analogue in his motivation – the wealthy sixteenth-century merchant from the state of Brandenburg is one of the *rechtschaffensten* of men and is driven to murder by his *Rechtsgefühl*[6] – but layers of irony accrue to Doctorow's text from the colour-blindness of the intertexuality. As 'history' Coalhouse's actions are impossible, but the implausibility of the story itself challenges the blandness of histories such as Jacob Riis's adulatory biography of Theodore Roosevelt, in which there were, indeed, no Negroes. Riis's *How the Other Half Lives* (1890) is quoted verbatim on the 'crazy quilt of humanity' in the Manhattan immigrant settlements. The callow tone of his *Theodore Roosevelt* (1903) may be one of the many 'historical' elements that are 'ragged' in Doctorow's fiction. What Doctorow has called his 'mock-historical or ironic-historical tone'[7] in *Ragtime* has led to the charge of frivolity or mere cleverness. The novel, according to Cushing Strout, lacks an integrating point of view.[8] In comparison with Doctorow's other historiographic metafictions, *Ragtime* may well seem a slight work, but – as I hope to show – it shares with them an impressive power to insist on a re-examination of American myths.

FOWLES, HISTORY AND 'CLASS'

Fowles's *The French Lieutenant's Woman* (1969) has been seen as the 'exemplary' work of the sixties in its attempted reconciliation of the self-sceptical modern novel with the traditional one. Put another way, Fowles's book is (in Malcolm Bradbury's words) a 'pastiche novel, a novel of ironic counterpointings' in which the present is allowed no easy triumph over the past in the name of progress.[9] This reading makes *The French Lieutenant's Woman* both a formal imitation of a Victorian novel and a work in which the distance between the modern reader and the Victorian past is itself a major concern. The mixture of past and present, real and imaginary, in the novel has the effect – according to one theorist of the new genre of historical fiction – of involving the reader in the moral issues, for s/he cannot abstain from judging by writing off the world of the novel as Victorian.[10] This is a plausible explanation of the effect of those 'frame breaks' in which the twentieth-century narrator obtrudes his presence, not merely to claim recent ownership of the toby jug brought to her Exeter hotel by Sarah but also to stare impolitely at Charles in his railway carriage. The ontological confusion caused (what level of fictional reality are we on?) plainly does not permit a passive consumption of the text. As readers we must confront the question of the status of the events described. More pointedly, the provision of alternative endings disturbs the reader's relationship with the text as it calls into question the authority of the writer. Facing his fictional creation in the railway compartment, the narrator distances himself from the conventions of closure in Victorian fiction and subverts the notion of the novelist's godlike power over his creatures. But, as Fowles has frankly admitted, to pretend that characters are free 'can only be a game', for 'the reality of the situation' is the writer's power to 'strike out developments' at any point in the book.[11]

Fowles's narrator not only controls his characters, he also appears to have absolute authority over 'history', for he tells us unequivocally that when Charles stared into Sarah's eyes after watching her abandoned sleep on the Undercliff, 'the whole Victorian Age was lost'. His authority is illusory however, and seems to me to be the corollary of the *author's* deferential attitude to 'real' history. *The French Lieutenant's Woman*, we remember, is concerned not only with the Victorian novel but also with Victorian history.

The intertexts are not only Hardy's *A Pair of Blue Eyes* but also the *Children's Employment Commission Report* (1867), E. Royston Pike's *Human Documents of the Victorian Golden Age* and Marx's *Capital*. The historical referents include the Second Reform Bill and the Tolpuddle Martyrs. The quality of the novel's version of Victorian history is a matter of some contention. What to Sheldon Rothblatt is 'deeply' historical, Patrick Brantlinger – in a companion article – considers simplified, in that it makes sexuality the *primum mobile* of history.[12] A.S. Byatt is more severe. She judges Fowles's understanding of Victorian life as crude, being derived from Bloomsbury's rejection of it.[13] My own view is that Fowles takes 'history' (in the sense of academic history) very seriously indeed, but does not take it at all seriously in his fiction. The plot of *The French Lieutenant's Woman* turns – before the reversal of Charles's fortunes – on Fowles's conception of the social history of Victorian England. Class plays a crucial role, for Charles is a gentleman who becomes fascinated by – and infatuated with – a young woman who is definitely not a 'lady'. Sarah's father's social pretensions not only ruined him; they also educated her above her class and made her sexually vulnerable. The analogy, of course, is with Hardy's Tess, though the closer intertext is *A Pair of Blue Eyes*. That intertext should help us to see how 'history' and fiction negate each other in *The French Lieutenant's Woman*.

A comparison of Fowles's 'Victorian' novel with Hardy's fictionalised version of his relationship with Emma Gifford reveals common incidents, characters and character relationships, as well as a number of prominent motifs (eyes, fossils, geological time). Noting that Charles's fascination with Sarah's eyes has much in common with the exchange of glances between Stephen and Elfride in Endelstow churchyard, A.A. DeVitis and W.J. Palmer have argued that Fowles's 'imitation' of the past both recreates and parodies it, since he feels the need to free himself and his characters from the novelistic conventions he has inherited.[14] A closer look might reveal that Fowles has, in a sense, depoliticised his intertext, since – for all its apparent concern with class– *The French Lieutenant's Woman* is a fable in which liberated sexuality defeats the feeble survivals of caste and economic divisions.

Hardy's tale is structured on class divisions. Elfride is led into the compromising situation that will cause her misery through the class difference between her suitor and herself. Her father's peremptory refusal to consider the young architect (Smith) as her suitor and his angry dismissal of the young man to what becomes exile is the immediate result of his knowledge that Smith's parents are members of the rural labouring class. Elfride is then susceptible to the attractions of Smith's social superior Henry Knight, who has acted as an intellectual patron to the aspiring proletarian. The story of Charles's fascination with Sarah frees the Victorian 'gentleman' from the bonds of his inherited class prejudices (his inbred tendency to see lower-class women as sexual objects purchasable with his money), but does this by transforming the socially outcast Sarah Woodruff into the Pre-Raphaelite new woman, Mrs Roughwood. As a gentleman, we are told, Charles is a social fossil, a living ammonite. His type, which is too disinterested to be really concerned with possessions and status, will survive in the modern world in the form of the totally dedicated pure scientist. Not only does this scenario divorce the idea of the gentleman from historical realities of economic and social privilege; it also offers a casually depoliticised version of science in the modern world.

As we have noted, class is ostensibly a major concern in *The French Lieutenant's Woman*. Charles is presented as the son of a man who successfully invested in railway stock and lost his fortune in gambling, yet Charles has been educated to consider trade vulgar and to feel an unassailable social superiority to the *nouveau riche* Mr Freeman (Ernestina's father). The narrator's class-consciousness is evident in his comments on Ernestina's philistinism when she responds to the possibilities of the Winsyatt estate, in Chapter 22. Moreover, in his role as social historian, the narrator has forceful things to say about the horrors of rural poverty and the exploitation of the labourer in Victorian England (Chapter 19). The exploitation of the servile classes in bourgeois Victorian society is vividly represented by the domestic slavery we witness in the Poulteney household (Chapter 4) where the unfortunate domestics are remorselessly bullied through their 100-hour working week. Since several of the chapters have epigraphs derived from Karl Marx's writings, it might seem perverse to argue that *The French Lieutenant's Woman* renders the class issue insignificant. Chapter 30, for example, is prefaced by a quotation from *The German Ideology* on the hegemonic power of the ruling class and its illusions. Yet not only is the 'gentleman' here shown as a fossilised relic in an age of irresistible social change (Darwin is a more significant presence in the novel than Marx); the story of Sam Fowler's economic and social rise from the role of a Sam Weller to that of an enterprising lower-mid-dle-class haberdasher offers a bland account of upward social mobility. The projection of the Fowler family fortunes into the present of the novel's enunciation (1967) makes Sam's great-great-grandaughter a successful film star, emblem of a Britain in which all class divisions have fallen before the allure of mass entertainment. In my view, the fiction does not compel its readers to re-examine history and recognise the myths embodied in conventional versions of the past; rather, the logic of the fiction is totally indifferent to that of the history intercalated with the fictional text.

In *The Aristos* (1964), Fowles gave a clear statement of his own version of Genesis: 'Adam is stasis, or conservatism; Eve is kinesis, or progress.' The version of history he offered here made the Victorian period one in which 'the man and the father, male gods, exact strict obedience to established institutions and norms of behaviour'. Victorian society, then, was an 'Adam society'. In contrast, 'Eve societies are those in which the woman and the mother, female gods, encourage innovation and experiment, and fresh definitions, aims, modes of feeling. The Renaissance and our own are typical such ages.'[15] The passage provides an obvious gloss on *The French Lieutenant's Woman*. Sarah represents change and experiment; Charles carries a load of established institutions and norms of behaviour from which he is permitted a painful escape in an alternative ending to the story. History here is envisaged as progress, for Victorian authority gives way to modern existential freedom. Fowles's politics, then, are sexual politics, not in the sense that he reduces all history to sexual motivation but in their programmatic transformation of the actualities of political power and economic privilege into a gender-determined myth of progress.

DOCTOROW, 'HISTORY' AND MYTH

In his 'Notes on an Unfinished Novel' (1969), while explaining that he did not consider *The French Lieutenant's Woman* an historical novel, Fowles also stated that the work began as a visual image. 'A woman stands at the end of a deserted quay and stares out to sea. That was all.'[16] Doctorow's *Loon Lake* (1979) also had its origin in an image, according to its author: an image of a private railroad train going through the forest (in the Adirondack Mountains) 'taking a party of gangsters to the mountain retreat of a powerful man of great wealth'. When the idea occurred, Doctorow, by his own account, had no notion what it meant, but he developed the image through the consciousness of Joe 'of Paterson', the fatherless poor boy whose 'visions of an incandescent splendor' included an image of a beautiful naked woman looking at herself in a mirror on a gangster-laden train.[17] The story of Joe Korzeniowski is a story of the Depression years, but its historical referents include the Seattle General Strike of 1919. This event is evoked for the reader in the prose of Warren Penfield, one of Joe's surrogate fathers, whose own father was a wage-slave in the Colorado mines. Even if, as Doctorow has stated, the multiple voices of *Loon Lake* 'turn out to be the work of one narrator',[18] The use of Penfield's voice to recount such events adds poignancy, for Warren Penfield is a failed believer in the cause of the common man as well as a failed poet. The feeling of camaraderie he experienced in Seattle, and his sense of the dignity of the ordinary working men, contrasts with his awareness of the futility of his life as the tame poet, tolerated as a guest by the very tycoon (F.W. Bennett) he once set out to kill in a symbolic act of vengeance for the many lives ruined by Bennett's ruthless exploitation.

The 'one narrator' of *Loon Lake* is Joe, the boy of proletarian origins whose dream of splendour leads him to become the 'son' of F.W. Bennett. Shifts from first to third person narrative work to put into question the objectivity of the telling and to problematise the distance between the voice that speaks and the protagonist who acts. Joe is an intermittently unreliable narrator because he is a mixture of idealism and crude ambitiousness, acute sensitivity to injustice and exploitation (as in his outrage at the fate of the Fat Lady in the carney) and ruthless betrayal of those who befriend him (among them the fat Scandinavian woman from whom he steals). Joe's quest for a father is not only signalled by the polyglot pun (Pater-son) latent in his assumed name; it is foregrounded throughout the narrative. Entering the private estate of Bennett, a 'wilderness as luxury' created for such 'rich patrons' as the industrial tycoon, Joe feels as if he is reflecting the clear arrogance of the owner. Almost as soon as he enters this 'province of wealth' Joe consciously adopts its customs. To amuse Libby, one of the domestics, he plays at being F.W. Bennett. Dressing in Bennett's clothes he feels like the rich man's son, though this charade takes place not long after Joe was savaged by the wild dogs that roam the estate. When Joe steals Bennett's clothes, his girl and his car, he feels a 'peculiar conforming of life' to his desires. Joe is already living out his dream, and his dream is already corrupted. The culmination of that corruption will be not merely Joe's inheritance of the Bennett power and fortune, but also his apology for those historical giants of industry, the Rockefellers and Carnegies, when Joe speaks as the historian of capitalism. Before this, Joe will have drifted towards Jacksontown, where he will become a part of the workforce in the appropriately named 'Bennett Autobody' works. Joe will become part of the body; he will act out the part of the worker-puppet whose life and fate are absolutely under the control of the master. Before Warren Penfield leaves on the aeroplane flight that will result in his death, he bequeaths all his papers to his 'son' Joe. But when Joe acts out Penfield's creed – his belief that words constitute the self – he claims to be Bennett's son. This is one of the heaviest ironies in a novel laden with ironies.

In an interview at the University of Heidelberg Doctorow referred to the immense impact Hawthorne had on him as a student. Hawthorne, whose works he read closely, 'did not give you ordinary life but a precipitate of it', according to Doctorow. Contrasting the Hawthorne romances with the patient accumulation of data in the realist novel, Doctorow said that Hawthorne's vision of fiction suited him very well.[19] He was referring primarily to *Welcome to Hard Times* (1960) a work obviously closer to the fable than the realist novel, but the comment throws light on the mixture of realism and abstraction in Doctorow's other fictions. Perhaps it is significant that Hawthorne favoured the 'twice-told' tale, for some of Doctorow's own tales retell stories that are essentially American legends, *Loon Lake* retells the story of James Gatz's service of a 'vast, vulgar and meretricious beauty' and his rise from poverty to 'greatness'. Fitzgerald's *The Great Gatsby* is the unmistakable intertext in the story of Joe's dream and its fulfillment, but the effect of the retelling is to demythologise (or deglamorise) the fabulous wealth of the boy who springs from his 'Platonic conception of himself'. Fitzgerald lets his readers glimpse Gatsby's sordid association with the underworld (in particular with Meyer Wolfsheim), but Nick Carraway's narrative has the effect of mystifying Gatsby's riches. Further, though Tom Buchanan, the representative of immense fortunes, is arrogant and brutal in his personal relationships (particularly with his working-class mistress Myrtle), his money is 'non -olfactory'; the reader does not get a scent of its taintedness. In contrast, *Loon Lake* insists on the dependence of the Bennett empire on the services of the appropriately named Tommy Crapo and his hired thugs. The gangsters on the train in Doctorow's first image of the story prove to be comically overawed by the conspicuous wealth of Bennett's estate, but they are not comic when we watch them at work at Jacksontown, murdering a working stiff who dared to defy Bennett's authority. Crapo Industrial Services is an integral part of Bennett's system.

Doctorow's most recent novel, *Billy Bathgate* (1989) seems to be a retelling of *Loon Lake* in a simpler, and more powerful, narrative mode. The diverse styles (including computer language) and methods (including annotations) of the earlier gangster tale are replaced by the one voice of Billy, the poor boy from the slums, this time in the Bronx, who names himself from his place of origin and who is fatherless in the sense that his natural father has left him and his mother (a beautiful Irish immigrant) to struggle against squalor and poverty on their own. Billy's mother has retreated into madness while he goes on his quest for a father and finds him in the shape of the gangster Dutch Schultz (Arthur Flegenheimer), the hero of all the poor boys in the neighbourhood and symbol of the power and splendour of wealth acquired by brute force and lack of moral scruple. Billy longs for recognition by Schultz, even while he fears him and when he is brutalised by him (Billy's nose is broken to provide an alibi for the blood caused by the murder of Julie Martin). At last Billy finds Schultz's hand on his shoulder 'like a father's hand', though this is shortly before the Dutchman is gunned down by killers from a rival gang. After witnessing the murder of his gangster-hero, Billy feels 'fatherless' and returns to the Max and Dora Diamond Home for Children considering himself an orphan. Schultz's rambling and incoherent speech as he lies dying seems to include unmistakable allusions to an Oedipal theme: 'the boy came at me. Yes, he gave it to me. Come on, he cuts me off, the beneficiary of his will, is that right? A father's son.'

Interestingly, some of the fictional Schultz's dying words – and those that seem most obviously determined by the pattern of fictional relationships

Doctorow has invented – are taken from an historical record of the gangster's life and death. The historical Dutch Schultz, like the fictional gangster, murmured 'Oh Mamma, Mamma, Mamma, oh stop it' as he lay dying in hospital. He also babbled 'the boy came at me', though he had no Billy Bathgate as surrogate son. The source of a number of incidents and some dialogue in *Billy Bathgate* is a series of articles by Dixie Davis, in *Collier's Weekly* in July and August 1939. Under the title 'Things I Couldn't Tell till Now', Dixie Davis confessed to his association with Schultz's mob and gave graphic accounts, not only of the killing of the Dutchman but also of the murder of Jules Martin, which provides one of the most vivid episodes in Doctorow's novel. Davis's story contains no suggestion of a liaison between the gangster and a beautiful, amoral, high-society woman, nor does it give any hint that such a romantic interest was possible for the crude, brutal killer he shows Schultz to have been. The first instalment, in the 22 July issue of *Collier's*, begins with his eye-witness account of the Dutchman's impulse-killing of Julie Martin in the Old Harmony Hotel, Cohoes, New York. Schultz 'wore his pistol under his vest, tucked inside his pants, right against his belly. One jerk at his vest and he had it in his hand. All in the same quick motion he swung it up, stuck it in Jules Martin's mouth and pulled the trigger.' Doctorow's eye-witness Billy is a more innocent, and more interesting, observer than the historical Dixie Davis, a man who had made his career out of legal services for mobsters, yet Davis was young enough at the time of the events he recalls to have been known as 'the Kid Mouthpiece' of the Schultz mob.

In *Loon Lake*, as Richard King astutely noted,[20] Doctorow wrote an American version of the 'family romance' according to Freud and Rank. Joe's quest for a father is a quest for legitimacy; for a place in the social order. In *Billy Bathgate*, Doctorow retells the story of the American quest for an ideal object, accentuating the ironies of the contrast between Billy's sense of the beauty and excitement of existence and the excremental significance of the actual object pursued: money. Schultz's 'criminal enterprise', his 'business' of crime literally makes 'shit' of human lives, packing up the remains of his victims in garbage cans for disposal amid 'the odorous crap of the glamorous night'. Schultz hides his fortune amid the 'shit of the beer drop' where Billy discovers it, only to entrust it to Arnold Garbage's care.[21] In this retelling of the quest, Fitzgerald's archetypal story of romantic American yearning (and *his* retelling of the Alger story and of Benjamin Franklin's *Autobiography*) is present as an intertext without which Doctorow's story loses its full resonance. American history, for Doctorow, is recent history. *Welcome to Hard Times*, his mock-Western, takes us no further back into the past than the late nineteenth century. Consequently, the issues raised tend to impinge on the present, and Doctorow's treatment always gives them a sense of urgency for any reader concerned with the present state of American society. Taken out of context, his well-known assertion, in 'False Documents', that 'there is no fiction or nonfiction as we commonly understand the distinction: there is only narrative' could be interpreted as postmodernist confession of belief in the indeterminacy of all narratives and hence an admission that historical truths are forever unattainable. Taken in context, however, Doctorow's emphasis is plain: 'history shares with fiction a mode of mediating the world for the purpose of introducing meaning, and it is the cultural authority from which they both derive that illuminates those facts so that they can be perceived'. Here Doctorow borrows a phrase from Roland Barthes to make his point: 'historical discourse is essentially a product of ideology, or rather of imagination'.[22] In his Heidelberg interview, he used his own formulation: 'I think history is made; it's composed. There is an objective event, but until it is construed, until it is evaluated, it does not exist as history.'[23]

In *The Book of Daniel* (1971) the 'objective event' must be the execution of the Rosenbergs. Their guilt, or innocence, is still a matter of speculation. The construing, or evaluation, of that event becomes Doctorow's most powerful and disturbing fiction; a fiction that will not allow its readers to close the book of recent American history. In some ways, *The Book of Daniel* is Doctorow's closest approach to a realist novel. In his own words, 'it was the characters and their complexity that moved me – the historical intersection of social and personal agony, history moving in Daniel'. [24] Taken together with his account of the 'saving' of the book by realising that it had to be done in Daniel's voice, this comment would seem to justify interpretations of the novel in terms of the creation of that voice.[25] Daniel's tirades against the reader, as well as his cruelty to his young wife, can then be understood in terms of the psychopathology of the son of parents executed for treason. Yet *The Book of Daniel* is Doctorow's most self-reflexive work; more than any other of his novels it calls attention to its own fictionality and insists that the reader engage with the problems of responding to it as a text.

When, in the second paragraph of the novel, we read 'This is a Thinline felt tip market, black. This is Composition Notebook 79C made in USA by Long Island Paper Products, Inc', we are confronted with the physicality of the book in front of us as well as the'physicality' of the 'book' in which the fictional Daniel is writing. The epigraphs should have alerted us to the possibilities of books as prophecies, Jeremiads, examinations of the conscience of the nation. When, at the conclusion, Daniel submits his life as his book, we must again think of the biblical Daniel, whose Book contained the interpretation of dreams. Doctorow told one interviewer that he was not aware that the novel's Daniel had a relationship to the biblical Daniel until he 'found him . . . going into the Bible to look up the original'[26] The reader of *The Book of Daniel* reads Daniel reading the *Dartmouth Bible* and must respond to the resonance of 'a Time of Persecution'.

Historical referents abound in *The Book of Daniel*. They enter the text in Daniel's asides on the intense victimisation of radicals, dissidents and immigrants in the United States *after* wars, in his brief allusions to knouting in Russia, in his note to himself to explore the history of corporal punishment as an instrument of class repression, and pre-eminently in the analogy between the execution of the fictional Isaacsons and that of the historical Rosenbergs. 'History' is a recurrent theme in Daniel's sardonic 'Many historians have noted'. These references, allusions and hints exist in the text undistinguished from the vivid passages in which Daniel records his (and his sister Susan's) childhood experience of the terror and anguish of a 'time of persecution'. Among the most powerful passages in the novel is Daniel's evocation of life in the East Bronx Children's Shelter: 'All the surfaces were hard and the din was often unbelievable. To quieten us down he blew a whistle which left points of pain in my ears.' Daniel can hear his sister's screams of rage coming through the walls as he lies awake after lights out, but he cannot comfort her since she is imprisoned in the girls' section of the home. The smells of the institution are a mixture of vegetable soup (associated with impoverishment and deprivation by the mature Daniel) and vomit: 'There was always a lot of vomiting. Kids were always getting sick and throwing up.' This is a moving and authentic account of the fictional Daniel's youthful misery, yet the section is introduced by the caption 'ALONE IN THE COLD WAR with Franny and Zooey'. Linking with an earlier allusion to *Catcher in the Rye*, this reference self-consciously signals that we are experiencing, as readers, the 'David Copperfield kind of crap' that Holden Caulfield said he eschewed. Daniel, then, breaks the frame of his own narrative to remind his readers that his evocation of past suffering is a *literary* creation: an exercise of the imagination. This is the Daniel who will taunt the reader with his capacity to 'do' the execution of his own parents. Of course, he was not present at the scene, yet his words create a scene so harrowing that it will not let its readers disengage from the moral dilemma of surrogate witnesses of officially sanctioned state repression and violence.

In offering us Edgar Allan Poe as the archetypal traitor – the arch subversive – Daniel is inviting us to consider the role of art as that of subverting the official truths and certainties of the society to which the artist belongs. Calling Daniel a 'hero – or a criminal of perception', Doctorow leaves no doubt that he believes in the moral responsibility of the artist. Narrative determines the way we apprehend 'history', but if we respond treacherously to those stories society tells itself about its past (that is, if we perceive the presence of ideology in the fictions) we may free ourselves from a form of enslavement and may accept our own moral responsibility.

DOCTOROW, MYTH AND HISTORY

By his own account, Fowles's *A Maggot* (1985) is not an historical novel. In his Epilogue to the novel, Fowles not only rejects the possible classification of the book as historical, but also distinguishes categorically between fiction and what he calls 'real history'. His novel, he says, is 'almost all invention', though he took the names of some of his characters from 'real history'. Further, the book makes no attempt to reproduce 'known history'. In the same passage, Fowles expresses the greatest respect for 'exact and scrupulously documented history', which he regards as an exacting discipline and 'essentially a science'. We could hardly be farther from Doctorow's conception of history; nor could we easily find a more sharply contrasting view of its relationship to fiction. To John Fowles, as he makes clear in his afterword to *Locating the Shakers* (1990), 'historians proper' (by which he means professional or academic experts) have a knowledge of the past to which the historical novelist cannot aspire. It follows, then, that the novel 'can never do what good historiography can, by the standards of serious history'.[27] Instead, the historical novel can present a vivid and impressionistic picture of a period. It can also present the writer's feelings and thoughts about that period, and suggest what it may mean to the present. The implications are clear: 'real' history lies in the domain of science; it has an objective existence that can be represented adequately in the writings of professional historians whose methods must be empirical. The only history the fiction writer can offer will be subjective: being 'invented' it will lack the authority of the impersonal academic-scientific history Fowles respects. Recent American fiction has been spectacularly lacking in respect for the 'history' it has absorbed into itself (Robert Coover's *The Public Burning* must surely be the outstanding example of such disrespectful, anti-authoritarian, treatment of the historical record, but Kurt Vonnegut's *Slaughterhouse Five* shows as little deference to 'serious history').

A Maggot had its origin in an image (so its author tells us). Fowles was haunted by a vision of travellers on an unspecified quest and, since they rode horses, he knew only that they belonged to the past. Whereas Doctorow's *donnée* for *Loon Lake* (gangsters on a train) came laden with sociopolitical connotations, Fowles's image acquired some specificity by association with the face of a young woman represented in a watercolour dated 1683; a face that haunted the novelist by its 'presentness' – its 'refusal to die'. That face, in turn, became linked in the novelist's mind with the face of Mother Ann Lee, the Shaker leader Fowles had long admired, and *A Maggot* became a fable of the redemption of Ann's own mother, the fictional Rebecca Hocknell, a former prostitute who *may* be credited with a vision of Holy Mother Wisdom, the mother, widow and daughter of Christ and the coeval of God. Her interrogator Ayscough certainly does not credit her with anything but delusion, but he is the arch conservative, defender of the establishment in religion as in politics, a Man of Law who dreads any and all change and sees religious dissent as the road to social anarchy or – the ultimate horror – democracy. The story of Rebecca's transformation becomes a retelling of Fowles's version of Genesis. Ayscough is an Adamic figure in his hatred of change. He lives by the 'unspoken *idée reçue* of his age. Change means not progress, but . . . decline and fall.'[28] As in *The Aristos*, 'Adam is stasis, or conservatism'. The England of 1736, the year in which the tale is set, is one in which society exacts 'strict obedience to established institutions and norms of behaviour'. In an explicitly historical aside, the narrator of *A Maggot* notes that English society at that time worshipped property; the true religion of the country was vested in 'a profound respect for right of property'[29] rather than reverence for the church. A corollary of this religion (or 'idolatry', as the narrator terms it) was an unquestioning belief in the sacredness of 'rank and natural respect'[30] in other words, a commitment to an unchanging system of caste.

In her role as 'Fanny' the London prostitute, Rebecca is used by rich – and 'noble' – men as an object or animal on whom they can prove their sexual prowess. She lives in a world whose conditions are 'more inexorably fixed than we can imagine'[31] a world in which personal destiny is 'fixed' to a degree a modern consciousness would find intolerable; in which, being a whore, she exists only as a sexual object to men of the class that exploits and categorises her. In that world, men such as her husband John Lee exist as 'a tool or a beast' exists, because the world for them is 'entirely preordained'.[32] But, as even the unredeemed Jones (alias Farthing) testifies, after her vision of the maggot, 'there was some great change upon her' and 'Fanny-Louise' became 'another woman'. Rebecca's experience of June Eternal teaches her the true lesson of Christ: 'man may change of his own will; and by His grace, so be redeemed'. It also teaches her that society may change, for her vision of the 'happy land' is, patently, a vision of a Shaker society in which there is no private property, no distinction of rank or circumstance, as well as no carnal marriage. To Ayscough, the 'happy land' of the Shakers is nothing other than a hell where the common mob rules; it is a vision of his dreaded 'democracy'. His version of Genesis is patriarchal: 'Eve came of Adam's seventh rib'. Rebecca's threatens all his settled, immovable assurances in its sexual insubordination: 'Nor was Eden born, nor Adam nor Eve, were Holy Mother Wisdom not there at the first with God the Father'.[33]

As Fowles makes clear in his Epilogue, *A Maggot* is a fable of the 'painful breaking of the seed of self from the hard soil of an irrational and tradition-bound society'. He sees the first stages of the growth of the modern ego in the outburst of religious dissent and enthusiasm in England in the late 1730s.

John Wesley and Ann Lee shared a vision of what was wrong with their world. Both were part of an emotional enlightenment that is undervalued in our histories of the 'intellectual (and middle-class) enlightenment' of the age. Dissent, at this period, was a manifestation of 'an eternal biological or evolutionary mechanism' that is always needed, and 'in our own age more than ever before'.

Evidently we are back in the intellectual world of the narrator of *The French Lieutenant's Woman*; a world in which progress towards modern existential freedom is (paradoxically) pre-ordained because it is part of the evolutionary mechanism. The freedom is, then, as illusory as the freedom of the characters in the literary text on which Fowles commented in his interview with Campbell. In *A Maggot* the metafictional devices (the repeated allusions to role-playing, to the theatre, and to plots) and the narrative method (the progressive shifts – through a series of crossexaminations – closer to the emotional reality of Rebecca's problematic encounter with God the Father, God the Son and God the Mother) serve to put in question the authority of the text as well as the authenticity of names and character parts. On oath, Mr Francis Lacy, the actor who played the part of 'Mr Bartholomew's' uncle, tells Ayscough that he assured his 'nephew' that he 'was not in some fixed story, as it were in a tragedy, where all is antecedently doomed'.[34] Yet 'Mr Bartholomew', or 'his Lordship' – though he is the true radical in his belief that God is 'eternal motion' – seeks to know the secrets of time to come. Those secrets are known – in the fictional world – to its author, however tentative his method and however determinedly he problematises the reality of the maggot.

FOWLES, HISTORY AND FABLE

'Real history' is present in *A Maggot* not only in the form of allusions to John Wesley and Mother Ann Lee but also in facsimiles of pages from the 'Historical Chronicle' sections of the *Gentleman's Magazine* for 1736. Intercalated with the pages of the fiction, these fragments of history act as repeated frame-breaks as well as implicit acts of authentification. The 'Chronicle' contains ample evidence of the repressiveness of the class system in the England of 1736 and of the brutality with which the national religion of reverence for property was enforced. The entry for Friday 9 April records the hanging of Wm Bithell and Wm Morgan at Worcester for cutting down Ledbury Turnpikes. On Monday 10 May, Stephen Collard was sentenced to death for stealing a silver watch, Jos. Glanwin was condemned to death for stealing twelve handkerchieves, while Daniel Malden received the death sentence for stealing a silver tankard, and Chris. Freeman for stealing 'wet Linnen'. Collard and Glanwin were reprieved for transportation, but 'wet Linnen' and a tankard seem to have kept their value, which in both cases was a human life. These extracts from the 'Chronicle' in the *Gentleman's Magazine* counterpoint Ayscough's interrogation of witnesses who can be browbeaten and threatened because their social status makes them vulnerable to the immense power of the master Ayscough serves – the 'Your grace' to whom his sycophantic letters are addressed.

In *A Maggot*, as in *The French Lieutenant's Woman*, class is a major concern. In Fowles's story, the emergence of the modern self was possible only when the rigidities of the social hierarchy were broken. Religious dissent was a means to social progress in this version of eighteenth-century English history since the emotional awakening of the common people was effected by the messages of such prophets as Wesley and Ann Lee. Implicit in Fowles's view of history is the belief that the highest point on the evolutionary scale is the existential freedom achieved by the modern individual who has become totally liberated from the conditioning factors of economics and politics. Such transcendental individualism being taken as the culmination of history, the actualities of social injustice in the past (recent or remote) can have no urgent relevance to the present. So the 'respect' for history noted by Bergonzi becomes a means of disengagement from the issues (moral and political) involved in the construction of that history. This can be seen as precisely such an abdication as Walter Benjamin warned against in his 'Theses on the Philosophy of History': a failure to 'wrest tradition away from a conformism that is about to overpower it'.[35]

NOTES

* 1.   Martin Green, 'Nostalgia Politics', *The American Scholar* (Winter 1975–76): 841–3. Green's other examples of the new fiction were John Berger's G and J.G. Farrell's *The Siege of Vishnapur (sic)*. Presumably this is a misprint for *The Siege of Krishnapur*.

2.   Robert Scholes, *Fabulation and Metafiction* (Urbana, Chicago and London, 1979), pp. 208–9.

3.   Bernard Bergonzi, 'Fictions of History' in Malcolm Bradbury and David Palmer (eds), *The Contemporary English Novel* (New York, 1980). Bergonzi refers to the work of David Caute and B.S. Johnson as well as Berger and Farrell.

4.   Fredric Jameson, 'Postmodernism, or the Cultural Logic of Late Capitalism', *New Left Review* 146 (1984): 68–71 (reprinted in Jameson's *Postmodernism, or the Cultural Logic of Late Capitalism*, London and New York, 1991, pp. 1–54), and

'Postmodernism and Consumer Society' in *Postmodernism and its Discontents*, (ed.) E. Ann Kaplan (London and New York, 1988).

5. In an interview in Thomas Le Clair and Larry McCaffery (eds), *Anything Can Happen: Interviews with Contemporary American Novelists* (Urbana, Chicago and London, 1983), Doctorow says of Tateh: 'I love that character, but I also understand him'. He goes on to say that 'as compassionate as we feel for Tateh and as much as we love him, here's a man who has betrayed his principles and gotten ahead that way' (p. 103). This interview is reprinted in Richard Trenner (ed.), *E.L. Doctorow: Essays and Conversations* (Princeton, 1983).

6. Heinrich von Kleist, *Michael Kohlhaas*, (ed.) F.W. Wilson (London, 1910), p. 1.

7. Doctorow uses the words in his interview with Larry McCaffery in *Anything Can Happen*. See above, note 5.

8. Cushing Strout, 'Historicizing Fiction and Fictionalizing History', *Prospects* 5 (1980): 423–37.

9. Fowles's novel is described as exemplary in Bradbury and Palmer's Preface to their *Contemporary English Novel* (1980). Bradbury's other formulation occurs in his *Possibilities* (London, 1973), p. 258.

10. Linda Hutcheon, 'The Real World(s) of Fiction: *The French Lieutenant's Woman*' in Ellen Pifer (ed.), *Critical Essays on John Fowles* (Boston 1986). Hutcheon's essay is reprinted from *English Studies in Canada* 4, No. 1 (1978), 81–94. Hutcheon's theoretical writings on 'historiographic metafiction' are extensive. The most useful, in my view, is her *A Poetics of Postmodernism: History, Theory, Fiction* (New York and London, 1988).

11. Fowles talks of the 'game' of 'pretending' his characters are free in an interview with James Campbell, *Contemporary Literature* 17, No. 4 (1976): 456.

12 The Brantlinger and Rothblatt articles are parts of '*The French Lieutenant's Woman*: A Discussion' in *Victorian Studies* 15 (1972): 339–56.

13. A.S. Byatt's 'People in Paper Houses: Attitudes to "Realism" and "Experiment" in English Postwar Fiction' is included in Bradbury and Palmer (eds), *The Contemporary English Novel*.

14. '*A Pair of Blue Eyes* Flash at *The French Lieutenant's Woman*', *Contemporary Literature* 15 (1974): 90–101.

15. John Fowles, *The Aristos* (London, 1964; 1989), p. 157.

16. Fowles's essay appears as part of *The Novel Today: Contemporary Writers on Modern Fiction*, (ed.) Malcolm Bradbury (London, 1977). See, especially, p. 136.

17. Doctorow has told the story repeatedly. The interview in Charles Ruas's *Conversations with American Authors* (London, Melbourne and New York, 1984: 1986) contains the reference to the train as 'incandescent' (p. 206). The account of the 'party of gangsters' comes from the interview in Le Clair and McCaffery's *Anything Can Happen*, p. 99.

18. Ibid.

19. Herwig Friedl and Dieter Schulz (eds), *E.L. Doctorow: A Democracy of Perception*.

A Symposium with and on E.L. Doctorow (Essen, 1988), p. 195.

20. Richard King, in a review of *Loon Lake* in the *Virginia Quarterly Review* 57 (1981): 341–50. See also King's 'Between Simultaneity and Sequence' in *A Democracy of Perception*. For an excellent account of Doctorow's treatment of the 'American Dream' see Arthur Saltzman, 'The Stylistic Energy of E.L. Doctorow' in Richard Trenner (ed.), *E.L. Doctorow: Essays and Conversations.*

21. The quotations are to be found on pp. 82, 319 of the Macmillan edition (1989). On the theme of money as excrement in Doctorow's writing see David S. Gross's excellent 'Tales of Obscene Power: Money and Culture, Modernism and History in the Fiction of E.L. Doctorow' in Trenner.

22. Ibid., p. 24.

23. Friedl and Schulz, *A Democracy of Perception*, p. 184.

24. Le Clair and McCaffery (eds), *Anything Can Happen*, p. 98.

25. One such interpretation is Sam L. Girgus's 'In His Own Voice: E.L. Doctorow's *The Book of Daniel*' in *A Democracy of Perception*.

26. Ibid., p. 191.

27. *Locating the Shakers*, ed. Mick Gidley and Kate Bowles (Exeter, 1990), pp. 147, 150. Fowles here refers approvingly to Katherine Tarbox's discussion of *A Maggot* in her *The Art of John Fowles* (Athens, Georgia, 1989). In her account of the novel Tarbox stresses its author's 'god games'. To her, it is 'a game of titillation, a sensuous interplay of cause and effect, stimulus and response' (p. 143).

28. John Fowles, *A Maggot* (London, 1985; 1986), p. 319.

29. Ibid. p. 233.

30. Ibid. p. 302.

31. Ibid. p. 56.

32. Ibid. p. 389.

33. Ibid. p. 380.

34. Ibid. p. 174.

35. Walter Benjamin, *Illuminations*, (ed.) Hannah Arendt (London, 1970), p. 257. I am indebted to Richard Godden's paper ' "So That the Dead May Not Be Killed Again": Doctorow and the Poetics of a Persecuting Society', given at the 1991 conference of the British Association for American Studies, for its approach to *The Book of Daniel* in terms of Benjamin's 'Theses'.

FURTHER READING

Marguerite Alexander, *Flights from Realism: Themes and Strategies from Postmodernist British and American Fiction* (London, 1990).

Walter Benjamin, *Illuminations*, (ed.) Hanna Arendt (London, 1970).

Malcolm Bradbury, *Possibilities* (London, 1973).

——(ed.), *The Novel Today: Contemporary Writers on Modern Fiction* (London, 1977).

——and David Palmer (eds), *The Contemporary English Novel* (New York, 1980).

Herwig Friedl and Dieter Schulz (eds), *E.L. Doctorow: A Democracy of Perception. A Symposium with and on E.L. Doctorow* (Essen, 1988).

Mick Gidley and Kate Bowles (eds), *Locating the Shakers* (Exeter, 1990).

Linda Hutcheon, *A Poetics of Postmodernism: History, Theory, Fiction* (New York and London, 1988).

Fredric Jameson, *Postmodernism, or the Cultural Logic of Late Capitalism* (London and New York, 1991).

E. Ann Kaplan, *Postmodernism and its Discontents* (London and New York, 1988).

Tom Le Clair and Larry McCaffery (eds), *Anything Can Happen: Interviews with Contemporary American Novelists* (Urbana, Chicago and London, 1983).

Ellen Pifer (ed.), *Critical Essays on John Fowles* (Boston, Mass., 1986).

Charles Ruas, *Conversations with American Authors* (London, Melbourne and New York, 1984; 1986).

Robert Scholes, *Fabulation and Metafiction* (Urbana, Chicago and London, 1979).

Richard Trenner (ed.), *E.L. Doctorow: Essays and Conversations* (Princeton, 1983).

CHAPTER FOURTEEN

Carver Country

Brian Scobie

> Once it was important to see myself as a writer from a particular place. It was important to me to be a writer from the West. But that's not true any longer, for better or worse. I think I've moved around too much, lived in too many places, felt dislocated and displaced, to now have any firmly rooted sense of 'place'.
>
> (Raymond Carver, *Paris Review* (1983), pp. 218–19)

Within contemporary American fiction, Raymond Carver has undoubtedly established a province of his own, distinctive and identifiable. To a great extent this has been a matter of content, of the kinds of situations – largely emotional and psychological situations in the lives of couples – that they record. Critics have not been slow to coin labels for his fictional world – Hopelessville,[1] or the world of 'low-rent' tragedies,[2] for instance – as well as seeing it as part of a general movement (where he was linked with Ann Beattie, Richard Ford, Tobias Wolff, Frederick Barthelme) in contemporary American fiction – Minimalism, K-Mart Realism, Dirty Realism, Downside Neo-Realism.

Yet among critics it has usually been accepted that his world (the world of *Will You Please Be Quiet, Please*, 1976, and *What We Talk About When We Talk About Love*, 1981) had its correspondent reality not only in Carver's own personal life (these were stories written during the years of determined alcoholism) but in contemporary American society at large. Carver was credited with giving us access to a neglected part of the social landscape in which people were indeed leading 'minimal' lives, the inarticulacy and marginality of which had meant they had gone largely overlooked or neglected. Carver himself has encouraged this wholesale mimetic approach to his writings in his essays (and in interviews he gave) both by confirming the autobiographical basis of his art and by assigning himself the role of one who reports from just such a neglected social hinterland.[3]

He speaks, for example, at the end of his *Paris Review* (1983) interview about 'bringing the news from one world to another' by fiction. It was an idea fundamental enough to his way of thinking about fiction that he repeated it in 'On Writing' in *Fires* – 'they want to carry news from their world to ours', he said of writers in general.[4] It hardly constitutes a radical aesthetic. He suggests that those who are too taken up with innovation produce writing that 'gives us no news of the world', and offers the hope that 'Maybe writing fiction about particular kinds of people living particular kinds of lives will allow certain areas of life to be understood a little better than they were understood before.'[5] It is a suitably modest claim that simultaneously positions itself against the so-called 'fabulist' tendency of postmodern American fiction, and also against any pretence that you can change things through fiction. Echoing Auden, he said, 'Art doesn't make anything happen.'[6] Realist indeed.

In a later interview with Kasia Boddy, Carver was again leery about attributing any political or sociological significance to his works, realist though they be. He demurred even at so unspecific a suggestion as that the stories were offered as 'comments' upon American society! But he did allow that he had a tendency to write about 'working class people, and the dark side of Reagan's America. So in that regard I suppose the stories can be read as a criticism, as an indictment.'[7]

However, the social or political dimension of contemporary life was evidently never one of his explicit concerns, as he made clear in the 1987 interview published in *Frank*: 'My stories take place on a personal level as opposed to a larger political or social arena. . . . Chekhov said once that there are two poles in a story, "him" and "her", the North Pole and the South Pole.'[8] This latter remark is resonantly taken up in 'Why Don't You Dance?' in a way that tells us much about the economical nature of his so-called minimalism:

> In the kitchen, he poured another drink and looked at the bedroom suite in his front yard. The mattress was stripped and the candy-striped sheets lay beside two pillows on the chiffonier. Except for that, things looked much the way they had in the bedroom – nightstand and reading lamp on his side of the bed, nightstand and reading lamp on her side.
> His side, her side.[9]

His was an essentialist or universalist view of human nature, if his response to the next question is anything to go by. He was asked, 'So, essentially, people don't change even when their social and political environment does?' His answer was, 'No, they don't.'[10] One way to read those statements, and one that surely works in an obvious sense, would be to see the American location of the vast majority of his stories as ultimately irrelevant. The absence of detail and the prevalence both of the generic and of 'polarisation' serve universalist ambitions. Minimalist tactics, maximalist strategy.

Even a more local sense of place was something he claimed not to have in his stories after the early years, during which he had thought of himself as a Western writer and in a loose sense had offered a Northwestern locus for his stories. Mona Simpson, who conducted the *Paris Review* interview with Carver, noted (perhaps with some satisfaction) that his house in Syracuse was furnished with items bought in a single day, all matching. (Even his most immediate environment seemingly a matter of indifference to him). The walls were painted white and, like the rest of the house, were almost entirely bare of decoration. Tess Gallagher's collection of peacock feathers (one thinks inevitably of 'Feathers') provided the only evidence of personal intervention in this interior. He was non-committal in his responses to her questions about whether he felt more at home there, in Syracuse, or in the Pacific Northwest, where he and Gallagher also kept a house.[11] Certainly, on the face of it, Simpson seemed to have confirmed (or implied a confirmation of) the consistency between aspects of Carver's life and those of the transients that people his fiction, rootless characters in generic environments – impersonal apartment buildings, motels, suburban houses or trailer parks.

Carver country appears not to be a matter of geography, or even of physical environment at all (except in so far as it is marked by that dominance of the generic and mass-produced), but rather of social and cultural or psychological (and even spiritual) location. We are invited to enter not a 'place' but a predicament. The question remains how far that predicament is culturally determined. This formulation of the question allows for the possibility that, on the one hand, Carver presents a very American phenomenon, that the (broadly) cultural (i.e. social, economic and psychological) identification of Carver country is symptomatically 'American': that he is therefore an 'American writer' whose work belongs to something we can perhaps still think of as 'American Literature', indeed that locates itself within 'American Literature'. Yet to be American in this sense might indeed mean having minimalised relations with locality or history, and also with cultural practice in any but a postmodern sense, on the grounds that to European eyes it is precisely a diminished (or at any rate a radically transformed) sense of historical, local or cultural determinants or constraints that characterises American literature(s).[12]

On the other hand, we may prefer to believe that he is therefore simply an existential writer (like Beckett, say, or Kafka) whose landscape is defined by psychological or spiritual parameters rather than national or cultural ones, with the implication that he addresses transcultural, ahistorical, transcendent realities. The North Pole and the South Pole. It may be that we can get no further with the question about the Americanness of Carver's fiction than to point to the absence of any sense of place. To this silence about issues of national, regional, communal identity. To its yielding to the postmodern proliferation of the generic. If some such sense of *America as postmodern* is one way of defining the mode of Carver's Americanism, it is not (conspicuously) something about which his art is conscious or explicit.

VARIANTS OF REALISM

I don't like to read about the experience of writing, the self-reflective thing of writing fiction about writing fiction and so forth.

(Raymond Carver, interview in *Frank* (1987–88), p. 12)

But Carver's fiction has also been identified by the very deliberate and even aggressive return to realism which he shares with a number of other recent American writers, and which has constituted a reaction against the 'fabulist' tendencies of fiction writing in the United States. What has made his kind of fiction seem somehow *more* real has been (as ever) the minimising in it of evidences of 'literariness', and the way it offers itself as a 'witness' of real lives.[13] This quest for neo-realism has had a certain kind of consequence in Carver's fiction, particularly for his handling of plot and narrative voice. He contrives to offer us stories which are less evidently 'stories' (i.e. plotted constructs with beginnings, middles, ends, climaxes and catastrophes, etc. – as prescribed by Aristotle and confirmed by traditional practice).[14] And he tells the 'story' either through the agency of a first person narrator, or by a narrative focalisation almost coincident with one of the characters. Thus, he denies himself the larger perspective of narrator/author, by means of which the author might intervene between the reader and the story or characters in order to shape, share or modulate responses, creating thereby an ordered hierarchy of significance of the kind implied by the now perhaps passé literary term *point-of-view*. On occasions when he employs an omniscient narrator, · he yet retains a reserve which makes no overt judgement. There are Carver-situations and Carver-perplexities, there is not a Carver point-of-view in these fictions. Not explicitly. Neither as plotter nor as commentator and interpreter is the author's presence readily detectable. Neither of these formal strategies is, of course, innovative; but they and their tendency are highly characteristic.

Carver's stories invariably miss the climactic event, perhaps with the inference that in reality there are no climactic events by which we can measure and mark out the tenor of our lives. Or that, if there *are* events that are significant, their significance is most often obscured, or they themselves so insignificant and lacking in *moment* that they pass barely recognised, so that there is a discrepancy between (to borrow the language of Saussure) the signified and the signifier. The short story as a genre has since Chekhov and Joyce been seen as well suited to this kind of brief, epiphanic 'glimpse' of larger transcendent meaning. Carver admired and repeatedly cited V.S. Pritchett's definition of the short story as 'something glimpsed from the corner of the eye',[15] with its suggestion of both brevity and liminal presence. What he spoke of as 'illumination, consequences and meanings' are not in his texts epiphanically revealed, however much the fictions themselves may strain towards illumination. The distinction between (transcendent) epiphany and (secular) glimpse may be precisely the difference between the modernist and the postmodernist writer here.[16] So agnostic is Carver that he sets aside the question of meaning for the question of empirical accuracy and truth – clear and specific language will allow his glimpse to speak for itself of illumination, meaning, etc. Carver's aesthetic seems therefore to proceed in realist terms, respecting the actual and refusing to subject it to either the resonances that derive from plot, or those that owe their identification to the narrative voice, far less from the 'insights' of the characters. Events must speak for themselves without the benefit of amplification. This author is not wiser than his characters, nor apparently using his story to persuade the reader of anything, any programme or agenda. The refusal to deploy all the resources of plot, and to impose (or even reveal) interpretation upon the actualities so faithfully reported, is part of his so-called minimalism (a term about which he expressed his own dissatisfaction).[17] It is as though latter-day realism will inevitably involve some measure of minimalism.

'Tell the Women We're Going', though not one of Carver's strongest stories,[18] provides an interesting variant on his often minimalist realism and an accessible route to his textual strategies. It has a plot, at least in the sense that in it events follow a sequence of chronological stages to a cataclysmic conclusion. As we know, in fiction chronological sequence has at least the implication of causal sequence, and therefore of *consequence*, to use Carver's word. (*Post hoc, ergo propter hoc.*) Indeed, the double murder with which the story ends (although of course the text is in fact not quite as specific as that about how matters end!) is hardly something glimpsed out of the corner of the eye. Although the chronology of the narrative leads us towards the final violence, the causality is obviously inadequately or incompletely expressed at the explicit level. We are made aware that events are *driven* by some powerful motives at work in Jerry but we do not have access to what these might be, at any rate none of the traditional fictional means of allowing access. Focalisation in the text, for example, falls entirely upon Bill. The conscious-ness of the murderer remains closed. The final lines read: 'He never knew what Jerry wanted. But it started and ended with a rock. Jerry used the same rock on both girls, first on the girl called Sharon and then on the one that was supposed to be Bill's.'[19]

As has already been suggested, the text is here discreet and tactful to the point of evading the naming of the act to which it refers. It practises instead a kind of circumlocution, metonymic in character – 'it started and ended with a rock. . . . used the same rock' – and again in the sustained final phrase, 'and then on the one that was supposed to be Bill's'. This tendency to evasion and circumlocution is consistent with other features of the text – with the deflected focalisation, for example, and with the inarticulacy, silence and reticence that characterise the dialogue. That there is a narrator we cannot doubt. He (or she) moves us economically through all the formative years of the friendship of Bill and Jerry to bring us with narrative efficiency to that Sunday. Apart from providing that background and offering the focalisation upon Bill, the narrator is remarkably cool, perhaps maintaining that coolness by the evasions we have noted. The narrative proper begins with a flat statement: 'It was Sunday at Jerry's place the time it happened.'[20] The reference to 'it' is without antecedent, which itself fosters anticipation, drives the reader forward by withholding knowledge – knowledge this time of the final action. When the narrator (or the text) at last supplies the final action (though in the oblique manner we have remarked), it is not of course sufficient. The narrator seems to discharge responsibilities once the actions are merely narrated (without being *related*, except minimally – i.e. chronologically, sequentially). Insight, significance, meaning, illumination and consequence all remain to be supplied. In Barthes's terms, the proairetic code provides the chief means by which the text is organised, that is, the action is unfolded in a deliberate manner. The hermeneutic code, on the other hand, is asserted by silence, and by allusions to silence. Ultimately, it is by far the more powerful.[21]

John Barth likewise spoke of the 'extrospective' character of minimalist fiction such as Carver's[22], and what he had in mind seems well enough illustrated in this case: the text's attentive record of action, and its scrupulous refusal of interpretation or comment. The inscrutability of Jerry to Bill and to the reader – 'He never knew. . . .' – has of course been prepared in a couple of passages that concern 'not knowing' (as did the narrator's 'it'):

> Bill was thinking how Jerry was getting to be deep, the way he stared all the time and hardly did any talking at all.
> Bill moved in his chair and lighted a cigarette.
> He said, 'Anything wrong, man? I mean, you know.'
> Jerry finished his beer and then mashed the can. He shrugged.
> 'You know,' he said.[23]

That the definition of 'deep' equates it with silence is itself revealing. Given the importance in Carver's text of what does not get articulated and therefore cannot be known, (i.e. what it all 'means'), the presence here as phatic gesture of precisely these words (mean/think/know) – as merely ironic tokens in limited discourse – surely brings us to a recognition of the text's strategies (as well as functioning as an important episode in the syntax of the plot). 'You know' foregrounds the whole process of revealing and concealing that attracts and arrests the reader, rendering the entire question of 'interpretation' problematic for the (now thoroughly activated) reader who is thereby given the responsibility for 'illumination' or 'meaning and consequence', and must read the text's foregroundings in these seemingly casual demotic phrases. The casual has become the causal.

There is a later passage which serves the same function, offering an opportunity for reflection or illumination (where another or an earlier author might have arranged that characters achieve a measure of self-consciousness, and the reader might pick up on the kinds of significances that are being traded in). It is plainly linked to the earlier passage. It takes place two or three hours later in the story, when the young men are through playing pool and are in the midst (for Jerry at least) of a nostalgic attempt to recapture the simplicity of their lost youth – pool being one of the rituals of the male bonding apparently so important in American fiction (together with drinking, hunting, fishing) – and to release themselves from the responsibilities that enter their lives with women, marriage, children. (That, of course, is how I read the passage, supplying to it specific cultural codes. For the moment my interest is more in the extent of the encoding involved in the text than the decoding of its specifically American cultural language. Neither the narrator nor the characters help the reader out here.) The text brings us back to that self-referential issue: How can Jerry read himself? How can Bill read Jerry? How do we read the text?

> Bill said, 'So what do you think, Jerry? I mean, what do you think?' Bill said.
> Jerry drained his can, mashed it, then stood for a time, turning the can in his hand.[24]

The chiasmus ('Bill said / what do you think? / I mean / what do you think? / Bill said') reinforces the foregrounding of the textual strategy, while the mimetic demand for a real record of a 'real' inarticulate conversation is satisfied at the same time. The other aspect of the foregrounding at work here concerns the silent response of Jerry, which as before focuses on the crushing of the can in his hand. The story works by playing this gesture as evidence of inner conflict and potential for violence. What it does is to displace the ultimate violence by displacing the word he uses in both instances here ('mash') from its proper location in the final scene, where its place has been taken by the now powerful and charged restraint and neutrality of 'used'. Both 'mashed' and 'hand' are powerful presences in the text's final lines as a result of a careful, literary or rhetorical, economy of the narrative line. As my next section will propose, such stories ultimately demand cultural decoding. The restraint and neutralisation of violence become real-life possibilities. So that a critic like Barbara Henning can perhaps with justification write of Carver's story 'Preservation' that it asks the reader 'to care, simply to care about the characters and their predicaments'.[25] Such characters 'along with millions of other Americans, want and need . . . economic stability, a political purpose, a sense of community, or a spiritual belief' (what seemingly amounts to a reassertion of one version of the American Dream in inauspicuous times).

TEXTUAL STRATEGY AS CULTURAL COMMENTARY

The characters construct their reality starting from the signs they receive, just as we construct the fiction starting from the text we read: their apprenticeship to the world is an image of ours to the book.

(T. Todorov, *Introduction to Poetics*, Oxford, 1969, pp. 55–6)

As has been suggested, it would have been more characteristic of Carver to have deprived us of the climactic event altogether, for there can be little doubt that the maximal character of the final event inevitably renders the minimal details that precede it *significant*, however much the text evades or disguises its interpretative strategies (in the way that forensic discourse reconstructs plot and produces evidence). The reader is activated by a very sensational shock – the murders. This is to raise explicitly the question of closure in Carver's texts. In the same way as the murder in 'Tell the Women' closes the text at one level while, as it were, ensuring that it remains open at other and more important levels (of interpretation), so Carver's texts frequently offer closure of this ambiguous kind. I want to consider two texts of which this is certainly true – 'Fat' and 'Why Don't You Dance?' In both cases the endings open questions of how we ought to interpret the stories themselves. In fact, both end with the kind of perspectival shift that Carver liked to apply, and that incorporates into the texts the problematised process of 'reading' them. It is perhaps first worth briefly mentioning the best example in his work of this shift – the story that was published as both 'Distance' and 'Everything Stuck to Him'.[26] In this case the story is about a story and achieves its effects by the intertextual relations at work within the larger text. In fact, Carver's choice of 'Distance' as one of the alternative titles for the alternative versions of this story seems itself to allude to this process of assessment within a new perspective, the distances being temporal, spatial and emotional, And narrative. It creates a *mise-en-abyme*.[27] Framing a text and making shifts from frame to story (hyperdiegesis to diegesis) is naturally one way of throwing into relief those aspects that have (continuing or revealed) significance. Given the paucity of indicators as to how we are to sift the meticulous record of details, the difficulty of reading the codes, such shifts become naturally of great textual moment.

In both 'Fat' and 'Why Don't You Dance?' the endings make the claim that what has 'happened' in the story is *significant*, but in both cases that significance remains elusive. It is not confirmed in the superficial way that the murders at the end of 'Tell the Women' seem to confer importance on what has passed, hinting at the depth beneath the extrospective surface. Rather these two texts close with ironic notions of insight, on the brink of a revelation but without a way of giving it a name. It is a textual strategy that is of course designed to discomfit and (especially) to activate the reader. The question then becomes one of the extent to which the text can bear the reader's scrutiny, the extent, that is, to which it is indeed 'coded' and not mere contingent 'garbage' (to borrow a computer term).

The act of narration may be an attempt (as it is for the girl in 'Why Don't You Dance?') to find the meaning, to 'get it talked out', or it may be (as in 'Fat') an attempt, having found it, to communicate it, to 'bear witness'. At the end of the latter story, the nameless first person narrator says of Rita, the audience for whom she has told the story of the fat man, 'I can see she doesn't know what to make of it'. (We should note the provision of two narratees as well as the author/narrator complexity. The narrator is here addressing the implied reader, not Rita, her audience.)

> I feel depressed. But I won't go into it with her. I've already told her too much.
> She sits there waiting, her dainty fingers poking her hair.
> Waiting for what? I'd like to know.
> It is August.
> My life is going to change, I feel it.[28]

The suggestion that the audience has been told 'too much' may seem sardonic to the reader, who is struggling to connect 'My life is going to change' with the apparently inconclusive story about the fat man. The narrator seems to have said too little, not too much.

The story has obviously been about excess and over-indulgence, as well as betraying anxiety about its own excess as a text. Once again Carver seems to connect the ostensible matter with the processes of narration. And again it is by the deployment of a narrative framing device that these levels are related. At the diegetic level – the story the text tells – the narrator waits on the fat man, serving him with a kind of fascination at the embodiment he offers of the process of consumption in which she has her (professional) place. His use of the pronoun 'we' is appropriate to his bulk, to his representative-ness, and to the sense of complicity and guilt he occasions. He brings out the waitress in her. He embodies what waiting and serving serve. She fusses over his order, suggests he remove his coat, accepts his caveats about the excep-tional nature of his eating, is compliant, apologetic, assiduous, eager. The teasing that goes on in the kitchen over her inferred sexual attraction to him simply reflects the ambiguities of service. Her role as waitress/servant persists when she goes home to serve the comforts of Rudy, first preparing tea that he can enjoy in front of the TV, then relinquishing her own wishes to his sexual importunity in the bedroom (where Rudy's 'unbuttoning' seems linked in the text to the suggestion she had earlier made to the fat man to take off his coat in the restaurant, and to that curious remark she offers in mid-story, 'Rudy has his apron and hat off, if you see what I mean'), until she suddenly feels that she is swollen, puffed up (to use the appropriate but displaced term from the text).[29]

The text at this level also insists upon assembling (and serving up) what amounts to an excessive parade of characters, all themselves functionaries in this process of service: Herb, Leander, Rudy, Margo, Harriet and Joanne, as well as the narrator herself. The narrative is overfed, but in the kind of orderly way that the menu is also full.

If we shift to the hyperdiegetic level, to the frame of the *récit*,[30] we can easily read this too as a kind of service, a kind of feeding of detail to Rita, ordered and full but strangely empty of meaning. Nothing happens in her story – 'Nothing else' is all she can offer Rita's whetted appetite. So Rita doesn't know what to make of it. The final image of her is of her dainty fingers poking her hair, contrasting with the fat man's, 'three times the size of a normal person's fingers – long, thick, creamy fingers'. She is waiting; the narrator is, after all, a waitress. This perplexity of Rita's has also, though in a different way, been the narrator's: 'I know now I was after something. But I don't know what', she says, and 'Rudy, he is fat, I say, but that is not the whole story.' The reader is no better off when she admits, 'a feeling came over me', because she is never any more specific about what that might be. As readers too we are fed, but we are not satisfied.

The narrator's frustrated desire to 'gain', and then her unexpected and sudden feeling that she is fat, might be interpretable as her desire to have children. She feels her stomach in the shower and thinks about what it would be like to have a child who 'turned out to look like that, so fat'. Fatness seems here to be associated with pregnancy. Her feeling of her own fatness comes, moreover, when Rudy is making love to her. Is the change then the change that pregnancy would bring? It seems to me rather that fatness is in the text associated with indulgence/consumption and submission to service roles which are ultimately unsatisfactory, unfulfilling or empty. That the text, in short, valorises what is absent – including the absent pregnancy (which would constitute a meaningful fatness, a real gain). The narrator's sudden sense of fatness is a realisation of the need for change. Such a reading is of course very susceptible to a number of feminist articulations, and that would surely be entirely appropriate. What might be called a cultural reading, of which feminist insights undoubtedly form a significant part, would certainly offer another way of looking at the text, and throw emphasis upon contemporary America's 'service industry' culture of the post-industrial, postmodern age.

That Carver placed 'Fat' at the beginning of his first major collection suggests, in the light of what has been said, that he perhaps regarded it as a kind of manifesto (though a characteristically oblique one). The collection certainly seems dedicated to literary *leanness* and to notions of absence. Texts are hollowed out so that we are confronted by what is *not* there.

As mentioned previously, 'Why Don't You Dance?' (from *What We Talk About When We Talk About Love*, his second major collection) is another text that ends with a shift in perspective, and a failed attempt to give articulation to the significance of events that (once again) have been meticulously recorded. The girl acknowledges in the proleptic section with which the text ends that there was 'more to it', but she gives up trying to find out what that more might be. In contrast to 'Fat', the central figure (the man) is not one who has 'gained' to an extraordinary degree, but one who has lost, and who epitomises relinquishment, or renunciation. The boy and the girl indeed practise their own kind of reduction – 'offer ten dollars less' – reduction, that is, of the money they're prepared to offer on the sale items; but, of course, they do this in order to gain material advantage, to make a better deal in this impromptu market. They are loading up for a life together; the man is abandoning the material trappings of just such a life. He retreats; they advance. Yet it seems plain that it is not in these external and material conveniences and comforts that any real transaction takes place. The very notion of an interior laid out in the yard, inside outside, is the essence of emptiness defined by (material) presence. The man, moreover, is absent when they first stop. Even when he has returned there is another absence – that of the implied wife.

It is notable that, of the two young people, it is the girl who has the keener sense of how to bargain; but also that she is the one who has the greater sense of romance, and of the tragedy of romance – 'You must be desperate', she says to the man as they dance. However, she is the one who has recognised that that tragedy might be something she can make capital out of – 'Whatever they ask, offer ten dollars less . . . besides, they must be desperate or something.' She not only wants to kiss the boy on the bed, notices the star and wants to dance, but she is the leader in the couple's keenness to pick through the leftovers of a marriage, the furnishings of just such an attempt on life as they are about to make. The text acknowledges that ambiguity: 'He looked at them as they sat at the table. In the lamplight, there was something about their faces. It was nice or it was nasty. There was no telling.'[31]

If 'Fat' is concerned with the emptiness that lies behind excessive consumption and service, this story seems to be concerned both with the renunciation of the material (the sadness of things) and with some kind of extraordinary and paradoxical process of material recycling and emotional regeneration that speaks (ironically) to the human capacity for hope and survival. What the man ultimately seems to want them to have is the music, the record-player, the records, the dancing. The girl's subsequent cynical, self-protective consumerist/materialist reduction of the experience is one that offers a false perspective, because it leaves her too dissatisfied. It is ironic that the concession the text makes about the limits of her final attempt to get it talked out invokes the consumerist discourse of contemporary advertisement: 'And MORE!!!' (the American advertisement's strident way of admitting its own discursive limitations). The possibility of that intertextual play goes some way towards confirming for me the cultural specifics of the textual strategies I have been describing in Carver. (To that observation I would simply want to add that the text also constitutes a 'telling' which is itself 'no telling'.)

With any observation of the specifically American character of the issues dealt with in the text we approach one of the major issues that *Forked Tongues* addresses. The yard sale is a peculiarly (perhaps quintessentially) American phenomenon; if American society is conspicuously committed to consumption of goods (as of services), the yard sale is its necessary domestic consequence. At some level of textuality, Carver seems to be working with/against the consequences of a society dedicated to consumption and incapable of achieving satisfaction. His textual strategies are wholly mimetic of America as Text: famine amidst the superfluities of the Reagan years.

NOTES

1. D. Newlove, 'Fiction Briefs', *Saturday Review* (April 1981), coined the phrase, which was then taken up by W.L. Stull in one of the better critical articles on Carver, 'Beyond Hopelessville', *Philological Quarterly* 64 (1985): 1–15.

2. See R. Towers, 'Low Rent Tragedies' in the *New York Review of Books*, 14 May 1981.

3. See the essays in *Fires* (London, 1985) and interviews with Carver collected in *Conversations with Raymond Carver* (Jackson, Mississippi, 1990), ed. M.B. Gentry and W.L. Stull.

4. *Fires*, p. 24.

5. *Paris Review* 25:88 (1983), 'The Art of Fiction LXXVI' (Interview with Mona Simpson): 192–221. p. 221.

6. Ibid. p. 220.

7. *London Review of Books*: (15 Sept. 1988): 16.

8. David Applefield, 'Fiction and America: Raymond Carver', *Frank: An International Journal of Contemporary Writing and Art* 8–9 (1987–88): 6–15. p. 9.

9. *Stories of Raymond Carver* (London, 1985), p. 187.

10. Applefield, op.cit, p. 9.

11. *Paris Review*, p. 193ff.

12. Carver's 'minimalism' (and minimalism in general) has been the object of much hostility and occasioned expressions of regret, for the most part. The most useful discussion of the movement in general appeared in the minimalism issue of the *Mississippi Review*, 40–41 (1985). An attempt to link the formal characteristics of so-called minimalism with the contemporary American cultural situation in the context of Carver's writing was offered in Barbara Henning's 'Minimalism and the American Dream: "Shiloh" by Bobbie Ann Mason and "Preservation" by Raymond Carver', *Modern Fiction Studies* 35:4 (1989): 689–98. John Barth's short article is the most succinct introduction to the subject. See below, note 22.

13. See, for example, the remarks in the Introduction to *American Short Story Masterpieces*, (ed.) Carver and Tom Jenks (New York, 1987), which offered as a criterion for selection the formula 'short stories which on occasion had the ambition of enlarging our view of ourselves and the world . . . that in some important way bear witness to our own lives'. In the editors' view this excluded stories that lacked a 'strong narrative drive' as well as 'further samples of what some have hailed as the "new fiction" – self-reflexive, fabulist, magical realist, as well as mutations, offshoots, and fringe movements thereof' (p. xiii).

14. It has to be said that Carver himself distinguished between postmodernist metafictional writing and the movement of 'writers who have begun to write "stories" again, trying to create recognizable people and place them in life-like circumstances' (see *Frank* interview, p. 9). He certainly saw himself as belonging to the latter group. My argument is in large measure a qualification of his own judgement.

15. See *Fires*, p. 26.

16. See A.A. Brown, 'Raymond Carver and Postmodern Humanism' in *Critique* 31:2 (Winter 1990): 125–36. He contrasts Carver with Hemingway, who 'never loses sight of his frame of reference, his values'. For Carver, and for postmodern writers in general, 'There is no universal referent, no code of ethics or uncontestable values, no resource of significant events to draw from. . . .' (p. 131).

17. See Applefield, op.cit. p. 8–9.

18. W.L. Stull, 'Beyond Hopelessville', thought it one of the two weakest stories in *What We Talk About When We Talk About Love*, the other being 'Popular Mechanics'. (His view of the latter is not one I would dispute.)

19. *Stories of Raymond Carver*, p. 226.

20. Ibid., p. 222.

21. See Barthes, *S/Z* (Paris, 1970; trans. London, 1975).

22. John Barth, 'A Few Words about Minimalism' in *New York Times Book Review* (28 Dec. 1986): 1.

23. *Stories of Raymond Carver*, p. 222.

24. Ibid, p. 223.

25. Henning, loc.cit., p. 698.

26. Carver published revised versions of a number of his stories, of which the most discussed is probably 'The Bath'/'A Small Good Thing'. These revisions are often taken as a recantation of minimalism sins. See again W.L. Stull's 'Beyond Hopelessville', loc. cit., which detects a movement from 'existential realism' to 'humanist realism', from 'crass causality' (in 'The Bath') to 'a story of spiritual rebirth' ('A Small Good Thing'). Or M.J. Bugeja, 'Tarnish and Silver: An Analysis of Carver's *Cathedral*' in *South Dakota Review* 24 (1986): 73–87, which also offers a comparison of the two versions of 'The Bath'/'A Small Good Thing' and speaks approvingly of 'stories with genuine up-beat endings' which 'enhance' *Cathedral*.

27. See one of the first (and still one of the most useful) articles published on Carver: D.Boxer and C. Phillips, 'Will You Please Be Quiet, Please?: Voyeurism, Dissociation, and the Art of Raymond Carver', *Iowa Review* 10 (1979): 75–90. They quote (relevantly) from 'Put Yourself in My Shoes': 'Her voice seemed to come from him from a great distance. . . .'

28. *Stories of Raymond Carver*, p. 16.

29. The fat customer 'puffs' throughout.

30. As noted above, there is in fact more than one level of framing narration; we are told about the telling of the 'story' to Rita.

31. *Stories of Raymond Carver*, p. 190.

FURTHER READING

D. Boxer and C. Phillips, 'Will You Please Be Quiet, Please?: Voyeurism, Dissociation, and the Art of Raymond Carver' in *Iowa Review* 10 (1979): 75–90.

A.A.Brown, 'Raymond Carver and Postmodern Humanism' in *Critique* 31:2 (Winter 1990): 125–36.

M.J.Bugeja, 'Tarnish and Silver: An Analysis of Carver's *Cathedral*' in *South Dakota Review* 24 (1986): 73–87.

Raymond Carver, *Fires* (London, 1985).

Marc Chenétier, 'Living On/Off the Reserve' in *Critical Angles*, (ed.) Chenétier (Carbondale, Illinois, 1986), pp. 170ff.

Marshall B.Gentry and William L.Stull (eds), *Conversations with Raymond Carver* (Jackson, Mississippi, and London, 1990).

Sam Halpert (ed.), . . . *When We Talk About Raymond Carver* (Layton, Utah, 1991).

Barbara Henning, 'Minimalism and the American Dream: "Shiloh" by Bobbie Ann Mason and "Preservation" by Raymond Carver' in *Modern Fiction Studies* 35:4 (1989): 689–98.

Adam Meyer, 'Now You See Him, Now You Don't, Now You Do Again: The Evolution of Raymond Carver's Minimalism' in *Critique* (1989): 239–51.

Paul Skenazy, 'Life in Limbo: Ray Carver's Fiction' in *Enclitic* 11 (1988): 77–83.

William L. Stull, 'Beyond Hopelessville: Another Side of Raymond Carver' in *Philological Quarterly* 64 (1985): 1 –15.

IV Gender and Race: D.H. Lawrence to Philip Roth

'And how had it ever happened here with the chances so good for diversity?', asks a bewildered Oedipa Maas at the climax of Thomas Pynchon's *The Crying of Lot 49* (1966), faced with that wasting of all difference that has reduced the American dream to the dead level of modern reality. In this section of the volume, difference is a prominent issue. Oedipa's anguished sense of marginalisation, of being excluded from the promised land of plural forms of freedom and self-fulfilment, returns us to the questions raised in Hermione Lee's reflections on Willa Cather, about the 'marginal man' and the possibility for participation in any national identity where difference is so strenuously asserted and defended. For, as Linda Hutcheon claims in *A Poetics of Postmodernism* (New York and London, 1988, p. 12), 'The centre no longer completely holds': multicultural America, multiracial Britain, cannot be 'the homogenous monolith (that is middle-class, male, heterosexual, white, western) we might have assumed'. Comparative analysis of the two literatures will therefore have to reflect this shift toward recognition of difference, of the transnational categories of gender, class and race which articulate individual and cultural identity, and away from the aspiration to pit totality against totality. This section may be deemed in one respect eccentric, since it lacks the single focus of the preceding groupings, but the 'ex-centric', as Hutcheon calls it, whatever resists the homogenisations of a centred and settled conception of national and cultural identity, may now be considered the dynamic of our cultural formations, more immediately visible and influential in the United States, as the essays here tend to suggest.

A word on class, the transnational category which is not directly addressed in this section. It can hardly in practice be divorced from exploration of the significance of gender and race in the texts and contexts under consideration. Representations of class difference are plainly compounded with representations of sexuality, for example, in Alistair Stead's examination in the first essay of pastoral romances. Consider the misalliances in Lawrence's *Lady Chatterley's Lover*, L.P.Hartley's *The Go-Between*, even Cather's *A Lost Lady* (all those ladies . . .). In the very different setting of the black woman's struggle for survival and respect in the sixties and seventies in both Britain and America, as Olga Kenyon points out in the second essay, classism is a component of their racial oppression, although the Nigerian-born Buchi Emecheta is typically compelled by the British scene into a very illuminating self-consciousness: 'In London classism divides us; because many immigrant women do menial jobs, they feel too awkward to talk to me, and white feminists do not fully understand our problems.' Paulina Palmer's survey of women's representations of women in the city draws on several writers alive to the part played by social status in their dramas of feminist adaptation to city life, not just the British realist Zoë Fairbairns but Marge Piercy, who has written: 'I am one of the few contemporary American novelists consciously and constantly preoccupied with social class . . .' (*Contemporary Novelists*, 5th edn; (ed.) Lesley Henderson, Chicago and London, 1992, p. 730).

If anything unites the diverse studies of ex-centric perspectives in this section it is the recurrence of the dual process of myth-making and myth-breaking. Myths of national identity may themselves be in play, but it is usually what Adrienne Munich in *Making A Difference: Feminist Literary Criticism* (ed. Gayle Green and Coppélia Kahn, London and New York 1985, p. 224) calls 'the working myths of culture', the subsidiary and complexly interrelated fictions that the literary texts convey, which are the focus of these studies. Stead's essay associates the pastoral myths (of the superiority of country to city, the psycho-sexual energies of life in the woods) with the constructions of childhood, masculinity and cultural identity. Pastoral myth surfaces again, replayed and revised, in Olga Kenyon's exposition of Emecheta's ideal and experienced motherhood in rural Africa and metropolitan Britain, and in Paulina Palmer's presentation of the city as attractive to women seeking economic and sexual independence but also as locus of masculine control and aggression, discordant space from which one might need to retreat, like the radical feminists in Sally Gearhart's Utopian fantasy *The Wanderground*. American feminists have frequently built their revisionary Utopias on the bucolic or Edenic images of other worlds recurrent in science fiction, from Charlotte Perkins Gilman's *Herland* (1915) to Ursula Le Guin's *The Word for World is Forest* (1977), whereas British women have more commonly produced anti-pastoral comedies of manners, exposing patriarchal complicity with Karl Marx's 'rural idiocy' (Fay Weldon's *The Heart of the Country*, 1987) or mocking experiments in communal living in the countryside (Janice Elliott's *The Honey Tree*, 1978). One particular myth about woman's relation to the city which Palmer is anxious to dispel is the assumption that the lesbian is the product of urban life, tied to the lesbian 'scene' by the sexual imperative. Bryan Cheyette's essay, the last in this section, shows his Jewish novelists, British and American, struggling against the 'narrow and excluding' racial stereotypes imposed and disseminated by their own communities (the Jew as emblem of bourgeois respectability) and toward the re-invention of themselves in 'imaginary homelands'. In the process, Philip Roth's fictional *alter ego*, Nathan Zuckerman, in *The Ghost Writer*, swings between surrogate fathers, the appetite of Abravanel and the asceticism of Lonoff, in a way which characteristically compounds the sexual with the racial, while the enthusiasm of the male Jewish novelists, Roth and Sinclair, for displacement to textual homelands is counterbalanced by the cautious allegiance to history of the female novelists, Cynthia Ozick and Elaine Feinstein.

Stead's essay begins, in its scrutiny of Robin Hood and Pan as peculiarly complex and persistent figures of pastoral discourse, with the most traditional sense of myth (tales many times retold from the world's treasure-house of story), and Kenyon touches on this in observing Alice Walker's exploitation of the African Mother-Goddess in *The Temple of My Familiar* (where Lissie, one of several narrators, recounts her many incarnations reaching back through Isis, Medusa and the Black Madonna). Medieval Robin Hood, unlike classical Pan, has often been seen to hover between fantasy and history, and in British reinterpretations, in particular, to become an embodiment of a masculinist national myth. In the hands of writers like D.H. Lawrence and John Fowles the figure becomes a peculiar kind of sexual outlaw, merged with the disruptive and minatory shape of Pan the goat-god, hiding out in psychic reserves of the woods. Here one might see common ground between the modern pastoral myth in America, too: representations of the male need to escape temporarily from the pressures of the city into the regenerative freedoms of the country, often envisaged, whether directly or indirectly, in heterosexual or homosexual terms. In 1990, for instance, Robert Bly's immensely popular non-fictional *Iron John* was matched by Michael Cunningham's fictional design for living *A Home at the End of the World*. The Panic, or satyrical, pastoral is, in recent times, more attractive to the Americans, who tend to produce wilder, raunchier fabulations veering between the sinister male chauvinism of the 'sex-singer' of John Hawkes's *The Blood Oranges* and the exuberant polymorphous perversity of Guy Davenport's Fourierist Utopian fantasies in *Eclogues* and *Apples and Pears*.

One of the complementary aspects of the pastoral myth is the woman's converse need to escape from the confinement of the country into the economic opportunity and anonymous pleasures of the city. Cather's Lost Lady takes her place with the more obvious early-century rebels against the village in her fiction (Thea, Lena, Lucy) as representative of a deeply divided American response to the alluring city. But this pattern is discernible in both Paulina Palmer's study of Marge Piercy's *Small Changes* and in Olga Kenyon's account of Buchi Emecheta's autobiography and fiction. In both essays the city appears to be a site of contradictions. For the heroine of *The Joys of Motherhood*, and Emecheta herself, the city is inhospitable and alien, but it becomes for the novelist, after terrible suffering at the hands of a brutal husband and a racist society, a place of achievement where the single-parent mother-worker is finally vindicated by her determination and her literary gift. For the American black woman writer it presents a double face too: Alice Walker's ambivalence in 'The Black Writer and the Southern Experience' (in *In Search of Our Mothers' Gardens*, London, 1984, p. 21), hating the hardship of Southern black country, but hanging on to the pastoral distinction. Walker's statement that: 'in the cities it cannot be so clear to one that he [*sic*] is a creature of the earth', can be compared with Toni Morrison's conviction, in 'City Limits, Village Values: Concepts of the Neighbourhood in Black Fiction' *Literature and the American Urban Experience*, (ed.) Michael C. Jaye and Ann Chalmers Watts, Manchester, 1981, pp. 35–43), that black pro-urbanism, and the automatic association of so much black culture with the personal freedoms of the city, risked the loss of the life-line to 'the ancestor' in the village. It is the enriching contact with the community, with roots, that sustains the African-American writers (not the women only, but most notably these), directly or through history and fiction (as in the impact of Zora Neale Hurston's fiction on Alice Walker, and Walker's own researches into the folkways of her people), and is denied to the uprooted and more narrowly educated Emecheta. Emecheta's fictions, inspired by the 'social realities' of British realist work by women in the fifties and sixties, and starting out in journalism, have lacked the vernacular verve and lyrical idiom that Walker shares with generations of black artists reared on the blues, jazz and biblical cadences. Her latest novel, *Gwendolen* (1989), however, incorporates Caribbean patois and begins to rival Walker's memorable image of the fate of Celie, heroine of *The Color Purple*, in its depiction of incestuous horror and the triumph over appalling male brutality.

The contrast in styles that Kenyon highlights in her comparison of African-American Walker and Black British Emecheta echoes that drawn by Peck in his comparison of Agee and Orwell earlier in volume, but in Palmer's enquiry into women's writings about city life it is the diversity of styles and modes, cutting across the different racial, political and sexual identifications, that is most impressive. Analysis of the pairs of writers across a range of fictional modes (realist, magical realist, lesbian crime fiction) attests to the depth and vitality of imaginative response to the urban as a contested and challenging space for women. Differences between the British and American approaches to urban issues tend to be intellectual and ideological (with Americans more optimistic about the opportunities opened up, the British more attentive to the undeniably grim realities), reflecting, Palmer suggests, the different kinds of feminism prominent in the United States and the United Kingdom in the past twenty years.

Palmer's demonstration of the British contribution to energetically engaged representations of city life might go some way to qualifying Martin Amis's impassioned promotion of the superior ambition and effort of (exclusively male?) American novelists: 'they get the novel out of the house and on to the streets, into the institutions, into the places where society is really shaped' ('The Great American Mix', *The Observer*, 16 February 1986). Philip Roth would be numbered among the writers given this accolade. Amis remarkably makes no reference to African-American novelists – no Ralph Ellison, no Toni Morrison – but declares that 'American fiction is dominated by Jewish-American fiction'. The last essay in this book pays tribute to both the American-Jewish and the British-Jewish novelists, (Roth and Cynthia Ozick, Clive Sinclair and Elaine Feinstein), and it is worthy of note that the British fictions, fine as they are, do not occupy the same conspicuous position in British culture as Roth's. Cheyette, however, argues for a great deal of common ground between these writers in their efforts to transcend parochial and repressive Jewish identifications and fictional stereotypes: vivid imaginations of counterlives, variously located in 'imaginary homelands' where the customarily split self of the displaced Jewish protagonists can achieve some kind of integration in terms of their shared European history (the shadow of the Holocaust haunts all the texts.) Cheyette draws interesting distinctions, however, between Roth's and Sinclair's views of America, as resistant and plastic terrain, and between the gendered readings of the status of the 'imaginary homelands', which for Ozick and, less emphatically, Feinstein possess 'the insurmountable "borders" of history'.

Finally, this essay curves back to the concerns of the first essay in this section and the first essay in the volume, to the pastoral and to cultural identity. Only Bernard Malamud, among American-Jewish novelists, has much use for pastoral romance, in *A New Life* (1961) and *Dubin's Lives* (1979), employing it ironically as part of his revision of the myth of Americanisation. (*Dubins Lives* combines features of modern pastoral with the kind of international, intertextual fiction practised by Lurie through the scholar-hero's ironic identification with his British biographical subject, D.H. Lawrence, and his putative subject, Thomas Hardy). The heroes of Howard Jacobson, the British-Jewish novelist, in *Coming From Behind* (1983) and *Peeping Tom* (1984), are also typically alienated from the British literary heritage of the country walk, the whole 'rural plot'. In *The Counterlife*, Roth appears to reverse Jarman's exposure of the Achilles' heel of Pound and Eliot, tracking anti-Semitism now to a specifically British and rural lair. Turning on the narrow stifling world of British gentility and lingering prejudice against Jews, Roth's Zuckerman sees Britain generically: 'The pastoral is not my genre . . . the pastoral stops here and it stops with circumcision' (p. 323). But the American male's rejection of the 'cozy and strifeless' (p. 317) is equally the project of Elaine Feinstein, suspicious of little Briton self-preoccupation, looking to an international stage for the acting out of the still troubling, always unfinished business, of forging or affirming a cultural as well as personal identity.

CHAPTER FIFTEEN

Pastoral Sexuality in British and American Fiction

Alistair Stead

ALLUSIONS BY A SINGLE WORD SOMETIMES SHOW THAT A MAN HAS BEEN IN ARCADIA.[1]

In Bret Easton Ellis's *American Psycho* (1991), the psychopathic narrator Patrick Bateman fails to get his secretary into a trendy New York restaurant and has to settle for 'the near empty dining room in Arcadia'. Distractedly answering her question about the name, he reels off a Classical Dictionary entry on the ancient region of Peloponnesus, Greece, with its capital Megalopolis, then, less casually, informs her that Pan was worshipped there: 'His revels were very similar to those of Bacchus. . . . He frolicked with nymphs at night but also liked to . . . frighten travellers during the day. . . . Hence the word *panic*'.[2] An undetected serial killer, Bateman offers up in coded form his obscene proclivities, his choice of pastoral terminology outrageous in the new Megalopolitan context. In this Baudrillardian nightmare of image-mastered consumerism 'Arcadia' is just another trivially motivated brand name, dislocated from any coherent moral or cultural framework. The literary allusion serves to present Bateman as a *reductio ad absurdum* of postmodern information society (all data, no wisdom) and a recklessly patronising sadist. It also aligns the supposed reader with his terrible knowingness. To what use then is Ellis putting this cultural nostalgia? What connects the name of paradise on earth with Bellow's 'moronic inferno'? Here, the reference to Pan holds a clue. Superficially, Bateman is representing himself as the playboy god, randy and mischief-making reveller, almost coincident with his public image as an upwardly mobile Wall Street dealer. He suppresses the genial, often comic Pan, the country god of shepherds and music-making. He only hints at that modern sinisterly sexual creation, the violent and vindictive demon who has sprung from the Christian identification of Pan with Satan and been an agent of Gothic fantasy since *The Great God Pan* (1894) by the British story teller Arthur Machen.[3]

Slight as it is, in the context of an overextended novel, Ellis's allusion may still be potent. Allusions to pastoral in modern fiction are surprisingly frequent and functional, and motifs of Pan and Robin Hood with which I intend to deal, laying emphasis on their association with erotic idylls, are strangely resilient in modern and postmodern fiction on both sides of the Atlantic. In an important essay, 'Pan in America' (written in 1924), D.H. Lawrence retold the old Plutarch story of the death of Pan, of how mysterious voices were heard crying at the beginning of the Christian era, 'Pan is dead! Great Pan is dead!' Lawrence, however, is not convinced: 'But Pan keeps being reborn, in all kinds of strange shapes.'[4] He was surveying a long tradition of intertextual play in this pastoral *topos* and was to continue to contribute to it himself in the later twenties. He was the harbinger of later twentieth-century variations, particularly when they foregrounded sexuality. 'Pan in America', with its claim that Pan as symbolic of man's living relation to his natural environment finds the New World a more congenial home, also anticipates the American bias toward the Pan myth in the later century. Similarly, the title of a recent historical fantasy by the British novelist Peter Vansittart, *The Death of Robin Hood* (1981), would seem to repeat the Plutarchian gesture. This extended elegy on the hero of Sherwood as a manifestation of wild nature that constantly threatens the corruptions of civilisation tracks his incarnation from primeval forest origins to the outbreak of the Second World War. But as in Lawrence, the entropic pattern is subverted: Hood's energies are transmuted, malignly, into the Nazi appropriations of his forest-god primitivism, benignly into the rite of passage of Roy, the adolescent hero of the novel's final section. The Green Man Lives! Even as Vansittart writes 'The Death', the image of Robin Hood is resurrected in British fiction and American movies. In the brief compass of this essay I cannot do justice to all the resurrections of the celebrated pair; I can only focus on exemplary cases of their metamorphoses in this century, demonstrating that recurrent allusions and intertextual tropings, interesting in themselves as testimony to their potency as cultural symbols, throw light on both the shared and distinguishing perspectives of the British and American writers who employ them.

PUTTING THE COMPLEX INTO THE SIMPLE

William Empson famously epitomised the business of pastoral in this formula in *Some Versions of Pastoral* (1935), and in this spirit I will endeavour to condense the long, complicated history of the genre. In its early European and highly conventionalised form, from Alexandrian Greek to Renaissance neoclassical, it represented the life of shepherds and other country folk in the (comparatively) trouble-free zone of Arcadia or the Golden Age (in later Christianised forms it might be Eden, the time of prelapsarian innocence), where in a *locus amoenus* (lovely place) their chief occupations were singing, making love and tending their flocks. A paradoxical form, artfully produced by a sophisticated urban sensibility to assuage the burdens of that complex consciousness in nostalgia and nature-worship, it composed an image of the simpler, juster, happier life in harmony with nature that only achieved significance in terms of implied or overt contrast with the power-obsessed, industrious, commercial, striving world of the court or the city.

In the eighteenth century, pastoral's limited repertoire of idealising conventions seemed effete and exhausted, and its ethos (where it was not simply rejected) was adapted to more plausible, mundane circumstances and settings. From the Romantic period onwards, pastoral fictions might be said to address, as Peter Marinelli has put it, 'the complexities of human life against a background of simplicity'[5] this is the modern form that Edward L. Ruhe has called 'displaced pastoral',[6] where the desirable simplicity is no longer to be sought among herdsmen but among humble workers, children, *ordinary* people, and the setting need not be paradisal, not even the countryside itself, wild or cultivated, but some vestiges of these or whatever seems, in comparison with the modern industrial scene, less socialised, closer to the paradigm of simplicity and naturalness. Post-romantically, the nostalgic component of pastoral remains: it is the 'art of the backward glance',[7] but the longing to return to innocence, childhood, untrammelled desire is increasingly subject to ironic exploration, or the sceptical re-views born of an age ideologically determined by Darwin, Marx, Nietzsche and Freud.

Writers of modern fictions operating within the age's realistic predisposition tend to produce mock-pastoral and counter-pastoral, heightening the traditional awareness that nature is only a construction of the civilised mind, that the country life is hard labour, that there can be no disconnection from the sphere of politics or the economy of the marketplace, that there are no human relations without tension. The pastoral project always failed, foundering on mortality (*Et in Arcadia ego*: Even I, Death, hold sway in Arcadia). But such melancholy and unease are also countered in much modern pastoral writing by new versions of the classic hopefulness of, say, Virgil's fourth Eclogue (the Golden Age will return through the intervention of a child-saviour) where the Arcadian shades into the Utopian impulse, or memory, as in Proust, miraculously repairs the ravages of time through a complex aesthetic translation. In Britain, contemporary pastoral flourishes discreetly in the romances of Iris Murdoch, John Fowles and the later work of Peter Ackroyd, where the great prototype of Thomas Hardy casts a long shadow. In America, patentee of a Postmodernism arguably hypersensitive to issues of genre, pastoral fiction announces itself more boldly, whether to burlesque in Gilbert Sorrentino's *Blue Pastoral* (1983) and satirise in T. Coraghessen Boyle's *Budding Prospects: A Pastoral* (1984), or to recover in John Gardner's *Nickel Mountain: A Pastoral* (1973) and reanimate in Guy Davenport's *Eclogues* (1981). But pastoral may survive only as an episode, a brief encounter, not 'meant to last' as the eponymous hero of Beryl Bainbridge's *Sweet William* (1975) informs his latest conquest[8] or as a remote, implied perspective, barely discernible, in the plethoric satire of novels like Thomas Pynchon's *The Crying of Lot 49* (1967) or *Vineland* (1990).

Pastoralism has done much to shape the self-images of British and American cultures. Britain, longer-historied and islanded, saw itself early as an enclosed garden under siege (John of Gaunt's 'demi-paradise'). As the first industrial nation it had good reason to recoil into compensatory, nostalgic fantasies of a 'green and pleasant land'. Romantic nature poetry and Victorian 'pastoral novels'[9] exhibit resistance, both radical and conservative, to an increasingly mechanised, materialist, rootless urban society. By the beginning of the twentieth century, the construction of 'Englishness' seizes on a dream of 'Merrie England' and the imperialist idolisation of 'home'. Well into this century even liberals and socialists have tended to locate culture in a pre-industrial 'past'.[10] Britain remains an urban society with rustic pretensions, where Little Englandism, conservation, antimodernism and much Toryism displace

expressions of sentimental patriotism on to the landscape, as Raphael Samuel has argued: 'The pastoral version of the national myth – the idea that the "real" England is in the countryside – has never been more widely popular.'[11]

American experience has repeatedly been interpreted by intellectual and cultural historians in terms of pastoral. America was originally a European dream of a New Eden, with Adam and Eve granted their second chance in the Garden of the West, or an old Arcadia, a recoverable Golden Age. Jefferson's Virgilian agrarian dream of a yeoman republic confirmed the ruralist bias of the national self-image. Westward exploration and settlement was constantly interfused with a pastoral ideology in the nineteenth century, but even twentieth-century studies of 'The Urban Nation' have taken note of the tenacity of romantic populist myths of the country, and, in spite of a developed literature of city and suburban life, so much of canonical American literature from Fenimore Cooper and the Transcendentalists to Faulkner and Updike has primitivist, agrarian and pastoral inflections. Leo Marx, perhaps the most influential of American critics on this theme, recognised its radical as well as its more obviously conservative potential: 'Pastoralism seems to be the alternative program to the established order most attractive to Americans.'[12]

A CULTURE IS NO BETTER THAN ITS WOODS

That was mid-Atlantic Auden's conclusion to 'Woods' in his *Bucolics* of 1953, and woods have played a significant part in the pastoral production of a national identity for both countries. Pan and Robin Hood, prominent in sylvan iconography, both make comically reduced appearances in Angela Carter's *jeu d'esprit* 'Overture and Instrumental Music for *A Midsummer's Night's Dream*' (*Black Venus*, 1985), a disenchanted look at the archetypal wood of Shakespearian pastoral as mediated by Victorian romanticism. She steeply contrasts the purely finite, temperate English *wood* with the haunted depths of the trackless Northern European *forest*. Apart from the hauntedness, the contrast might well be between British and American imaginative structures. Britain lacks wilderness in the American sense.[13] Long ago the great forests succumbed to agriculture and other economic usage. (*Lady Chatterley's Lover* makes reference to the felling of trees for the First World War effort.) Trees, originally an obstacle to economic progress soon acquired aesthetic value in British culture. An imaginary forest has filled its dreams with Green Men, Robin Goodfellows, Jack-in-the Greens, Lobs and the like, and some notion of an undomesticated retreat has thrown up the greenwood of 'Merrie England' and the Wild Wood of Kenneth Grahame's classic fantasy *The Wind in the Willows* (1908).[14] Most of these spaces are comparatively tame, as Carter implies, and it takes strenuous efforts on the part of her contemporary Robert Holdstock in *Mythago Wood* (1984) to forge a new version of the British 'haunted wood' story in which a remnant of ancient wild woodland provides an unstable heterotopic habitat for folkloric archetypes such as a shockingly violent Robin Hood. America's vast tracts of forest, however, are *the* national heritage, source of 'a variety of complex, and at times, contradictory myths and symbols, general ideas and emotions, which have fused to become part of the collective American moral and cultural imagination'.[15] Folkloric heroes like Paul Bunyan and Johnny Appleseed, Fenimore Cooper's Natty Bumppo, Thoreau's idealisation of the backwoodsman as an Adam in Paradise, are representatives of the mythic lode. In enunciating his influential Frontier thesis on national development, Frederick Jackson Turner had claimed that American democracy 'came out of the American forest', by-product of the pioneer conquest of the wilds.[16] Conversely, Thoreau's praise of the wilderness and George Perkins Marsh's classic of ecological thought *Man and Nature* (1864) helped to shape a powerful conservationist ideology. In modern American literature elegy and protest recurrently concern themselves with the loss of trees, from *The Big Woods* stories of William Faulkner to the 'ecotage' propaganda of Edward Abbey.[17]

Consonant with Carter's expression of the English wood as 'the common garden of the village' is her playful revision of Pan and Robin Hood: 'Robin

Wood, the fertility spirit, lurks in the green shade', and, she drily adds, 'this wood is kind to lovers', while Puck, polymorphously perverse, commits unprintable gross acts 'down in the reeds by the river, as he is distantly related to the great bad god Pan' – gross acts familiar in an English public school.[18]

Pastoral is the humble genre (*humile genus*) and Carter duly humiliates. But Robin Hood and Pan both rose from very humble origins: Robin as a yeoman outlaw popular in medieval balladry and Pan as a 'comic-grotesque little country god'.[19] As a much older source Arcadian Pan is also a more global myth. Robin Hood, appearing as a legendary ballad hero in the Middle Ages, has always hovered on the edges of history, a local hero (from Barnsdale, then Sherwood Forest) and a peculiarly English myth. Pan, the cosmopolitan traveller, has been more consistently associated with the erotic. Lord of the woods, god of shepherds and hunters, inventor of the pan-pipes, his semi-goatish nature linked him from the start to chasing nymphs or goddesses as well as terrifying travellers. Patricia Merivale has reviewed the many meanings accruing to his name, culminating in the Pans of D.H. Lawrence in the first quarter of the century, which tend to respect the goat-god paradox, recreating it in a combination of pagan, often sinister force with a sense of the spiritual or divine in nature. Yet it is only comparatively recently that the benevolent rustic god has been accorded sexuality as his central literary characteristic.[20]

Both figures originally lacked strong narratives, playing parts in a series of sometimes cruel or violent pranks and jests. The Elizabethan drama put Robin in pastoral stories and Scott integrated him into historical romance (*Ivanhoe*, 1819) contributing to his conversion into 'a literary symbol of a vanished and largely illusory medieval Arcadia'.[21] Elevated from yeoman hero to dispossessed aristocrat by the Elizabethans, this daring and generous figure soon grew as paradoxical as Pan: anti-clerical but devoted to Our Lady, loyal to the king, but at odds with authorities, susceptible to radical and conservative interpretation. It was Joseph Ritson in the 1790s who finally fixed the class-conscious British myth by making our hero rob the rich to give to the poor. The sexualised image of Robin enters with the fifteenth-century May games when Maid Marian is imported from France. With a mistress or wife in the ballads and plays, Robin was established as pastoral swain. But apart from the spirited heroine of Thomas Love Peacock's *Maid Marian* (1822), the lovers were routinely anodyne in nineteenth-century romance and 'in the absence of any strong sexual connotations',[22] Robin's adventures furnished the stuff of successful juvenile literature. Since later nineteenth-century anthropology unscientifically identified him as a fertility god, he has become the Green Man, mascot of ecological concerns.

In the sexual discourse of Angela Carter's English wood the versions of Pan and Robin, polarised as sensual and sentimental icons of the erotic, but associated as images of masculinity, announce my focus. In the review of the pastoral sexuality encoded in these figures and developed in many British and American texts, I shall be attending to masculine (often masculinist)[23] myths in male-authored fictions, with the exception of Cather's Peacockian reorientation of the greenwood myth toward Marian. I shall look first at the modern use by Forster and Lawrence of these myths for articulating English wildness; then compare American and British Marians in novels by Cather and Hartley; and, in contemporary fiction, contrast the British contribution via Robin Hood to a nativist pastoral of secrecy, notably in John Fowles, with the American postmodern reformulations of a satyrical (or Panic) pastoral that centres in sexual experimentation.

WILD MEN

Her wilderness is a greenwood, her wild man Robin Hood
(Henry David Thoreau, 'Walking', 1862)

Why has not England a great mythology? Our folklore has never advanced beyond daintiness, and the great melodies about our countryside have all issued through the pipes of Greece. Deep and true as the native imagination can be, it seems to have failed here. It has stopped with the witches and fairies.
(E.M. Forster, *Howards End* (1910), Chapter 23)

Forster's fourth novel seems to echo Thoreau's claim that English literature lacked the means to express wild nature and turns away from the etiolated anti-suburban terrorism of his own and other later Victorian fantasies of Pan, satyrs and fauns.[24] It was not until *Maurice* (written in 1913–14, but not published until 1971) that he found the myth to match the wild within to that sense of the country's wilderness. Rejecting the more commonplace neopagan code for same-sex love (Virgil's second Eclogue), he articulated the gay romance of suburban middle-class Maurice and the gamekeeper Alec in terms of the greenwood idyll. It is only in the second half of the novel that Maurice, betrayed by the man who has roused him to sexual self-awareness, sees himself as 'an outlaw in disguise', yearning for a Robin Hood-like counter-society of eroticised comradeship. His encounter with Alec, a man from the woods makes possible the actualisation of the dream; his new instinctual being, revolting against his old conformist self, opts for 'the forests and the night' for 'Sherwood' rather than the office. 'They must live outside class, without relations or money . . .'[25] Determined to give his criminalised lovers the happy ending so often denied them by society and literature, Forster appears to propel them into the 'simple pastoral' world of permanent retreat where they may find guilt-free gratification of desire in the recovered Golden

Age of Tasso's great chorus from *Aminta* (1573): '*S'ei piace, ei lice*' (If it pleases, it is lawful). 'Complex pastoralism', as Leo Marx argues, 'acknowledges the reality of history.'[26] Forster's cultural nostalgia may tend to simplify, as in his Terminal Note (1971) he looks back on the book's prewar England 'where it was still possible to get lost', but his evocation of 'a deserted valley for those who wish neither to reform nor corrupt' constructs a carefree *patria* whose typically calculated modesty offers resistance to the norms of responsibility that the imperial state would impose on its citizens.[27]

Although D.H. Lawrence was not to exchange Pan for Robin Hood as decisively as Forster, and the identities might blur, he extended in several fictions that 'last moment of the greenwood' to which *Maurice* belongs.[28] Common to their greenwood treatments of sexuality is the figure of the gamekeeper. Lawrence's Annable, a minor character in his first novel *The White Peacock* (1911) is compared to 'some malicious Pan',[29] but Mellors in his last novel *Lady Chatterley's Lover* (1928) is associated, like Alec, with the English myth. The gamekeeper has already been established as an Arcadian type of self-conscious virility in Richard Jefferies' *The Gamekeeper at Home* (1878); 'In brief, freedom and constant contact with nature have made him every inch a man: and in this nineteenth century of effeminacy may be seen some relics of what men were in the old feudal days when they dwelt practically in the woods.'[30] Such nostalgic masculinism still clings to Forster's and Lawrence's creations, more emphatically to the latter's, but they are not completely rural, are more socially unstable (Alec comes of small tradesmen, Annable is an ex-parson, Mellors has been a blacksmith and a soldier). What distinguishes Annable and Mellors from Alec is their articulate bitter disenchantment with modern civilisation. Annable, Pan-like, is a physically impressive, intimidating person, preaching the life of the 'good animal'.[31] A reputed devil, he believes the woods are an exclusively male preserve. Unlike Alec, both Annable and Mellors are refugees from failed marriages, but the latter's more complicated attitudes veer between tenderness towards his love, Lady Constance, and his regressive urge to dominate – preservative and destructive drives epitomised in the gamekeeper's social role.

Lawrence returned to his native English scene in *Lady Chatterley's Lover*, after many years of absence, with some of Forster's prewar sense of England's shrinking natural vitality, and found a more concretely realised *locus amoenus* in the familiar Midlands woodlands, half-historical, half-mythical, of Sherwood, what's left of the 'wild old England'. Mellors is Sir Clifford Chatterley's gamekeeper in woods that are 'the remnant of the great forest where Robin Hood hunted'.[32] This last refuge had already provided Birkin and Ursula, the lovers in *Women in Love* (1920), with a 'pastoral oasis' for the consummation of the mystical marriage.[33] Now Sherwood is more important to the complex idyll of Connie's and Mellors' affair. As Patrick Parrinder contends, 'Lawrence was re-writing in sexual terms, one might say, the myth of Robin Hood, bringing joy to the deprived.'[34] His heroine adventures into the woods, first perceived as her husband's property, then as the temporary retreat of her lover. In each version of the novel, there is a significant crossing from one zone (constrained) to the other (free) by an icy woodland spring ('where Robin Hood used to drink', 'called Robin Hood's Well', or 'John's Well', hinting at the Revelation to come).[35] All the sites connote refreshment and cleansing as well as a sinister coldness, heralding the ambiguity of the Robin Hood figure, a mature lover but sexually and socially vulnerable, who in seducing her from her symbolically crippled husband will regenerate both their passional selves and allegorically redeem *their* England from its affectless mechanised greed.[36] As his latter-day Lady Marian, she becomes identified with the woods ('like a forest'),[37] and its secret places, at first associated with him (the clearing, the hut) become 'the secret places' of her body that he explores.[38] But assimilation of Connie to the forest world is fraught with ideological danger. As in the older pastoral of happiness, the idyll is 'a private masculine world where woman is not a person but a sexual archetype, the eternal Eve'.[39] This passive and essentialised vision of woman is partly qualified by Lawrence's modern acceptance of his heroine's sensuality yet, as Mellors' horror at his wife's insistence on her own orgasms and his obliging Connie to exorcise sexual shame through submission to anal intercourse (he is more like Pan, 'a reckless devil' in his 'phallic hunting out')[40] tend to show, her sexuality is still subjected to the masculinist control of the phallic god. Meanwhile the social dream of Sherwood, of 'other men to be with, to fight'[41] the industrial blight, dwindles in Mellors' concluding letter to a William Morrisite fantasy of working men learning to live without spending; only Connie's pregnancy is a Virgilian pastoral focus of hope.

THE MAPLE AND THE BIRCH CONCEAL NO DRYADS, AND PAN HAS NEVER BEEN HEARD AMONG THE REED-BEDS . . . A GODLESS PLACE.[42]

Willa Cather needed no lessons from Lawrence's 'Pan in America' on the transfer of Old World gods to the New World. Her early experiments with translating old mythologies into American idiom, modelled on Heine's *The Gods in Exile* (1853), were lightweight; later theophanies became more subtly allusive, helping to imply a legendary depth to the apparent bland unhistoried surfaces of her native land, especially Nebraska where she was raised. In one of her best novels *A Lost Lady* (1923), she plays ironic variations on her retelling of Pan's enticement of Luna in 'The Bohemian Girl' (1912).[43] Marian Forrester, another fleet-footed moon-goddess (like Diana, queen of foresters), finds herself drudging for her ruined, invalid older husband, Captain Forrester, a former railroad pioneer, in their once pastoral summer home in Sweet Water, Nebraska, now their permanent impoverished retreat. No benign romantic Pan will rescue her. Niel, her youthful admirer through whom the action is most frequently focalised, proves Pan's anti-type in Virginian manners, sexual mildness, aesthetic and moral commitment. Pan's sexual power belongs to the 'coarse wordlings', Frank Ellinger to whom she is attracted and Ivy Peters on whom she depends financially, while Niel (a variant on Nigel, 'champion') is only a would-be chivalric saviour of the lost lady, unable as adolescent in Part 1, or young man in Part 2, to cope with this sexual degradation. Niel's only half-realised potential for feudal service alerts us to Cather's adaptation of the medieval myth of Sherwood.[44] The *locus amoenus* is the Forrester place, with its charming grove a miniature greenwood. The Forresters ('foresters' are early American pioneers) recall Robin Hood and Maid Marian (Tennyson's romantic Sherwood comedy of 1881 was called *The Forresters*). The aged Robin, Daniel Forrester, is a tree-like survivor of a Golden Age, and Niel, as his name implies, is only half the man, son-like aspirant to the role of Marian's guardian. Cather not only recasts the myth to aggrandise her Western fable about the end of a heroic era in national development (the Captain's vision, courage, courtesy and selfless generosity toward those for whom he feels responsible, grant him Robin's mythic status), but appropriating the male (epic) genre, refocuses the material from a feminine perspective. Marian, known variously as Maidy, Maid Marian, Lady Forrester, finds herself as she ages unable to keep to the script, implicit in the names, that she is the chaste heroine of a Victorian version of the romance. Niel's eloquent, misplaced demand that she resolve her paradoxes (both attentive wife and sensuous adulteress, gracious society hostess and at ease with simple country boys, a stylish charming woman ruthless in her struggle to survive), is rejected, and the chivalrous male text of the pastoral lady, Niel's 'bright impersonal memory' of the safely dead, is deconstructed by the elusive quality of her superior vitality: 'She mocked outrageously at the proprieties she observed, and inherited the magic contradictions.'[45]

Julian Moynihan has argued provocatively that it is a 'maiden-cult' that best focuses the pastoralism of British nineteenth-century novels, that the renaturing of a society whose values were invested in the 'permanent tradition of the country' but under threat from industrialisation, urbanism and plutocracy, is regularly symbolised in the 'caring for young ladies' from Jane Austen to the end of the line in *Lady Chatterley's Lover*, 'the essential post-war pastoral novel'.[46] Since Henry James's Isabel Archer is a major example it may well be that American novelists working along Jamesian lines may furnish corresponsive cases (Edith Wharton, Willa Cather, Scott Fitzgerald, for instance). In this context, *A Lost Lady* may be compared with a British novel: L.P. Hartley's *The Go-Between* (1953), in which, in the spirit of Moynihan's later examples, the 'sentimental notion of maiden rescue' is critically revised. Both books come at this through the now familiar Sherwood mythology.

The Go-Between tells how Leo Colston is traumatised for fifty years by his exposure as a thirteen-year-old to the lovemaking of his adored Marian Maudsley (an heiress about to marry a lord) and Ted Burgess (a local farmer), when on a summer visit to Brandham Hall, the Maudsley's country estate. The older Leo, as first-person narrator, refracts his experience through the extravagant symbolisations of the child, whose mythopoetic imagination, reading his new acquaintances through the idealising lens of the Zodiac, is strikingly coloured by the Robin Hood legend. The identification of himself with Robin, and so Marian (Virgo) with the Maid, is suggested to him by her purchase for him of a Lincoln green summer suit. His happy elaboration of the association enables Marian to exploit him as a messenger between her and Ted. Leo's green rebirth in the summer heat of 1900 (the past as a country promising a Golden Age) seems idyllic, but his self-conception as a servant to Our Lady is betrayed, his sexual and emotional being ruined, until in his sixties he is granted a 'joyful resurrection' through restored memory and a final 'errand of love' on behalf of Marian.[47]

Both Marians, misconstrued by their romantic rescuers, elicit ambivalent responses as 'fake' maidens whose survivals are morally dubious (Cather's departs and marries a rich protector, Hartley's bears Ted's child and marries her lord). But the titles confirm divergent interests: Cather's in the Lady, Hartley's in the Child. Cather, unresponsive to Freudian theory and treating Niel as androgynous convenience, lays very little stress on Marian's psychosexual impact on his development. Hartley almost melodramatically foregrounds the lifetime's damage done to amnesiac Leo and the Oedipal romance of Leo's ambivalence toward Ted and Marian as surrogate father and mother figures. But both novelists combine the 'Maiden-cult' pastoral with what Moynihan has tried to displace, 'The Child as Swain'. Hartley's expatiation on a short phase of his hero's childhood, his accent on the 'immunities of childhood', betokens a British obsession; while Cather, moving her equivalent character from childhood to the edge of manhood, puts American emphasis on the adolescent.[48] Furthermore, Cather's pastoral is not really about property, material inheritance, the typically British kinds of continuity: the Forrester place as architecture is not impressive and the Forresters are childless. Leo's reviving errand to ensure the continuance of the aristocratic line and his final symbolic re-viewing of the 'imposing facade' of Brandham Hall betray a British nostalgia apt to the time of writing, when the fate of country houses and estates was uncertain (before the National Trust had enabled the survival of so many); its immoderate expression had appeared already in the lushly elegiac Arcadianism of Evelyn Waugh's *Brideshead Revisited* (1945).

IT IS A MYTH BASED ON HIDING . . .

As a messenger, Leo is entrusted with secrets, but his secretiveness goes deeper than that: from keeping to himself his Robin Hood fantasy to the discovery of his diary of the 'past, lost self' he had been representing for years. This dwelling on secrecy harks back to the preoccupations of Forster and Lawrence with desire driven underground. The British passion for secrets is reflected most blatantly in its penchant for the spy story and thriller (the world of John Le Carré and Graham Greene). But John Fowles is the most notable recent contributor to what might be called a pastoral of secrecy, whose hero is Robin Hood.[49]

In an early essay, 'On Being English and Not British', Fowles launched a myth of the secret self.[50] Distinguishing Red-White-and-Blue Britain (a political concept) from Green England (a moral one), he attributed to the latter a mania for justice, with an archetypal hero in the Just Outlaw like Robin Hood (always in revolt, never in power). Now our trees have gone, the greenwood is a mental retreat, a mask of reticence or distracting manner that preserves the hidden authentically free life. A variant of the theory forms part of the half-serious meditations of the eponymous hero of *Daniel Martin* (1977).[51] As a cultural theory it soon attracted scorn: 'This Robin Hoodism business is something of an *idée fixe* with Fowles . . . [and in *Daniel Martin*;] one finds particularly trying the attempt to impose a personal fantasy on the national psyche.'[52] Yet this is to ignore the ways in which many British writers of the period have plundered the same store for cognate if not identical purposes. The eccentricity is common.[53]

The title story of Fowles's collection *The Ebony Tower* will exemplify his pastoral exploitation of the myth. A more realistic, scaled-down version of *The Magus* (1965; revised 1977), it repeats the romance pattern of a man's quest in a secret Edenic place for freedom dependent on a mysterious beautiful woman. David Williams, Op artist and art critic, comes to remote Brittany to interview in his forest-shrouded domain the rogue expatriate Henry Breasley, Grand Old Man of British art. Breasley, another of Fowles's magus-mentors, seems to David the green man in disguise, 'The wily old outlaw hiding behind the flamboyant screen of his outrageous behaviour'; behind 'his cosmopolitan influences' he was 'perhaps as simply and inalienably native as Robin Hood'. The 'surface wildness' of his affected mannerisms allows his 'real self to run free' and be creative. The *locus amoenus* of his manoir satisfies 'the old need to escape from the city, for a mysterious remoteness'[54] and associates aesthetic production with sensual freedom embodied in Breasley's attendant nymphs Diana (the Mouse) and Ann (The Freak). The paradoxes of Breasley and his earthly paradise are insinuated in its name: Coëtminais, literally translated as 'forest of monks', but punningly construable as 'forest of coitus', artistic dedication and erotic inspiration conjoined.[55] Breasley's Mouse (his Muse, as he crudely jests, with a hole in it) is aptly Diana of the forest-hunt, the moon pervading his great paintings of *The Moon Hunt*, Marian to his Robin. Exposure to Breasley's anti-establishment stance and anti-abstractionist aesthetic combines with the temptation of the romantic Diana to leave David still unable to break free of safe art and safe marriage. Alienated from the 'passion to exist' he perceives in the old man's creative individualism and the woman's sexual independence, he has only this momentary sight of 'his lost true self'.[56] Behind his woodland romance, Fowles draws again on pastorally familiar archetypes, of a static Adam, resistant to change, and a vital, dynamic Eve.[57] But this valorisation of the feminine collapses his protofeminism into an essentialising of sexual identities that blocks the radical transformation of his male protagonists. He repeatedly projects in his idyllic secret places, with psychoanalytic self-consciousness now, sites of the longed-for return to 'the lost sense of self and unity embodied in the mother figure'.[58] But here the maternal pleasance is presided over by the dangerously phallocratic father-figure (inherited perhaps from Lawrence). In the neighbourhood of Breasley, David is under a spell: just as he frames pictures of his experience in terms sympathetic to Breasley's art, he is afflicted with 'primeval male longing', rape-urges alien to his reason. Breasley now looks more like Pan: comic at first, 'a smiling old satyr in carpet slippers' presiding over a *déjeuner sur l'herbe* 'with a raffish old wide-brimmed panama hat on his head' (Pan-ama?); but darker aspected, in his Hitlerish appearance, his reactionary extremes, his manipulation of the devotion of his 'nurses'. Once more the refugee Robin is dubiously conflated with priapic Pan.[59]

LIKE ALL GREEKS HE WANTED TO GO TO AMERICA[60]

Just as Pan is rarely exploited in contemporary British fiction, so Robin Hood only occasionally figures in adult American literature.[61] He makes a guest appearance in Peter S. Beagle's Thurberish fantasy *The Last Unicorn* in 1968, but has made more impact in the movies; the latest version, Kevin Costner's

Robin Hood, Prince of Thieves (1991), keeps up the American cinematic tradition of completely ahistorical fantasy, gestural political topicality (post-Vietnam), and minute shifts in the sexual politics (Marian fights a little, is allowed a giggly Lawrentian vision of Robin bathing in the nude). The burgeoning of American Pans since the liberalising sixties may have something to do with Raymond M. Olderman's claim that sex became 'fabulous' in the last decade, that is, grotesque or comically absurd.[62] He cites John Barth's *Giles Goat-Boy* (1966), probably the weirdest re-formation of the Pan–satyr figure in American fiction since the hero is half-goat and half-machine, but the Pan inspiration is lost to view in the baroque overlay of mythic resonances and farcical excursions. Since the sixties too, pastoral fictions, with an occasional reversion to realism like John Gardner's *Nickel Mountain*, have been 'fabulations': self-consciously shaped, artfully textured, preoccupied with ideas.[63] Many are also *satyrical* invoking a typology of satyrs and fauns and mocking or countering traditional bucolic solemnities. I want to draw attention to three diverse instances of these postmodernist Panic pastorals, where, more exuberantly and inventively than their English counterparts, they explore the new world, if not of authentic sexual freedom, then some prodigious discourse of sex.[64]

Tom Robbins's cult 'serio-comic novels' (his own term)[65] are counter-cultural after-images of the sixties and his revival of Pan in three books is done with Beat playfulness and equivocal missionary intent. In *Another Roadside Attraction* (1971), a sceptical drop-out dreams that Tarzan, a goat-riding harmonica-playing hippie champions the displaced Pan's union of flesh and spirit against the supplanting Jesus's patriarchal moralism. In *Even Cowgirls Get the Blues* (1976), Pan is reincarnated in pastoral space in Montana as 'The Chink' or the 'old goat', a cackling hermit-guru, who seducing the picaresque heroine Sissy, instructs her in Oriental philosophy and the history of Pan (a bawdy goat-man identified with Krishna and misread by Christians as the Devil).[66] *Jitterbug Perfume* (1984) tells of a search for an immortalising perfume involving the transportation of Pan himself, still conventionally sensual but in a stinking decline since the Christian triumph, to America to found 'a new Arkadia'. By the end Wiggs Dannyboy, an 'electronic shaman' resembling Timothy Leary, has a pastoral vision of evolution out of old reptilian and animal consciousness (Pan) into new floral consciousness (Jesus and Buddha) and so into a new Golden Age.[67]

Far from this whimsical knockabout is John Hawkes's ornately poetic Arcadia. *The Blood Oranges* (1971) is set in Illyria, passably a southern European resort where two middle-aged American expatriate couples summer in idleness, allusively the imaginative world of *Twelfth Night*. 'Illyria' confounds Elysium and delirium as Hawkes mixes his erotic idyll with Gothic fantasy. The first-person narrator Cyril, self-styled 'sex-singer', is a 'pastoral person' (Shakespeare's Feste, the lyric shepherd, a satyr) who projects in the idealising terms of 'idyll', 'faun', 'sylvan', etc., an experiment in open marriage, involving his own adultery with Catherine and his endeavours to make her husband Hugh sleep with Cyril's wife Fiona. But Hugh, Cyril's antithesis, as a crippled voyeurist and autoeroticist (Malvolio, Christ, St Peter), is reluctant to comply. The book is a half-comic, half-sinister Nabokovian study in solipsism, in which Cyril, a preening male chauvinist trying to camouflage his sexual imperialism by compelling others into 'sexual extension', ends up as a dispossessed Pan, having helped to bring about the death of Hugh, his wife's desertion, his mistress's trauma, with only his 'song' to console him.[68]

Cyril questionably sees himself as a man of 'sensuous rationality',[69] but this is a better description of Guy Davenport and his narrators, including Adriaan van Hovendaal, a Dutch Epicurean philosopher instinct with Whitmanian pansexualism.[70] For if Hawkes is possessed by the spirit of de Sade, Davenport's Gallic affinity is with Charles Fourier, the nineteenth-century French socialist who dreamed of New Harmony, a wonderfully systematised world of co-operative labour and commitment to play pitted against the decadent 'civilisation' of his day.[71] 'Apples and Pears' (1984), Davenport's only novel-length fiction, starts from reflection on Fourier's hoped-for restoration of the Golden Age: 'In our time we long not for a lost past but for a lost future.'[72] Davenport, too, creates Arcadian Utopias; in a brilliantly pictorial style (he interleaves his own graphic art), he aims 'to paint one perfect pastoral landscape with figures, an eclogue',[73] and draws heavily on the traditional classical pastoral lexicon: Adriaan in 'Apples and Pears', for instance is a flute-playing hedonistic bisexual Pan.[74] His Fourier-coloured experiment with the tribal family and sexual licence is, however, relocated in a Northern Europe of the mind, more tolerant of sexual diversity than – implicitly – puritan America. At the core of the book, effectively Adriaan's part-analytic, part-narrative journals, is his 'complex friendship' with his protegé Sander, a beautiful young artist. Socratic at first, with Adriaan as intellectual, aesthetic and sexual mentor, the relationship expands benignly into bizarre permutations of homo- and hetero-eroticism, to include Sander's sister Grietje and numerous adopted ephebes in the rapturously happy libertarian household of an 'outlaw family'.[75] It is perhaps the most extraordinary pastoral of happiness ever, revelling in masturbation, exposed genitalia, complaisant minors, and athletic congress (although there is a strange coyness about sodomy and lesbian sex), and the domain of Pan, verging on a paedophiliac Utopia, is celebrated in a style, rich in intertextuality, aureate diction, and urbane self-consciousness, that strenuously, grotesquely, Americanly, strives toward a new 'ceremony of innocence'.

NOTES

1. 'Maria Edgeworth's Notes for Essay on the Genius and Style of Burke', quoted in Appendix III, Maria Edgeworth, *The Absentee*, (ed.) W.J. McCormack and Kim Walker (Oxford, 1988), p. 282.

2. Bret Easton Ellis, *American Psycho* (London, 1991), p. 263.

3. Patricia Merivale's *Pan the Goat-God: His Myth in Modern Times* (Cambridge, Mass., 1969) is the classic thematological study to which I am deeply indebted. But its focus is on the period 1890–1926 only, and it is too restrictive in its interpretation of allusion.

4. Edward D. McDonald (ed.), *Phoenix: The Posthumous Papers of D.H. Lawrence* (London, 1936), pp. 22–31. (pp. 22, 23).

5. Peter V. Marinelli, *Pastoral* (London, 1971), p. 3.

6. Edward L. Ruhe, 'Pastoral Paradigms and Displacements With Some Proposals', in Richard F. Hardin (ed.), *Survivals of Pastoral* (Lawrence, Kansas, 1979), pp. 103–50. (p. 122).

7. Marinelli, op. cit., p. 9.

8. Beryl Bainbridge, *Sweet William* (London, 1975), p. 48.

9. See Michael Squires, *The Pastoral Novel: Studies in George Eliot, Thomas Hardy and D.H. Lawrence* (Charlottesville, Virginia., 1974) and Shelagh Hunter, *Victorian Idyllic Fiction: Pastoral Strategies* (London, 1984).

10. See Iain Chambers, *Popular Culture: The Metropolitan Experience* and *Border Dialogues: Journeys into Postmodernism* (London, 1990).

11. Raphael Samuel, 'Little Englandism To-day', *New Statesman and Society* (21 October 1988): 27–30.

12. Leo Marx, 'The Puzzle of Anti-Urbanism in Classic American Literature', in *Literature and the American Urban Experience: Essays on the City and Literature*, (ed.) Michael C. Jaye and Ann Chalmers Watts (Manchester, 1981), pp. 63–80. (p. 78). Corrective to Marx's classic *The Machine in the Garden* (New York, 1964) are Annette Kolodny's feminist readings of American pastoralism in *The Lay of the Land* (Chapel Hill, 1975) and *The Land Before Her* (Chapel Hill, 1984).

13. See Thomas Hinde, *Forests of Britain* (London, 1985) and contrast Max Oehlschlaeger, *The Idea of Wilderness* (New Haven, Connecticut, 1991).

14. On British tree-worship, see Kim Taplin, *Tongues in Trees* (Hartland, 1989).

15. Michael Williams, *Americans and Their Forest: A Historical Geography* (Cambridge, 1989), p. 9.

16. Frederick Jackson Turner, *The Frontier in American History* (New York, 1962), p. 293.

17. Edward Abbey, *The Monkey Wrench Gang* (1975; London, 1978). 'Ecotage' is the Luddite activity of militant American environmentalists.

18. Angela Carter, *Black Venus* (London, 1985), pp. 68, 70.

19. Merivale, op. cit. p. 227. He is, however, son of Hermes, the trickster god having strong associations with Eros and theft.

20. Ibid., Chapter 6, 'Culminations: D.H. Lawrence', p. 226.

21. R.B. Dobson and J. Taylor, *Rymes of Robyn Hood: An Introduction to the English Outlaw* (London, 1976), p. 58.

22. Ibid.

23. For a useful distinction between 'masculine' ('masculinity') and 'masculinist' ('masculinism'), see Arthur Brittan, *Masculinity and Power* (London, 1989). The former refers to aspects of men's behaviour that fluctuate over time, the latter to the idea of a male essence, something innate.

24. But Alan Wilde in 'The Naturalisation of Eden' (in *E.M. Forster: A Human Exploration: Centenary Essays*, (ed.) G.K. Das and John Beer, London, 1979, pp. 196–207) argues cogently for a subtly extended presence of an ambiguous Pan throughout Forster, without, however, correlating this with the Robin Hood myth in *Maurice*.

25. *Maurice* (Harmondsworth, 1972), pp. 120, 187–8, 192. Forster associates their love with Pan only in suggesting that their sexual union has exposed them to fear, fear that breaks down and opens up the old self: 'Physical love means reaction, being *panic* in essence . . .' (p. 198; my italics).

26. Leo Marx, *The Machine in the Garden*, p. 363. Simple, or sentimental pastoralism, normally defines itself by the absence of any return from the retreat from civilisation.

27. E.M. Forster, *Maurice*, p. 221. For *patria*, see the Introduction to this volume, p. 6. The ritual of male bonding in the woods belongs to the homo-eroticism of the masculinist adventures into the wilderness of classic American literature as influentially analysed by Leslie. A. Fiedler in *Love and Death in the American Novel* (New York, 1960; rev. edn, 1966). But, for all the 'Whitmannic' influence on Forster, his idyll is culturally different: openly homosexual, not taking place on any plausible Frontier (which the empire could have afforded), and is across class rather than race.

28. *Maurice*, p. 221.

29. D.H. Lawrence, *The White Peacock* (Harmondsworth, 1987), p. 189.

30. Richard Jefferies, *The Gamekeeper at Home* (Oxford, 1979), p. 12.

31. *The White Peacock*, p. 208.

32. D.H. Lawrence, *Lady Chatterley's Lover* (Harmondsworth, 1990), on pp. 46, 44.

33. 'Pastoral oasis' is Renato Poggioli's term for a pastoral episode within another genre, say, epic: 'The Oaten Flute', *Harvard Library Bulletin* XI (1957): 147–84. See *Women in Love* (Harmondsworth, 1989), Chapter 23 'Excurse', pp. 402–3. Cf. John Alcorn in *The Nature Novel From Hardy to Lawrence* (New York, 1977, p. 97): 'Birkin has at last located the modern English Eden: it is the forest home of the pastoral ballad hero-rebel, Robin Hood.'

34. 'A Ruthless Frontiersman of Literature', review of *The Letters of D.H. Lawrence: Vol. 7* and two critical studies, *THES* (14 December, 1979): 15.

35. *The First Lady Chatterley* (Harmondsworth, 1973), p. 42; *John Thomas and Lady Jane* (Harmondsworth, 1973), p. 92; *Lady Chatterley's Lover*, p. 91. On the relations among the three versions, see Michael Squires, *The Creation of 'Lady Chatterley's Lover'* (Baltimore, 1983) and Derek Britton, *'Lady Chatterley': The Making of a Novel* (London, 1988). I concentrate on the final version as the fullest, more ambitious exploration of the classic Lawrentian themes.

36. The patriotic dimension is notably exhibited in Connie's much-quoted drive through the mining district (Chapter 11), where 'one England blots out another' and only remnants of 'the England of Robin Hood' can be glimpsed (op. cit., pp. 162–3).

37. Ibid., pp. 144.

38. Lawrence further identifies the revelatory goal of the novel with the eroticised landscape (the spring, the secret places): 'for it's in the *passional* secret places of life, above all, that the tide of sensitive awareness needs to ebb and flow' (Ibid, p. 105).

39. Renato Poggioli, 'The Oaten Flute', op. cit., p. 160.

40. *Lady Chatterley's Lover*, p. 258.

41. Ibid., p. 126.

42. *Letters of America by Rupert Brooke*. With a preface by Henry James (London, 1916), Letter 13, p. 155.

43. On Cather's adaptation of Heine's idea of pagan deities living in disguise among ordinary people to Virgilian myth, see Bernice Slote(ed.), *The Kingdom of Art: Willa Cather's First Principles and Critical Statements, 1893–1896* (Lincoln, Nebraska: 1966), pp. 101–2.

44. For more detail about this pastoral model, see Hermione Lee's first-rate study, *Willa Cather: A Life Saved Up* (London, 1989), pp. 202–4.

45. *A Lost Lady* (London, 1980), pp. 174, 75.

46. Julian Moynihan, 'Pastoralism as Culture and Counter-Culture in English Fiction 1800–1928: From A View to a Death', *Novel* VI, no. 1 (Fall, 1972), pp. 20–35. Moynihan is taking issue with William Empson's fifth chapter to *Some Versions of Pastoral* on *Alice in Wonderland* as 'The Child as Swain', which puts the emphasis on childhood rather than maidenhood as the thematic preoccupation of nineteenth-century pastoral.

47. *The Go-Between* (Harmondsworth 1953), pp. 270, 279.

48. Ibid., p. 146. This contrast between British nostalgia for childhood and American nostalgia for adolescence is supported by Jasper Griffin in a review of two books on childhood in Classical Athens and the Roman Empire: see 'Ancient Kids', *New York Review of Books* (25 October 1990): 20.

49. John Fowles, *Daniel Martin* (St Albans, 1978), p. 289.

50. *Texas Quarterly* VII, nos 3–4 (Autumn 1964): 154–62.

51. *Daniel Martin*, 'The Sacred Combe', pp. 289–96. Compare also Fowles's theorising in *The Tree* (1979; St Albans, 1992) on the Green Man.

52. Kerry McSweeney, *Four Contemporary Novelists: Angus Wilson, Brian Moore, John Fowles, V.S. Naipaul* (Kingston and Montreal, 1983), pp. 146–7.

53. See Alan Sillitoe, *The Death of William Posters* (London, 1965) and *Raw Material* (London, 1982). Both link Robin Hood to General Ludd, as do Andrew Sinclair in his *Albion Trilogy* (*Gog, Magog, King Ludd*, London, 1967, 1972, 1988) and Peter Vansittart in *The Death of Robin Hood* (London, 1981). See, too, David Storey's play *The Restoration of Arnold Middleton* (London, 1967), Robert Holdstock's *Mythago Wood* (London, 1984) and David Pownall's *The White Cutter* (London, 1988).

54. *The Ebony Tower* (St Albans, 1975), pp. 83, 82, 77. Cf. Fowles's vision of the artist as 'the "green man" hidden in the leaves of his or her unique and once-only being'. *The Tree*, op. cit., p. 47.

55. *The Tree*, p. 63, Fowles sees woods as erotic because they are 'places that isolate and hide'.

56. *The Ebony Tower*, pp. 103, 111.

57. John Fowles, *The Aristos* (London, 1965; rev. edn 1968), 'Adam and Eve', pp. 165–6.

58. Fowles, quoted in Bruce Woodcock, *Male Mythologies: John Fowles and Masculinity* (Brighton, 1984), p. 78.

59. *The Ebony Tower*, pp. 76, 57. The conflation goes back to the seventeenth-century association of Pan, Fauns and Satyrs with Robin Goodfellows. See Merivale, op. cit., p. 246, n. 65.

60. Ernest Hemingway, *In Our Time* (New York, 1925), the last line.

61. Merivale (op cit., pp. 221–1) finds only Lawrence Durrell of interest here among British contemporary novelists.

62. Raymond M. Olderman, *Beyond the Waste Land: A Study of the American Novel in the Nineteen-Sixties* (New Haven, Connecticut, 1972), p. 20.

63. Robert Scholes's term, launched in *The Fabulators* (London, 1967), p. 12.

64. See Michael Foucault's argument in Vol. 1 of *The History of Sexuality: An Introduction* (Harmondsworth, 1990) against the commonly received ideas of 'Victorian' repression and 'modern' liberation, and for recognition of an extended 'putting into discourse of sex'.

65. Quoted in *Contemporary Novelists*, 5th Edition, ed. Lesley Henderson (Chicago and London, 1991), p. 771.

66. *Even Cowgirls Get the Blues* (London, 1991), pp. 231–2.

67. *Jitterbug Perfume* (London, 1991), pp. 166, 320–6. Robbins's books revert to Lawrence's point in 'Pan in America', that Pan is associated with the new land and the Indian as most closely identified with its chthonic energies.

68. *The Blood Oranges* (London, 1971), pp. 3, 183, 147. Cyril's identification of Hugh

as Pan (p. 182) is ironic; it is Cyril who welcomes the role of satyr (p. 150), but this is for his wife who regularly calls him 'baby'. Hawkes evidently takes Cyril more seriously in his own comments upon the novel.

69. Ibid, p. 203.

70. Adriaan, Davenport's *alter ego*, appears in other stories. Davenport explains his symbolic name in 'Ernst Machs Max Ernst', in *The Geography of the Imagination: Forty Essays* (London, 1984), p. 381: 'Hadrian, the garden-keeper, i.e. *Epikouros.*'

71. On Davenport's extensive reference to Fourier, see Bruce Bawer, 'The Stories of Guy Davenport: Fiction à la Fourier', *The New Criterion* 3, No. 4 (1984): 8–14.

72. *Apples and Pears*, op. cit., p. 63.

73. 'On Some Lines of Virgil', *Eclogues: Eight Stories* (1989; London, 1984), p. 232.

74. *Apples and Pears*, p. 128. Davenport's Arcadians may recall the late nineteenth-century use of 'Arcadian' for homosexual which hovers over British pastorals by men from Forster to Waugh. See Brian Reade, *Male Homosexuality in English Literature from 1850 to 1900* (New York, 1971), p. 8.

75. *Apples and Pears*, pp. 63, 283.

FURTHER READING

Arthur Brittan, *Masculinity and Power* (London, 1988).

R.B. Dobson and J. Taylor, *Rymes of Robyn Hood: An Introduction to the English Outlaw* (London, 1976).

Richard F. Hardin (ed.), *Survivals of Pastoral* (Lawrence, Kansas, 1979).

Annette Kolodny, *The Lay of the Land: Metaphor as Experience and History in American Life and Letters* (Chapel Hill, 1975).

Peter V. Marinelli, *Pastoral* (London, 1971).

Leo Marx, *The Machine in the Garden: Technology and the Pastoral Ideal* (New York, 1964).

Patricia Merivale, *Pan the Goat-God: His Myth in Modern Times* (Cambridge, Mass., 1969).

CHAPTER SIXTEEN

The City In Contemporary Women's Fiction

Paulina Palmer

INTRODUCTION

Life in the modern city, as feminist critics and writers illustrate,[1] confronts women with a number of problems and contradictions. On the one hand, it offers them an escape from the confines of the family unit and the restrictions of the domestic role by giving them scope for paid employment, 'anonymous wandering and sexual freedom'.[2] On the other, however, it carries risks of poverty, sexual exploitation and loneliness. The fact that urban institutions and social structures are male-defined and dominated creates a major barrier to female fulfilment and success. While free to take advantage of the opportunities for education and employment which the city provides, women are frequently excluded from full participation in public life. Having achieved a degree of autonomy and independence, they find themselves in the frustrating situation of being barred entry into the higher echelons of politics and business, those twin bastions of patriarchal power.

Contemporary American and British women writers, in representing the city in novels and stories, explore these problems and contradictions in a variety of different ways. A passage from an essay by Marge Piercy highlights the prominence which the motif assumes in their work, while also pinpointing some of the different modes and approaches (quasi-documentary, historical or speculative) which they employ. Piercy observes that:

> Fiction builds us alternative cities superimposed on the city whose streets we walk or drive. Some of these paper cities seem close to our own, evoking the pleasures of reading a story set in a Boston you remember, or an Upper West Side of Manhattan you live in. But some of these cities are exotic, threatening, enticing – cities of the dead and cities of the unborn.[3]

The different perspectives on the city which, as Piercy points out, women writers adopt, reflect, of course, the proliferation of discourses treating urban issues which is a feature of modern culture. In the past thirty years or so the city has become the focus of a notable amount of debate and controversy in the United Kingdom and North America. Town-planners, architects and community-action groups, along with feminists and postmodernist theorists, have contributed to this exchange of ideas.[4] The commentaries on urban life and institutions which they have produced provide the context for and in some cases, as we shall see, directly influence the works of American and British fiction reviewed in this essay.

Three different approaches to the city are discernible in contemporary women's fiction. The American Marge Piercy, the British Zoë Fairbairns and other writers who employ the realist mode concentrate on exploring from an explicitly feminist point of view the material and social aspects of urban life. Appropriating feminist theoretical analyses of the hazards which women encounter in an urban environment, such as poverty, homelessness and incidents of male violence, they foreground in their novels the physical and economic struggles women wage to survive. The city functions in their fiction as a key site of feminist struggle. It represents, in fact, a contested space which women strive to claim and win from the forces of patriarchy.

Very different from the fiction of Piercy and Fairbairns, with its emphatically social slant, are novels by the American Phyllis Burke and Andrea Dworkin, and the British Angela Carter and Jeanette Winterson. The fiction of the last four writers may be loosely termed 'postmodernist' in character. By experimenting with genre and style, they advertise both the fictionality of the texts they create and their strongly ideological focus. The images of the city which appear in the works of these writers, while differing in many respects, reveal certain common features. All four, as well as projecting a view of identity and culture as 'construct' or 'process', display an interest in the parodic reworking and 'recycling'[5] of motifs from earlier texts. They also explore and rehabilitate the history of ethnic minorities and underprivileged sections of the community. The images of the city they create are, in some cases, based on urban scenes with which we are familiar. In other cases, they are, to quote Piercy, 'exotic', taking the form of 'cities of the dead and cities of the unborn'.

Lesbian fiction produced in the United Kingdom and North America illustrates yet a third approach to the city which contemporary women writers adopt. Examples include novels by Sally Gearhart and Anna Wilson, which rework from a lesbian feminist perspective the traditional motif of the polarity between city and country; and contributions to the genre of lesbian crime fiction by Rebecca O'Rourke and Mary Wings. Writers of lesbian fiction, both British and American, display an exceptionally acute awareness of the interplay of danger and pleasure which city life holds for women. While depicting the depressing and violent aspects of urban existence, they also give an affirmative account of the social and economic independence which an urban environment can allow. Representations of the city in lesbian fiction are, in fact, remarkably eclectic and diverse. They illustrate many of the formal and stylistic approaches cited above. Wilson and O'Rourke employ the realist mode, Gearhart experiments with utopian fiction, while Wings adopts a postmodernist stance.

As we shall see, interesting differences emerge between the treatment of urban themes in American and British fiction. American writers maintain on the whole a tension between the positive representation of the city as a place of opportunity for women and the negative view of it as the site of female oppression and exploitation. British writers, on the contrary, adopt a more negative point of view. They concentrate on describing the grim and disturbing aspects of urban life.[6]

Differences also exist between the particular kinds of feminist perspectives which American and British writers appropriate and reproduce in their novels. American fiction tends to be influenced by radical feminist and cultural feminist attitudes, while its British counterpart frequently reflects a socialist feminist viewpoint.

THE CITY AS THE SITE OF FEMINIST STRUGGLE

Piercy's *Small Changes*, published at the early date of 1973, is one of the first novels to explore women's experience of urban life from the viewpoint of contemporary feminism. Her treatment of the topic inaugurated a tradition, setting the agenda for subsequent works examining women's response to urban institutions and structures. Fiction of this kind includes American novels such as Gloria Naylor's *The Women of Brewster Place* (1980) and Alix Kates Schulman's *On the Stroll* (1981), and British ones such as Zoë Fairbairns's *Benefits* (1979), Pat Barker's *Blow Your House Down* (1984) and Sue Townsend's *Rebuilding Coventry: A Tale of two Cities* (1988).

In depicting the city as the arena of feminist struggle and focusing attention on women's acts of collective resistance to patriarchal power, Piercy, Fairbairns and the other writers cited above are strongly influenced by the feminist movements which originated in the early seventies – the radical feminist and socialist feminist movements in particular.[7] Radical feminist theorists such as Susan Brownmiller[8] and Susan Schechter,[9] concentrating attention on the topics of male violence and the sexual exploitation of women, discuss rape, battery and the prostitution system which operates in many cities. Socialist feminist theorists such as Michèle Barrett[10] and Lynne Segal,[11] on the other hand, explore the social and economic aspects of women's urban situation. As well as investigating women's position in the family and paid employment, they analyse the part which the state plays in regulating women's lives.

Both the radical and the socialist feminist movements, it is important to note, balance their theoretical analyses of women's oppressed and exploited circumstances with an emphasis on practical strategies of survival and resistance. These are generally collective in nature. The setting-up of women's communal houses, rape-crisis centres and refuges for battered women are notable examples. Piercy, Fairbairns and other writers working in the tradition they established appropriate and reproduce the emphasis on practical group activity, as well as the theoretical perspectives, which characterise these movements.

The delineation of the urban environment in Piercy's *Small Changes* and Fairbairns's *Benefits*, the two novels on which I intend to focus, is notable for its immediacy and documentary vivacity. By referring to contemporary urban problems, such as the lack of adequate, reasonably-priced housing, and to controversial features of modern architecture, such as the high-rise tower block, they make their accounts of city life highly topical. The images of Boston and London which they create are easily recognisable, enabling the reader to enjoy the pleasures of identification.

Small Changes is located in the Boston of the sixties. This is, the period of the Sexual Revolution and the so-called 'Permissive Society', the era immediately preceding the advent of the Women's Liberation Movement. As well as describing the excesses of male chauvinism rife in the period, Piercy illustrates how, in response to this oppressive climate, women started to develop strategies of resistance and self-defence.

In the opening chapters of *Small Changes* Boston represents a place of opportunity for the two central characters, Beth and Miriam. Beth, who has working-class roots, has come to the city to escape from a violent marriage and survives financially by taking a job as a secretary at the Massachusetts Institute of Technology (MIT). Miriam, who is middle-class, has the advantage of a university education. As a graduate student in computer science at MIT, she looks forward to economic independence and an intellectually rewarding career.

In portraying Beth's and Miriam's experience of life in Boston, Piercy foregrounds the theme of male dominance. In *Small Changes* she argues persuasively that men dominate the realms of technology and science, denigrating their female colleagues and ridiculing and exploiting the female secretaries. They also control the city's social life. On arrival, Beth quickly perceives that access to companionship and cultural activities depends on her forming a relationship with a man. This is vividly illustrated by an episode in which Tom Ryan, a computer scientist from MIT who has taken her to a film, escorts her on a guided tour of the city:

> After the movie he said, 'Come on, we'll do the guided-tour bit, the Square, Harvard and the environs, walk along the Charles by moonlight, phantom sculling, Georgian brick, etc. You aren't one of those overdelicate females who can't walk on their feet, are you? . . .' He gripped her by the elbow, his fingers like clothespins. Propelled her along. She hardly understood half of what he was saying but he would not let her interrupt for questions. The only pause in the swirl of words was when he chuckled at one of his remarks.[12]

Tom's insensitive and domineering behaviour typifies for Piercy the power which men enjoy in an urban environment. Under the guise of protecting Beth and showing her round, he treats her in an arrogant and patronising manner. He dominates her intellectually and verbally, and (as the 'clothespin' grip he exerts on her arm indicates) even controls her pace and movements.

Whereas the middle-class intellectual Tom is portrayed as dominating the city streets by means of education and verbal articulacy, the working-class hippie Phil, another character whom Beth and Miriam encounter, achieves power by means of brute force and sexual manipulation. This is apparent from an episode in which, feeling disgruntled because the advent of the Women's Movement has made the women in his life less amenable to control, he sits on a street bench contemplating the female pedestrians with an appraising eye. While engaged in this typically male pastime, he remembers an incident in his youth when he and his buddies met in a similar street in order to perpetrate a gang rape.

Piercy interprets the episode of the rape from a radical feminist perspective. She describes it as motivated not by a desire for sexual pleasure or release but by the men's macho determination to prove their virility and achieve a sense of camaraderie. As Phil himself admits, 'It had been a ritual, it was feeling powerful and being men together. . . . Whose idea? Anybody's? The idea belonged to the streets. Pissed on all day in school, they were going to be men that night' (pp. 288, 285). The memory of the incident, combined with the sudden recognition that he is growing old, has a disturbing effect on Phil, making him feel uneasy and insecure. He consoles himself by turning his attention to finding a woman: 'He started looking. It was rule one that you could always find a woman. Men were off at jobs in the daytime but women were around waiting. . . .' (p. 289). The streets, Piercy implies, represent for the predatory male a hunting-ground and place of entertainment, but signify for women a place of victimisation and exploitation.

Male displays of arrogance and aggression, of the kind in which Tom and Phil engage, form the backdrop against which the female characters in the novel strive to resist oppression and forge for themselves a degree of hard-won independence. Their acts of resistance take two different forms – individual and collective. Middle-class Miriam relies on her own personal abilities. Although these initially appear adequate, in the long run they are ineffectual in challenging the chauvinistic climate of city life. Her increasing sexual dependence on men, combined with the unhappy marriage she makes, result in her losing autonomy and self-respect.

The strategy of resistance which Beth adopts is more successful. Recognising the value of collective action, she helps to initiate the women's commune movement. The aim of the communal housing which she and her friends organise is, as she unpretentiously puts it, to provide 'a warm place' for herself and other women to live (p. 262). It offers an alternative form of living structure to both the conventional family unit and the permissive mixed households which flourished in the sixties. These, as she knows from personal experience, often entrap women in a net of sexual exploitation and domestic drudgery.

By the end of the novel Beth has succeeded in achieving not only social independence from men but also sexual independence. She embarks on a lesbian relationship with Wanda, the leader of a feminist theatre troupe, assisting her in the battle she is waging to win custody of her children.

Small Changes, as my discussion of Piercy's treatment of the contrary fortunes of Miriam and Beth indicates, has a symmetry of design and an explicitly ideological focus, which give it the air of a feminist fable. By structuring the novel in this manner, Piercy successfully demonstrates the value of a feminist approach to life, but creates a narrative which appears on occasion simplistic and over-contrived. The novel, though realist in style, aims primarily to instruct the reader in concepts of sexual politics. Like other novels written in a similar mode, it merits, as I argue in greater detail elsewhere,[13] the designation 'fiction of ideas'.

In contrast to Piercy's *Small Changes*, which approaches Boston from a quasi-documentary viewpoint, Fairbairns's *Benefits* depicts London in a futuristic, dystopian light. *Benefits* centres on the imagined attempt made by the right-wing British government to exert control over women's domestic labour and child-bearing capacities by paying them, on a selective basis, a financial 'Benefit'. The scheme as one would expect, has disastrous consequences. A number of women lose their jobs and, as a result, their financial independence. They are driven back into the home – and a predictable escalation in domestic violence occurs. Unlike Piercy, who treats women's oppressed domestic circumstances from a radical feminist perspective, Fairbairns adopts a socialist feminist approach. Whereas Piercy describes women's unpaid labour in the home, such as housework and childcare, as being performed in the service of men, Fairbairns portrays women as carrying out these labours not only for men but also for the state.

At the centre of *Benefits* is the conflict between the London Women's Movement, which seeks to resist the government-imposed Benefit scheme, and the establishment coterie of male politicians and social workers, who wish to enforce it. The key arena of sexual politics in the novel is not, as in Piercy's *Small Changes*, the city street, but that symbol and eyesore of modern urban architecture – the high-rise tower block.

Collindeane Tower, the London tower block in question, assumes a number of different functions and meanings in the course of the novel. Ironically, as Fairbairns remarks in the opening chapter, Collindeane is out of date from the very moment of its construction since it was built at a time when 'planners, builders and social workers were already losing faith in tower blocks'.[14] It stands empty and derelict, a symbol of the failure of the male, middle-class planners and architects to cater for the needs of working-class families.

Collindeane Tower, however, does not stand empty for long. A group of homeless women in search of a place to squat move into it and make it their home. In its newly acquired role of women's commune Collindeane represents an example of creative 'recycling'. 'Recycling' is a concept associated with the culture of the seventies, feminist culture in particular. Marshall Berman defines it as the art of 'finding new meanings and potentialities in old things and forms of life'.[15] This sums up the way the women treat Collindeane. They fill the Tower with sticks of furniture and use it as the basis for a new style of living, one which, though it may strike the outsider as anarchic and structureless, none the less has its own distinctive pattern and rhythm. In providing a focus for the women in the London area, Collindeane fulfils a variety of uses. It functions as a children's nursery and playschool, a refuge for battered women and, as women converge from different areas to challenge the Benefit scheme, a centre of feminist resistance.

Collindeane Tower thus shifts in significance during the course of the novel from being a symbol of the patriarchal mismanagement of the housing situation to one of feminist community. It is increasingly identified with the Women's Movement and the contradictions which the Movement embodies. While the trailing ferns and floral window boxes, which the women introduce to adorn the walls, carry connotations of a peaceful, rural economy, the guard with a leashed dog patrolling the perimeter signifies a state of defence and warfare. 'The notes of music' and 'wail of a baby', described by Fairbairns as emanating from its windows, indicate that it provides a home for different kinds of creativity – cultural as well as biological (p. 73). Though derelict and on the verge of collapse, it successfully withstands the assaults of the elements and the representatives of the patriarchal status quo. It serves as a beacon, both literal and metaphorical, for the women living in the neighbourhood. As one of them observes on approaching, 'The battered old tower was ablaze with lights, winking from behind makeshift curtains and through cracks in the wall' (p. 73).

POSTMODERNIST PERSPECTIVES

The novels by Burke, Dworkin, Carter and Winterson, which I discuss in this section, merit the designation 'Postmodernist' in a number of ways.[16] All four writers, influenced by feminist and psychoanalytic theory, concentrate on denaturalising certain concepts and phenomena, such as femininity, patriarchy and heterosexuality, which have traditionally been seen as natural and unchanging. This focus on denaturalisation is accompanied by the foregrounding of the constructed aspect of sexuality and gender. Emphasis is placed on the fragmented and constructed nature of subjectivity and culture, which are perceived to be in a state of process and flux.

The narrative styles which the four writers employ, though differing considerably, reflect their recognition of the constructed nature of culture and identity. By experimenting with genre, the writers emphasise the fictionality of the text and its ideological focus. They also reveal a preoccupation with parody and pastiche. These features of their texts are more than merely decorative. By reworking imagery and tropes from earlier, more conventional narratives, they both re-evaluate their perspectives and highlight their limitations.

The role which the city plays in the four novels also displays links with Postmodernist and feminist currents of thought. Urban experience is described as epitomising the contradictions of aspiration and disillusion which modern life involves. As Berman cogently remarks, to live in the modern city is 'to find ourselves in an environment that promises us adventure, power, joy, growth, transformation of ourselves and the world – and, at the same time, that threatens to destroy everything we have, everything we know; everything we are.'[17] The city as well as representing a social and architectural construct, signifies to the four writers in economic terms the site of capitalist consumerism and, from an ontological point of view, life as a ceaseless process of change and flux. It also denotes the site of the construction of gender, and the arena in which struggles relating to sexual and racial politics take place.

Burke's *Atomic Candy* (1989) and Dworkin's *Ice and Fire* (1986), the two examples of American Postmodernist fiction which I've chosen to consider, are intriguing texts to compare. Both writers concentrate on re-evaluating a similar period of American history – from the fifties to the eighties. This era holds obvious interest for the woman writer, since it gave rise to a series of rapidly changing social movements, culminating in the advent of contemporary feminism. These include the Civil Rights Movement of the late fifties, the Sexual Revolution and Hippie Movement of the sixties, and the Women's Liberation Movement of the seventies.

In representing American urban life in this period, both Burke and Dworkin focus on particular ethnic sections of the community. Burke concentrates attention on Irish Americans, and Dworkin on Jews and blacks. It is, however, the themes of gender and sexual politics which they chiefly address. A central topic in their novels is the interaction which occurs between the construction of femininity and female sexuality, on the one hand, and urban culture, on the other. This culture, and the materialistic values it embodies, are described as all-encompassing, exerting a stranglehold on the entire globe. In *Atomic Candy*, in fact, they appear to extend beyond the globe, going so far as to pollute the moon. On reporting the landing of the Apollo spacecraft, the TV commentator unexpectedly observes, 'There is a lot of lunar junk up there. Sort of like a big spacecraft wrecking yard. There are also a lot of cupcake liners.'[18] The bounds of American culture are further extended by the naming of a lunar mountain 'Mount Marilyn' in honour of the national sex symbol, Marilyn Monroe!

In depicting American urban life, Burke and Dworkin seek primarily to convey to the reader its fragmented and decentred nature, along with the contrary emotions of excitement, glamour, anxiety and fear which it evokes in the individual. They create sharply etched vignettes of typical urban scenes, such as city streets, restaurants and department stores. Fredric Jameson's description of postmodernist culture as characterised by 'the transformation of reality into images, the fragmentation of time into a series of perpetual presents'[19] is, in different ways, applicable to the styles and perspectives of both writers.

Yet the reader, though aware of certain superficial affinities between the images of city life which Burke and Dworkin create, is chiefly conscious of the differences they display. Burke, taking Boston as her location, gives a humorously satiric exposé of the materialistic values which dominate the lives of the citizens, and the ruthless pursuit of pleasure and power in which they engage. *Atomic Candy* investigates, in fact, a remarkably wide spectrum of society; it interweaves the public events of presidential campaigns with the private lives of call-girls and Woolworth's counter-assistants. Dworkin, in contrast, adopts a radical feminist viewpoint and focuses on a narrower section of the community. Powerfully capturing the desperation of city life, she gives an emotionally raw account of the economic deprivation and the racial and sexual discrimination experienced by the poorer residents of Camden and New York.

The oxymoronic title *Atomic Candy*, which Burke chooses for her novel, signals to the reader the paradoxes of American culture which she examines. The palaces of pleasure which cater for the desires of the consumer society of Boston, such as the Blue Lagoon Club, Filenes Department Store, and the humbler Woolworth's, are built, she illustrates, on foundations that conceal atomic fall-out shelters. The American psyche, she implies, combines the contradictory impulses of a lust for pleasure and power with a terror of imminent destruction. The title *Atomic Candy* also hints, of course, at the paradoxical nature of male images of female sexuality. Female sexual attraction, exemplified in the novel by Marilyn Monroe and her namesake Marilyn Albion, gives rise on occasion to explosive effects. These include not only the pleasures of orgasm but also, as the characters discover to their cost, violent events such as physical assault, mental breakdown and suicide.

The key image which Burke chooses to characterise the city of Boston and the culture it produces is the fake and the synthetic. Synthetic substances form, in fact, a link between different dimensions of life. The products on display at the annual Tupperware party, a major event in the Boston social calendar, are manufactured from plastic, while the breasts of the ladies who sell them, so the rumour goes, are enlarged with silicone. The family-tree of this tickytacky consumer society aptly celebrates the fact that 'Bakelite begat Tenite II, Tenite II begat Lucite, Lucite begat Plexiglas, Plexiglas begat Polystyrene, Polystyrene begat Nylon . . .' (p. 121). Woolworth's functions, literally and symbolically, as the centre of this synthetic culture. Neither the orangeade nor the lemonade sold at its counters, Burke ironically comments, 'have been sullied by real oranges or real lemons' (p. 41). Woolworth's also functions as the site of the construction of femininity and the transformations which it involves. It is here that the young Marilyn Albion, daughter of Joe Albion, the Mayor of Boston, is taught to conquer her guilt-feelings about female vanity and 'to make friends with her reflection'. She also learns from the counter-assistants the fashionable art of 'girl-talk', a style of discourse epitomised by the aphorism 'Beyond good and evil there's a little dab of makeup' (p. 45).

Unlike Burke, who employs imagery of the fake and the synthetic to represent the materialistic, phoney values of American urban culture, Dworkin introduces elemental imagery signifying ideas of contradiction and flux to evoke the atmosphere of the city. The title of her novel *Ice and Fire*, another exercise in oxymoron, represents the extremes of cold and heat which the poorer sections of the population suffer on the streets of Camden and New York. It also signifies the alternating states of drug-induced stupor and sudden eruptions of violence which Dworkin sees as typifying contemporary urban life. Each, she emphasises, is similarly destructive in effect.

Ice and Fire displays as a text certain superficial affinities with the feminist confessional novel popular in the period of the seventies.[20] However, the novel's style and structure are considerably more complex and sophisticated than the format of seventies' confessional fiction. The narrator's subjectivity is portrayed as fractured and decentred, as opposed to unitary. This effect is achieved partly by means of the juxtaposing of her past and present identities, and partly by the frequent shifts of pronoun from 'I' to 'you' to 'we' in certain episodes. While the use of 'you' has the effect of involving the reader in the experiences recounted, and encourages her to identify with them, the use of 'we' transforms the text from a personal, confessional-style narrative to a collective, group account.

The motif of the city is, in fact, integral to the design of *Ice and Fire*, since the various stages of the narrator's life which the novel describes are represented by her encounters with a series of different cities. One of the most original episodes is the account of her childhood in Camden, New Jersey, which occurs in the opening pages. Here Dworkin creates a brilliantly impressionistic description of the city streets, as perceived through the eyes of a child. The streets in the afternoon and early evening, with the women indoors and the men at work, take on the appearance of a vast playground. Engrossed in a game of hide-and-seek, the narrator comments: 'If you were a child, you would see that the adults were far away, and that the streets stretched into a million secret hidden places.'[21]

Dworkin's representation of childhood is notably unsentimental. The games the children play and the activities in which they engage are, she illustrates, by no means innocent but, on the contrary, reflect and reproduce the racial and sexual power-struggles of the adult world. In exploring the streets in the vicinity of her home, the narrator quickly discovers that both the city and her movements within it are covertly mapped and zoned by racial and religious divisions:

> There were Jewish blocks and Catholic blocks and black blocks. We were supposed to stay off the black blocks, though it was never put that way. We were always just showed how to walk, down which streets, and told where not to go, which streets. The streets we weren't supposed to go on just had that in common: black faces, black children . . . (p. 19).

Since the narrator is a rebellious, independent-minded child who, as she admits, 'liked to go where I wasn't supposed to' (p. 19), she initially ignores the rules and prohibitions imposed by these divisions. However, the prejudices engrained in urban culture prove in the long run too strong for her to combat. The friendships which she forms with the Polish Catholic boy Michael and the black girl Nat are disrupted by the ridicule of her peers and the pressure of public opinion.

325

The activities in which the children engage, as well as reflecting racial and religious prejudices and divisions, also reproduce contemporary power relations between the sexes. The terrifying game of 'witch', that they play in the twilit streets of Camden, is a particularly vicious example. It takes the form of a sadistic game of hide-and-seek in which the boys pursue the girls with the aim of capturing them and incarcerating them in a wooden cage. Dworkin pinpoints the double bind in which the girls who participate in the game become entrapped. Though desiring to attract the boys and be pursued, the girls are scared at the prospect of capture and incarceration. If caught, they are reduced to the role of victim, while, if not caught, they are ridiculed and made to feel unattractive and unwanted. This double bind, Dworkin suggests, epitomises the contradictions inherent in woman's position in a patriarchal society.[22]

The narrative strategies which British exponents of Postmodernist fiction, such as Carter and Winterson, employ, differ markedly from those of their American counterparts Burke and Dworkin. Carter and Winterson take as the context of their novels celebrated periods of British history, pictured in the popular imagination as quaint or magnificent, and, by utilising the device of parody, reappraise these periods and the cultural images associated with them. Their approach to history supports Linda Hutcheon's contention that in Postmodernist fiction 'the parodic reprise of the past of art is not nostalgic; it is always critical'.[23] In describing late Victorian London in *Nights at the Circus* (1984), Carter exposes the codes of male dominance and the oppressive stereotypes of womanhood current in the era. Winterson, in representing Elizabeth and Jacobean London in *Sexing the Cherry* (1989), investigates through the experiences of her heroine the Dog Woman the misogynistic fears and fantasies of a phallocentric culture.

Fevvers, the central figure in Carter's *Nights at the Circus*, is a Cockney music-hall entertainer and aerialiste. The pair of wings which she is reputed to possess result in her acquiring the title 'bird woman'. The image of 'bird woman' is by no means unitary in significance but carries a number of contrary meanings. While the female characters interpret it as signifying liberation, the male figures assign to it meanings which are oppressive or exploitative. They celebrate Fevvers on a transcendental level as 'queen of ambiguities' and 'angel of death', but also denigrate her as 'spectacle' and 'freak'.

The contrary images and meanings which in the course of the narrative accrue to Fevvers and her marvellous wings are also applied, it is interesting to note, to the city of London. London, like Fevvers, is identified with entertainment, spectacle and manipulative cunning. It is humorously described as 'a little village on the Thames of which the principal industries are the music hall and the confidence trick'.[24] The questions 'Is she fact or is she fiction? Nature or art?', which people ask about Fevvers, are equally relevant to the city.

The richly baroque imagery which Carter uses to depict London and its buildings strikes the reader on occasion as somewhat bizarre and grotesque. For example, Fevvers describes the dome of St Paul's Cathedral as 'the divine pap of the city, which, for want of any other, I needs must call my natural mother' (p. 36). She proceeds to personify the city as 'London, with one breast, the Amazon Queen' (p. 36). Yet, though from a visual point of view these images appear incongruous, they appropriately highlight the artifice of both urban culture and the fictional text which Carter is creating. They also effectively foreground the feminist perspective which she applies to the city. London, she emphasises, as well as catering for male pleasures with an assortment of clubs, theatres and brothels, is also the birth-place of the Women's Suffrage Movement. Ma Nelson, Fevvers's foster mother, is a staunch feminist, and the brothel where the two women work becomes during the day, in the absence of male clients, a woman's commune, bustling with feminist activity.[25]

Winterson in *Sexing the Cherry* also concentrates on re-evaluating earlier periods of history and on deconstructing the images commonly associated with them. Her delineation of Elizabethan London deflates and undermines the usual romanticised accounts. Instead of presenting the city as quaint or splendid, she focuses on scenes of squalor and violence. As the Dog Woman, a Londoner born and bred, laconically remarks, 'London is a foul place, full of pestilence and rot.'[26]

The Dog Woman is a gloriously exuberant figure; her antecedents include the Baron Munchausen and characters from Rabelaisian fiction. She performs a number of different functions in the novel. She is a vehicle for Winterson's deconstruction of conventional codes of femininity, as well as for the denaturalisation of heterosexual relations. Portrayed as a giantess, she carries out a series of incredible feats. Her exceptional strength and huge stature enable her to toss elephants in the air and to pick up men by the scruff of the neck 'the way a terrier does a rat' (p. 88). Though aware that her height, flat nose and heavy eyebrows are at odds with conventional ideals of female beauty, she none the less prides herself on being built 'in proportion'. A writer with a patriarchal viewpoint would no doubt treat her as the butt of ridicule, but Winterson portrays her in a warmly sympathetic light. The description of the Dog Woman's one and only experience of sexual intercourse, a bizarre event in which her male partner, on account of her enormous size, 'felt like a tadpole in a pot' and is reduced to 'burrowing down the way ferrets do', does not make her look ridiculous (pp. 106–7). On the contrary, it has the effect of defamiliarising the sex act, making it, not her, appear grotesque and absurd. It also cleverly parodies the male fantasy of the vagina dentata.

Winterson's treatment of the motif of the city is, in fact, the most inventive and varied of all the examples discussed in this essay. It illustrates the woman writer's ability, remarked on by Piercy, to create cities which are 'exotic, threatening enticing – cities of the dead and cities of the unborn'.[27] As well as taking as her theme Elizabethan London, Winterson also treats the motif of the city in a symbolic and speculative light. She describes, for example, 'a city of words', a fantasy realm where people move around on tightropes over a bottomless abyss. Employing imagery verging on the Swiftian, she describes how: 'The words [of the inhabitants], rising up, form a thick cloud over the city, which every so often must be thoroughly cleansed of too much language. Men and women in balloons fly up from the main square and, armed with mops and scrubbing brushes, do battle with the canopy of words trapped under the sun' (p. 17). In this passage Winterson wittily parodies the Postmodernist obsession with the problematic nature of language, highlighting the capacity of words to mystify and confuse.

THE CITY IN CONTEMPORARY LESBIAN FICTION

Whether or not lesbianism is a predominantly urban phenomenon is a controversial question. The theorist Elizabeth Wilson describes it – in my opinion erroneously – as the product of city life. Commenting on the emergence of lesbianism in nineteenth-century Paris, she writes:

> The lesbian is an inhabitant of the great cities, first glimpsed by Baudelaire in Paris, 'capital of the nineteenth century' (W. Benjamin, *Baudelaire*, 1973). A new kind of woman emerges from the restless anonymity of the crowds, aloof from the sullen aimless excitement of the thousands that drift along the pavements and surge through the squares, a figure whose mystery and danger is that she is alone. The lesbian stands outside family, yet is not simply a worker. Her sexuality necessarily defines her.[28]

However, although the lesbian 'scene', centering on commercial bars and clubs, is generally located in an urban environment, to identify lesbianism *per se* with 'the great cities', as Wilson does, is to ignore the facts. Lesbian partnerships and social groups flourish not only in the city but also in towns and villages. Moreover, collections of lesbian essays such as the American publication *For Lesbians Only: A Separatist Anthology* (Onlywomen Press, 1988) and the British *Out the Other Side: Contemporary Lesbian Writing* (Virago, 1988) include contributions from country-dwellers as well as city-dwellers. Since women who identify as lesbian are to be found in every occupation, class and age-group, to associate lesbianism with a single environment, whether urban or rural, is clearly incorrect.

When we turn to the topic of lesbian fiction,[29] we find that writers concentrate attention on both the city and the countryside. Frequently they bring together the two locations within a single text, effectively juxtaposing and contrasting them. A number of lesbian novels rework, from an innovatory point of view, the traditional motif of the polarity between city and country. While the images of the city they create tend to be pessimistic, foregrounding oppression and loneliness, their representations of the countryside display significant differences. They vary from idealised vignettes of pastoral happiness to grim delineations of rural hardship and isolation. *The Wanderground* (1985) by the American Sally Gearhart and *Altogether Elsewhere* (1985) by the British Anna Wilson, two novels which link sexual politics to ecological issues, illustrate these two contrary approaches. Gearhart, writing from a cultural feminist viewpoint and employing fantasy, highlights the contrast between urban and rural economies and ways of life. Wilson, on the other hand, combines a radical feminist perspective with a Marxist feminist one, and writes in the realist mode. Emphasising the all-pervasive influence of urban values, she describes the countryside not as separate from the city but as an extension of the capitalist urban economy. By so doing, she deconstructs and collapses the traditionally perceived differences between city and country.

Gearhart's *The Wanderground*,[30] an example of utopian fiction located in an unspecified period in the future, brings together themes of lesbian separatism, women community, and the transformation of male and female consciousness. The novel centres on the adventures of the Hill Women, a group of radical feminists who have moved from the city to the country. They have developed over the years powers of telepathy and telekinesis, and now enjoy the ability to communicate with animals and birds. Their decision to move from an urban to a rural environment was prompted, we are told, by the oppressive and brutal nature of city life. Gearhart draws a stark contrast between the behaviour of the city-dwellers, which is characterised, in the case of both sexes, by violence and competition, and the gentle, caring attitudes prevalent in the country.

The Wanderground has proved exceptionally popular with feminist readers, achieving, in fact, the status of a 'cult novel' in North America and the United Kingdom. In identifying urban culture with violence and death, and portraying women as moving to the countryside to start a new life, Gearhart evidently has her finger on the pulse of contemporary lesbian experience and myth. Some of the autobiographical essays in the American collection *For Lesbians Only*, it is interesting to note, introduce a similar set of themes and even utilise similar imagery. One writer describes how, having encountered incidents of sexual violence, she decided to move from an urban environment because 'I felt like I was dying internally, and that I was going to die, literally, if I continued to stay in the city.'[31] She joins a separatist farming commune and, like the characters in Gearhart's novel, values the experience as 'an act of creating something new' and constructing 'a healing environment for wimmin and the earth' (p. 253).

Wilson's *Altogether Elsewhere* differs radically from Gearhart's novel, since it is realist in style and set in the recent period of the eighties. However, the image of city life which it presents is similarly grim. Taking as her location the London Inner City, Wilson describes in a deliberately minimalist, honed-down style, 'decaying buildings, the city degenerating. Crushed waitresses leaning on smeared tables, people walking the streets without purpose.'[32] *Altogether Elsewhere* focuses on a group of women, some hetero-sexual and other lesbian, who differ in age, race and occupation. Brought together by a desire to challenge male violence, they form themselves into a vigilante group. Under the leadership of the middle-aged Elsie, they patrol the streets at night in pairs, with the aim of protecting women from rape and assault. Wilson rejects the temptation to idealise or sentimentalise women's community. On the contrary, she explores the difficulties which the women, on account of their different backgrounds and ethnic origins, experience in communicating and achieving a sense of unity.

Familiar urban locations such as the public baths, the underpass, the high-rise block of flats and the lesbian bar form an appropriately drab context for the activities of the women. The supermarket alone gleams with lurid, artificial light, its display of goods offering the shopper an illusion of choice and plenty. As Elsie, interpreting the ideological message of the display, bitterly remarks, 'The violent lights and these gigantic bins of produce, they are there to tell us that we live in a sunny, abundant world' (p. 61).

The urban context of *Altogether Elsewhere* is punctured on occasion by the introduction of episodes set on the coast or in the country. However, instead of employing these rural scenes to provide a contrast to and a respite from, the oppressive aspects of city life, Wilson utilises them to highlight the all-pervasive nature of the capitalist urban economy and its depressing effect on the psyche. Sitting on the promenade, gazing listlessly at the sea, Gloria, a young black women burdened with family responsibilities, despondently perceives that 'She is not on holiday, after all. Wherever she goes, she must think the same thoughts' (p. 20).

Elsie's memories of working as a farm-hand in her youth are by no means liberating. She mentally contrasts the optimistic cliché 'Take a breath of fresh air and forget your troubles' (p. 66) with the harsh reality of working on the land. Her memories of farm life consist not of idyllically peaceful landscapes but of 'dry stubborn cows and hay-bales too heavy to life, and plodding home across the fields exhausted')p. 67). Farming in the twentieth century, she recognises, is premised on a 'brutish simplicity' involving the ruthless exploi-tation and destruction of animals. It consists of 'draining cows of milk, of calves, finally of meat, their bodies shoved, impregnated, kicked, transported, sliced' (p. 67).

In representing the brutal nature of the capitalist consumer economy and its oppressive effects, Wilson draws a series of striking analogies between ecological issues and sexual politics. She powerfully compares and contrasts acts of cruelty to animals with male victimisation of women.

A more varied and mixed picture of lesbian urban life than that created by Gearhart and Wilson is provided by a genre of fiction which has become increasingly popular in the eighties and nineties. This is lesbian crime fiction.[33]

The numerous thrillers and detective novels which comprise this genre have provoked controversy among feminists. Critics argue about whether or not lesbian writers succeed in transforming the chauvinistic, patriarchal attitudes and values which characterise the traditional-style thrillers of Raymond Chandler and Dashiell Hammett so that they accord with feminist principles.[34] However, while critics disagree on the perspectives of lesbian crime fiction and its relation to feminist politics, they agree on the vivid and compelling account that it gives of city life.

Writers of lesbian crime fiction, such as the British Rebecca O'Rourke and the American Mary Wings, pinpoint with exceptional acumen the interplay of pleasure and danger which city life holds for women. Their fictional representation of these topics gains strength from the fact that it is based on and reflects the contradictions of lesbian urban life in North America and the United Kingdom today.

An urban environment holds certain obvious attractions for the woman who identifies as lesbian. As well as offering opportunities for paid employment, it affords the protection of sexual anonymity and provides access to a social life focusing on women's centres and on the commercial 'scene' of clubs and bars. Simultaneously, however, it carries prominent risks and dangers. The lesbian, since she lacks male protection and the economic security of marriage, is especially vulnerable to both physical assault and poverty. Her sexual identity, if discovered, makes her a likely target for abuse. It may also result in her losing her job and, if she lives in rented accommodation, in being evicted from her home.

O'Rourke and Wings treat this cluster of topics in very different ways. O'Rourke in *Jumping the Cracks* (1987) focuses on the bleak and depressing aspects of lesbian urban existence. Employing a socialist feminist perspective, she gives a critique of the social injustices which typify life in the United Kingdom. Wings' *She Came Too Late* (1986), on the contrary, reflects a liberal feminist stance. Wings celebrates the pleasures of independence, socialising, and forming personal relationships, which city life affords the lesbian who enjoys a modicum of financial security. The contrasting approaches adopted by the two writers give rise to interesting differences in narrative style. O'Rourke, writing realist fiction, creates a text that offers the reader the pleasure of identification. Wings, on the other hand, by basing the adventures of her sleuth Emma Victor on those of Chandler's Marlowe and parodying Chandler's style, uses Postmodernist conventions to create a brilliantly stylised display of pastiche and wit.

The discussion of lesbian fiction is an appropriate topic with which to conclude this study of the representation of the city in contemporary women's fiction. It brings together some of the different styles and modes of writing, such as realism, fantasy and Postmodernist experimentation with parody and genre, which have been considered separately in earlier pages. It also illustrates certain significant intellectual and ideological differences that exist between British and American approaches to urban issues. O'Rourke's *Jumping the Cracks*, with its focus on unemployment and the tragic decline of the cities in the United Kingdom in the eighties, exemplifies the propensity of British writers to concentrate attention on the grim and oppressive aspects of urban life. Wings's *She Came Too Late*, on the contrary, in celebrating the scope for independence and social exploration, which city life often affords women, typifies the more optimistic viewpoint which American writers tend to adopt. A contrast is also apparent between the socialist feminist perspective employed by O'Rourke and Anna Wilson, and the cultural and liberal feminist perspectives adopted by Gearhart and Wings. These ideological and political differences are, I suggest, not merely personal but reflect the different kinds of feminism which, in the past twenty years, have achieved prominence in the United Kingdom and North America.

The images of women's response to the urban environment which appear in contemporary women's fiction are, in fact, exceptionally varied. They fully match up to the spectrum of approaches and styles described by Piercy, giving rise to the fictional creation of cities which are, to quote her words, 'exotic, threatening, enticing – cities of the dead and cities of the unborn'.

NOTES

1. See Susan Merrill Squier, *Women Writers and the City: Essays in Feminist Literary Criticism* (Knoxville, 1984).

2. Ibid., p. 7.

3. 'The City as Battleground: the Novelist as Combatant', in Michael C. Jaye and Ann Chalmers Watts (eds.), *American Urban Experience: Essays on the City and Literature* (Manchester, 1981), p. 209.

4. Studies of the city include: Marshall Berman, *All that is Solid Melts into Air: the Experience of Modernity* (1982; London, 1983); Malcolm Bradbury, 'The Cities of

Modernism', in Bradbury and James McFarlane (eds), *Modernism: 1890–1930* (Harmondsworth, 1976), pp. 95–104; Mike Davis, 'Urban Renaissance and the Spirit of Postmodernism', in E. Ann Kaplan (ed.), *Postmodernism and its Discontents: Theories and Practice* (London, 1988), pp. 79–87; Jane Jacobs, *The Death and Life of the Great American Cities* (New York, 1961); Jo Little, Linda Peake and Pat Richardson, *Women in Cities: Gender and the Urban Environment* (Basingstoke, 1988).

5. See Berman, *All that is Solid Melts into Air*, op., cit., p. 337.

6. Squier makes a similar distinction in *Women Writers and the City*, op. cit., p. 8.

7. For reference to contemporary feminism and its influence on fiction, see Hester Eisenstein, *Contemporary Feminist Thought* (London, 1984); and Paulina Palmer, *Contemporary Women's Fiction: Narrative Practice and Feminist Theory* (Hemel Hempstead, 1989).

8. *Against Our Will: Men, Women and Rape* (New York, 1975).

9. *Women and Male Violence: The Visions and Struggles of the Battered Women's Movement* (London, 1982).

10. *Women's Oppression Today* (London, 1980).

11. *Is the Future Female? Troubled Thoughts on Contemporary Feminism* (London, 1987).

12. *Small Changes* (New York, 1973), p. 52. Subsequent references are to this Fawcett edition and are in the text.

13. See Palmer, *Contemporary Women's Fiction*, op. cit., pp. 6–11.

14. *Benefits* (London, 1979), p. 3. Subsequent references are to this edition and in the text.

15. *All that is Solid Melts into Air*, op. cit., p. 337.

16. For discussion of Postmodernist fiction, see Hal Foster (ed.), *Postmodern Culture* (London, 1983); Linda Hutcheon, *The Politics of Postmodernism* (London, 1989); Meaghan Morris, *The Pirate's Fiancée: Feminism, Reading, Postmodernism* (London, 1988).

17. Berman, *All that is Solid Melts into Air*, op. cit., p. 15.

18. *Atomic Candy* 1989) (London, 1990), p. 153. Subsequent references are to this Pandora edition and are in the text.

19. 'Postmodernism and Consumer Society', in E. Ann Kaplan, op. cit., p. 28.

20. For reference to the feminist confessional novel, see Elizabeth Wilson, 'Tell it Like it is: Women and Confessional Writing', in Susannah Radstone (ed.), *Sweet Dreams: Sexuality, Gender and Popular Fiction* (London, 1988), pp. 21–45.

21. *Ice and Fire* (London, 1986), p. 9. Subsequent references are to this Secker and Warburg edition and in the text.

22. Dworkin also explores woman's position in a patriarchal society in her theoretical works *Our Blood: Prophesies and Discourses on Sexual Politics* (New York, 1976; London, 1981); and *Pornography: Men Possessing Women* (New York, 1981; London, 1981).

23. Linda Hutcheon, *The Poetics of Postmodernism*, op. cit., p. 93.

24. *Nights at the Circus* (London, 1984), p. 8. Subsequent references are to this Chatto and Windus edition and in the text.

25. The second part of *Nights at the Circus* centres on St Petersburg. The city is portrayed as displaying extremes of poverty and riches. Though personified by the female figures of the Sphinx (p. 96) and The Sleeping Beauty (p. 97), it is, in actual fact, as male-dominated as London. Women are exploited either as domestic drudges or objects of display.

26. Jeanette Winterson, *Sexing the Cherry* (London, 1989), p. 13. Subsequent references are to this edition.

27. 'The City as Battleground', op. cit., p. 209.

28. 'Forbidden Love' in Wilson, *Hidden Agendas: Theory, Politics and Experience in the Women's Movement* (London, 1986), p. 169.

29. For further discussion of contemporary lesbian fiction, see Palmer, 'Contemporary Lesbian Feminist Fiction: Texts for Everywoman', in Linda Anderson (ed.), *Plotting Change: Contemporary Women's Fiction* (London, 1990), pp. 42–62.

30. London, 1985.

31. Iandras Moontree, 'An Interview with a Separatist', in Sarah Lucia Hoagland and Julia Penelope (eds.), *For Lesbians Only: A Separatist Anthology* (London, 1988), p. 252.

32. *Altogether Elsewhere* (London, 1985), p. 112. Subsequent references are to this edition and in the text.

33. For reference to lesbian crime fiction see Sally Munt, 'The Investigators: Lesbian Crime Fiction', in Susannah Radstone (ed.), op. cit., pp. 91–119; and Palmer, 'The Lesbian Feminist Thriller and Detective Novel', in Elaine Hobby and Chris White (eds.), *What Lesbians Do in Books* (London, 1991).

34. Anna Wilson gives a negative view of the lesbian thriller ('Lesbian Gumshoes, *Bay Windows*', Vol. 6, no. 7, (18 Feb. –24 Feb. 1988): 1–2), but Rosalind Coward and Linda Semple describe it as a suitable vehicle for treating feminist themes ('Tracking Down the Past: Women and Detective Fiction', in Helen Carr (ed.), *From My Guy to Sci-Fi: Genre and Women's Writing in the Postmodern World* (London, 1989), pp. 39–57).

FURTHER READING

Pat Barker, *Blow Your House Down* (London, 1984).

Marshall Berman, *All that is Solid Melts into Air: The Experience of Modernism* (New York, Simon and Schuster, 1982; London, 1983).

Phyllis Burke, *Atomic Candy* (New York, 1989; London, 1990).

Angela Carter, *Nights at the Circus* (London, 1984).

Andrea Dworkin, *Ice and Fire* (New York, 1986; London, 1986).

Zoë Fairbairns, *Benefits* (London, 1979).

Sally Gearhart, *The Wanderground* (Massachusetts, 1980; London, 1985).

Sarah Lucia and Julia Penelope Hoagland, (eds.), *For Lesbians Only: A Separatist Anthology* (London, 1988).

Christian McEwen and Sue O'Sullivan (eds), *Out the Other Side: Contemporary Lesbian Writing* (London, 1988).

Gloria Naylor, *The Women of Brewster Place* (New York, 1982; London, 1983).

Rebecca O'Rourke, *Jumping the Cracks* (London, 1987).

Paulina Palmer, *Contemporary Women's Fiction: Narrative Practice and Feminist Theory* (Hemel Hempstead, 1989).

——'The Lesbian Feminist Thriller and Detective Novel', in Elaine Hobby and Chris White (eds), *What Lesbians Do in Books* (London, 1991).

Marge Piercy, 'The City as Battleground: The Novelist as Combatant', in Michael C. Jaye and Ann Chalmers Watts (eds.), *American Urban Experience: Essays on the City and Literature* (Manchester, 1981), pp. 209–17.

——*Small Changes* (New York, 1973).

Alix Kates Shulman, *On the Stroll* (New York, 1981; London, 1983).

Susan Merrill Squier, *Women Writers and the City: Essays in Feminist Literary Criticism* (Knoxville, 1984).

Sue Townsend, *Rebuilding Coventry: A Tale of Two Cities* (London, 1988).

Anna Wilson, *Altogether Elsewhere* (London, 1987).

Mary Wings, *She Came Too Late* (Watsonwill, California, 1986; London, 1986).

Jeannette Winterson, *Sexing the Cherry* (London, 1989; New York, 1989).

CHAPTER SEVENTEEN

Alice Walker and Buchi Emecheta Rewrite the Myth of Motherhood

Olga Kenyon

MYTHS ABOUT MOTHERS

From Richard Wright, Ralph Ellison and James Baldwin in the United States to Chinua Achebe, Ben Okri and Ngugi wa Thiong'o in Africa, black male writers represent the predicaments of men with compassionate complexity. Despite cultural diversity, they portray mothers as long-suffering victims, devoted to religion and family and resembling such stereotypes in white literature as Faulkner's black servant Dilsey, in *The Sound and the Fury*. Such images prevented black men from seeing the individuality of their women-folk, till black women themselves began writing, publicly deconstructing stereotypes in order to re-envision their lives, their potential, their language.

Their deconstruction raises questions about the politics of representation in patriarchal culture. Is it easier for black women born in the United States to resist male stereotyping than for Afro-British immigrants? Societal and fictional concepts seem more restrictive for black Britishers than for Americans, as the greater experimentation in the American novel encourages a less unitary view of fictional form and representation of self. I shall address some of these issues through a comparison of the writing of Alice Walker, from Georgia and Buchi Emecheta, born in Nigeria.

Walker is proud of her community's speech-styles and her Southern heritage, whereas immigrants are exiled from culture and language, often despised by the host nation. National myths also play their part; American myths stress sexual and economic roles, while the 'new' immigrant woman in England has given rise to fewer myths, except those of being uncommu-nicative or 'too fertile'. The contempt for mothers of large families (also expressed in the United States, in government reports[1] blaming black mothers for poverty) adds to the alienation felt by black women, and contrasts to the praise expressed in their own cultures. These contradictions are represented by Walker and Emecheta implicitly in their fiction, explicitly through their journalism.[2] Their texts are admired and bought by the range of feminists, yet they distance themselves from white feminists whom they both consider too middle-class to be sufficiently critical of patriarchal contempt of mothers. This indicates that classism is as rife in America as Britain. Or is it racism that causes them greater marginalisation, as mothers and/or writers?

Buchi Emecheta and Alice Walker both rethink stereotypes about mothers, but in intriguingly different ways. These differences stem partly from distinct upbringing: Walker was born in Georgia to devoted sharecroppers; Emecheta, an Ibo, was orphaned young, brought up by relatives, virtually a servant in their house because she was merely a girl. She gained short-lived prestige by marrying into a well-to-do family and promptly producing two sons. When she followed her young husband to Britain, she discovered that her fertility in promptly producing three more children, relegated her to poverty and ostracism, experiences which shaped her early writing. Walker admired her mother, adopting her 'parole' for Celie in *The Color Purple* (1983), while Emecheta seldom includes parental speech rhythms in her early writing, except in her autobiography *Head Above Water* (1986) (in Chapter 2, 'The Miracle'). Now equally politicised, *both* pay tribute to their cultures, particularly the creativity of the hard-working, story-telling women. Their fiction of the early eighties foregrounds *material* values, the supporting of children emotionally and often financially.

The contrasts in their writing are as striking as the similarities. Walker gained a scholarship to school, then a place at Spelman College; English is her mother tongue, with which she feels free to experiment. For Emecheta English is a third language, lacking the metaphors and (for her) the flexibility of her native Ibo, or the Yoruba of central Nigeria. She was not taught to write in her mother tongue, only Yoruba 'more suitable for dramatists, such as Wole Soyinka.'[3] Walker expresses a culture-specific indebtedness to other writers, black and white, male and female, which is not paralleled in Emecheta. Both grew to love the English literature they were exclusively taught. Yet Walker felt able to break away from school-imposed structures, while Emecheta tends to keep a more traditionally English approach to story-telling, with analysis of moral dilemma through character. America offered a tradition of freer forms of prose, and, currently, participation in black rediscovery of powerful black slave narrative; in contrast, the British examinations system decreed a canon which still restricts the approach of many British novelists to their craft.

One of the few critical books to handle both writers, the pathbreaking *Black Feminist Criticism* by Barbara Christian (1985), stresses that the idealisation of maternity in African culture paradoxically marginalises mothers. The proverbs which Emecheta interweaves certainly underline the imprisoning effect of community sayings such as 'The joy of being a mother is the joy of giving to all your children': 'A woman without a child for her husband is a failed woman.' Until recently, black male writers considered that women fulfilled (and redeemed) themselves through marriage and motherhood. Today we see another male-created stereotype emerging, that of the 'liberated' urban women, who uses her sexuality to gain slightly greater control over economic resources. Male writers denigrate her, Walker praises her in 'characters' such as Blues singer Shug; Emecheta represents the suffering caused by the double bind of wanting to please a man, yet having to compete with him in the market-place.

In Africa it is women novelists, pre-eminently Bessie Head in Botswana who have led the re-envisioning of the woman, both as an individual in her own right, with a rich interior life, and as a significant contributor to alternative values in a newly emerging country. Head protested against sexual inequality through highly charged metaphors of madness and redemption. Emecheta examines these topics, in a more 'realistic' framework, of mothers leashed with children and submission. However, both began writing in the European form of the romance, Head in *Maru* (1971), Emecheta in *The Bride Price* (not published until 1976).[4] Falling in love is not central to African story-telling and ill fits the aims of African writers. When they broke away, they developed fiction better adapted to represent social destructiveness.

Emecheta supported her children from journalism, and studied sociology. Matter-of-fact discourse and documentary inform *Second-Class Citizen* (1974). Her language has a directness based on factual observation, which strengthens her polemics. Head in her final great novel experiments imaginatively, to take us into the mental agony of a marginalised single parent. Both represent women's worth through the protagonists of *The Joys of Motherhood* (1979) and *A Question of Power* (1974). Their heroines undergo periods of near madness when their physical and mental wretchedness is intensified by societal rejection of their worth as people – and mothers. Recent South African writing is far more politicised.

The icon which influences our unconscious divorces sexuality from motherhood. In Europe Christianity stressed the Virgin mother. In most African cultures motherhood has been central, with greater eminence given to fertility. The Mother Goddess reigns over agriculture, tribal life and many aspects of religious worship.[5] Hence a major culture clash for Emecheta. The relatively high status of mothers (of boys) has positive effects but their areas of work are still restricted. Most African women are workers in the home, *and* the fields and small-scale trading, that is in non-influential areas. This of course links the situation of mothers in Africa with black mothers in the

Southern states of America, a link emphasised by Alice Walker when she talks of the 'mother/worker' in her article on Emecheta. 'She reasons that since her children will someday be adults, she will fulfil the ambition of her life not only for herself, but also for them. Since this novel is written to the adults her children will become, it is okay with her if the distractions and joys they represent become part of it. In this way she integrates the profession of writer into the cultural concept of mother/worker that she retains from Ibo society.'[6] Walker widens her analysis, too much at times, by referring to both African-American and Native American religious models; Emecheta, possibly more restricted by her culture, refers to the Nigerian women she sees working in the fields when she returns every summer, to teach creative writing. African-American and African religions, particularly the icons of mother-goddesses, emphasise the need for a point of view that values *all life*. Yet while celebrating maternal ancestors' strength and sacrifice, Walker also insists that mothers have the right to be individuals, and that any sacrifice should be means to deeper life, not just an end in itself; if the ideology of motherhood does not value women, a culture loses the particular gift of seeing the world from the angle of continuation, necessary for any meaningful struggle to health and freedom. Now that Emecheta has reached a certain eminence, she also stresses our vital need to respect this planet, our earth. 'Our people do not claim to own it, but receive it in trust, to be cultivated for their own use only, not exploited; then passed on to subsequent generations.'[7]

Perceiving herself as an African-American, Walker makes substantial use of African images of women, relishing the fact that the earliest African religious image was mother earth. She is still revered as the source of life in Africa, and is represented in many female figures in Walker's more recent novel *The Temple of My Familiar* (1989). The mother-goddess is even an alternative icon for 'green' movements alarmed by the implications of pollution for the entire human race. Women are told to stay in subsistence farming, which is far less destructive to ecology.[8] Many black women writers protest skilfully in fiction against the customs of their traditional societies in thus relegating too many women to near subsistence (physically) and silence (politically).

To highlight this inequality, in *The Slave Girl* (1989) Emecheta uses the symbol of the slave for most women. And, like Walker in *The Color Purple*, she condemns the over-specialisation of gendered spheres – woman in homestead work, man earning wages. It is only when Celie's brutal husband sits beside his wife sewing that he begins to redeem himself. Emecheta cannot envisage the possibility of redemption for males in her native or immigrant cultures; she suggests the need to live without them. Both writers portray the tension between the 'two spheres' which have subordinated women by subtle condemnation of female language as gossip, and behaviour as 'stupid', 'girlish', etc. They show woman used as scapegoat, called backward when she conforms, 'immoral' when she tries to better her life, or even exercise some element of choice. Their heroines, especially Walker's Meridian, and Adah in *Second-Class Citizen* suffer the double domination of whites and their own males. Both find sexism as restricting as racism.

FICTIONAL STRATEGIES FOR SOCIAL REALITIES

They analyse some of the causes of this, fictionalising the topic of motherhood, which until recently had remained the great *unwritten* story. Being a mother is the experience of most women, but the *institution* of motherhood is still under the control of men, and interpreted through mainly male myth, religion, science, politics, economics. Walker rejects male icons through the mouth of Shug, a blues singer. The mother goddess is taken from her problematical pedestal when Celie is taught to appreciate the godhead *within* herself, thanks to Shug's lesbian love. Similarly, Adah learns to value her own ability to survive and even study while providing for her five children, virtually unaided. Yet Emecheta's approach remains less ambitious, not a remythologising, but a documenting, to expose. She seems to lack the American idealism that Walker so patently exhibits.

Both examine what it means to be a woman in our patriarchal societies, where thought is structured in the simplistic polarities of male/female, active/passive, rational/irrational. The second term is considered the negative version of the first, and used to belittle or exclude women. White feminist literary critics stress the destructiveness of such Aristotelian thinking, and encourage us to read the hitherto excluded. Emerging black feminist critics, however, refuse to be subsumed with their white sisters. They claim that knowledge of black history and culture is the necessary 'context' for the study of their literature.

Walker has given us valuable knowledge of her background in her essays *In Search of Our Mothers' Gardens* (1983). There she praises the mother who laboured beside her father in the fields, from dawn to sunset, yet always found time to attend to her seven children's needs. Emecheta also gives details of frustrated creativity, illness, hunger and exhaustion, but less polemically, as if apprehensive that a British reader might not accept her writing if it strayed from meticulous recording of 'social realities'. To an extent she was right, in that she spent a whole year posting her manuscript to editors before it was finally accepted. Such perseverance and belief in self is rare, especially in a battered wife. When questioned she put her persistence down to Ibo tenacity: 'We Ibos are very stubborn', she told me.

She can now be a role model for immigrant girls, who even come to her and ask advice on making a career in writing. She tells them they must be prepared to live for three years without money, and have extraordinary self-discipline, with almost no social life, until they have published two or three books, when it becomes possible to live by writing in Britain. In Nigeria it would be impossible for a woman, 'because not enough people read and because I'm too outspoken to see all my works printed in Lagos, where other women are not supportive enough.' As immigrant, Emecheta has no supportive community, having lost the original (which would have been disinclined to support a girl writer), *and not able* to create a new one. 'In London classism divides us; because many immigrant women do menial jobs, they feel too awkward to talk to me, and white feminists do not fully understand our problems.'[9]

In order not to be subsumed by white feminism, Walker developed a form of black feminism – 'womanism' – which she claims, 'appreciates and prefers women's culture, women's emotional flexibility . . . women's strength. [And is] Committed to survival and wholeness of entire people male and female.'[10]

The Color Purple represents Celie slowly learning to become more womanist, more courageous in her dealings with an exploitative husband. It is only *after* she has rejected the role of worker-mother that she can develop. The nuclear family proves too destructive for this mother, but she can find love in the extended family that develops as her step-children grow up. As each mother feels the need to develop part of herself, she can leave her children with the women still in the homestead at that moment. That cannot yet happen in Africa where, according to Emecheta 'half of our problem rests with women, bitching about one another, unlike western women who tied themselves to poles to get the vote for all'.[11]

The suffering of Celie's daughter-in-law Sofia provides insight into what happened to caring black mothers who voiced too much independence in the United States. When the mayor's wife admired her dressing of her children, and asked her to work for her, Sofia answered, 'Hell no' – an understandable reply from any mother who wants to look after her own offspring. Whites make her suffer for nineteen years for this rebellion, symbol of injustices meted out to ex-slave mothers, which they are expected nevertheless to overcome, and mother whites' children with no rancour. This helps to explain why black women distance themselves from white feminists.

Through Sofia, and above all Celie, Walker memorialises her own step-great-grandmother who had to cope with seven children, all their illnesses, and a husband who never even called her by her name. (In memory of the slave great-great-great-grandmother who walked to freedom with two babies, she keeps the name Walker.)[12] With sister Americans she studied the lives of such women while working for welfare rights in Mississippi in the sixties. She collected their folklore stories – and was told of the work of Zora Neale Hurston. Hurston's research released both herself and Walker from the often condescending records of white folklorists, and inspired their growing respect for the achievements of black women. Walker acquired a wider range of role models than the orphaned Emecheta, and greater acquaintance with black knowledge. Her personal admiration for Hurston is also political, in that she is working for the recovery of 'lost' reputations.

Emecheta's aims in her first novel, *Second-Class Citizen*, were not political, but personal: just to recount her story, though distanced, in the character of Adah. She follows her young Nigerian husband to London and produces five children, only to find herself despised by British society and battered by her penniless student husband. Despite his violence and being rejected even by fellow Nigerians, she succeeds in supporting herself and her five children – working full-time as a librarian – and, remarkably, sustains a writing career.

Central is Emecheta's unquestioning acceptance that caring for her children is the essential part of her life, even while working full-time, and studying to improve her prospects. The topic of caring motherhood came to the fore in much women's writing of the sixties, in America and Britain. Americans often stressed political and gynaecological dimensions, from Betty Friedan to Mary MacCarthy. Popular young British novelists such as Margaret Drabble and Penelope Mortimer created a climate where discussion of the value and cost of motherhood, both personal and social, could be foregrounded in novels. At about the same period British television produced documentary plays such as Nell Dunn's *Cathy Come Home*, about a homeless young mother with three small children. (Emecheta has written three plays for television.) Emecheta was impressed by their recording of 'social realities'. It proved propitious for her, whose ear and upbringing fail to give her the lyricism noticeable in Soyinka, Okri and much African-American writing, male and female, indebted to their communities' musical traditions. With all its oppressive shortcomings Britain expanded Emecheta's mind where Africa had failed to educate her ear.

These British novelists of the sixties considered themselves in the tradition of the nineteenth-century social novel (Barthes calls it 'readerly'), which Emecheta's colonial school had taught her. This 'realism' is less experimental or 'writerly' than the American exploration of fictional alternatives, and facilitated Emecheta's acceptance in Britain. White male critics praised her, and she was chosen as one on the 'Best Twenty Writers under forty' in 1983. Since then publication has proved much easier, while our Equal Opportunities policies in inner cities have encouraged the reading of black writing. (Walker came from a more supportive community, and a country with more

Black and Women's Studies, yet *The Color Purple* was scarcely noticed until it won the Pulitzer Prize.) Yet in spite of critical acclaim and a fairly wide readership, Emecheta did not receive a year's good income until her grand tour of America in 1989. She told me that teaching creative writing in American universities pays far better than any other work she does. [13]

The influence of African culture on Emecheta is most marked in the dedication to her children, the writing for them, not in spite of their needs and noise. 'Emecheta is a writer and a mother and it is because she is both that she writes at all', states Alice Walker, who admits that the novel, while good, is heavily autobiographical and not stylistically exciting. She praises Emecheta's view of her situation from a cultural perspective which precludes self-pity and above all makes us rethink 'traditional Western ideas about how art is produced. . . . It raises fundamental questions about how creative and prosaic life is to be lived and to what purpose, which is more than some books, written when one's children are banished from one's life, do.'[14]

I suggest that Emecheta is widely read because she synthesises the fictional and historical modes. As David Lodge remarked in *The Novelist at the Crossroads* (1971), such synthesis *is* modern British 'realism'. A Marxist critic might say that, unlike many American novelists she interprets the forces that have restricted women like herself, in representing setbacks as social evils, not ineradicable ones. She also bears witness to a class of women still under-represented: working-class. Some of my white adult women students consider that she is recounting their problems while describing her own. Such identification is less likely with Walker, who feels the right to incorporate elements of slave narrative, erudite discourse of the missionary sister, patterning metaphors, misspellings.

In some ways, the two writers can both be compared to eighteenth-century women novelists who supported themselves from their professional earnings, using elements from the few genres available. Indeed, Walker adopts the epistolary form, as did the first professional novelist, Aphra Behn, but feels free to adapt it to the 'parole' of her community, breaking away from literary registers. Her discourse is at once more colloquial and more polished than Emecheta's, as passages from each writer about the longing to go to school suggest:

> The first time I got big, Pa took me out of school. He never care that I love it.
> Nettie [her sister] stood there at the gate holding tight to my hand. I was all
> dress for first day. You too dumb to keep going to school, Pa say. . . . But Pa,
> Nettie say, crying, Celie smart too. Even Miss Beasley say so . . . Pa say, Who-
> ever listen to anything Addie Beasley have to say. She run off at the mouth so
> much no man would have her. That how she come to have teach school.
>
> (*The Color Purple*, p. 11)

343

This letter is written to God by a pubescent girl, too lonely to have any friends. Her short staccato sentences are dramatic and vivid. The artful vernacular forms of speech of her culture are made to work *for* the revaluing of this speech. Emecheta's heroine, Adah:

> School – the Ibos never played with that! They were realising fast that one's saviour from poverty and disease was education. Every Ibo family saw to it that their children attended school. Boys were usually given preference, though. So even though Adah was about eight, there were still discussions about whether it would be wise to let her stay long. 'A year or two would do, as long as she can write her name and count. Then she will learn to sew' Adah heard her mother say.
>
> (*Second-Class Citizen*, p. 9)

Emecheta's commentary adopts something of a sociological register: 'the Ibos', 'every Ibo family' but she can be sloppy, as in her repetition of 'though', suggesting the run of speech. Her small piece of dialogue is enough to give us a glimpse of difficulties with the mother, though less than what we glean of Walker's 'Pa'.

Emecheta attended that school, and was successful at English exams. However, she was never once given an African book to read – she told me that she only began to read African writers once she arrived in London. Whereas Walker had three years at College, loved the European writers she studied, and quotes from Rilke and Camus in her books. In spite of racism, she has had greater chances in the United States to concentrate on writing – she took a year to think about these characters, while Emecheta, an immigrant, laboured to support and bring up five small children.

Walker points out that *Second-Class Citizen* is 'heavily autobiographical, but no less valid as a novel' (p. 703). Its sequel, *Head Above Water* (1986), follows the tribulations of Adah's story with the account of how she successfully emerged from condemned housing to a dignified, fulfilling life. It began as journalism, a series of articles in *The New Statesman*. In a recent interview to me, Emecheta stressed her aim of offering a constructive image of a black immigrant mother refusing to accept the few denigrating categories first thrust on her. *Head Above Water* depicts a slow improvement, not in her own situation alone: 'There are more Blacks going to university, more Afro-Caribbean studies, more books by black writers studied in schools – though seldom on show in bookshops or libraries and the media. I still consider myself marginalised. In my present book I deal with the many problems and prejudices which exist for immigrants in Britain now.'[15]

Significantly, immigrant novelists such as Emecheta and Joan Riley (from the Caribbean) have been criticised by their communities in Britain for purveying destructive images of girls, although these are based on their personal experience. They have now, in recent novels, decided to follow examples of Walker in experimenting with spoken rhythms, in both cases an adopted 'patwah' of Jamaica. Interestingly, it is not their vernacular, but the language of their grandmothers, grandmothers whose creativity and resourcefulness is finally being publicly praised.[16] (But in some ways this is a regressive manoeuvre, forced on Emecheta by the hostile reception of her contemporary linguistic strategy.)

Ironically, at the very time that the stories of 'grandmothers and aunts who brought me up' are being resuscitated by black women novelists, story-telling is ceasing in immigrant groups 'because mothers work such long hours and have to leave their children alone, as I did, with no female relatives near'. The rich African traditions of fable, animal imagery, oralcy, moralities, spoken tales, are dying out in Britain, though they remain a powerful force in many writers who stayed in Africa, such as Wole Soyinka. In America blues and the black musical tradition continue to feed male and female writing, noted for its lyrical vein, from Hurston to the youngish Gloria Naylor (whom Emecheta taught briefly in a Creative Writing course). Emecheta is less lyrical, cut off from African music and from orality with its competitions in riddles or all-night parable-telling. She tries to recapture these by returning to Lagos University in the summer. 'The dream of African immigrants is to go home, and stay there. The weather is so much better in Lagos, it helps you to relax. But you can only afford to do that if you find a well-paid job. I manage the summer there, so at last I keep my two worlds, my two cultures.'[17] This financial capacity for return visits, and public pride in the ability to possess two cultures are recent for immigrants.

Emecheta's early cultural experiences in Nigeria were of a colonised country. 'We all sang Rule Britannia at school and looked on England as our mother country.'[18] At that time the American South was struggling to implement anti-racist legislation. The Civil Rights movement gave the American blacks a profile and a pride which has not been equalled for black Britishers.

Walker's second novel *Meridian* (1976) foregrounds a Civil Rights worker. Though torn between the demands of her community and political struggle, she is more 'liberated' than the women in Walker's first novel, *The Third Life of Grange Copeland* (1970), which represented two generations of black women, downtrodden and humiliated by their husbands. Only the third generation is saved – by the murder of an irredeemable father.

Meridian foregrounds the problems faced by Southern black women when trying to fulfil the expectations of both their community and themselves. Meridian has a mother who is psychologically incapable of mothering her, in part because having a baby 'shatters her emerging self' but, above all, because society has left her, like most of Emecheta's protagonists, in ignorance about the frustrations caused by proclaiming motherhood as sanctified while leaving the reproducers in the lowest economic positions.

Meridian takes a boyfriend because 'it saved her from the strain of having to respond to other boys' (p. 54). She marries him only to discover (like Adah) that racism has made him 'always a boy'. Furthermore she 'did not know what a man should be' (p. 64). Society has given her no knowledge to guide a central relationship. She throws herself into the Civil Rights Movement, where she reflects on the meaning of motherhood. Soon she is placed in a tragic dilemma by having a baby which she must give up if she is to go to college. Two friends voice the opposing views struggling inside her: Delores, an activist, claims 'You have a right to go to college' (p. 83); the other woman, mother of six children, made pregnant at fourteen, states 'It's just selfishness' (p. 86). Although Meridian acknowledges intellectually that by giving away her baby she may be saving 'a small person's life', she continues to feel 'condemned' because she cannot repudiate these conflicting societal images. Meridian is obsessed by this sin against black motherhood – an obsession which finally leads to her madness.

Walker's skilful structure opens with Meridian crazily leading a group of children in against a tank. Slapstick and irony underscore society's judgement of women. The author then examines why the heroine has been reduced to this action. Emecheta uses a similar technique of flashback in *The Joys of Motherhood*, which also opens with an attempt at suicide. But her heroine cannot equal Meridian in attempts to explore a way out, and 'to judge the world by standards that would apply beyond her natural life' (p. 189). Politicised by Civil Rights, Walker establishes a relationship between the effects of slavery, of racism and sexism in the oppression of mothers – which must be described to be fought.

OUT OF AFRICA

Emecheta was brought up in a more overtly sexist society, and under a military dictatorship at times. For political and personal reasons she keeps to the psychological and social in her description of material oppression. The very title *The Joys of Motherhood* indicates the contradictions of motherhood which she represents realistically and ironically. This wide-ranging African novel opens in the middle of the story when Nnu Ego runs out of her home in horror on seeing her longed for baby son dead on the floor. Not only does the death relegate her to the lowest position, of complete failure as a woman, she loses her will to go on struggling in an alien, capitalist city.

This novel highlights aspects of women's intimate wretchedness seldom represented in the male literature of her country. Emecheta explains some of the contradictions which Nnu Ego can never fully resolve. Her father Agbadi is an important man in his village, partly because of his farm, partly because of his farm, partly because he has the qualities expected of a male in that rural society. He has neglected his wives, but adored his child Nnu Ego. He intends a good match for her, but once she is married and fails to produce an heir promptly, she is rejected. Although her father takes her back, he soon marries her off again, to a worker in Lagos whom she has never seen. She despises him for earning his living as washerman in a white household. Only when he has fathered her first son can she begin to feel affection for this fat, self-absorbed male. Once she has produced five children, her community appears to value her. But the husband takes another wife, and she has to work so hard to support them all that she dies in her forties, haggard, alone. By then the children have all left; they return to give her 'the greatest funeral ever seen' (p. 224).

This is Emecheta's most African novel, enriched with African proverbs, African beliefs, African words. The structure represents the complexity of Nigerian culture, by swinging from a chapter on the supportiveness of village life, to one revealing sexism which makes rural women into chattels. She now feels able to exploit varying modes of writing. There is less British shaping in the cultural images of women bowed down by their labour for people who give little affection or understanding.

The Joys of Motherhood represents both the social value, and male under-valuing, of women in village life. Unlike Walker in America, she perceives little relief in cottage industry, which saves Celie – a solution condemned as sentimental by some critics. Work in the city, though an experience of many American blacks, is glossed over by Walker, whereas Emecheta stresses a mother's loss of status in urban wage-earning society. Her heroine learns to adapt, like other mothers, by selling on street or market, when competition allows. Yet male writers such as Robert Staples still maintain 'In Afro-American culture motherhood represents maturity and the fulfillment of one's function as a woman.'[19] Respected it may be, but only when it conforms to the norms imposed on it by males in power. The mother is praised when overburdened with children, especially male, yet scorned, even rejected for another wife if she fails to produce enough healthy children. At least the African urban mother can find some support from other mothers, whereas the immigrant is ostracised in foreign ghettoes in *Second-Class Citizen*.

In the United States, slavery virtually destroyed the concept of black motherhood, replacing it with that of breeding; the slave woman was valued as 'producer' of products that could be sold. Walker represents a historical vestige of this in the opening letters of Celie, recounting the treatment of Celie by her step-father. Like the nineteenth-century slave-owner, he uses her for his sexual needs, selling her babies without telling her; she is left with milk running down her breasts. That is one reason why in *The Color Purple* the love/sex relationship between Celie and Shug is central, represented as natural. It strengthens both women, who were rejected by the very fathers of their children when merely young mothers. It is their lesbian love which teaches Celie to value herself – and that sexuality can be satisfying. Emecheta, already censored in Lagos, dare not approach such a topic, though she does analyse sexual abuse in her latest novel.[20] In between two cultures, she runs the risk of satisfying neither, while Walker had the luck to please Spielberg and see her novel a box-office success.

Black women writers in the United States emphasise female culture as a means to self-development. However, novels analysing the dilemmas of immigrants, from the brilliant *Brown Girl, Brownstones* (1959) by Brooklyn-born Paule Marshall (whose family came from Barbados) to Emecheta's texts, represent mothers *separated* from each other by long hours of work. They portray a destructive interiorisation of bourgeois values and an overt classism undermining mother–daughter relationships and female friendships. There is an undercurrent of hostility toward motherhood even noticeable in Walker, occasionally. This aspect is commented on by Diane F. Sadoff in a recent article[21] arguing for a non-Oedipal tradition for women writers. However, in *The Color Purple*, Walker foregrounds the supportiveness of mothers towards each other. Her attitude to women's friendships might be criticised as senti-mental, but it is based on her childhood experience of a close-knit supportive southern community. And, like Emecheta, she believes that life dictates art.

The Color Purple is an outstanding work of fiction and witness, exploring a vast range of topics. The use of letters is significant, enabling Walker to demonstrate the powerful directness of the language of apparently 'semi-educated' black women. The resourcefulness of this hitherto scorned idiom revalues their medium of expression, transforming it into an art form, and a forceful tool for rethinking and re-examining myths. Walker reviews the roles of men and women, in and outside the family, in America and Africa, to explore less divisive ways of living together. She has had more time to study African civilisation than her overworked Ibo sister.

It is Walker, romantic about Africa, not Emecheta, who offers the example of men in Africa sewing, weaving and making 'beautiful quilts which are full of animals and birds and people' (p. 159). Celie's husband finds peace finally when he begins to sew, beside the woman he had despised. They smoke a pipe together, further transcending cultural stereotypes. Such previsioning of gender leads to a rethinking of societal myths. Though she praises the black church in which she was brought up, Walker questions Christian mythology in order to free blacks from its 'mind-forg'd manacles'. Celie has to stop writing to a patriarchal God, to reject the myth of a white-bearded Father before she can become an autonomous person.

Though black Christian missionary work is appreciated, Walker boldly resorts to African myths in order to free our minds of destructively rigid Christian concepts. The Olinka believe that 'after the biggest of white folks no longer on earth, the only way to stop making somebody the serpent is for everybody to accept everybody else as a child of God, or one mother's children. . . . These Olinka worship the snake, they say it's the smartest, cleanest, slickest thing they ever seen' (p. 233). Walker's method is to reverse and re-envision the Christian concept of the snake and thus of evil. She also does this to 'Mr——' who finally becomes a named person – Albert. The apparently incorrigible husband is transformed by changing his perception of himself and ceasing to submit to a macho mythology.

Emecheta is, in her way, as emancipated and as idiosyncratic in her religious beliefs as Walker. She recognises that the Methodist church her family attended was rigid, but does not consider it paradoxical to adhere to much of its moral teaching. Some of its tenets, such as 'finish whatever you thought fit to begin', aid her writing. She accepts Methodist attitudes to sex and will not allow her children to disobey them. But her mind is not colonised; she has translated Christian faith into a form compatible with an African outlook: 'Heaven is down here, on earth. When someone dies they go back into the earth. The land was here before we came, we are all just passing through. . . . I try to go to church every Sunday, and praying I equate with the African way of talking to oneself. A mother will say "God, make my child be in a good temper today." It's making prayer work, God's spirit inside you.'[23] This African spirituality resembles Shug's in *The Color Purple* – though Emecheta has not yet transmuted it into her fiction, except in a few parts of *The Rape of Shavi* (1983), her fourth book, written when feeling more confident. It was published by her own firm, set up with her eldest son.

FROM ALIENATION TO EMPOWERMENT

After the hard labour of bringing up five small children on her own, while working and studying sociology at the London School of Economics, Emecheta now has a little time at last to read. Her education in Africa had been so traditionally English that it was only in London that she began the stimulating discovery of black writers. She particularly enjoys Zora Neale Hurston, Maya Angelou and Toni Cade Bambara.

> I love the way they use their colloquial language, it's meant to be read aloud, it's so musical. And there's a younger woman, whom I taught in Creative Writing classes, Gloria Naylor – she uses lively, experimental English. I never read Alice Walker till I met her in 1989, when we both taught Creative Writing at Yale University. I

liked her as a person, and I now like her writing. Though I think she has been fortunate with her connections. The novelist I admire most is Toni Morrison, because of her brilliant metaphors.[24]

Time for reading and teaching on an MA course has crystallised Emecheta's perceived cultural priorities. At school she had accepted the idea of the Devil as black, but now freeing language from pejorative images and improving images used for women are her articulated aims. In recent writing she includes more discourses than her own, particularly that of Jamaicans she hears in London: 'I have tried to incorporate Jamaican rhythms, such as "God dies for the truth" while writing about the dilemmas of blacks born in Britain. At last I have the courage to say "I write for blacks." '[25]

White economic policy attempted to impose birth control on African-American mothers. In the United States and Britain newspaper articles have commented on blacks as 'over-running the country'. In Africa the World Bank advocates the benefits of birth control without taking account of deeply rooted convictions such as 'Immortality is given by having many children.' Motherhood is even more problematical for black than white women. White women are nowadays seen as wives first, only later in relationships as mothers. But for American blacks with their terrifying past as slave producers of babies (to sell!) the possession of a virgin is precious. Wanting the best for their children is often seen, according to Walker, as a threat, even to white women. Being able to keep their children at home represented an advance after the deprivations imposed by slave owners.

Alice Walker, Toni Morrison, Maya Angelou, the black writers who attract public attention, are all mothers, and all pay tribute to the extra dimension this experience has given them. They agree in renouncing the icon of the Black Mammy, and representing the variety and dignity of the many black mother-figures they have known. Angelou's Southern grandmother not only owned the town store, she lent money to needy whites. When persecuted by the unruly children of these whites, she sang hymns loudly, calmly, giving her grandchildren a magnificent role model. Grandmothers as role models are also praised by Emecheta in her article on the women who led the Aba riots in the twenties. Yet for most mothers, large families meant physical and emotional suffering, in the Southern states, and even more so in Africa – to judge by statistics such as life expectancy and infant mortality.

The problematic situation of mothers in Africa is represented by Nettie in her letters from Africa. The village women press her to marry, yet they look worn down by unending hours of home and field labour. Their role of mother may be sanctioned by patriarchal words, yet it does not endow them with quality of life, nor consideration from a husband, even when he is chief. Nettie's discourse was learnt at a white-dominated school like Emecheta's;

their efforts at 'correctness' implicitly reveal their experience of overcoming the sense of alienation in a colonising language.

Both Emecheta and Walker record dramatically the marginalisation of young worker-mothers. Walker's 'writerly' freedom contrasts with the sociological approach of Emecheta. Yet both share didactic and increasingly polemical intentions. African story-telling often had a didactic content; for instance, the animal fables aimed to teach children (an American inheritance which can be seen in Joel Chandler Harris's Brer Rabbit, only recently being reassessed, its myths reappropriated by blacks).

The Temple of My Familiar (1989) praises the spirituality of mothers for over a thousand years. Poetic registers transform the hard-working 'characters' into wise, interesting, even beautiful goddess figures. The earth mother has been restored to her position of icon, worshipped for her values of caring. These goddesses care not for individuals, but for the future of our planet. *The Temple* testifies to the continuing desire of black women writers to work for causes, which here include ecology and world peace. Walker's latest book, *Possessing the Secrets of Joy* (1992), returns to African materials and characters from *The Color Purple* and *The Temple* and addresses the issue of female circumcision. Emecheta, increasingly 'committed' in journalism[26] rather than fiction, advocates study of traditional techniques to help African women and farmers. Both these show how commitment to community leads them to propose global measures to improve the quality of human life.

Both now advocate study of black history, symbols and discourse as a basis of literary creation, and criticism. They differ vastly in their approach to texts and in idioms used, from experimental to traditional. Yet both share a belief in the power of fictions to offer mother-workers a range of liberating role models. They represent women growing from humiliation to potential, from alienation to empowerment.

NOTES

1. Such as the Moynihan report, 1954.

2. Their journalism is contained in volumes such as Walker's *In Search of Our Mothers' Gardens* (New York, 1983). Emecheta's first published writing was in the form of articles in *The New Statesman*, later to be turned into her first published work, the semi-autobiographical *In the Ditch* (1972). Both continue with journalism as well as fiction.

3. It could be claimed that Emecheta is more alienated from her parents' culture than an orphan boy might have been. She stated in interview: 'I can't write stories in my own language, so I have to use English' (Adeola James (ed.), *In Their Own*

Voices: African Women Talk, London, 1990).

4. Emecheta told me that the first book she began writing was a 'happy-ever-after romantic story.' Her husband destroyed the entire manuscript, which she decided to rewrite. It is based partly on her mother's experience and called *The Bride Price* (1976).

5. C.A. Diop, *The African Origin of Civilisation* (Westport, Connecticut, 1974), pp. 143–5.

6. Walker, 'A writer because of, not in spite of, her children', in *In Search of Our Mothers' Gardens* (London, 1984), p. 69.

7. Interview given to me in June, 1989.

8. Denise Paulme (ed.), *Women of Tropical Africa* (London, 1963).

9. Interview, June 1989.

10. Walker, *In Search of Our Mothers' Gardens* (London, 1984), p. 122.

11. Interview given to me, 10 June 1990.

12. Walker, 'Choice: A Tribute to Martin Luther King Jr', *In Search of Our Mothers' Gardens*, p. 142.

13. Interview, June 1989.

14. Walker, 'A writer . . .', op. cit., pp. 67, 69–70.

15. Interview, June 1990.

16. Grandmothers often had to spend long hours looking after the offspring of overworked mothers. They obviously play a vital part in transmitting oral traditions, and skills. They are praised by Walker, Emecheta and Maya Angelou.

17. Interview, June 1990.

18. Interview, June 1989.

19. Robert Staples, *The Black Woman in America* (Chicago, 1973), p. 153.

20. The sexual revolution in the United States has allowed far more open discussion of sexual topics, creating a climate where Walker felt able to portray lesbian love as fulfilling. Nigeria proved more puritanical, producing both censorship and self-censorship. Furthermore, until the eighties there have been elements of legal restrictions and sexual reserve in Britain. Yet even in the United States the film of *The Color Purple* toned down the love between the two women considerably.

21. See 'Black Matrilineage: the Case of Alice Walker and Zora Neale Hurston' in Micheline R. Malson et al. (eds), *Black Women in America: Social Science Perspectives* (Chicago and London, 1990), pp. 197–219. Sadoff remarks on the undercurrent of hostility toward motherhood in some of Walker's novels, in Toni Morrison's *Sula* (1974) and Gayl Jones's *Corregidora* (1988).

22. Claudia Tate, *Black Women Writers at Work* (Hertfordshire, 1985), p. 185.

23. Interview, June 1990.

24. Ibid. Her incorporation of Jamaican rhythms shows both an admiration for

Caribbean culture and a desire to be part of the British Caribbean community. Her latest novel *Gwendolen* (1989) is set in sixties' Jamaica.

25. Her articles appear in journals such as *New Society*, *West Africa* and *Granta*. On 30 November 1991 she noted to me that she had been published by most British newspapers, particularly *The Guardian*, but never *The Daily Telegraph*.

FURTHER READING

Barbara Christian, *Black Feminist Criticism* (New York and Oxford, 1985).

Adeola James (ed.), *In Their Own Voices: African Women Talk* (London, 1990).

Olga Kenyon, *The Writer's Imagination: Interviews with Major International Women Writers* (London, 1992).

Micheline R Malson et al. (ed.), *Black Women: American Social Science Perspectives* (Chicago and London, 1990).

Denise Paulme (ed.), *Women of Tropical Africa* (London 1963).

Claudia Tate (ed.) *Black Women Writers at Work* (Hertfordshire, 1987).

Susan Willis, 'Black Women Writers: Taking a Critical Perspective' in *Making a Difference: Feminist Literary Criticism*, (eds.) Gayle Greene and Coppélia Kahn (London and New York, 1985).

Selected Works: Buchi Emecheta

In the Ditch (London, 1972).

Second-Class Citizen (London, 1989).

The Bride Price (London, 1976).

The Slave Girl (London, 1977).

The Joys of Motherhood (London, 1979).

Destination Biafra (London, 1982).

Double Yoke (London, 1983).

The Rape of Shavi (London, 1983).

A Kind of Marriage (London, 1986).

Head Above Water (London, 1986) Autobiography.

Gwendolen (London, 1989).

Selected Works: Alice Walker

Once (New York, 1968) Poems.

The Third Life of Grange Copeland (New York, 1970).

Revolutionary Petunias and Other Poems (New York, 1973).

In Love and Trouble: Stories of Black Women (New York, 1973).

Meridian (New York, 1976).

Good Night, Willie Lee, I'll See You in the Morning (New York, 1979) Poems.

You Can't Keep a Good Woman Down (New York, 1981) Stories.

The Color Purple (New York, 1982).

In Search of Our Mothers' Gardens: Womanist Prose (New York, 1983).

Living by the Word: Selected Writings 1973–1987 (New York, 1988).

The Temple of My Familiar (New York, 1989).

Possessing the Secret of Joy (New York, 1992).

CHAPTER EIGHTEEN

Philip Roth And Clive Sinclair: Representations of an 'Imaginary Homeland' in Postwar British and American-Jewish Literature

Bryan Cheyette

Let me suggest that Indian writers in England have access to a second tradition, quite apart from their own racial history. It is the culture and political history of the phenomenon of migration, displacement, life in a minority group. We can quite legitimately claim as our ancestors the Huguenots, the Irish, the Jews; the past to which we belong is an English past, the history of immigrant Britain. Swift, Conrad, Marx are as much our literary forebears as Tagore or Ram Mohan Roy. America, a nation of immigrants, has created a great literature out of the phenomenon of cultural transplantation, out of examining the ways in which people cope with a new world; it may be that by discovering what we have in common with those who preceded us into this country, we can begin to do the same.

('Imaginary Homelands' (1982) in *Imaginary Homelands: Essays and Criticism 1981–1991*, Salman Rushdie, 1991)

Salman Rushdie's contrast between his 'own racial history' and an alternative cultural and political tradition of migration and displacement – which includes 'the Jews' among other immigrant groups – is a telling one. For Rushdie, a possible 'strategy' to overcome the 'narrowly defined cultural frontiers' of his Indian background is to assimilate into an international community of displaced writers. He wishes both to remake the English 'past' to accommodate his own minority Indian culture and, at the same time, to construct America as an exemplary 'nation of immigrants' which has 'created a great literature out of the phenomenon of cultural transplantation'. As Rushdie himself recognises, this ideal of an 'imaginary homeland', beyond a writer's particular national community, has been an increasingly significant aspect of British-and American-Jewish fiction over the past two decades.[1] I want to examine four Anglo-American writers – Philip Roth, Clive Sinclair, Elaine

355

Feinstein and Cynthia Ozick – in the light of Rushdie's seminal formulation, as his essay, to a large extent, has set the agenda for a reading of the textual 'Jewishness' of these writers. The need to escape the narrow and excluding stereotypes of a racialised 'Jewish identity'; the remaking of an 'English past' in the light of minority experience; the idealisation of America as a 'nation of immigrants'; and, above all, the representation of an imaginary homeland as a sphere in which a displaced writer can be fully integrated; these will all be seen to be key characteristics of the recent Anglo-American Jewish novel. It should be emphasised from the outset, however, that these attributes are by no means an unproblematic part of the literature under discussion. Rushdie himself recognises in his essay that his 'identity is at once plural and partial'. Sometimes he feels that he 'straddles two cultures'; at other times that he 'fall[s] between two stools' (p. 15).

PHILIP ROTH: 'CHAINED TO MY DWARF DRAMA'

In his series of 'Zuckerman' novels (from *The Ghost Writer*, 1979, *Zuckerman Unbound*, 1981, *The Anatomy Lesson*, 1983, and *The Prague Orgy*, 1985, all collected in *Zuckerman Bound*, 1989, to *The Counterlife*, 1987, and *Deception*, 1990) Philip Roth can be said to have played, relentlessly, with the 'plural and partial' identities of his writer-persona.[2] *Zuckerman Bound*, which is made up of four individually published works, begins with *The Ghost Writer*. In this meticulously crafted novel, a young Nathan Zuckerman (aged twenty-three) goes in search of a surrogate literary father after being rejected by his real father and the leaders of the Newark Jewish community for writing a short story based on a family scandal. The antagonistic response to Zuckerman's fiction in *The Ghost Writer*, as Roth notes in his autobiography, is not dissimilar to the reaction which he himself encountered from Jewish communal leaders when he published the stories collected in *Goodbye, Columbus* (1959). Roth was even asked at a hostile public meeting at New York's Yeshiva University whether he would write the same stories if he were living in Nazi Germany – a question which Judge Leopold Wapter, a Newark elder, repeats to Zuckerman in *The Ghost Writer*.[3] As Roth later comments, his 'bruising' public exchange at Yeshiva University 'constituted not the end of my imagination's involvement with the Jews, let alone an excommunication, but the real beginning of my thralldom. . . . My humiliation before the Yeshiva belligerents . . . was the luckiest break I could have had. I was branded' (pp. 129–30).

Like Roth, Zuckerman is a 'controversial' novelist born in Newark in 1933, but this does not mean, as is often thought, that *Zuckerman Bound* is an 'autobiographical' text. It is, precisely, this too easy relationship between what Roth has called 'the written and the unwritten world' that is exploded in his later fiction. This elusive association has preoccupied Roth since his earliest short stories culminating in his description of himself as a 'walking text'. In one sense, as Clive Sinclair has argued, Zuckerman is 'the Semite-obsessed writer Roth's Jewish detractors imagine him to be'.[4] Zuckerman embodies, in other words, the confusion of those that can not differentiate between the 'written and the unwritten world'. As Roth recounts in his autobiography, the 'fanatical security' of his lower middle-class Newark childhood has, in the monomaniac misreading of his early fiction, been conflated with the 'fanatical insecurity' engendered by the Holocaust:

> This group whose embrace once has offered me so much security was itself fa-
> natically insecure. How could I conclude otherwise when I was told that every
> word I wrote was a disgrace, potentially endangering every Jew? Fanatical secu-
> rity, fanatical insecurity – nothing in my entire background could exemplify
> better than that night [at Yeshiva University] how deeply rooted Jewish drama
> was in this duality.
>
> (pp. 129–30)

It is this unresolved 'duality' that entraps Roth's 'plural and partial' fictional *alter ego*. In *The Ghost Writer*, Zuckerman attempts to transcend the narrowness of his Newark Jewish background by associating himself with an international literary tradition which is embodied in the writer E.I. Lonoff. Along with the egomaniacal Felix Abravanel (another of Zuckerman's potential surrogate literary fathers), Lonoff is viewed by Zuckerman as an 'American cousin' (p. 47) of the Russian-Jewish writer, Isaac Babel. Lonoff, unlike Babel, is the 'Jew who got away': 'You got away from Russia and the pogroms. You got away from the purges – and Babel didn't. You got away from Palestine and the homeland. . . . You got away from New York' (p. 50). Leaving New York after three months for the solitude of New England, the ascetic and deracinated Lonoff has renounced the unwritten world: 'I turn sentences around. That's my life. I write a sentence and then I turn it around. Then I look at it and turn it around again. Then I have lunch' (pp. 17–18). Abravanel, on the other hand, has a superabundance of 'life': 'Beautiful wives, beautiful mistresses, alimony the size of the national debt, polar expeditions, war-front reportage, famous friends, famous enemies, breakdowns, public lectures, five-hundred-page novels every third year . . .' (p. 53). These two extreme kinds of novelist (based loosely on Bernard Malamud and Norman Mailer) conform to Philip Rahv's characterisation of the American writer as either a 'paleface' or a 'redskin'. Lonoff is clearly a Jamesian 'paleface' who has a 'refined estrangement from reality' and Abravanel is clearly a Whitmanesque 'redskin' whose 'reactions are primarily emotional, spontaneous, and lacking in personal culture'. Roth, in a formative commentary on Rahv's polar opposition, describes himself as a 'redface', an uneasy reconciliation of these two 'seemingly inimical realms of experience'.[5]

The Ghost Writer deploys the aesthetics of the 'redface' as Zuckerman attempts to reconcile the extreme possibilities of Lonoff and Abravanel. The sequestered Lonoff, living in New England, and mediated through James's short story 'The Middle Years', has, in the end, what he calls a limited 'range of imagination' (p. 33). Zuckerman remembers Babel's definition of the Jewish writer as a 'man with autumn in his heart and spectacles on his nose', but secretly adds 'and blood in his penis' (p. 49) to this description. The typically 'Lonovian' hero is 'a nobody from nowhere, away from home where he is not missed, yet to which he must return without delay' (p. 14). While Babel's stories are located in history, Lonoff's carry the 'burden of exclusion and confinement' (p. 12). Abravanel, to be sure, has the 'unruly personal life' and 'turbulence' (p. 33) – not to mention the 'blood in his penis' – which is located in Zuckerman's writing but, stuck in the 'egosphere', Abravanel was 'not in the market for a twenty-three-year-old son' (p. 66). Neither the aestheticism of Lonoff nor the egocentricity of Abravanel are adequate models for Zuckerman, as a 'redface', to engage with the history which has caused the 'fanatical insecurity' of Newark Jewry. A purely aesthetic 'imaginary homeland', in other words, is eschewed as a rather facile means of transcending Zuckerman's narrowly defined cultural frontiers. For this reason, *The Ghost Writer* and *Zuckerman Bound* as a whole are both split between the transfiguring world of the imagination and the unremitting homeland of history.

This split can be seen in the figure of Amy Bellette who perceives herself – and is perceived by Zuckerman – as a reborn Anne Frank who has survived Bergen-Belsen death camp. On one level, as Hannah Wirth-Nesher argues, Anne/Amy 'is the paragon of both Jewish suffering and of renunciation on the holy altar of art' who, more than anyone, is able to absolve Zuckerman of the guilt of 'betraying' his family and community:[6] 'Oh, marry me, Anne Frank, exonerate me before my outraged elders of this idiotic indictment! Heedless of Jewish feeling? Indifferent to Jewish survival? Brutish about their wellbeing? Who dares to accuse of such unthinking crimes the husband of Anne Frank!' (pp. 170–1). This fantasised use of the history of Anne Frank by Nathan and also by Amy (in relation to Lonoff) and Judge Wapter (who recommends to Zuckerman that he see the Broadway production of *The Diary of Anne Frank*) points to the nature of the Holocaust 'ghosts' which haunt Zuckerman's quest for a redemptive 'imaginary homeland'. On the other hand, the split between Anne Frank and Amy Bellette indicates the general disparity between Zuckerman's Newark Jewish background and this Holocaust-centred construction of Jewishness: 'Ma, you want to see physical violence done to the Jews of Newark, go to the office of the plastic surgeon

where the girls get their noses fixed' (p. 106). Set against the historically-in-
duced monomaniacal (mis) reading of Zuckerman's (and Roth's) stories, *The
Ghost Writer* is constructed as a peculiarly imprecise fiction. Narrated by a
rather bemused Zuckerman, twenty years after the event, this work contains
a wide variety of competing voices and texts which, as in Nathan's equivo-
cation over his potential surrogate fathers, are of uncertain 'authority'.
Precisely because the elder Zuckerman ironically debunks the pretensions of
his younger self – 'Nathan Dedalus' – it is impossible to judge exactly what
credence one should give to any one 'text' in the novel.[7] It is this split in the
narrative voice of Zuckerman that is repeated throughout *Zuckerman Bound*.

In a 1973 'interview with myself', collected suitably enough in *Reading
Myself and Others* (1975), Roth describes the 'self-conscious and deliberate
zigzag that my own career has taken, each book veering sharply away from
the one before' (p. 84). Roth at this time was comparing, in particular, the
earnestness of *Letting Go* (1962) and *When She was Good* (1967) with the
carnivalesque *Portnoy's Complaint* (1969), *Our Gang* (1971) and *The Breast*
(1972). But this 'zigzag' method is never more apparent than in *Zuckerman
Bound*. The 'epilogue' to this volume, called *The Prague Orgy*, literally
prefigures *The Ghost Writer* as its precise chronology (which begins on 11
January, 1976) takes place before Zuckerman has supposedly written his
earlier work.[8] The circular relationship of Roth's 'epilogue' to the beginning
of *Zuckerman Bound* is also reinforced by situating Zuckerman in Czechoslo-
vakia in a redemptive search for the lost manuscripts of a Yiddish writer killed
by the Nazis (based loosely on Bruno Schulz). Here, the method of *The Ghost
Writer* is writ large as Zuckerman, in *The Prague Orgy*, once again attempts
unsuccessfully to use the high seriousness of art – foregrounded in its
references to James's *The Aspern Papers* – to transcend his narrow personal
culture in America. By setting this story in Prague, the historical landscape of
Jewish suffering, Roth is able to place Zuckerman momentarily in an
authentic 'imaginary homeland'. But, before he is able to achieve this, he has
Zuckerman undergo a hilarious 'crisis of solipsism' in *Zuckerman Unbound* and
The Anatomy Lesson. It is this zigzagging tension between 'self' and 'history'
that splits Zuckerman asunder in his eponymous novels.[9] At the end of
Zuckerman Unbound, Zuckerman discovers himself to be truly alone: 'You are
no longer any man's son, you are no longer some good woman's husband,
you are no longer your brother's brother, and you don't come from
anywhere, anymore, either' (pp. 404–5). Such is the devastation that his
best-selling novel *Carnovsky* (supposedly reminiscent of *Portnoy's Complaint*)
is meant to have caused. Bereft of a family, community, wife and childhood,
Zuckerman in *The Anatomy Lesson* undergoes a painful inner journey right
to the tips of his 'frazzled' nerve ends (p. 501). Zuckerman's comic self-obsession,
in other words, is caused by an intense fear that his writing, after all, did

merely reflect the narrow, communal preoccupations that besiege him. At one point in *The Anatomy Lesson*, Zuckerman considers whether to make Jaga, a Polish refugee, the material for an ameliorative novel provisionally entitled *The Sorrows of Jaga*. But he drops the idea almost as soon as it is considered.

> Hopeless – and not only because of the grass and the vodka. If you get out of yourself you can't be a writer because the personal ingredient is what gets you going, and if you hang on to the personal ingredient any longer you'll disappear right up your asshole. Dante got out of hell easier than you'll escape Zucker- man – Carnovsky. You don't want to represent her Warsaw – it's what her Warsaw represents that you want: suffering that isn't semi-comical, the world of massive historical pain instead of this pain in the neck. War, destruction, anti- semitism, totalitarianism, literature on which the fate of a culture hinges, writing at the very heart of the upheaval, a martyrdom more to the point – some point, *any* point – than bearing the cocktail-party chitchat as a guest on Dick Cavett. Chained to self-consciousness. Chained to retrospection. Chained to my dwarf drama till I die.
>
> (pp. 550–1)

This contrast between Zuckerman's 'dwarf drama' and the 'world of massive historical pain' structures Roth's *Zuckerman Bound*. Zuckerman needs – but cannot achieve – a dramatic 'imaginary homeland' that can 'dwarf' his sense of constriction and insularity. In the words of the Czech border guard, which ends Roth's 'epilogue', he is finally sent 'back to the little world around the corner' (p. 784). That Zuckerman feels himself to be confined to a 'little world' or 'dwarf drama' is also central to Roth's own sense of constricted Jewishness. It is axiomatic for Roth that in the novels of Saul Bellow, which sound not unlike the stories of E.I. Lonoff, 'renunciation is Jewish and renunciation is all'. He also argues that his own *Portnoy's Complaint* was part of this Bellovian (or Lonovian) 'nightmare of bondage' and 'mood of baffled, claustrophobic struggle'. Alexander Portnoy's 'complaint' is, after all, defined as 'a disorder in which strongly-felt ethical and altruistic impulses are perpetually warring with extreme sexual longings'. It is this combination of, what Roth has called, the 'Jewboy' and the 'Nice Jewish Boy' – appetite and renunciation – that has long since defined the doubleness of his textual Jewishness.[10] By assuming the identity of Milton Appel, for instance, Zuckerman in *The Anatomy Lesson* becomes simultaneously both a pornog- rapher and a would-be doctor. The social acceptance and measured worthiness of Henry Zuckerman, Nathan's dentist brother, similarly fore- grounds the 'little world' of repressed bourgeois Jewishness which Zuckerman's *Carnovsky* and Roth's *Portnoy's Complaint* are written against. These warring oppositions, as shall be seen, were eventually given their literary apotheosis in *The Counterlife*.

CLIVE SINCLAIR: 'EVERY PEOPLE HAS ITS STORY'

It is, I want to argue, exactly this formative sense of constriction – which received representations of Jewishness have placed on a writer's imagination – that Roth especially has in common with his British counterparts. The commonplace moralising of Jews as emblems of bourgeois respectability has, for over a century, deformed the British-Jewish novel into, at its worst, either tame apologetics or comedy of manners satire. Clive Sinclair, a British novelist born in 1948, has particularly utilised American-Jewish writing to overcome the limitations inherent in the British-Jewish novel form. From his earliest collection of short stories, *Hearts of Gold* (1979) and *Bedbugs* (1982), Sinclair has attempted to 'write fiction that owes nothing to any English antecedents' and has, therefore, self-consciously located his 'national' history as a Jew in Israel, America and Eastern Europe.[11] At the same time, Sinclair's fiction is playfully aware of the dangers of solipsism in this displacement of an 'English' identity on to a Judaised 'imaginary homeland'. 'Ashkenazia', collected in *Bedbugs*, is both a fictitious Yiddish-speaking country situated somewhere in central Europe and, also, the sum of Sinclair's writer-narrator: 'Many of my fellow-countrymen do not believe in the existence of God. I am more modest. I do not believe in myself. What proof can I have when no one reads what I write? There you have it; my words are the limit of my world. You will therefore smile at this irony; I have been commissioned by our government to write the official English-language *Guide to Ashkenazia*' (p. 238). By the end of this story, all that remains of 'Ashkenazia' is a 'field of wooden skeletons' and Sinclair's deranged persona truly becomes bounded by his words, 'Now the world will listen to me, for I am the guide to Ashkenazia. I am Ashkenazia' (p. 248). This conflation of selfhood with nationhood is, on one level, the necessary solipsistic response of an author who displaces an historical narrative on to what Roth has called a 'useful fiction'. For the post-Holocaust writer, however, an 'imaginary homeland' can not merely be constituted by words alone as Europe is littered with 'fields of wooden skeletons'. A purely textual 'Ashkenazia' is an act of writerly megalomania precisely because Sinclair's narrator thinks that he can bring these 'skeletons' to life. This simultaneous need to imagine more interesting homelands, which can never be fully possessed by the writer, is the subject of Sinclair's early fiction. 'The Promised Land', for instance, is a story told by a fool – or 'schlemiel' – who wishes to possess Hannah Ratskin, who lives in Tel Aviv. Considered an 'irrelevance' by Hannah who loves a handsome Israeli warrier, Ami Ben Tur, the 'schlemiel' of the story is in a state of unrequited love which also defines his diasporic relationship with the actual 'promised land' of Israel. The opening line of the story is (*pace* Melville) 'Call me Schlemiel' and Sinclair's narrator later expands, lewdly, on this reference to *Moby Dick*:

'To tell you the truth, I want to fuck Israel. Okay, so Ahab was obsessed with Moby Dick; well, my Promised Land is only an Israeli cunt' (p. 20). A non-Hebrew-speaking Jew in Israel is, according to this story, the ultimate outsider, 'I am Jewish but my tongue is not circumcised' (p. 18). Unlike the writer-narrator in 'Ashkenazia', who deludes himself into making a 'homeland' out of language, Sinclair's 'schlemiel' turns into a Nazi-rapist by thinking that his sense of existential displacement can have an all too literal biological solution.

In his *Diaspora Blues: A View of Israel* (1987), Sinclair defines himself as having a 'dual loyalty' to 'the language of England and the history of Israel' and argues that, for a writer, there is 'something to be gained from having a language but no history, a history but no language'. Unlike his relation to England, his interest in Israel has provided him with a 'narrative' in which to situate himself. According to Sinclair, the 'accidental structure' of his first novel, *Bibliosexuality* (1973), meant that it could only be 'terminated arbitrarily' with the novel's hero and lover randomly disappearing.[12] Instead of following this 'parthenogetic form', his next two novels, *Blood Libels* (1985) and *Cosmetic Effects* (1989), take to its logical conclusion the reproductive union, in his stories, of selfhood with nationhood. Both novels, that is, are personal histories which have national consequences. As in one of Sinclair's later stories, 'Kayn Aynhoreh', hypochondria is the natural condition of those who place the imagination at the centre of nationhood. Jake Silkstone, the Sinclairian alter ego in this story, reappears in *Blood Libels* and describes his various Scriptophobic and Dermagraphic ailments as 'the psychosomatic approach to history': 'Just as the mind, knowing the symptoms, has no need of bacillus or virus to counterfeit an illness, so history does not need facts to proceed. What people believe to have happened is more important than what actually did' (p. 188). 'The psychosomatic approach to history' has especially telling consequences in *Blood Libels*, resulting in the emergence of the fascistic 'Children of Albion' in England and the 1982 Israeli invasion of Lebanon. In this novel, Sinclair deliberately undermines the idea of history as the 'pseudo-scientific study of facts' (p. 188) by treating well-known political events in Israel as grotesque fantasy and by turning grotesque fantasy in England into seemingly plausible historical narrative. In *Cosmetic Effects*, the centrality of the imagination in the creation of historical and political 'facts' becomes the subject of the novel. This can be seen especially in the involvement of Sinclair's protagonist, Jonah Isaacson – a teacher of Film Studies at the fictional University of St Albans – with the making of a Biblical Western in Israel called *The Six Pointed Star*. The director of this film, Lewis Falcon (based loosely on John Ford and Howard Hawks), is quite explicit about the fictionality of his 'America':

Every people has its story . . . which is not the same as its history. It is this story that roots them on the land, that sustains their sense of identity. It may not be. the truth, but it is believed. I have lived all my life in the twentieth century, I am not ignorant of the importance of truth, but I am an artist and my first responsibility is to the story – the story of the American people.

(p. 163).

Sinclair's own short story called 'America' anticipated Falcon by showing that the idea of America, based on a series of puns and word-plays, is always liable to inventive reinterpretation. The depiction in *Cosmetic Effects* of 'America' as being not only a nation-state but a 'state of mind' (p. 61), not unlike Sinclair's Israel or 'Albania' (named after St Albans), interestingly reverses Roth's well-known account of the difficulties of writing American fiction. For Roth, 'the American writer in the middle of the twentieth century has his hands full in trying to understand, describe and then make *credible* much of American reality. It stupefies, it sickens, it infuriates, and finally it is even a kind of embarrassment to one's meagre imagination?' Unsurprisingly, much of Roth's fiction attempts to control and give meaning to what Hermione Lee was rightly called a 'vertiginous America'.[13] Zuckerman's infuriating 'celebrity' status in *Zuckerman Unbound* – as illustrated by Alvin Pepler, his crazed game-show *doppelgänger* – is no less a fantastic version of the novelist than the monomaniacal (mis)readings of Judge Leopold Wapter in *The Ghost Writer*. Whereas Sinclair places his 'America' at the heart of the literary imagination, Roth needs a cool Jamesian aesthetic to distance himself ironically from American 'reality'.

Far from being beyond the grasp of the 'imagination', Sinclair's 'America' in *Cosmetic Effects*, like much else in the novel, is a metaphor that eventually becomes 'real'. Jonah Isaacson recognises this when he proclaims, 'give my imagination a metaphor and it'll have the mise-en-scène worked out in no time' (p. 5). Isaacson, in fact, comes to embody the competing stories which, as he shows, are literally fighting it out to the death in the Middle East: 'Although I have only one arm I really feel like two people – a smooth man and a hairy man – two people in a single body, like the Israelis and the Palestinians are two people in a single land; there's Jonah Isaacson, the good husband, here to watch over his pregnant wife, and there's his double, the anonymous philanderer, who simply wants to fuck Stella Richmond' (p. 204).

Cosmetic Effects deals with the possibility of Jonah Isaacson being unwittingly turned into a human bomb by his Palestinian doctor, Said Habash, who fits him with a prosthetic arm. Whether Isaacson is a 'Son of Ishmael' (the name of a terrorist group) or the son of Isaac (an Israeli national hero) is deliberately left open to question. Isaacson loses his memory for much of the novel and thus has a number of competing national stories imposed on him. His animalistic desires and domestic constraints embody this terrorising or civilising doubleness, but are also part of a conscious narrative 'pluralism' which encourages 'a proliferation of stories and interpretations [so that] the future won't be fascistic' (p. 45). For Sinclair, the imagination 'bind[s] more strongly than kinship' and, like Roth's *The Counterlife*, he therefore constructs a multiplicity of possible 'counter-lives' and national identities for his increasingly fractured and decentred alter ego.

COUNTER-LIVES: BEYOND ENGLISHNESS

The Counterlife can be said to enact, quintessentially, the split in *Zuckerman Bound* between the fixed binary oppositions – appetite and renunciation or history and selfhood – that bedevils Zuckerman. Along with the extreme Zuckermanic alternatives articulated at Roth's leisure in the four books which make up *Zuckerman Bound*, *The Counterlife* constructs, at break-neck speed, a bewildering series of potential 'selves' for Nathan Zuckerman and his brother, Henry. Rather like *The Ghost Writer*, where the elder Roth is an ironic, debunking reader of his younger self, *The Counterlife* is full of deliberate and playful misreadings and 'texts' which wilfully lack authority. The 'counterlives' in each section of the novel – whether situated in America, Israel or England – are skilfully undermined and transformed throughout the novel into a superabundance of possible stories. It is not only Zuckerman's indeterminate selfhood which is random and arbitrary in the novel but the supposedly stable national contexts which are equally split between the rival insights of Nathan and Henry. In this way, as Mark Shechner has rightly noted, Roth has successfully yoked together theatricality with history in *The Counterlife*.[14] To take just one example, Henry in 'Judea', living in an Israeli West Bank settlement, makes out a case for 'we' and not 'I', 'a world of ideology, of politics, of history . . . defined by *action*, by *power*' as opposed to the world of the domestic 'self' which he has just rejected (p. 140). It is not 'Judea', however, but England – in the 'Gloucestershire' and 'Christendom' sections – that ironically transforms Nathan into a 'Jew' without a 'self': 'England's made a Jew of me in only eight weeks, which, on reflection, might be the least painful method. A Jew without Jews, without Judaism, without Zionism, without Jewishness, without a temple or an army or even a pistol, a Jew clearly without a home, just the object itself, like a glass or an apple' (p. 324). By the time of *Deception* Roth, who has spent nearly two decades living part of his year in London, is quite explicit about defining England as a place of constriction where a 'Jew' can only be defined negatively. His foregrounding of racialised images of 'the Jew' in *The Counterlife* – especialy the tradition of English literary anti-Semitism – is eventually contrasted with his description, in his subsequent novel, of New York comprising of 'Jews with force . . . Jews with appetite. Jews without shame. Complaining Jews who get under your skin. Brash Jews who eat with their elbows on the table. Unaccommodating Jews full of anger, insult, argument and impudence' (p. 204). The 'Roth' figure in *Deception* has never 'felt more misplaced in *any* country' (p. 109) than in England.

This antagonism between 'America' and 'England' is not unlike the critical distinctions between the American and English literary tradition in Richard Chase's *The American Novel and its Tradition* (1957) which Ann Massa has usefully applied to the widely differing prewar British- and American-Jewish novel.[15] According to Chase, the American novel 'tends to rest in contradictions and among extreme ranges of experience' whereas the English novel 'gives the impression of absorbing all extremes, all maladjustments and contradictions into a normative view of life'. To be sure, 'Englishness' – that is an English 'national culture' – has been understood, historically, as having a peculiarly fixed construction of the past as a 'settled present'. According to Philip Dodd, it was in relation to this fixed Englishness that ethnic minorities 'were invited to take their place, and become spectators of a culture already complete and represented for them by its trustees'. By contrast, the American novelist is able constantly to re-imagine or re-mythologise its relationship to a (European) past in a much less 'normative', less harmonious, manner.[16]

The perceived alienness of English national culture was indicated by Roth in a 1985 interview with Hermione Lee, collected in *Reading Myself and Others*, who asked him whether he intended to write about his time spent in England. Roth's stern reply was that he should be asked that question 'twenty years from now' when, around the year 2005 or 2010, he might 'dare' to 'set a story in a wine bar on Kensington Park Road' (p. 161). Two years after this interview, Roth published *The Counterlife* which was not only partly set in London and rural England but contained the important (and suitably named) genteel 'English' voice of Maria Freshfield. In his 1985 interview, Roth went on to say that one of the main reasons that he was unable to conceive himself writing on 'England' is that he had no 'culture-grievances' with England, 'nothing drives me crazy here, and a writer *has* to be driven crazy to help him *see*. A writer needs his poisons. The antidote to his poisons is often a book' (p. 161). What drives Zuckerman and 'Philip' 'crazy' about England in *The Counterlife* and *Deception* is precisely the English 'normative view of life' which accommodates even the most 'extreme' (anti-Semitic) feelings. What is interesting, however, is that Roth (through Zuckerman) accuses himself of exactly this lack of extremity in his autobiography. Zuckerman's 'letter' to Roth at the end of *The Facts* notes that his autobiography refuses 'to explode' as the reader is not given any sense of the intense motivations for Roth's 'voyage out' of 'a series of safe circles – home, neighbourhood, fraternity, Bucknell?' (pp. 162–5). Roth's trajectory from his provincial 'Weequahic Jewish' origins to metropolitan New York is clearly that of a great many assimilating, universalising third-generation American immigrants. As Zuckerman says, *The Facts* could be the life-story of 'anybody, almost' (p. 165). The disruptive presence of the 'Semite-obsessed' Zuckerman, in other words, is there to qualify a narrative which emphasises Roth as a 'normative' assimilator, exactly the kind of 'good boy' (p. 167) that his fiction debunks.

By the end of *The Facts* it is not just Nathan Zuckerman but his 'wife', Maria Freshfield Zuckerman, who indulges in the most savage dismissal of Roth's autobiography: 'the mask of Philip [is] too nice. He's the little boy nuzzling mama's sealskin coat. It's no wonder he begins with that' (p. 191). Continuing on from his autobiography, *Deception* is best described as a dialogue on Roth's Zuckermanic preoccupations – including his 'dissatisfactions with England and Englishness' (p. 50) – which takes place, for the most part, between 'Maria' and 'Philip'. At the beginning of this novel, 'Philip' is told that after spending all day sitting in his room he does not have any 'new experience': 'We might as well be holed up in an attic like the Frank family' (p. 24). Once again, we have the combination of Roth's sense of solipsism with his equally compelling, if unsettling, sense of the Holocaust as the necessary 'thematic architecture' behind his fiction.[17] Only the cool, Jamesian, womanly voice of 'Maria' is able to dissent fully from these mutually supporting antagonisms which structure Roth's *Zuckerman Bound* and *The Counterlife*. The 'exhaustion with masks, disguises, distortions, lies' (p. 6) or endless textual play, which Roth complains about at the beginning of *The Facts*, results in him taking refuge in facticity – as in his autobiographical *Patrimony: A True Story* (1991) – as well as the 'other' voice of Maria. But it is Maria, and not the supposed veracity of biographical 'truths', who is best able to cut the male artist down to size and counter the certainties that 'Philip' or 'Zuckerman' have with respect to their uncertain identities.

Sinclair, in his latest novel *Augustus Rex* (1992), similarly begins to question radically the limits of imaginative reconstruction at the same time as he creates his most comprehensive 'imaginary homeland' in sixties' and seventies' Sweden. Sinclair's fiction brings August Strindberg back to life, after half a century in the grave, with the devilish temptation that he will once again become an all-powerful writer and unbridled lover of women. The novel is narrated by Beelzebub, Lord of the Flies, who uses sexualised women to tempt the resurrected Strindberg to over-reach himself with Faustian consequences (he is turned into a fly). Following on from the megalomaniacal storyteller of 'Ashkenazia' – who thinks that he can breath life into Europe's 'skeletons' – *Augustus Rex* sets out to constrain the supposedly unlimited power of Strindberg's death-defying art. By the end of the novel, Strindberg's uncontrollable jealousy and his anti-Semitic loathing of his wife's lover, Emmanuel Adler, proves to be his downfall. As with the Professor of Philosophy in Sinclair's 'Titillatio' (who is torn between Spinoza and spermatozoa, Kant and cunt), Strindberg's intellectual sense of 'detachment' (p. 196) is unable to dissociate itself from the physical presence of his wife's body. In this way, Sinclair once again exposes the pretensions and self-delusions of the male imagination. Far from endlessly re-inventing themselves, as Clare Hanson argues with regard to Sinclair's storytelling protagonists, *Augustus Rex* demonstrates the feminised boundaries which limit the seductive power of the masculine aesthetic. The final image of Strindberg buzzing around his wife's body privileges in unequivocal terms the physical presence of women over the megalomaniacal fantasies of the male artist.[18]

CYNTHIA OZICK AND ELAINE FEINSTEIN: LITERARY 'IDOLATRY' AND THE LIMITS OF THE MASCULINE IMAGINATION

As well as Roth and Sinclair, two important women writers, the British-Jewish Elaine Feinstein and the American-Jewish Cynthia Ozick, have both consistently made use of 'imaginary homelands' – or what Ozick has called Central European 'verbal landscapes' – in their fiction. Ozick, significantly, differentiates her 'verbal landscapes' from George Steiner's ideal of an 'extraterritorial' Jewish textual tradition and Feinstein's Central European 'spiritual homeland' can also be distinguished, fundamentally, from that of her male counterparts. In her book of essays *Art and Ardor* (1984), Ozick rejects what she calls 'Literature as Idol' which foregrounds a surface aestheticism that is defined as 'a-thing-that-subsists-for-its-own-sake-without-a-history'. Ozick, unlike Roth and Sinclair, is quite explicit about opposing such Hellenistic or 'pagan' writing with a Hebraicised sense of historical judgement. Far from Rushdie's or Steiner's purely textual 'imaginary homeland', Ozick's fiction wishes precisely to show the dangers of such literary 'idolatry' and the potentially narcissistic textuality of the male imagination.[19]

The perils inherent in an aestheticising Hellenism are embodied in the figure of Joseph Brill, the protagonist of Ozick's novel *The Cannibal Galaxy* (1983), who is a French-Jewish survivor of the Holocaust. He ends up as the Principal of the pointedly 'middling' (p. 5) Edmund Fleg Primary School in Middle America. Brill spent the war years in hiding in a French convent where he was saved from deportation to Auschwitz. While in the cellar of the convent he discovered the work of Edmund Fleg (née Flegenheimer) who, rather like Matthew Arnold, postulated a grand synthesis between Hebrew and Hellene or the Christian and Jewish traditions. It is this ideal that he institutionalises in the 'Dual Curriculum' of his conspicuously mediocre Edmund Fleg Primary School. Fleg becomes Brill's exemplary but, in the end, rather mundane 'imaginary homeland'. What is interesting, however, is that the unreality of his harmonising ideals – which he arrogantly attempts to impose on Middle America – are brought home to him in explicitly gendered terms by the writer Hester Lilt and her daughter, Beulah. Whereas Brill attempts to transcend the Holocaust by, literally, reaching for the moon (through his early interest in astronomy), Hester Lilt, also a Holocaust survivor, is an 'imagistic linguistic logician' who creates an interpretative space so that others can discover her meaning: 'The more she delivered, the more she withheld. . . . She was all future; she cut the thread of genesis' (p. 92). Hester Lilt's enigmatic otherness challenges Brill's too easy cultural synthesis as her own books – *Metaphor as Exegesis; Divining Meaning; Interpretation as an End in Itself;* or *An Interpretation of Pedagogy* – all require a life-giving interpretative community to be of use. Instead of an egocentric transcendence of the Holocaust by Brill, Hester Lilt embodies a living history that each must reinterpret for themselves. Unlike the fiction of Roth and Sinclair, where the split between self and history takes place within the consciousness of an individual male protagonist, Ozick is at pains to situate this opposition in relation to the redemptive values of Hester Lilt. Her all-consuming maternal affinity towards the silent figure of Beulah fatally disrupts Brill's illusory Dual Curriculum, and is the necessary supplement to his synthesising or 'middling' imagination.

In her *The Messiah of Stockholm* (1987), Ozick rewrites Bruno Schulz's lost manuscript, *The Messiah*, by re-interpreting it through a reparative woman's voice. The novel is dedicated to Philip Roth who was the General Editor of the Penguin 'Writers from the Other Europe' series which republished Schulz's fiction in America. What is more, Roth had previously evoked the possibility of a *Messiah*-like masterpiece, destroyed by the Nazis, in his *The Prague Orgy*. But whereas the discovery of this work was meant to situate an ironically redeemed Zuckerman within the historical landscape of Jewish suffering, it is the impossibility of this imaginative displacement that concerns Ozick. Lars Andemening, the chief protagonist of her novel, is a third-rate Swedish literary critic and survivor of the War who adopts Bruno Schulz as his father. The bookseller Heidi Eklund, like Hester Lilt, shatters Andemening's fictionalised view of himself and, in so doing, she is able to 'see through to the skeleton' (p. 155) of Andemening and her other refugee customers. It is, as Joseph Lowin has noted, not Schulz's stories but the story of Schulz's brutal murder (at the hands of the SS) that Heidi privileges. Unlike

Andemening or Zuckerman or Sinclair's megalomaniacal writer-persona, Heidi Eklund does not wish to transcend the 'skeletons' of the past through story-telling but locates a very 'real' murder at the heart of her rewriting of Schulz's *The Messiah.*[20]

For the past two decades the British-born Elaine Feinstein, like Cynthia Ozick, has constructed Central Europe as a site on which to project a textual Jewishness which eclipses the parochial representations and received images of Anglo-American Jewry. Unlike Ozick, however, Feinstein does not deploy a fixed aesthetic in her fiction to distance herself from the merely 'imaginary'. Nonetheless, when Feinstein's early novels were thought of as a species of contemporary 'Gothic' – along with fiction by Angela Carter, J.G. Ballard and Emma Tennant – she was quick to differentiate herself from what she thought of as this 'steely rejection of humanism, a fashionable resistance to compassion which I believe is as much a luxury of our English innocence as the euphoria of the flower generation'. It was as the translator of the poetry of Marina Tsvetayeva and, later, of Margarita Aliger, Yunna Moritz and Bella Akhmadulina that Feinstein discovered her voice as a 'European' writer. In this sense, her writing was consciously opposed to an early influential group of Essex University poets (including Lee Harwood and Tom Pickard) who wished to foreground their common 'Englishness' and 'de-Europeanise' themselves. But the gendered limits of Feinstein's European humanism are also clear from her novels. Since her earliest work she has situated 'magical' father-enchanters at the heart of her fiction. These figures are always thoroughly ambiguous, both breathing 'life' into her female protagonists and, at the same time, threatening to make them 'dead with dependence'. In *The Shadow Master* (1978), the seventeenth-century Jewish false messiah, Sabbatai Zevi, is the ultimate historical expression of this double-edged enchantment. By the time of her *The Border* (1984) and *Loving Brecht* (1992), Feinstein was to situate Walter Benjamin and Bertolt Brecht in this 'magical' role. If the source of this life-giving 'magic' is the 'music of words', as suggested in *The Circle* (1970), then male writers are peculiarly uncertain embodiments of this imaginative 'refuge' for her women personae.[21]

In *The Border* Walter Benjamin – 'a Marxist who is not a materialist' (p. 57) – is a 'mystical' synthesising figure which the novel deliberately fragments. Set in Vienna before the *Anschluss*, this work is written as a tryptich in diary and epistolary form and this allows for three equally passionate accounts of an erotic triangle. Far from a single, male consciousness, the multiple, hallucinatory sense of reality in this novel – which is split along the lines of gender, poetic emotion and scientific reason, and political idealism and *realpolitik* – comes into play even when the main characters are faced with the threat of Nazism. The Spanish border at Port Bou in 1940, where Benjamin committed suicide, by the end signifies both his tragically fixed place in history and his internal fissures which are writ large in the novel. This is acknowledged in the form of *The Border* which reads an arbitrary version of its own story back from a contemporary perspective. By situating a great many different kinds of texts in a historical novel Feinstein, like Roth, establishes the possibilities for re-imagining a European past in terms of limitless 'magical' word-play as well as acknowledging the insurmountable 'borders' of history. But this is not, as Mark Shechner has argued, merely a 'journey of self-integration' into the European past for the Jewish novelist.[22] On the contrary, it is the lack of a sense of 'integration' into an historical other-world that each of the writers under discussion have highlighted in their fiction. Unlike Roth and Sinclair, Ozick and Feinstein also foreground gender difference to emphasise the gap between the imagination and history in their 'imaginary homelands'. But faced with the Anglo-American bour-geois certainties concerning their Jewishness, all of these writers evoke an indeterminate Jewish past precisely to help us rethink the present.

NOTES

1. Salman Rushdie, *Imaginary Homelands: Essays and Criticism 1981–1991* (London, 1991) p. 20 and pp. 9–21. This volume contains articles on the American-Jewish writers Grace Paley, Isaac Bashevis Singer, Saul Bellow and Philip Roth. Further references to this volume will be in parenthesis in the body of the text.

2. Further reference to these works, all published in New York, will be in parenthesis in the body of the text.

3. *The Facts: A Novelist's Autobiography* (New York, 1988) p. 127 makes this connection. For a detailed account of the Jewish communal reaction to Roth's early fiction see idem., pp. 113–30 and his *Reading Myself and Others* (Harmondsworth, 1985 expanded ed), pp. 205–30. Further references to these volumes will be in parenthesis in the body of the text.

4. Clive Sinclair, 'The Son is Father to the Man', in Asher Z. Milbauer and Donald G. Watson (eds), *Reading Philip Roth* (London, 1988), p. 169. Roth cites Paul Goodman's distinction between 'the written and the unwritten world' in his Preface to his *Reading Myself and Others* (p. ix), and Zuckerman describes Roth as a 'walking text' in *The Facts* (p. 162). For the implications of this latter term, see my 'Tales of a Walking Text', *Times Literary Supplement* 17–23 February, 1989): 159.

5. On *The Great American Novel* in his *Reading Myself and Others*, op. cit., pp. 82–4. Roth is citing Philip Rahv, 'Palefaces and Redskins' (1939) collected in *American Critical Essays* (ed.), Harold Beaver (Oxford, 1959). For a useful reading of this aesthetic in relation to Roth's fiction in general see Hermione Lee, *Philip Roth* (London, 1982).

6. Hannah Wirth-Nesher, 'From Newark to Prague: Roth's Place in the American-Jewish Literary Tradition' in Milbauer and Watson (eds.), *Reading Philip Roth*, op. cit., p. 26. This article also usefully compares Roth's evocation of Franz Kafka in his *The Professor of Desire* with the supposedly reborn Anne Frank in *The Ghost Writer*.

7. For this argument see Patrick O'Donnell, 'The Disappearing Text: Philip Roth's *The Ghost Writer*', *Contemporary Literature*, vol. xxiv, no. 3 (1983): 365–78.

8. Sinclair, in Milbauer and Watson (eds), op. cit., p. 170 rightly argues that 'since *The Ghost Writer* takes place in December 1956 and was composed more than twenty years later, it is clear that Zuckerman must have written it some months after the eponymous visit to Prague'.

9. Roth describes Zuckerman's 'crisis of solipsism' in an interview with Hermione Lee collected in *Reading Myself and Others*, op. cit., p. 165. See also Michael Woolf, ' "Oh, to be a center fielder": Philip Roth and *Zuckerman Bound*', The *Jewish Quarterly*, vol. xxxiii, no. 1 (1986): 35–9.

10. The definition of Alexander Portnoy's 'complaint' opens the novel. See also his ' "How Did You Come to Write That Book, Anyway?"', in *Reading Myself and Others*, op. cit., pp. 33–41 and pp. 209, 301.

11. ' "On the Edge of the Imagination": Clive Sinclair interviewed by Bryan Cheyette', The *Jewish Quarterly*, vol. xxxi, nos 3–4 (1984): 26–9. Sinclair's stories have been republished as *For Good or Evil: Collected Stories* (London, 1991). Further references to this volume will be in parenthesis in the body of the text. For the historical deformation of the British-Jewish novel see my 'The Other Self: Anglo-Jewish Fiction and the Representation of Jews in England, 1875–1925', in David Cesarani (ed.), *The Making of Modern Anglo-Jewry*, (Oxford, 1990).

12. *Diaspora Blues: A View of Israel* (London, 1987), pp. 50–3, p. 65, p. 202. Further references to this volume and to Sinclair's *Blood Libels* (London, 1985) and *Cosmetic Effects* (London, 1989) will be in parenthesis in the body of the text. For a general account of the importance of 'narrative' to ideas of nationhood see Homi K. Bhabha (ed.), *Nation and Narration* (London and New York, 1990).

13. Hermione Lee, *Philip Roth*, p. 45 and Chapter 2 *passim*; Roth, 'Writing American Fiction', in *Reading Myself and Others*, op. cit., p. 176.

14. Mark Shechner, 'Zuckerman's Travels', in his *The Conversion of the Jews and Other Essays*, (London and Basingstoke, 1990) Chapter 9.

15. Ann Massa, 'Fictions of the Ghetto: A Trans-Atlantic Comparison', The *Jewish Quarterly*, vol. xxxv, no. 4 (1989): 21–4.

16. Philip Dodd, 'Englishness and the National Culture', in Robert Colls and Philip Dodd (eds), *Englishness and Culture 1880–1920* (London, 1986), p. 22. See also Richard Chase, *The American Novel and its Tradition* (New York, 1957), pp. 1–2.

17. 'Interview with the London *Sunday Times*' in *Reading Myself and Others*, p. 137. Roth emphasises in this interview that Zuckerman, in *The Anatomy Lesson*, carries around with him the word 'Holocaust' which his mother has written while dying of a brain tumour.

18. For a limited but stimulating reading of Sinclair's short fiction in terms of endless textual play (breaking down the boundaries between 'fiction' and 'reality') see Clare Hanson, *Short Stories and Short Fictions. 1880–1980* (London, 1985), pp. 166–9. For a more convincing account of Sinclair's flawed and manipulative storytellers see Malcolm Bradbury, *No, Not Bloomsbury* (London, 1987), pp. 352–8. See also Murray Baumgarten and Barbara Gottfried (eds), *Understanding Philip Roth* (Columbia, 1990), p. 84 and *passim* for an account of Roth's definition of masculinity 'against a prototype of American maleness'.

19. Cynthia Ozick, *Art and Ardor: Essays* (New York, 1984), pp. 155, 225 and pp. 151–77. I will be referring to Ozick's *The Cannibal Galaxy* (London, 1984) and *The Messiah of Stockholm* (London, 1987) in parenthesis in the body of the text. See also George Steiner, *Extraterritorial: Papers on Literature and the Language Revolution* (London, 1972), Chapter 1 and his 'Our Homeland, the Text', *Salmagundi*, no. 66 (Winter – Spring, 1985): 4–25.

20. For this reading of Ozick see Joseph Lowin, *Cynthia Ozick* (Boston, 1988), p. 155 and Chapter 10 *passim*.

21. Elaine Feinstein, *The Circle* (London, 1970), p. 164. See also Peter Conradi, 'Elaine Feinstein: Life and Novels', the *Literary Review* (April, 1982): pp. 24–5, which cites Feinstein's account of her early influences, and the entries on Feinstein in Jay L. Halio (ed.), *British Novelists Since 1960* (Detroit, 1983) and Glenda Abramson (ed.), *The Blackwell Companion to Jewish Culture* (Oxford, 1989). References to Feinstein's *The Border* (London, 1984) will be in parenthesis in the body of the text.

22. Shechner, 'Zuckerman's Travels', op. cit., p. 100.

FURTHER READING

Roth's fiction has been published by Penguin Books in Britain and Farrar Straus Giroux in America.

Sinclair's fiction is also readily available in Penguin editions in Britain but remains shamefully underpublished in America.

Feinstein's poetry and fiction are published by Hutchinson in Britain but she is also shamefully underpublished in America.

Ozick's fiction is published by Alfred A. Knopf in America and, in part, by Jonathan Cape in Britain. Not all of her fiction, however, has been published in Britain and this, too, needs to be rectified.

Other than works cited in the notes, the following are useful:

Harold Bloom (ed.), *Philip Roth: Modern Critical Views* (New York, 1986).

Harold Bloom (ed.), *Cynthia Ozick: Modern Critical Views* (New York, 1986).

David Leon Higdon, *Shadows of the Past in Contemporary British Fiction* (London, 1984).

Peter Jones and Michael Schmidt (eds), *British Poetry Since 1970: A Critical Survey* (Manchester, 1980).

Holger Klein (ed.), *The Second World War in Fiction* (London, 1984).

Sanford Pinsker, *The Uncompromising Fiction of Cynthia Ozick* (Columbia, 1987).

Sanford Pinsker (ed.), *Critical Essays on Philip Roth* (Boston, 1982).

Efraim Sicher, *Beyond Marginality: Anglo-Jewish Literature after the Holocaust* (New York, 1985).

Contents Arranged Historically

★ These essays range across more than one period.

Index